Con Coughlin was born in L
at Christ's Hospital, Horsham and Brasenose College, Oxford. Since joining the *Daily Telegraph* in 1980 he has travelled extensively as a foreign correspondent, and since 1983 he has specialised in the Middle East where he was the *Daily Telegraph*'s correspondent in the region until 1988. He is currently chief foreign correspondent for the *Sunday Telegraph*, and a regular contributor to the *Spectator*.

Acclaim for Con Coughlin's HOSTAGE:

'Thoughtful, incisive . . . this withering portrait, while it will disturb those who think of (Terry) Waite as a hero or saint, is based on cold observations'

– *The Times*

'An admirable book'

– *The European*

'Excellent'

– *Private Eye*

'A comprehensive study'

– *Time*

'The most extraordinary story . . . I do not think that I can remember a case in the political or secular sphere where an eminent public figure has been quite so devastatingly candid about his or her low opinions of a colleague'

– A. N. Wilson,
Evening Standard

'Provides for the first time a fascinating account of the historical and political background to the crisis as it unfolded – highlighting the failure of the West to understand the cultures and concerns of the area'

– *Daily Mail*

'An almost old-fashioned tale of vanity, ineptitude, occasional acts of courage and the byzantine workings of Middle East politics'

– *Daily Telegraph*

'Fascinating'

– *Spectator*

'Remarkable'

– *Western Mail*

'Deftly written and expertly paced . . . his book also provides an unprecedentedly coherent insight into the identity, motives and character of the extremists who held not only innocent Westerners but many of the world's governments, hostage for so long'

– *Jewish Chronicle*

'The definitive story of the Lebanese hostage crisis'

– *Lancashire Evening Post*

'As honest appraisal as will come from the West'

– *Oxford Times*

HOSTAGE

The Complete Story of the Lebanon Captives

Con Coughlin

WARNER BOOKS

A *Warner* Book

First published in Great Britain in 1992
by Little, Brown and Company
This updated edition published by Warner Books in 1993

A CIP catalogue record for this book is available from the British Library.

Picture research by Linda Silverman.

ISBN 0 7515 0244 8

Typeset by Hewer Text Composition Services, Edinburgh
Printed in England by Clays Ltd, St Ives plc

Warner Books
A Division of
Little, Brown and Company (UK) Limited
165 Great Dover Street
London SE1 4YA

For my mother and in memory of my father

CONTENTS

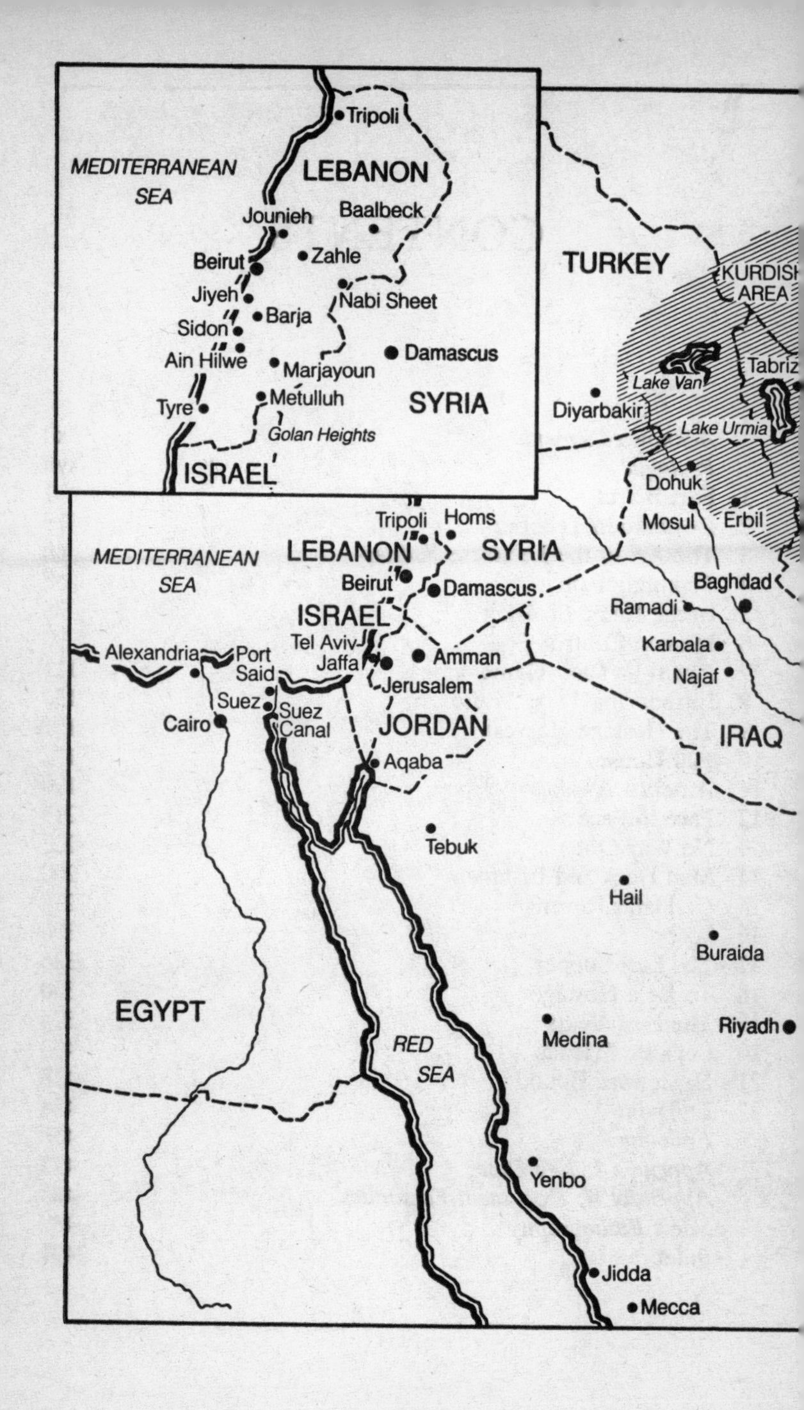
Tripoli
MEDITERRANEAN SEA
LEBANON
Jounieh
Baalbeck
Beirut
Zahle
Jiyeh
Nabi Sheet
Barja
Sidon
Ain Hilwe
Damascus
Marjayoun
Metulluh
Tyre
SYRIA
Golan Heights
ISRAEL
TURKEY
KURDISH AREA
Tabriz
Lake Van
Diyarbakir
Lake Urmia
Dohuk
Mosul
Erbil
Tripoli
Homs
LEBANON
SYRIA
MEDITERRANEAN SEA
Beirut
Damascus
Baghdad
Ramadi
ISRAEL
Tel Aviv
Alexandria
Port Said
Jaffa
Amman
Karbala
Najaf
Jerusalem
Suez
Cairo
Suez Canal
JORDAN
IRAQ
Aqaba
Tebuk
Hail
Buraida
EGYPT
Medina
Riyadh
RED SEA
Yenbo
Jidda
Mecca

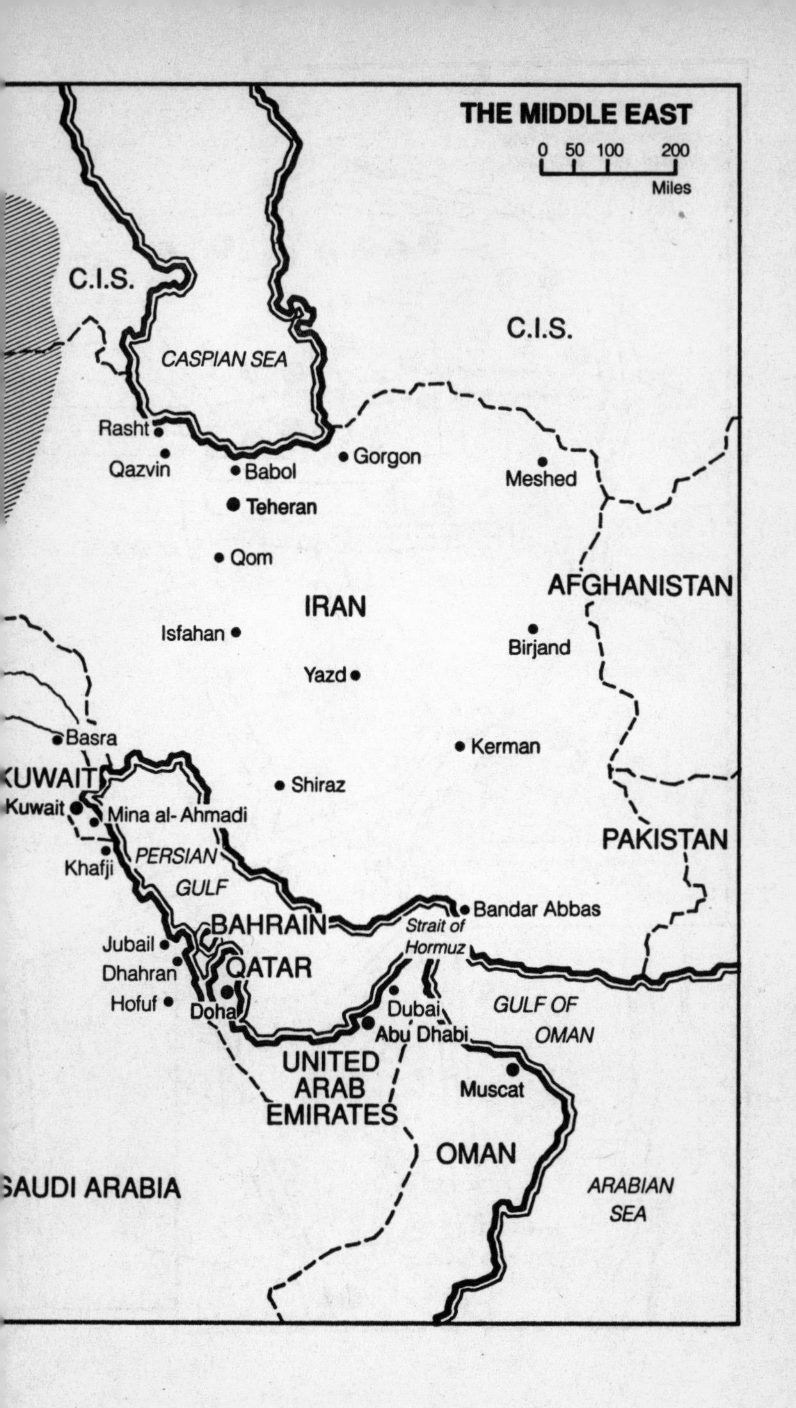
THE MIDDLE EAST
0 50 100 200
Miles
C.I.S.
CASPIAN SEA
C.I.S.
Rasht
Qazvin
Babol
Gorgon
Meshed
Teheran
Qom
AFGHANISTAN
IRAN
Isfahan
Birjand
Yazd
Basra
Kerman
KUWAIT
Shiraz
Kuwait
Mina al- Ahmadi
PAKISTAN
Khafji
PERSIAN
GULF
Bandar Abbas
BAHRAIN
Strait of
Hormuz
Jubail
Dhahran
QATAR
Hofuf
Doha
Dubai
GULF OF
OMAN
Abu Dhabi
UNITED
ARAB
EMIRATES
Muscat
OMAN
SAUDI ARABIA
ARABIAN
SEA

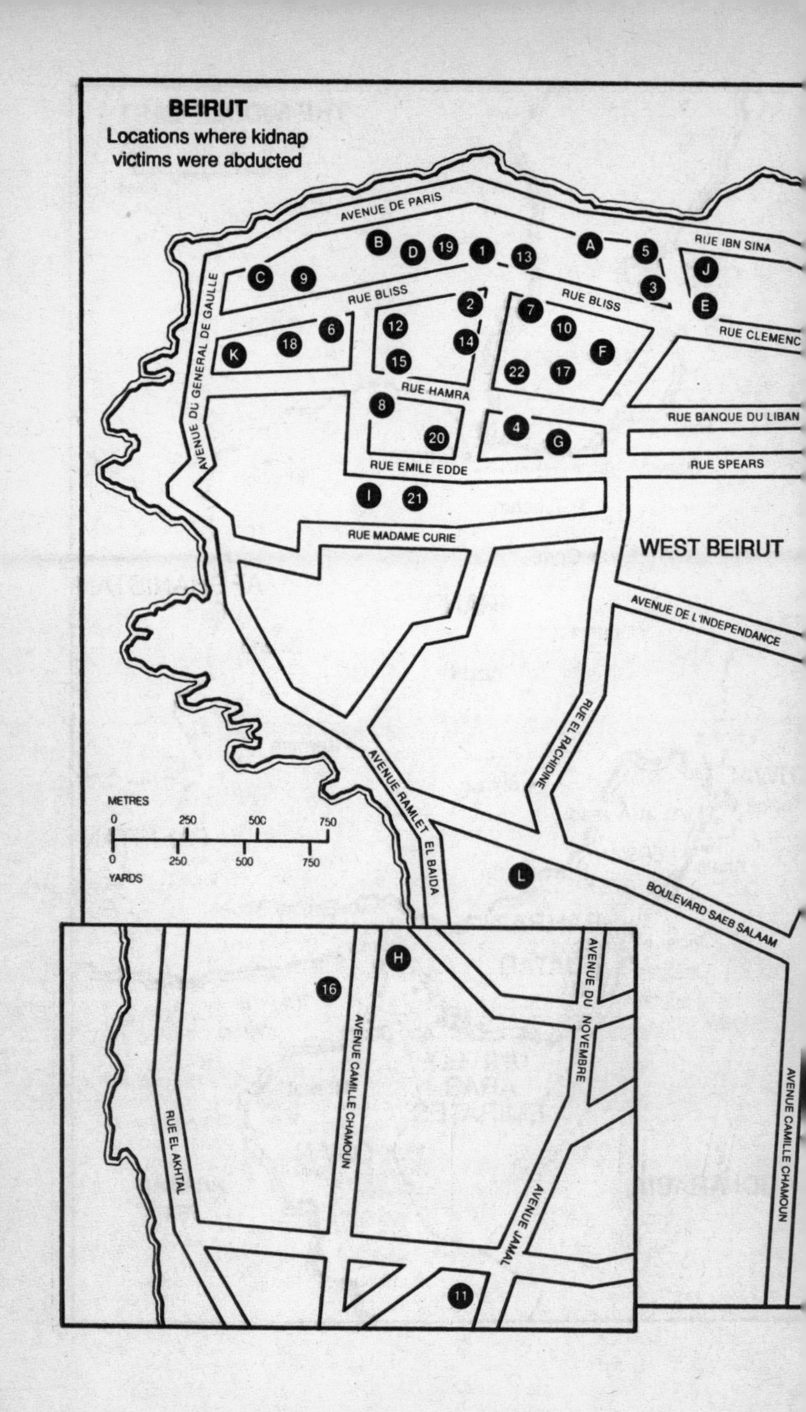
BEIRUT
Locations where kidnap victims were abducted
AVENUE DE PARIS
RUE IBN SINA
RUE BLISS
RUE BLISS
RUE CLEMENC
AVENUE DU GENERAL DE GAULLE
RUE HAMRA
RUE BANQUE DU LIBAN
RUE SPEARS
RUE EMILE EDDE
RUE MADAME CURIE
WEST BEIRUT
AVENUE DE L'INDEPENDANCE
RUE EL RACHIDINE
AVENUE RAMLET EL BAIDA
BOULEVARD SAEB SALAAM
METRES
0 250 500 750
0 250 500 750
YARDS
AVENUE DU NOVEMBRE
AVENUE CAMILLE CHAMOUN
RUE EL AKHTAL
AVENUE JAMAL
AVENUE CAMILLE CHAMOUN

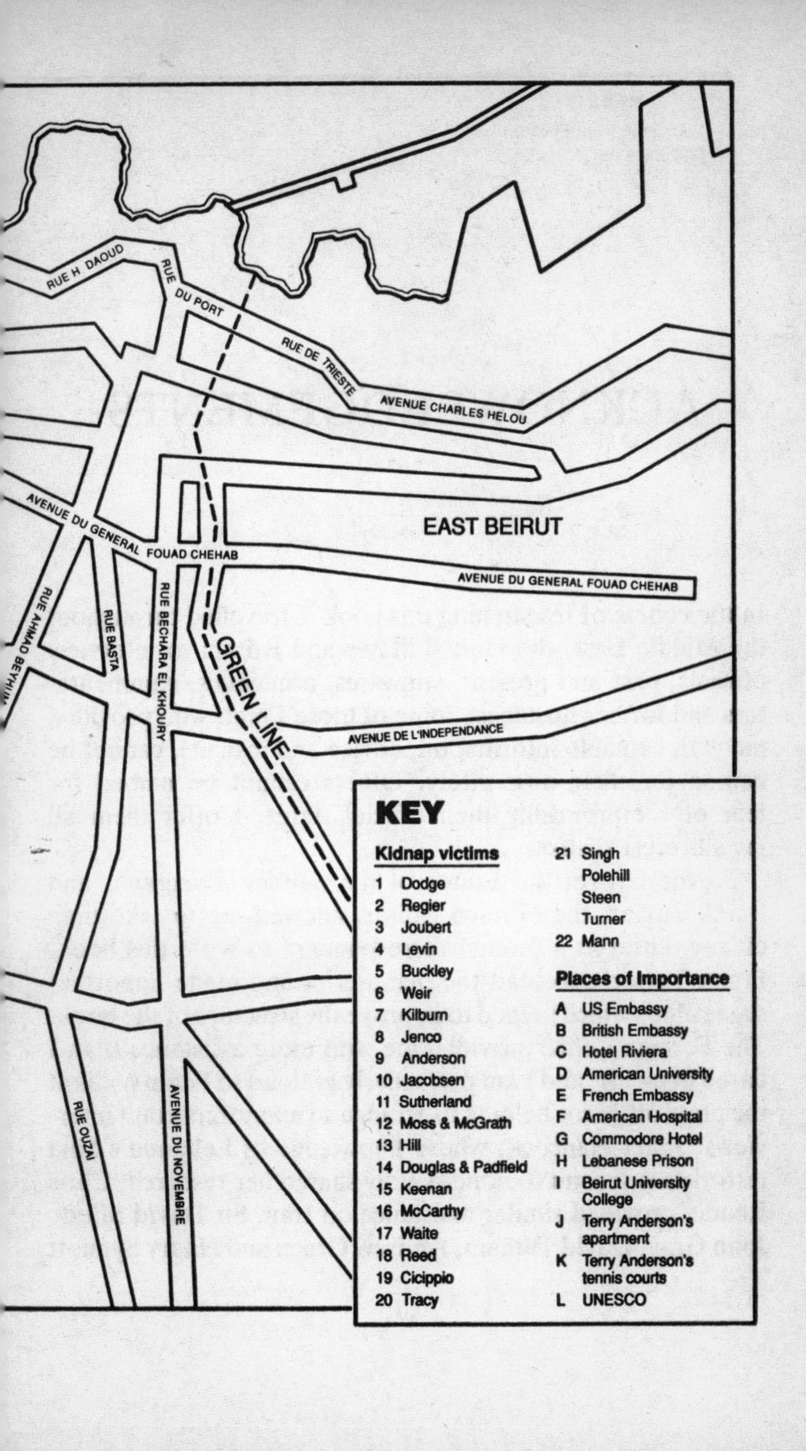
RUE H. DAOUD
RUE DU PORT
RUE DE TRIESTE
AVENUE CHARLES HELOU
EAST BEIRUT
AVENUE DU GENERAL FOUAD CHEHAB
AVENUE DU GENERAL FOUAD CHEHAB
RUE AHMAD BEYHUM
RUE BASTA
RUE BECHARA EL KHOURY
GREEN LINE
AVENUE DE L'INDEPENDANCE
RUE OUZAI
AVENUE DU NOVEMBRE
KEY
Kidnap victims
1 Dodge
2 Regier
3 Joubert
4 Levin
5 Buckley
6 Weir
7 Kilburn
8 Jenco
9 Anderson
10 Jacobsen
11 Sutherland
12 Moss & McGrath
13 Hill
14 Douglas & Padfield
15 Keenan
16 McCarthy
17 Waite
18 Reed
19 Cicippio
20 Tracy
21 Singh
Polehill
Steen
Turner
22 Mann
Places of Importance
A US Embassy
B British Embassy
C Hotel Riviera
D American University
E French Embassy
F American Hospital
G Commodore Hotel
H Lebanese Prison
I Beirut University College
J Terry Anderson's apartment
K Terry Anderson's tennis courts
L UNESCO

ACKNOWLEDGEMENTS

In the course of researching this book, I travelled throughout the Middle East, the United States and Britain to interview officials, past and present, witnesses, academics, commentators and former hostages. Some of those I met, who provided me with valuable information, advice and insights, cannot be named for their own safety. Others cannot be named for fear of compromising their official status. I offer them all my sincerest thanks.

Trevor Grove, the Editor of the *Sunday Telegraph*, and Frank Taylor, the Foreign Editor, allowed me to take time off my duties as a foreign correspondent to write this book. Frank Taylor also read the manuscript and made important suggestions which helped to improve the structure of the book. The Foreign Office provided me with more assistance than I dared hope for, and I am particularly grateful to Peter Willis at the press office for helping to arrange so many important interviews. Janet Hancock, whose knowledge of Lebanon's Shia terrorists is second to none, kindly shared her research; Chris Rendle provided similar assistance on Iran. Sir David Miers, John Gray, David Tatham, Andrew Green and Hilary Synnott shared their knowledge and expertise of the hostage crisis. Sir Charles Powell, Sir Geoffrey Howe, Anthony Teasdale and Douglas Hogg explained the formulation, implementation and realisation of Britain's hostage policy.

Brigadier Peter Woolley helped to fill in many gaps on the role of the British contingent in the multi-national force in Lebanon. Dr Peter Jones at the Department of Classics at Newcastle University helped to trace the ancient origins of hostage-taking; Nigel Churton of Control Risks provided a more up-to-date appraisal. Professor Paul Wilkinson explained the subtleties of terrorism in the Middle East. Robert Burke of World Television News, who devoted five years to trying to get John McCarthy released from Lebanon, provided a detailed account of the difficulties of getting someone released from Beirut. Peter Kemp recalled his close friendship with Leigh Douglas and Philip Padfield. I am particularly grateful to Freda and Edgar Douglas for summoning the courage to talk frankly about the loss of their son; Pat McCarthy revealed the joy of having his return. The late John Lyttle kept me well-informed as his mission to Lebanon progressed; Jonathan Petre of the *Daily Telegraph* kindly provided notes of his last interview with Lyttle. Kamal Khoury helped to piece together the last days of Waite's ill-fated mission to Lebanon. Lord Runcie was frank about the role of the Church. Brian Levick spoke for the first time about his ordeal as a hostage. Pierre Salinger of ABC News in London provided information he received from a dissident Palestinian leader about the murder of Alec Collett. Aernout Van Lynden shared his knowledge of the kidnap groups and arranged several important meetings in Lebanon. Patrick Bishop, my successor as the *Daily Telegraph*'s Middle East correspondent, brought me up-to-date on events I missed. The staff at the *Telegraph* library handled various queries with their usual efficiency and charm. Sue Neal did some valuable picture research and Joanne Roberts helped to arrange the interviews.

My trip to Lebanon would have been considerably more difficult without the assistance of Lena Kara and the hospitality of Steve Bent and Hala Jaber who put me up and sustained my enthusiasm during one of the wettest winters in Lebanon's history. Lena Kara was an invaluable guide who not only acted as a translator but shared many insights which helped to place the hostage crisis in its true context. Farouk Nassar and the staff of Associated Press shared their detailed knowledge of the hostage crisis with me, as did Peter Smerdon and Nadim Ladki at Reuters. Juan Carlos Gumucio of *El Pais* helped me to understand that nothing should ever be taken for granted in Lebanon. Jim Muir filled me in on what happened in Beirut during the years in which, for reasons of security, I was unable to venture into Lebanon. Akram Shehayeb explained the role of the Druze in protecting Waite. Dr Adnan Iskander, the vice-president of the American University of Beirut, gave a full account of the attacks the University suffered. Hassan Sabra, the editor of *Ash-Shiraa*, relived his world famous scoop. Sana Issa filled me in on the details of McCarthy's last days of freedom in Beirut. Sinan Birraj explained the difficulty of searching for 17,000 missing Lebanese.

In Cyprus Jonathan Wright related all the details of his abduction in Lebanon, as did Hazel Moss. Lynn and Gerald Butt recalled the horrors of having a young family in Beirut in 1984, while Chris Drake and the Memo staff once again facilitated my travel arrangements. In Israel Dr Clinton Bailey and Uri Lubrani gave generously of their time, while Rifka Zipper at the Government Press Office helped to arrange key meetings. Ian Black of the *Guardian* pointed me in the right direction when I most needed it.

Charles and Mia Laurence indulged me with their hospitality during my stay in New York, while Mary Curtius, Ori

Nir and Nellie Henderson were perfect hosts in Washington. Larry Pope, deputy head of counter-terrorism at the State Department, and Robert Oakley, the former head of the same department, gave me a detailed account of American diplomacy with regard to the hostage issue. Robert McFarlane explained at length his role in formulating US policy towards Iran and Lebanon in the mid-1980s. Tom Blandon at the National Security Archive helped me to sort through the mountain of documents on the Iran–Contra affair. David Dodge gave me the first full account of his abduction in Lebanon. Richard Murphy, the former head of the State Department's Near East section, was honest about miscalculations in American policy. Jo Cicippio and his delightful wife Elham entertained me to dinner at their new home in Princeton, New Jersey. Alann and Virginia Rose Steen agreed to let me visit them at their hideaway in the wilds of upstate Michigan. Tom Sutherland mixed more 'old-fashioneds' than were good for me and spared no detail of his experience as a hostage. Elaine Collett was frank about the frustration, seven years later, of not knowing what had become of her husband. Samir Habiby kept me up-to-date on his various schemes to get Waite released. John Rowan took time off from his congenial posting at the Irish Consulate in San Francisco to recall his efforts in Beirut and elsewhere on behalf of Brian Keenan. Father Charles Cesaretti revealed the mysteries of the bureaucracy of the Episcopal Church. Giandomenico Picco took me into his confidence and related his hair-raising escapades in Beirut to get the hostages released. My colleagues at the *Sunday Telegraph* and the *Daily Telegraph* made me welcome and allowed me the use of their facilities without complaint; in particular I offer Charles Laurence, Hugh Davies and Enda Jackson my thanks.

Marilyn Warnick helped me to negotiate the maze that is the publishing world. Gill Coleridge, my agent, had sufficient faith in this project to ensure its publication, while Alan Samson and Helga Houghton, my publisher and editor at Little, Brown, provided much-needed encouragement when the size of the task seemed overwhelming. To all the above and those not mentioned who provided equally valuable assistance, I offer my heartfelt thanks. All the interpretations and conclusions I have reached in the course of charting this immensely complicated subject are mine, and mine alone.

C.R.C.
London, 1992

PROLOGUE

Hell is empty, And all the devils are here.
– Shakespeare, *The Tempest*

As the tannoy system at Denver International Airport announced the final boarding call for his flight, Tom Sutherland did not display the slightest hint of unease as he kissed his wife goodbye and headed for the departure lounge. A stocky but fit man in his early fifties, with the rolling gait of someone who had enjoyed an athletic youth, there was still the faint trace of a Scottish brogue in his Americanised accent, which became distinctly more pronounced when he had sunk a few 'olds-fashioneds' while sitting on the porch of his home. A devoted family man, Sutherland had just spent an idyllic three weeks with his wife Jean and their three daughters at the family home in Fort Collins, an old frontier town in the foothills of the Rocky Mountains. Sutherland had flown home to attend the graduation of his eldest daughter, Kit, at the State university, and had taken advantage of the opportunity to take some leave. Now it was time for him to return to his teaching post at the American University in Beirut.

Sutherland had few qualms about flying back to a city which

had become synonymous in his home country with violence and lawlessness. In the two years he had been working at the university, he had made the trip from Denver to Beirut many times, and even when the fighting was at its height, he had never encountered any personal danger. He knew Beirut well enough not to take anything for granted. He knew how the seductive charms of the Mediterranean city could within minutes be transformed into another round of ugly blood-letting. He also knew that, even as an American citizen, if he took the necessary precautions, he was not personally at risk.

Sutherland had witnessed the disastrous deployment of the American armed forces into Lebanon with detachment. When 300 American and French soldiers were blown to pieces by two suicide truck-bombs, Sutherland had felt little sympathy. If they wanted to take sides in the Lebanese conflict, what did they expect? Similarly when Islamic fundamentalist extremists began kidnapping American citizens on the streets of Beirut, Sutherland had a ready explanation for why they would not bother him. Most of the American hostages had had jobs which exposed them directly to the dangers of life in Lebanon. Everyone knew that William Buckley, who had been kidnapped the previous year, was the Central Intelligence Agency's station chief in Beirut. Some, like Jeremy Levin and Terry Anderson, were journalists who exposed themselves to danger every working day. Apart from making themselves an easy target, it was more than possible that they had written or said something which had upset the leaders of the kidnap gangs. The same could also be said for churchmen like Lawrence ('Marty') Jenco and Ben Weir, who had taken a calculated risk by conducting Christian missionary work in the midst of an Iranian-inspired Islamic revolution. Whenever misfortune befell American citizens in Beirut, Sutherland had a string of excuses as to why he would not suffer a similar fate.

As Dean of Agriculture at the American University, Sutherland, in common with the small group of American teachers still working in Beirut, felt himself to be immune from the attentions of the kidnap gangs. During term he and Jean lived in a beautiful Ottoman stone villa on campus. On the rare occasions they went outside the university, they were taken in a chauffeur-driven car provided by the authorities. They usually spent holidays at Fort Collins. Sutherland, moreover, who had accepted the Beirut post in 1983 after a career at American academic institutions, felt he was making a constructive contribution to Lebanon's future, a contribution which he believed the Lebanese understood and appreciated.

Sutherland's job was to train future generations of Arab farmers and landowners in the art of husbandry and the latest technical advances in agrology, an invaluable task in a part of the world which wages a constant battle against the menace of the desert. Indeed, Sutherland had been imbued almost with a sense of mission by Dr Malcolm Kerr, an Arabist who had lived in the Middle East nearly all his life and the man who had persuaded Sutherland to come to Beirut. When Kerr was murdered in 1984 by an assassin who fired a silencer-equipped pistol at close range into the back of his head as he walked to his office on campus, this only strengthened Sutherland's determination to continue his work at the university. When Washington issued warnings asking, in the most persuasive tones, all American citizens resident in Beirut to leave at the first available opportunity, Sutherland scoffed at the notion, even more so when some of his fainter-hearted colleagues were only too willing to acquiesce. Sutherland was, after all, at heart a Scot, a race which is notoriously dismissive of unwarranted interference in its affairs.

During this leave, however, a development had occurred in Lebanon which had briefly caused Sutherland to question the wisdom of returning. Halfway through Sutherland's holiday in Colorado, he received the news that David Jacobsen, the administrator at the American Hospital in Beirut, had been kidnapped as he arrived for work one morning in late May, 1985. Apart from providing Beirut's main casualty facilities, the hospital was the university's teaching wing. Sutherland knew Jacobsen vaguely, having met him at university-associated social functions. In the current round of kidnappings, American staff at the university had been left alone. Jacobsen's abduction, however, might change all that. If the kidnappers held on to Jacobsen as they had the other American hostages, it might not be safe for Sutherland to return to Beirut.

The following morning Sutherland telephoned the university's offices in New York to get the latest information about Jacobsen, and to see whether he should return. Sutherland only had another three weeks of the semester to teach, and he was concerned about letting down his students. The officials in New York, who were in daily contact with Beirut, were able to put Sutherland's mind at rest. Jacobsen's abduction had apparently been a mistake, and they fully expected him to be released within the next few days. There was no reason why Sutherland should not return to Beirut. Just to be on the safe side, the university would ensure that there was an official car waiting at the airport to drive him to the campus.

Thus reassured, and thoroughly refreshed by his home leave, Sutherland boarded the aircraft for the eighteen-hour flight. He spent the early part of the flight reading and preparing the classes he would be taking, then caught up on his sleep. When he arrived at Beirut the next day on June 9, 1985, he made his way through the shambolic customs hall where, as expected, he was met by one of the regular university drivers. The road from Beirut airport to the city centre passes the outskirts of the southern suburbs, the slums inhabited in the main by Lebanese Shia Muslims, where those Americans who had already been kidnapped were thought to be held. As people had been kidnapped while travelling on the airport road, it was considered prudent for any foreigner travelling into the city to have a Lebanese escort. To Sutherland's surprise, his driver was driving a distinctive white Chevrolet Caprice, normally used by the university's president, Dr Calvin Plimpton. Sutherland's car was apparently out of action so, feeling slightly honoured, he climbed into the back of the Chevrolet for the twenty-minute drive.

The car had gone no more than a mile and was passing the southern suburbs when Sutherland noticed a brown Simca pull alongside him. Suddenly one of the men in the Simca pulled out a gun and waved at Sutherland's driver to stop. The gunmen wasted no time. While one held his gun at the driver's head, the others roughly pulled Sutherland from the back seat. Before Sutherland even had a chance to shout for help or attempt to fight off his assailants, they bundled him into the back of their car and sped off in the direction of the southern suburbs, leaving the terrified chauffeur by the roadside. The kidnappers were becoming expert at this game. Sutherland's abduction could have taken no more than thirty seconds. It was carried out in broad daylight on one of the busiest roads in Beirut, and no one took the slightest interest.

Sutherland soon regretted the luxury of the Chevrolet. Having been held for four days without knowing what was going on, he was brought before a short, broad-chested man. Imad Mugniyeh, a radical Islamic fundamentalist who had masterminded the campaign of terror against American interests in Lebanon, explained to him in broken English in his high-pitched, squeaky voice that the kidnappers had meant to kidnap Dr Plimpton, which was why they had intercepted Plimpton's car. It was only when they examined Sutherland's passport that they realised they had the wrong man. At this point Mugniyeh allowed himself a brief chuckle.

'You are a very unlucky man, Mr Sutherland. When we found out our mistake, we were going to release you. But now I think it will be better if we keep you.' Little did Sutherland then realise that as a result of this 'mistake' he would spend the next seven years as a hostage.

1

FORT BEIRUT

When word filtered through the base that London had called up on the military satellite with an urgent request to talk to the commanding officer, few of the soldiers guarding the beleaguered British position on the outskirts of Beirut were in much doubt what it meant. When they had flown to Beirut all those months before, they thought they were coming to Lebanon to do something useful, to help the Lebanese government get itself back on its feet after years of civil war. Lebanon might be a dangerous place – you could hardly miss the pictures of all that fighting on the television news. But they had joined the army to go to dangerous places, exciting places. If Mrs Thatcher thought it a good idea to send British troops to Lebanon, who were they to argue? After all, her achievement in the Falklands spoke for itself.

The circumstances, however, in which the 100 or so men of 16th/5th The Queen's Royal Lancers found themselves in early February 1984 bore little resemblance to their understanding of the peacekeeping role they had, with high optimism, been sent to fulfil by the British government. For the best part of a month they had been holed up in a disused, semi-derelict building on the outskirts of the Lebanese capital, doing their best to avoid the continual barrage of artillery shells, mortars and rockets landing all around them. All too frequently the high explosives fired by Lebanon's warring militiamen landed close enough to the British base to send showers of dirt and earth, not to mention deadly shrapnel fragments, over the battered redoubt. What made it worse was that, for all their training in the art of war, there was nothing the British soldiers could do to defend themselves against the onslaught, apart from taking to the shelters. They had been sent as peacekeepers, equipped with the barest of kit essentials. Apart from their rifles and a few anti-tank rockets – to be used only in an emergency – the soldiers had just about sufficient equipment to handle a mild outbreak of civil disobedience. The idea, after all, was that they were to act more as glorified policemen than soldiers. The continual barrage of hostile fire, however, suggested Lebanon had moved well beyond civil disobedience; this was full-blooded civil war, and it would require all their skill and expertise in soldiering simply to survive.

The final straw, the moment when it became abundantly clear the British contingent should start making plans to go home if it did not want to join Lebanon's ever-increasing mortality rate, had occurred a couple of days previously when a rare lull in the fighting enabled the men to venture from their bunkers. About thirty men had gathered in the small assembly area at the back of the compound to collect their laundry. They were indulging in the usual banter of men relieved to see daylight after so many hours underground when one of the look-outs on the roof suddenly sounded the alarm for everyone to get back to the shelters. The sheer professionalism of the men saved the day. There was no panic, simply a rapid but orderly evacuation of the exposed area. Seconds after the last shelter door was secured a rocket came crashing into the assembly area, filling it with shrapnel. Had the warning not been effective, the Thatcher government would have had a very difficult time trying to account for a major disaster.

The significance of this narrow escape was not lost on Lieutenant-Colonel Peter Woolley of the Prince of Wales's Own Regiment of Yorkshire, the forty-two-year-old commander of the force which now went under the unglamorous Whitehall-speak title of BritForLeb. Only a month previously Woolley had been commandeered from the army's staff college at Camberley and sent to Lebanon to take charge of the British contingent. He had been hand-picked by Sir Edwin Bramall, Chief of Defence Staff, who had specific requirements for the man he chose. This was not a job for the soldier's soldier type, the gruff, bluff military man who took a pride in carrying out orders, no matter what they might be. The immense complexities of the situation in Lebanon required someone with a more subtle, almost intellectual approach, someone who could come to terms with the conflicting interests of the various Lebanese factions while maintaining a cool head. Indeed, the job credentials suggested a candidate from the diplomatic corps rather than the army. Tall and handsome, with a reputation for being the thinking person's army officer, Woolley fitted the bill precisely, although even his cool exterior was somewhat flummoxed when he was told on the day of his arrival at Camberley to report in uniform to the Ministry of Defence Headquarters at Whitehall.

More surprises were to come when Woolley reported to London for briefings. Once the formal briefings were concluded, Woolley was rather taken aback to find the Field Marshal, a man of pleasant manner but steely will, asking him to step aside for a few confidential, quiet words. The Field Marshal, it soon became clear, had strong reservations about his men risking their lives in Lebanon.

Exactly why it was ever decided to send a hundred British soldiers on a peacekeeping mission to Lebanon in February 1983 has been lost in bureaucratic obfuscation. Clearly if the army had had its way, there would have been no British component in the multinational force sent to prop up the faltering government of President Amin Gemayel. The peacekeeping force was essentially Washington's idea, conceived after a group of fanatical Christian militiamen had embarked on one of the ugliest murder orgies even by the standards of the Lebanese civil war, killing hundreds of Palestinian civilians in Beirut's Sabra and Chatila shanty-town refugee camps. This incident in September 1982, carried out with the complicity of the Israeli army which controlled the area, deeply shamed the Reagan administration which had given its personal pledge to protect the Palestinians from precisely this eventuality. The Americans, by way of atonement, prepared to send a peacekeeping force to prevent further atrocities, and to help the newly-elected president to assert his authority after so many years of civil war. To give the force some semblance of international legitimacy, the Americans wanted as many other nations to contribute troops as possible. The French, with their recent colonial history in Lebanon and deep-seated suspicion of American expansionism, were on board from the start. The Italians joined up out of humanitarian concern for the Palestinians with whom they claimed, for a reason which remains obscure, some special affinity. The icing on the cake for the Americans, then, was to get the Brits on board.

Relations between Ronald Reagan, the American president, and Mrs Margaret Thatcher, the British prime minister, were cordial; the Washington establishment could always expect a favourable response when it floated an idea London's way. To be sure they did not miss the target on this one, however, the Washington planners threw in some good old-fashioned emotional blackmail, pointing out how, only the previous spring, the United States had fallen over backwards to help Mrs Thatcher's government during the crisis in the Falkland Islands, even though to assist a neo-imperial adventure in Latin America was not strictly in the national interest of the United States. Washington's pitch found a natural constituency at the Foreign Office, where the working day of career diplomats is governed by the immutable laws of *quid pro quo*.

There were vague diplomatic mumblings in London about security council responsibilities, the maintenance of historic ties in the Middle East and the need to fly the flag in a natural sphere of influence, although it is doubtful whether, if asked, anyone would have been able to give specific justification for risking the lives of British troops in Lebanon. When the idea was put to the army chiefs, they tried to knock it down as a nonsensical notion which would only result in British soldiers being killed. If the Americans wanted to fight the Lebanese civil war, that was up to them. But keep British soldiers out of it, the army protested. The Defence chiefs could not make the government see sense, however. Mrs Thatcher and her advisers succumbed to Reagan's emotional appeal rather than logic, and an unhappy compromise was reached which is all too often the essence of British diplomacy. If the army had to send British soldiers to Lebanon, the army would send the smallest possible force with the least amount of equipment, clearly in the hope that, if anyone noticed it was there, they would not consider doing it any harm. Thus when the Americans sent 2,000 of their best marines, the French 2,000 of their elite paratroopers and the Italians 2,000 infantrymen, the British government sent 115 reconnaissance squaddies from the Midlands.

A year later, in January 1984, when Woolley was leaving London to replace the outgoing commander, Bramall took the young Lieutenant-Colonel into his confidence.

'This thing's a busted flush,' remarked the Field Marshal, the only officer still serving in the British army to have taken part in the Normandy landings. 'We can't afford any British casualties on this one. Lebanon isn't worth a single British life. So if you have the slightest problem, don't hesitate to get in touch with me personally. Just phone straight through to me if things look as though they're getting dicey.'

For the first year the army's policy seemed to work, although those responsible for sending it to Beirut were rudely awoken from their insouciance when a pair of suicide truck-bombs blew apart the barracks of the American and French troops in September 1983, killing more than 300 soldiers. The truck-bombs also blew away what was left of the rationale that foreign troops could possibly maintain peace in a country as hell-bent on violence as Lebanon.

The rocket attack on the British base in early February 1984 persuaded Woolley it was time to activate his special channel to the Field Marshal. He decided against phoning Bramall, even though the British army's satellite communications systems was such that, from his bunker in Beirut, Woolley could get through directly to Bramall's office at the main Ministry of Defence building at Whitehall. Instead he attached a preface to the daily situation report to London, explaining in no uncertain terms the dangers the base now faced. 'In recent days there have been a number of developments which now constitute a serious threat to life . . . Within the last four days a large number of near misses from heavy artillery, mortars and rockets have been incurred. My conclusion is that the risk to life is considerably greater now than it was in the past.' The message was timed 1400 hrs, Monday, February 6, 1984.

The next day, exactly one year after the contingent had arrived in Lebanon, Field Marshal Bramall was on the phone asking to speak to Woolley. By now most of the soldiers at the base had heard of the contents of Woolley's last communication, and the fact that the most powerful military officer in the British Isles was now asking to speak to their commanding officer left them in little doubt they were about to receive their marching orders. When the call came through, Woolley was away from the base at a liaison meeting. On his return he called Bramall immediately.

'How soon can you move?' was the Field Marshal's brusque demand.

'About eight hours, sir.'

'Good. In that case you are being redeployed offshore,' replied the Field Marshal. 'I want you to liaise with the other forces, and I want you to let the Lebanese know what we're up to. Start moving as soon as you're ready and let me know when the manoeuvre is complete. And Woolley, good luck.'

The eerie silence which gradually settled over Beirut as dawn broke was in many ways as frightening as the non-stop artillery barrage which had rained down on the city for the previous forty-eight hours. At first it was difficult to know whether the fighting had stopped, or whether the gunmen were simply drawing breath in readiness for another round of fighting, or had been ordered to halt the carnage by one of the numerous ceasefires which seemed to dictate the city's destiny. After the panic of the past few days, it was difficult to adjust to the sudden atmosphere of calm. Was it safe to venture outside? And what would we find when we got there? Who was in control of the city?

There had been plenty of warnings that Lebanon was about to undergo a radical reversal in its fortunes. Ever since the New Year the writing had literally been on the wall as the Lebanese militias, increasingly frustrated at President Gemayel's failure to take a firm grip of his country, resorted to sticking up fly-posters offering their views on what the country needed. Each group had its own ideas about how to put the country right, and there was little common ground. Throughout the first few weeks of 1984 hardly a day passed which did not produce some development – all too often accompanied by an act of violence – which helped turn Lebanon into a pressure cooker waiting to explode.

The year opened in traditional fashion with an Israeli air raid on southern Lebanon which killed sixty Muslim civilians. Two days later an American marine was shot dead when his unit came under attack as they disembarked from their helicopter. Washington claimed the marine was killed by Lebanese 'terrorists'. A French paratrooper on sentry duty outside the French barracks was killed by a rocket-propelled grenade the following day. Meanwhile talks held in the Saudi capital Riyadh to try to salvage the legitimacy of the Gemayel government broke down because of Syria's demand that all American troops must first leave Lebanon. When Gemayel decided to press on with implementation of a new security plan, no one was surprised when Muslim soldiers started to desert in droves. By mid-January all Gemayel had achieved was to get the Americans and French involved in a massive firefight with Druze and Shia Muslim militiamen, the main opponents of the Gemayel government.

On January 17 the Saudi Arabian consul to Lebanon was ambushed in his car and kidnapped by six armed gunmen, apparently a gesture of thanks for the role the Saudis had played in trying to bring peace to Lebanon. Later that day hundreds of screaming, hysterical Christian schoolchildren were trapped in their classrooms when their school was subjected to a two-hour artillery barrage by the Druze. Twenty later required hospital treatment. On January 18 Dr Malcolm Kerr, president of the American University in Beirut, was shot dead outside his office. On the day that Ronald Reagan officially launched his campaign to seek re-election for the American presidency, Walid Jumblatt, the Druze leader, warned that he would seek Gemayel's resignation even if it meant 'the destruction of Lebanon'. By the end of January commanders of the peacekeeping contingents were receiving intelligence reports that the main Christian and Muslim militias were moving in reinforcements and artillery in readiness for a showdown. The month ended with a nine-year-old Lebanese girl being killed when her schoolbus was raked by machine-gun fire from an American marine position. 'We have no way of knowing what we hit and what casualties there are,' read a statement issued by the marines following the incident. Lebanon was about to topple over the abyss.

Despite all the warning signs, most people were taken completely by surprise when a rather panicky announcer interrupted the normal broadcast schedule on Beirut radio on the afternoon of Monday, February 6 to say that an immediate twenty-four-hour ceasefire was being put into effect. Anyone found breaking the curfew was liable to be shot on sight. The announcement caused pandemonium as thousands of Lebanese tried to get to pre-arranged destinations before the curfew took effect. But with so little time available, and the city centre virtually jammed with traffic, many people were stranded. Mothers found themselves marooned with young children in high-rise apartment blocks while their husbands were trapped in their offices, and when the shelling began, despite the announced ceasefire, everyone attempted to protect themselves by putting mattresses against the windows, or even by seeking refuge in the bath which, so long as the ceiling did not collapse, would afford good protection against shrapnel.

The ceasefire was part of a last-ditch attempt by the Gemayel government to hold the country together, but even before the deadline for its implementation had passed, Muslim militiamen had come onto the streets in a show of strength to make it clear that they had no intention of making concessions. Even as ordinary Lebanese made their way to the shelters, squads of Muslim militiamen were spreading throughout the city, moving with such alacrity and deliberate intent that whatever pockets of resistance they encountered at Lebanese army positions were either swiftly overcome or surrendered without a fight. By early evening the first wave of hand-to-hand fighting had died down. What followed was among the most savage and indiscriminate shelling of the city in the appalling history of the civil war as the Christian loyalists, enraged at being outsmarted by their Muslim foes, emptied virtually their entire arsenal on Muslim residential areas in West Beirut.

By coincidence thousands of ordinary British, American and French citizens also lived in this area of Beirut, once the cosmopolitan heart of the city, and before long the basement of the Commodore Hotel, which was now the unofficial focal point for the foreign community, began to fill up as terrified women and children, foreigners and Lebanese, were gathered up and brought in during brief lulls in the bombardment. Many people risked their lives to drive across the city to locate friends and relatives they knew to be trapped in apartments which offered no protection against such an onslaught. Children as young as three, some sobbing hysterically, were carried into the hotel wrapped in flak jackets. The Lebanese hotel staff, who had many years' experience of such eventualities, fussed about making everyone feel at home. Chairs were placed together to form makeshift beds for the children. Some adults slept propped up against walls or at their children's side. But the majority spent the next two days listening intently to the deep thud of the artillery shells being fired in the distance, and the shrill whine as they whistled overhead. Some believed that by counting the interval between hearing a shell fired and hearing it pass overhead, it was possible to tell how close we were to the target. But it was an inexact science, and sometimes a shell came crashing down without warning very close to the hotel, shattering the windows and sending shards of glass cascading across the lobby.

For anyone on the receiving end of that bombardment – there were still some 3,000 Britons in Beirut at the time – it was a truly terrifying experience, and it may well be that shock as much as anything explained the silence that settled over Beirut once the bombardment ended. After all, civilians do not often find themselves on the receiving end of a major artillery offensive. As people, unkempt and bleary-eyed, emerged from the shelters, the hotel staff did their best to restore spirits by raiding the food stores and producing an impromptu breakfast of tinned asparagus and smoked salmon. But for all the Lebanese sangfroid, most of us were more concerned with what was happening outside. According to rumours, the Shia Muslims' main militia, Amal, with help from the Druze militia, had carried out their threat to effect a de facto partition of the country. West Beirut and the Muslim enclave of Lebanon, where all the troops of the multinational force were based and most foreign residents lived, was now under the exclusive control of the Shia Muslims. All points of exit were closed, including the airport and the traditional crossing points at the Green Line which separated Christian East Beirut from Muslim West.

After waiting several hours to see if there was going to be any radical change in the security situation, curiosity got the better of some of us and, with some foreboding, we ventured out to examine what had become of the city. The streets were full of broken glass and masonry. The burnt-out wrecks of cars were strewn all around, and the only obvious movement of traffic was the constant procession of ambulances to the American University Hospital. In a twenty-four-hour period the hospital received 400-odd patients, of whom thirty-five were either dead on arrival or later succumbed to their injuries. Apart from the widespread devastation, the other noticeable feature about the city was that Shia Muslim militiamen had set up roadblocks at key intersections. At several checkpoints they had been joined by Lebanese army soldiers, many still wearing army uniform. At places the soldiers were instructing the militiamen in the use of the newly-acquired equipment, and it was not unusual to see a militiaman accidentally reversing an armoured personnel carrier through a shop window as he struggled to master the controls.

Far more alarming than this, however, was the appearance on the streets of groups of severe-looking young men with neatly-combed beards and a rather fanatical demeanour. For over a year there had been much talk about the secretive but effective methods employed by Lebanese Islamic fundamentalist groups, but very little was known about them. They had scored some spectacular successes the previous year by blowing up the American embassy and the American and French military bases, and were making life very uncomfortable for the Israeli forces occupying the south of the country. Yet their very success depended upon the clandestine nature of their activities. When I first came across a group of them manning a makeshift roadblock outside the American University, I mistook them for some of Walid Jumblatt's boys. When I inquired casually as to their precise loyalties, however, the group leader made no bones about it. 'I am a Khomeini Muslim,' he announced grimly, referring to the Ayatollah who had masterminded the Islamic revolution in Iran five years previously. 'Khomeini is our strength and our power,' he proclaimed as if by rote, and turned back to discussing some obscure point of Koranic doctrine. Others of the Islamic persuasion were not so passive. There were reports that groups of Shia Muslim fanatics were roaming Beirut smashing up bars and restaurants which sold alcohol; of women, both foreign and Lebanese, being harassed for dressing immodestly, all in the name of Khomeini. There were even wild rumours that an Islamic republic would soon be proclaimed in Beirut and, judging by the multitude of Khomeini banners and posters which seemed to appear almost overnight, these rumours might easily have contained a kernel of truth. It was not until a few weeks had passed, and Islamic fundamentalists had begun their campaign of taking Western citizens hostage, that we really began to understand their agenda for Lebanon.

Peter Woolley's first task after putting down the phone to Field Marshall Bramall was to contact his American counterpart, General Joy, commander of the US marine contingent.

'We're off,' Woolley pleasantly informed him.

'Really?' replied the American, his gravelly accent failing to disguise his surprise.

'And I've got some news for you,' Woolley continued. 'You're on your way home too!'

'*Really*?' the American replied, his surprise turning to anger. 'No one's told me anything about that.'

'Well I'd get on the blower if I were you, old man,' continued Woolley. 'Washington should have some idea what's going on by now.'

The experience of the American marines in Beirut could not have been more different from that of the British. While the men of the Lancers had contented themselves with monitoring the various ceasefire agreements between the rival factions – an increasingly futile occupation – the marines had effectively assumed the status of full-scale combatants. When the Druze and Shia Muslim militias launched their attack on Christian positions, US marine commanders got the old World War Two battleship *New Jersey* to shell the Chouf mountains, the Druze stronghold. By February 1984 the Americans were clearly seen to be taking sides, and it was not the side the Islamic fundamentalists were backing, a factor which was to have prolonged repercussions for Americans who continued to live in Beirut after the troops had left.

While Lebanon collapsed into chaos, hurried meetings were convened in Washington, London, Paris and Rome to discuss what to do with the 6,000 peacekeepers trapped in Beirut. In London, especially, awkward questions were raised in the House of Commons and elsewhere about the role British troops were supposed to be fulfilling in Lebanon. The general tenor of the remarks was, 'What on earth are they doing there in the first place?' – a question which evinced little response; those responsible for sending the contingent now declined to advance the arguments which had seemed so compelling the year before. This provided Bramall with the opening he had been seeking, and he wasted no time in persuading Mrs Thatcher that the only sensible course was to get his men out of Lebanon as fast as possible. So as not to lose face in the Middle East, however, it was decided that it would be unseemly to effect a unilateral withdrawal; that might look as though the British government was handing the Islamic fundamentalists some kind of moral victory. Instead it was decided that BritForLeb would redeploy offshore, i.e. to the Royal Fleet Auxiliary vessel *Reliant*.

Because people like Bramall had suspected from the outset that the venture would end in such an ignominious fashion, it did not take the British force long to pack up and leave. Unlike the Americans who had come to Beirut to stay, the British had arrived intending to depart at the first opportunity. It was simply a question of packing as much as possible in the Ferret scout cars, and heading for the safety of the port of Jounieh on the other side of Beirut, whence the whole unit, with equipment, would be transferred by Chinook helicopters to *Reliant*. The men set to work with relish to clear their belongings from the building they had nicknamed, with a certain irony, 'Fort Beirut'. There were lighthearted disputes over whether to pack the whisky at the expense of the satellite communications system, but within a remarkably short time BritForLeb was ready to leave. As a safety measure it was decided not to leave until the following morning – they didn't want to be mistaken for a hostile force. So at 7.30 am precisely the small British convoy set off through the rubble-strewn streets for the port. Woolley formally handed over what was left of the British base to the Lebanese army which, after all its advances against the nearby Druze positions, had more or less overrun the area anyway. The Lebanese commander, General Michel Aoun, signed a receipt for the fuel and supplies the British were unable to take with them; several months later an over-zealous Ministry of Defence clerk sent Woolley a bill for £126,000 for the supplies he left behind! As they moved out, a Lebanese woman thrust a note at one of the British soldiers. It was addressed to 'Mrs Thatcher and the British People,' and read: 'Mrs Thatcher. You came! What's For !!! You're Leaving! For what Reason !!!!!!!! Sincerely, A Lebanese Citizen.' As Woolley later privately observed, the note just about summed up the British contribution.

Woolley's last call was on General Ibrahim Tannous, commander of the Lebanese army, who had ordered the devastating bombardment of West Beirut during the previous two nights. The scene Woolley found at the Lebanese army headquarters was almost surreal. The complex had been badly damaged by shelling from the Druze and Shia militias, including Tannous's office which had had all its windows blown out. When Woolley arrived, however, he found Tannous the picture of composure, smartly dressed in his uniform displaying insignia and campaign medals, and sitting at his desk reading the morning newspapers. Woolley formally announced the decision of the British government to redeploy the peacekeeping force offshore.

'When are you leaving?' asked the Lebanese commander, showing no hint of surprise.

'In about ten minutes,' Woolley replied. 'The lads are outside with the engines running.'

'So soon,' opined the General. 'What a shame, Peter, we won't have a proper opportunity to thank you for everything you've done.' Then the General began to rummage through the drawers of his oversized desk. Presently he emerged with a look of triumph.

'Here, Peter, take these as a gesture of our thanks.' He handed Woolley a small black box. 'And have a safe journey home.'

Curious, the British commander opened the box. Inside were a pair of Lebanese army cufflinks.

The huge sigh of relief which swept through the corridors of Whitehall once the British force had been safely airlifted out of Lebanon was quickly followed by a major row in the Commons over the plight of the 3,000 British civilians who had been left behind. Richard Luce informed the House that the Foreign Office was 'assessing . . . very carefully the implications of what is happening' and considering 'calmly and rationally whether we continue to think we can make a constructive contribution.'

Denis Healey, the shadow foreign secretary, retorted bluntly by demanding to know why the British government was doing nothing for the Britons left behind. If the British government had troops in Lebanon, the least they could do was help British citizens trapped there. The biggest cheer, however, from both the Labour and Conservative benches, came when Enoch Powell made probably the most telling remark of the whole sorry episode. 'Why has it once again proved impossible for the Foreign Office to anticipate things which were so widely perceived by others?' he thundered. To loud Labour cheers he continued: 'How long will the United Kingdom continue to be dragged at the cart-tail of the disastrous misconceptions of United States policy?'

Nor were the other governments involved in the Lebanon débâcle having an easy time of it. At the Quai d'Orsay in Paris, French foreign office officials spoke lamely of maintaining France's 'historical and cultural' links with Lebanon, while in Washington President Reagan's campaign for re-election was getting off to a disastrous start. One day the Pentagon was proudly announcing that the battleship *New Jersey* had fired 200 16-inch shells – each said to be the size of a Volkswagen beetle – at 'rebel positions' in the Chouf mountains, the biggest display of American naval firepower since the Vietnam War. The next day officials were having to concede rather sheepishly that *New Jersey* had 'hit nothing of military value'. Such old-fashioned gunboat diplomacy did nothing to appease the growing American consensus that American troops had no reason to be in Lebanon and should be brought home forthwith. President Reagan's mounting confusion over American policy in Lebanon was further exposed when he began talking in terms of the whole population of Lebanon and Syria being 'terrorists' worthy of being shelled by the *New Jersey*.

Britain, it transpired, had acted unilaterally (i.e. Bramall had got his way) in ordering its troops home, but one by one, over the next few days, the other governments involved, starting with the Americans, announced they were also 'redeploying' their troops. Following the parliamentary row over the fate of foreigners trapped in West Beirut, the British Foreign Office began to organise an evacuation. The Foreign Office line from the start was to protest, 'They've all been warned before', but now the mandarins, under pressure from the politicians, were forced to act. The helicopters which had airlifted Woolley and his men to safety were asked to fly back to pick up the women and children.

They made a pathetic sight that chill February morning, the bedraggled remnants of the foreign community. Some had been trapped in their apartments throughout the ordeal with young children and no food. There were even dark hints of some being the victims of unspeakable acts carried out by militiamen who had taken advantage of the breakdown in law and order to rampage through the more exclusive residential districts. The evacuation had been organised at short notice. Word had been passed around that all those wishing to leave should present themselves outside the British embassy on the Beirut seafront the next morning. Each family was limited to two suitcases of luggage.

David Miers, the British ambassador, was on hand to make sure the operation ran smoothly. Even his wife, Imelda, it turned out, had been trapped in the official residence for twenty-four hours by the shelling until a detachment of security guards was able to rescue her. The chance of a rapid exit from Beirut appealed even to hardened veterans of nine years of civil war. There was a hard core of expatriates, many of whom had nowhere else to go, who refused to leave. But with gunmen rushing around sticking up posters of Iranian ayatollahs, and with most of the infrastructure destroyed by years of neglect, Beirut was no longer an attractive place to live. In many ways the gathering outside the embassy resembled a scene from some Third World crisis, except that these were British subjects clutching their worldly chattels. They were making the right decision. Beirut was never going to be the same again and, for those who decided to stay, the nightmare was about to begin. Within days of the evacuation, Islamic fundamentalists would kidnap their first victims.

2

DESTINATION TEHERAN

It was a beautiful summer's evening in Beirut, at that time when the gentle Mediterranean breeze begins to cool the piercing heat of a Middle East day in July. After a long day at work, David Dodge, acting president of the American University, set off across campus on his evening constitutional before dinner. For all the ravages war had brought to Lebanon, the American University still boasted one of the most beautiful campuses in the world. From his office in the main university buildings, constructed in the classical, arched style of the Ottomans, Dodge looked across a cluster of palm trees to the peerless blue of the Mediterranean.

It was July 1982, and Dodge had had few recent opportunities to take advantage of one of the most beautiful vistas in the eastern Mediterranean. The previous month, when the world was still preoccupied with the fortunes of the British armed forces in the Falklands, Israel had launched its own invasion of southern Lebanon in an attempt to destroy the powerbase of the Palestine Liberation Organisation, which had almost become a state within a state in Lebanon. Under the leadership of Ariel Sharon, the Israeli defence minister and a distinguished soldier, the Israelis had used troops, fighter aircraft and the Israeli navy to ensure that this time there would be no escape for the Palestinian fighters. Sharon's policy ultimately prevailed, and thousands of Palestinian fighters were evacuated by ship from Beirut later that autumn. But the price Sharon's policy exacted from Lebanon in terms of widespread devastation and the deaths of thousands of civilians profoundly changed the political landscape of Lebanon, mostly, as far as Westerners living there were concerned, for the worse. It was to clear up the mess the Israelis had made that the multinational peacekeeping force was dispatched to Beirut.

Nothing Dodge, a tall, wiry, softly-spoken man in his mid-fifties, had experienced in seven years of civil war in Lebanon could have prepared him for the might of the Israeli armed forces. Hardly a day passed without American-made Israeli fighter-bombers screaming over the centre of Beirut bombing targets at will. The Israeli navy quickly established a blockade of the port while the army set up a continual artillery barrage of the city. Dodge's primary responsibility, when he was not in the bomb shelter, was to ensure the safety and security of the university. His main concern was to keep Palestinian fighters off the campus. In the early days of the invasion Palestinian guerrilla commanders were convinced the Israelis would stage a sea-borne landing of Beirut, and the American University, with its spectacular vantage point over the Mediterranean, provided the best defensive position. One morning Dodge awoke to find that PLO gunmen had constructed an anti-aircraft battery on the outskirts of the campus and, despite the pleas of the university authorities, refused to budge. For days everyone expected the Israeli airforce to bomb the university to knock out the battery, but the attack never came. Possibly the Israeli military planners had weighed up the damage an attack on such a 'soft' civilian target might do to Israel's international reputation; they were also aware that the antiquated Palestinian anti-aircraft batteries were about as effective as throwing confetti against Israel's state-of-the-art fighter-bombers. Nevertheless, the presence of the Israelis in Lebanon for the past month had placed severe demands on Dodge's already onerous workload.

Dodge was well aware what a dangerous place the Middle East could be. He had worked in the region almost continually since joining Aramco, the main American oil company in Saudi Arabia, in 1949. Since 1956, he had lived in Beirut looking after the oil pipelines which, until the outbreak of civil war, pumped oil from the Saudi oilfields to ports on the Lebanese coast, providing easier and faster access to mainland Europe. As part of his job Dodge had even worked closely with the Shia Muslim communities in southern Lebanon, a unique experience at a time when most foreigners rarely strayed beyond the international jet set's playground in Beirut. One of the main pipelines from Saudi Arabia passed through southern Lebanon, and various deals had been negotiated between the oil companies and local tribal leaders to enable the pipeline to cross their territory. Occasionally rivalries between local Shia leaders would result in sabotage against the pipeline. One Shia leader bearing a grudge would sabotage the pipeline to get his rival into trouble, hoping the oil company would stop its payments in protest. At times like these Dodge would be called upon to intervene. He would travel around the south, drinking interminable cups of coffee with village elders, until the whole problem could be resolved amicably and the oil men could get on with shipping their product to Europe.

When David Dodge, together with thousands of other expatriates, had first travelled to Lebanon in the 1950s, his arrival coincided with the emergence of Beirut as a city of international dimensions after decades, if not centuries, of living in the shadow of Damascus, its close neighbour and chief rival for influence in the Levant. Under the suzerainty of the Ottoman Turks, who ruled the Arab world for the better part of 400 years, Beirut was a quiet backwater in the larger world of Ottoman influence, a quaint port which served as a capital for Lebanon's one million Christians and one of the region's foremost centres of learning. Towards the end of the Ottoman period, in 1866, a group of American missionaries decided to establish a college of higher learning in Beirut which would include medical training. The money was duly raised in the United States, despite the disruption of the civil war, and the authorities of New York State granted a charter for the new institution under the name of the Syrian Protestant College. In 1920, with the French running Lebanon, the trustees changed its name to the American University of Beirut. The university, with its headquarters in New York, was, according to its founder, Daniel Bliss, to provide higher education 'without regard to colour, nationality, race or religion. A man, white, black or yellow, Christian, Jew, Mohammedan or heathen, may enter and enjoy all the advantages of this institution for three, four or eight years; and go out believing in one God, in many Gods, or in no God.' The AUB, as the institution was to become known throughout the Middle East, quickly established itself as the foremost centre of learning and scholarship in the region, tutoring generations of Arab students who would rise to positions of power in politics, commerce, science and scholarship.

It was not so much the collapse of the Ottoman empire during the 1914–18 war, as the rise to power in Egypt of Gamal Abdul Nasser, in the aftermath of the 1939–45 war, which consolidated Beirut's rise to pre-eminence in the Middle East. Until Colonel Nasser seized control in 1954, Cairo was still basking in the reflected glory of having been a major administrative centre of the British empire. It was regarded as the region's premier political and intellectual centre. The high academic standards of the colleges and universities and the liberal social climate which prevailed under the Egyptian monarchy – save for the odd purge – not only enabled Cairo to sustain its central position in Arab affairs, it also provided an attractive home for the increasing numbers of Americans, British, French and other foreigners taking advantage of the business and commercial opportunities in the region.

Nasser changed all that. Committed to his fiery brand of Arab nationalism, Nasser lost no time in cleansing his nation of what he regarded as the undesirable influence of the West. Egypt was to be for Egyptians – or rather, Egyptians of the Nasserist viewpoint. Before long foreign businessmen, teachers and journalists were leaving Cairo in droves and, as they searched for a new home, Beirut, with its liberal academic reputation and laissez-faire economy, was quickly identified as a suitable domicile. Damascus, for all its traditional influence, suffered because of its close association with Nasser and his policies.

The arrival of so many talented and dynamic foreigners in Beirut complemented the emerging class of skilled Lebanese professionals who had taken full advantage of the first-class education facilities. Not for nothing did the Lebanese claim their roots back to the Phoenicians, the architects of Mediterranean commerce. When the growth of the oil industry in the Middle East increased the demand for bankers, engineers and managers, Lebanon had them in plentiful supply. By the 1960s, Beirut was the boom city of the Middle East. It also resembled an enormous building site. Every available acre was seized for high-rise apartment blocks and offices, with planning constraints only rarely applied. One day a buyer could purchase an expensive luxury apartment with an uninterrupted view of the Mediterranean. Within a few months the view would have been filled by another apartment block.

Everyone was so busy making money and enjoying the high life, that no one paid much attention to the underlying political problems in Lebanon, even though Lebanon boasted the most liberal press in the Arab world. In Beirut it was possible to find out anything about anyone. If you wanted to know which member of the Saudi Arabian monarch's harem was currently in favour, or who was behind the latest Palestinian terrorist campaign, you asked in Beirut. Kim Philby was by no means the only foreign agent active in Beirut in the 1960s. But no one seemed to take much interest in what was happening in Lebanon.

For the first thirty years of Lebanon's existence as an independent nation, the cosy carve-up of political power whereby the French had vested all the key powers of state in the Christians survived intact, despite occasional attempts to dismantle it, usually when the Christians attempted to hijack the constitution for their own ends. The most famous political crisis occurred in 1958 when American marines were actually dispatched to Lebanon to restore order. But for the most part, so long as the ruling élites were making a tidy fortune for themselves, few questions were asked about whether a system based upon such blatant political, economic and social injustice could survive. Although no Green Line as such existed to divide the communities, the Christians proliferated in East Beirut and the northern half of Mount Lebanon and the northern Bekaa Valley, while the Muslims tended to congregate in West Beirut, southern Lebanon and the southern half of the Bekaa. Back in the heady days of the 1960s and early 1970s, few among the tens of thousands of expatriates tripping the light fantastic in Beirut's nightclubs and restaurants paid much attention to Lebanon's politics. Apart from making a good living, expatriates, in common with many of Lebanon's commercial classes, paid no taxes. And Beirut was a place where money could buy anything.

Corruption may have been rife in Beirut, but it did not stop the city becoming by the 1960s the epicentre of banking, commerce and education in the Middle East. It is often said that one of the causes of the civil war was the profound jealousy the surrounding Arab countries felt at so high a proportion of the region's wealth being concentrated in one place. Until quite late into the civil war, Lebanon's banking sector virtually controlled the finance of the Arab world. Nor was Beirut pre-eminent only in banking. Any Arab seeking a good education would be expected to have at least one degree from the AUB; any Arab company with a problem would look to Lebanon to have it solved.

Perhaps the most surprising aspect of the Lebanese civil war was that it took so many people by surprise. One minute the beautiful people were hell-bent on their hedonistic pursuits; the next they were taking to the bomb shelters. Somehow no one had noticed the growing numbers of Palestinian refugees making their way into the outlying suburbs, whose presence threatened to swing the delicate demographic balance against the Christian hegemony in favour of the Muslims. Nor had too much attention been paid to the growing political influence which the Palestinians, under the leadership of the PLO, were starting to exert on Lebanon. The PLO's determination to fight for a fair deal for the Palestinians attracted much support among the leftist Lebanese Muslim groups who wished to achieve a similar goal for the Muslims in Lebanon.

When the civil war erupted in April 1975, many expatriates were reluctant to leave, no doubt finding it hard to believe the party was over. But once the Christians and Palestinians began massacring each other in earnest, the exodus of wealthy foreigners and Lebanese gathered pace. David Dodge was offered early retirement after the sharp rise in insurance premiums for the oil tankers put the Lebanese ports out of business. But after a year spent trying to adjust to life back in America, he decided in 1978 to return to Lebanon to work as an adminstrator at the American University, which he knew well. It was to become one of the great ironies of the hostage crisis that the one foreign institution genuinely concerned with serving the best interests of the Lebanese people, the AUB, should suffer so badly at the hands of the extremists. The early days of the civil war had taken their toll on the university, mainly by deterring many foreign students from travelling to Beirut for their higher education. Before the war, more than half its students came from outside Lebanon; after the war hardly any did, a development which inevitably had an adverse effect on academic standards and caused a sharp decline in foreign remittances. But in spite of these hardships, the board of trustees in New York was committed to maintaining standards, and one of their most important tasks was to continue to recruit academics of a high calibre to teach at the university. Dodge, who knew Beirut and the risks better than anyone, was happy to return to Lebanon and to play an active role in persuading fellow Americans to teach at the AUB.

Dodge arrived back in Beirut in 1978 and, until the Israeli invasion, the worst that had happened to him was when a group of rogue militiamen held him up and stole his car, an American make of station-wagon which just happened to be then in vogue among the more image-conscious militiamen. The experience of the Israeli invasion, however, was completely new. During the civil war, people were used to hearing small arms fire and the occasional shell. But they had never experienced the full might of a sophisticated war machine being used against them. It was probably because everyone was so obsessed with what the Israelis were up to that few people took much notice of an announcement made in Teheran that a detachment of Iran's Revolutionary Guards was being sent to Lebanon to help their Palestinian 'brothers' in their fight against Israel. At the time there was little for the hard-pressed Palestinians and Lebanese to get excited about in this statement. Iran was locked into an all-consuming war with Iraq, and was hardly in a position to break off hostilities and turn its guns against Israel. And the 500 or so Revolutionary Guards who eventually arrived in Baalbek, the capital of Lebanon's Bekaa Valley region, were hardly in a position to take on the thousands of Israeli troops which within a week were in complete control of southern Lebanon.

And because no one was paying much attention to the Iranians, few people took much notice either of the news that four Iranians travelling from Baalbek to Beirut had been kidnapped in early July 1982. The story merited only the briefest of mentions in the Lebanese press. Kidnapping, at least for the Lebanese, was a way of life, so why worry about a few Iranians? The Iranian group, which included Ahmad Motevaselian, the newly-stationed Revolutionary Guards commander at Baalbek, and Mohsen Musavi, the Iranian chargé d'affaires to Lebanon, was apparently on its way to Beirut for a reconnaissance mission to see how Iran could assist the resistance effort against the Israelis. Thinking their diplomatic credentials would facilitate their passage, the Iranians made the mistake of attempting to drive through a Christian checkpoint. The Christians, no friends of the Palestinians, were by then actively assisting the Israelis to set up a blockade of the Muslim area. Militiamen, especially Christians, have little truck with officialdom, and when the Iranians stopped at the checkpoint and presented their credentials, they were seized by the Christian militiamen and taken away. They were never seen again.

It was just a few days after the kidnapping of the Iranians that David Dodge, after weeks of confinement in the university basement sheltering from the Israeli air raids, was able to take his first evening stroll across the campus for some time.

It was July 19, 1982 and, after the Israelis had finally agreed to accept a ceasefire, the fate of Lebanon once more depended on the frenzied comings and goings of teams of international diplomats. As he was passing the main college hall, Dodge was aware of a group of young Lebanese coming up behind him. He moved to one side to allow them to pass when suddenly one of them knocked him to the ground with a forceful shove. Turning round, he saw a group of young men standing around him pointing their guns at his head. Although it was daylight, in the middle of campus at one of the busiest times of the day, no one did anything to help. His attackers were armed and did not give the impression they would take kindly to interference.

Dodge was bundled into the back of an American station-wagon, which had been coasting behind the kidnappers. He was made to lie face down on the floor while about half-a-dozen gunmen clambered onto the back seat, their guns sticking awkwardly into each other, their feet keeping him pinned to the floor. The car then sped out of the main university gates and headed off into the suburbs. Very quickly he found himself held in the kind of small apartment room which was to become very familiar to so many of his fellow-countrymen. The first shock to his system was that, after all the excitement of the kidnapping, nothing very much happened once he was locked in his makeshift cell. For the first two weeks almost no one spoke a word to him. His meals were brought at regular intervals, he was allowed one daily visit to the bathroom, but that was the sum of his contact with the outside world.

David Dodge was most probably kidnapped because, as acting president of the most prestigious American institution in Lebanon, he was considered a valuable target, someone the Americans would want desperately to have released. What was particularly confusing for Dodge, however, was that no foreigners had ever previously been kidnapped in Lebanon. For him there were no precedents. Unlike later hostages, he could not say to himself, 'Oh no, this is it,' because he had no idea what to expect. Foreigners in Beirut in the summer of 1982 knew next to nothing about Islamic fundamentalists apart from the odd piece of information they had gleaned about the Iranian Revolution. But Iran was hundreds of miles away, and why on earth would the distant Persians, with their ayatollahs and Koranic strictures, want to bother themselves with the superficial secularism of the Lebanese? Why would anyone want to hold an innocent American, or Briton, or Frenchman, hostage in a dank cell, chained to a radiator, with no communication with the outside world for an unspecified period of time? The foreigners were soon to learn the answers to these and many other questions about the nature of Islamic fundamentalists, their relations with Iran and their plans for Lebanon, all too frequently at great personal cost.

While in that first apartment, probably no more than three miles from the AUB, Dodge began to recall the odd items he had read in the Lebanese press about the arrival of the Revolutionary Guards and the kidnapping of the four Iranians. The guards were careful to conceal their identitities and who they were working for. Every time a guard came into his room, Dodge was required to cover his eyes with a blindfold. His suspicions were confirmed after two weeks when the guard who seemed to head the group had his first conversation with Dodge.

'You will go home soon. This will only be a short stay. But first we must get our four friends released.' The only other time he had any meaningful contact with the kidnappers was when Israeli warplanes renewed their attacks on Beirut.

'Mr David, these are your warplanes attacking us,' the guards would complain. It was difficult for Dodge to explain the subtleties of the international arms trade while being held captive in a dingy room.

A few days later the head guard returned and told Dodge he was being taken on a journey that would lead to his release. It would be necessary to drug him, so there would be 'no problems'. Dodge was blindfolded and bound, and then felt the prick of a needle entering his flesh. Within seconds he lost consciousness. When he awoke he was in a new apartment and, judging from the noises outside his cell, in a different location. Gone was the constant babble of city street noises which he had heard in Beirut, interrupted by the occasional Israeli air raid. Now all he could hear was the silence of the countryside, and the odd burst of birdsong. He had been placed in a room in what was clearly someone's house. All the windows had been covered by metal shutters, and the room was only modestly furnished, but it was an improvement on his cramped, and dangerous, quarters in Beirut.

The kidnappers, fearing the Israelis were about to enter Beirut, had decided to ship Dodge to the safety of the Bekaa Valley, which was well beyond Israel's jurisdiction and nominally under Syrian control. Exactly how the kidnappers managed to transport Dodge through the Israeli blockade of Beirut will always remain a mystery, but he was probably placed in a false floor under a lorry and driven over Mount Lebanon to the Bekaa Valley. In all probability the house in which he was held was within a few miles of Baalbek. Certainly from the moment he regained consciousness Dodge was acutely aware that his guards were very different from those who had held him in Beirut. They were much neater, wore green battle fatigues, and were polite to him. They were also extremely well disciplined. Whereas the guards in Beirut would occasionally open up and talk about their families, his new guards were careful not to say anything. 'We are here to guard you and take you to the bathroom. We are not here to talk to you,' they replied whenever Dodge tried to engage them in conversation. They were also more relaxed about his living conditions. He was allowed some books to read, although any contact with the outside world, such as a radio, was strictly prohibited. But he was never left in any doubt as to what would happen if he did not comply with their wishes. 'If you try to escape, we will kill you,' they often told him in a matter-of-fact way, almost as if they were discussing the weather. Occasionally when he heard them talking outside his room he thought they were speaking in an unfamiliar tongue. Dodge knew Arabic well enough, but this was a very different language. Could it be Farsi, perhaps, the language of the Iranians? For the eight months he was held in the Bekaa he could never be certain, but his suspicions were confirmed when he was moved to his next destination.

It was the middle of April 1983, about the same time that an Islamic extremist drove a suicide truck-bomb into the American embassy in Beirut killing more than sixty people and wounding hundreds more, when the head guard reappeared. 'We are going to release you,' the guard announced. 'We will have to drug you again because we have to take you back to Beirut and there will be security problems. But don't worry. Everything will be fine. When you wake up you will be a free man.' Dodge went through much the same procedure as before. He was bound, blindfolded, felt the injection, and passed out. But nothing could have prepared him for the shock when he came to his senses several hours later.

Rather than the noise of Beirut street life, the first sound Dodge heard as he regained consciousness was of a large aircraft making its final approach for landing. Even more alarming was the discovery, made as his ears adjusted to the whine of the hydraulic system, that he was being held bound and blindfolded in a crate. As he later wryly observed, he didn't exactly travel first-class to Teheran that trip. He was still struggling to come to terms with the implications of his unusual surroundings when the plane lowered its landing gear and made a precision landing. No sooner had the aircraft taxied to a halt than the cargo doors were flung open and he heard the excitement of men clambering through the hold towards the crate. There then followed the clatter of crow-bars as the men worked to prise open the bindings. The next thing he knew strong arms were lifting him out and helping him onto the tarmac. Someone reached behind him and untied the blindfold. Slowly he steadied himself after the long ordeal and his eyes began to come back into focus. It was cold, and judging by the faint hint of light in the night sky, dawn would soon be breaking. Then, as he looked over at a brightly-lit airport terminal on the corner of the apron, he could just make out an official noticeboard with something on it painted in English: 'Welcome to Teheran International Airport'.

From the moment Dodge arrived in Teheran, no one made the slightest effort to conceal from him that he was in Iran. By the same token his guards were not exactly falling over themselves to advertise his presence in the Iranian capital. Still dazed by the experience of being crated up and of awaking to find himself in Iran, Dodge was placed in the back of a large Mercedes which immediately sped off using a side exit and headed through the deserted, pre-dawn streets of the capital of the Islamic revolution. The car did not stop until they reached the gate to an imposing building in Teheran's northern suburbs. At this point Dodge was re-introduced to his blindfold and the party moved into the compound. Dodge heard the heavy iron security gates close behind him, and was then helped out of the car and led along a series of narrow passageways. The party again came to a halt while someone unbolted what was clearly a well-secured door. After a few moments of fumbling with keys, the door swung open and Dodge was led into a small room. As the locks were rebolted behind him, someone called, 'It's OK, you can take off the blindfold now.' Dodge found himself in a small but clean prison cell. Before long he would learn he was a guest at Teheran's notorious Evin prison, the Place de la Concorde of the Iranian Revolution, where literally thousands of Iranians had perished before the dawn firing-squads of the Revolutionary Guards. For David Dodge, however, his arrival at Evin in April 1983 was ultimately to provide his ticket to freedom.

Throughout the long history of the hostage crisis in Lebanon there were numerous claims that Western hostages had been shipped to Teheran for interrogation at the hands of Ayatollah Khomeini's henchmen. The truth of the matter, however, is that David Dodge was the only foreign hostage held in Lebanon who ended his captivity in Teheran. While there were no doubt occasions, especially when the fighting in Lebanon reached fever pitch, when the kidnappers must have wished they could place all their captives in the safety of Evin, this was not an option they were able to pursue, with one exception.

As with all their actions, the kidnappers never gave the hostages an adequate explanation of what was happening to them, so that the decision to ship Dodge to Teheran remains something of a mystery. It may have had something to do with the fact that the same group was implicated in the suicide truck-bomb attack on the American embassy and feared they would be the target for a reprisal raid. There is also the possibility that the commanders of the Revolutionary Guards in Teheran were becoming increasingly frustrated at their failure to locate the four Iranians kidnapped by Christian militiamen in July 1982. By transferring Dodge to Evin, they perhaps hoped this would bring more pressure to bear on the kidnappers to release the four Iranians. Certainly the authorities in Teheran remained so obsessed about the fate of the missing Iranians that resolving their fate remained one of their central demands right up to the final negotiations to resolve the hostage crisis years later.

In terms of his living conditions, Dodge's move from the Bekaa Valley to Teheran was a considerable improvement. Evin was much cleaner, the food was of a higher standard and delivered regularly, the guards were more friendly and there were even regular hot showers. The only oddity of the Evin regime was that the guards required all prisoners to wear blindfolds whenever they left their cells, even to go to the shower-room. For a couple of weeks Dodge even had a companion: a middle-aged Iranian, a small, well-mannered man who apparently had offended the mullahs with his political views, was placed in Dodge's cell. Though neither could speak the other's language, they managed to communicate through hand gestures, and play the odd game to while away the time. Despite the improvement to his habitat, however, Dodge's move to Teheran did nothing for his morale. Suddenly he felt a long way away from his friends in Lebanon, the friends he knew would be exploring every conceivable avenue to secure his release. He was also well aware that the American embassy no longer functioned in Teheran.

Furthermore, he was constantly threatened by the guards, who gave him the distinct impression that it would not be long before he joined the dawn execution chorus which was such an established part of the prison's daily routine. On several occasions he was ordered to put on his blindfold, and marched along corridors and up and down metal staircases until his escort reached the office of a senior Revolutionary Guards officer. He was then subjected to intensive interrogation. The officer wanted Dodge to tell him everything about himself, no matter how trivial. He wanted Dodge to tell him about all the people he knew in the Arab world, how he got to know them, what he thought of them. From time to time he would slap Dodge hard across the face and scream: 'You're a spy. We know you. You work for the CIA. We will kill you, don't worry.' Then he would settle down and tell Dodge to carry on. Nothing the American told him was very spectacular, just run-of-the-mill gossip about the Arab world any discerning reader could pick up from the local press. At times it was clear the interrogator was quite impressed by some of Dodge's viewpoints. Then he would be overcome with embarrassment for showing the prisoner undue deference, and would strike out again. At the end of each interview (Dodge thinks there were three in all), his tormentor would ask about the four missing Iranians. Dodge had no idea what had happened to them, and said so. This in turn prompted the same reply: 'Don't joke with me, they're dead. And you will be too before long.' His comments had the desired effect. Each time Dodge was led back to his cell, he was convinced his chances of release were worse than ever.

Thus when, on the morning of his 365th day as a hostage, a guard walked into Dodge's cell and announced he was going home, Dodge refused to believe what he was hearing. After so many broken promises, Dodge suspected this would be just another move to another cell. Only when he was taken to the main prison office and had his blindfold removed did he begin to believe this might indeed be his lucky day. He was handed the clothes he had been wearing on the day of his kidnapping, which he had not seen since (throughout most of his captivity he was dressed in old army fatigues). He was also handed back his own watch and the $600 in cash he had been carrying. Without further ado, he was driven back to Teheran airport where a Syrian Arab Airlines jet was about to leave for Damascus. A Revolutionary Guards officer escorted him onto the plane, and to Dodge's surprise, the two men settled into the first-class compartment. Noting Dodge's surprise at their superior travel arrangements, his escort quietly apologised for the indulgence. All the economy seats were apparently occupied by Revolutionary Guards on their way to Lebanon, and the authorities could not run the risk of Dodge being spotted by them in case they decided to intervene and prevent his release. Dodge also noted that sitting just a few seats in front of him in the first-class compartment was Farouk al-Sharaa, the Syrian foreign minister.

At Damascus airport he parted company with his Revolutionary Guard escort who bade him a cheery farewell. At no point during his release did any of his guards express the slightest hint of regret over the ordeal he had been forced to endure. An official Syrian delegation was waiting to meet him on the tarmac, and after a brief round of introductions he was driven out of the airport by the VIP exit. He was taken to a palatial house on the outskirts of Damascus where, he was later to learn, he was a guest of Rifaat al-Assad, the brother of the Syrian president. Dodge's belief that the Syrians were somehow behind his release was confirmed during the evening when he was called to the phone to take a call from Geneva. On the phone was Rifaat himself, politely inquiring whether he was being well looked after. The next morning, after a good night's sleep and his first bath in a year, Dodge was driven to the American embassy and formally handed over. Finally he was a free man.

In view of what was later to unfold in Lebanon, it is remarkable to consider that David Dodge's unpleasant encounter with the Iranian authorities happened several years before the hostage crisis in Lebanon really took hold over the imagination of the West. Everything that happened to David Dodge was a forerunner of the fate that awaited a future generation of foreigners kidnapped in Lebanon, while at the same time his abduction and captivity taught the kidnappers some useful lessons about how far they could and could not go in the way they ran their hostage operation. Few of the above details about Dodge's kidnapping have been previously published, mainly because he was sworn to secrecy by the Syrians after his release. The Syrians were concerned that details of their role in facilitating his release would not do them any favours in the eyes of other radical Arab states, for whom the very idea of assisting the US government was anathema.

And yet Dodge's story was of profound significance for the way the hostage crisis in Lebanon was to develop. One of the major issues throughout the hostage crisis, for example, was the question of exactly how much influence Syria had over the kidnappers. There is no doubt the Shia groups responsible for the kidnappings operated in territory nominally under Syrian control. Syria, for reasons which will be examined later, also had close relations with Iran, which was certainly funding, if not controlling, the hostage groups. The operation to transfer Dodge from Lebanon to Teheran would have entailed shipping him through Damascus airport. It later transpired that the whole operation to ship Dodge as an item of Iranian military cargo – and therefore subject to diplomatic immunity – was organised by Rafik Mohsen-Doste, the Iranian minister responsible for the Revolutionary Guards, who had trained with the PLO in Lebanon in the 1970s.[1] Apart from the position he held, Mohsen-Doste was highly influential in Teheran because he had driven Khomeini's car during his triumphant return to Teheran in 1979. In retrospect, of course, this was Iran's big mistake. Given the all-pervasive nature of the Syrian intelligence services, there is little doubt the Syrians were well aware of the contents of the unusual, human-sized crate being shipped by the Revolutionary Guards to Iran, but the Syrians clearly thought it better to wait their moment before making

[1]John K. Cooley: *Payback: America's Long War in the Middle East*, Brassey's (US) Inc., 1991.

a fuss. Dodge's arrival in Teheran caused untold problems for the Iranians. As he later candidly admitted when I met him at the AUB head office in New York: 'For the Iranians I was a nuisance, an expense and a liability. It got to the point where they either had to kill me or release me.'

Dodge's presence in Teheran denied the Iranians their favourite fall-back position, a position they were later to reiterate with frustrating frequency; namely that they did not control the kidnappers, they could only exert *influence* over them. This was hardly a tenable position for the Iranians once it became clear they had an American abducted in Lebanon sitting in the Iranian capital's primary jail. The Syrians were also less than pleased that the Revolutionary Guards should abuse their hospitality in such an unsophisticated manner. The Syrians were content to let the Revolutionary Guards extend their influence in Lebanon so long as by doing so they posed a constant source of irritation to Syria's enemies, in particular the Israelis. It was not part of the deal for the Iranians to start embarrassing the Syrians, which is how President Assad regarded the irregular techniques employed with regard to Dodge. Given the poor relations that existed in the summer of 1983 between Damascus and Washington, it is nonetheless surprising the Syrians should have responded at all to the constant badgering from the US embassy in Damascus to intervene on Dodge's behalf. With 2,000 American marines dug in around Beirut airport, less than a three-hour drive from the Syrian capital, and the *New Jersey* battleship cruising off the Lebanese coast, President Assad clearly felt no harm could be done by winning a few brownie points in Washington.

David Dodge's only regret after his release was that he was not more forceful in advising his American colleagues, who remained teaching at the AUB, to leave Lebanon. Dodge was friendly with Malcolm Kerr, who was murdered six months after his release, and knew several other American academics, such as Tom Sutherland, who fell victim to the next round of hostage-taking.

'I think the AUB should have been a lot more circumspect in sending people to Beirut,' Dodge later admitted. 'I was the only trustee who had any misgivings. After what happened to me it seemed obvious it would happen again, and the AUB was the softest target in the whole of Beirut. But the bottom line is that people legally have a right to do what they want to do. And if they want to go to Beirut and work for a worthy cause like the AUB, it is difficult to stop them.'

The happy collision of circumstances which resulted in Dodge's release was unique. For the Iranians, shipping Dodge to Teheran proved to be a profound miscalculation which resulted in the American being released three months later. It was a mistake the Iranians would not repeat.

3

THE ART OF THE LEBANESE KIDNAP

As Prince Bohemond I of Taranto, Prince of Antioch, was being dragged off in chains for a long and ignominious captivity in a remote dungeon in Asia Minor in the year 1100 AD, he probably had more pressing matters on his mind than to reflect that he was another victim of one of the oldest and most popular pastimes in the history of the Middle East. A formidable opponent, scourge of the Muslim armies throughout the triumphant procession of the First Crusade through the Holy Land, Bohemond, even as he was being taken captive by the Saracens, was working on an escape plan. When the Italian prince realised he had no chance of escape, 'he cut off a mesh of his yellow hair' and gave it to a trusted Crusader footsoldier to give to the newly-proclaimed King of Jerusalem, Baldwin of Boulogne, as proof of his identity, together with a passionate plea for Baldwin to launch a rescue mission before he disappeared off the face of the earth. Baldwin, however, more concerned for his own safety, made only a half-hearted attempt to recover his old friend and rival. He set off in pursuit of the Saracens with a party of some 140 knights, but when the Saracens retreated into the mountains of northern Syria, Baldwin gave up the chase. And so Bohemond, who, like so many before and after, had left his home country in search of fame and fortune in the exotic climes of the Orient, was abandoned to spend a long and uncomfortable period held hostage by Muslim extremists.[1]

In retrospect, it is odd to think that so many people, not least the hostages themselves, were so taken by surprise when the kidnapping of foreigners in Beirut began in earnest in the spring of 1984. To the uninitiated, Lebanon had always seemed one of the more civilised areas of the Arab world, a country where the people understood, appreciated and even aspired to Western values. But however much the chic, nouveau riche commercial classes in Beirut loved their large American cars and expensive French fashions, the underlying fascination with causing the maximum amount of distress and violence to one's enemies and rivals was never too far from the surface, as the countless atrocities committed in the name of the Lebanese civil war were to reveal. Hostage-taking was a tradition almost as old as the Middle East itself, and in the Levant old habits die hard.

Possibly the earliest record of someone being held against their will in the Middle East is to be found in chapter 14 of Genesis, verse 12: 'And they took Lot, Abram's brother's son, who dwelt in Sodom, and his goods, and departed.' Lot was captured during one of the intermittent battles between the various tribes of Canaan for control of the Jordan Valley, and even though Lot and Abraham had become estranged following disputes between their various camp followers, Lot's enemies clearly realised the extra bargaining power they would acquire by taking captive a blood relative of such an important

[1]Sir Steven Runciman: *A History of the Crusades*, vol. I, Cambridge University Press, 1951.

regional power-broker as Abraham. Any hopes that the capture of Lot would play to their advantage, however, were dashed by Abraham's swift response. 'When Abram heard that his brother was taken captive, he led forth his trained men, born in his house, three hundred and eighteen, and pursued as far as Dan. And he divided himself against them by night, he and his servants, and smote them, and pursued them unto Hobah, which is on the left hand of Damascus. And he brought back all the goods, and also brought again his brother Lot, and his goods, and the women also, and the people.' It seems Abraham was more expert at handling a hostage crisis than some modern-day Western governments.

Despite the enormous time-span covered by the Old Testament, however, there are surprisingly few references to what is currently known as hostage-taking. Perhaps the most famous biblical figure to be held against his will in a foreign land was Joseph; but he was sold into slavery in Egypt by his jealous brothers, so that those responsible for keeping Joseph in Egypt were not technically responsible for bringing him there. The most likely explanation for the dearth of hostages in the Bible is that, in those primitive times, it was easier to kill one's enemies than hold onto them, with all the responsibility of feeding and housing the captives.

It was the Greeks, Persians and Romans who actively sought to incorporate hostage-taking into their *modus operandi*. When in 490 BC the Persian army was making its way through Greece on its way to the battle of Marathon, the Persians first made the rounds of the islands in the Aegean, pressing troops for service and taking the islanders' children as hostages.[1] This was an eminently sensible precaution. When undertaking such a hazardous venture as marching on Athens, the Persians

[1]Herodotus: *History of the Persian Wars*.

could ill afford to run the risk of a military challenge from the sea. In those instances where the islanders refused to supply hostages, the Persians laid siege to the town and destroyed the crops in the surrounding country until they got their way. Not surprisingly, most islands provided hostages rather than precipitate the destruction of their land. In this and many other cases during the period, hostages were taken as a guarantee of good behaviour or allegiance.

It was during the Roman period that hostage-taking developed more as a tactic designed to achieve a specific goal. Take the case of the schoolmaster at Falerii which in 390 BC was being besieged by the Romans.[1] The schoolmaster had under his care the children of all the leading men in the town and one day, hoping that he could both end the siege and cover himself with glory, he led the boys out of the town giving them the impression they were going on a long hike, but instead led them straight into the camp of the Roman commander, Camillus. 'These boys' parents control our affairs,' the schoolmaster announced to an astonished Camillus. 'I have delivered them into your hands. So Falerii is now yours.' The schoolmaster had calculated that the parents would immediately submit to the Romans rather than allow any harm to come to their offspring. But the schoolmaster had underestimated the Roman sense of probity. Camillus found the schoolmaster's craven behaviour to be unworthy of the dignity of a Roman officer. Denouncing the schoolmaster as an unprincipled swine, Camillus had the traitor stripped and bound, gave the boys sticks, and told them to beat him all the way back to Falerii. If Rome was to defeat Falerii, Camillus observed rather priggishly, it would be through the traditional Roman arts of 'courage, persistence and arms'. In the event,

[1]Livy: *History of Rome*.

these qualities were not required as the Falerians capitulated without reservation, so impressed were they by the Roman sense of honour and justice.

From ancient times to modern, hostage-taking has flourished in the Middle East, as Bohemond and many other Crusader princes found to their cost. Throughout the Middle Ages, which in many respects could be said to have lasted in the Middle East until the discovery of oil at the start of this century, the taking of hostages adopted a variety of guises. Large areas of Arabia were left to their own devices for centuries, especially once the Ottoman Turks established their hegemony, because the ruling authorities had neither the resources nor the inclination to take much interest in parochial Arab affairs. It was left to the muftis and village chiefs to maintain the peace which, because Arab family ties were both extensive and binding, was forever being challenged by one dispute or another. In the absence of any easy redress of grievances through the government authorities, it often made sense for a family to kidnap a member of the clan with which it was in dispute and to hold him hostage until the aggrieved party received satisfaction. If no satisfaction was forthcoming, the hostage could either be released or killed. If this was how the culture of hostage-taking flourished in the Middle East at a micro level, exactly the same philosophy prevailed at the macro level of the Ottoman empire, the Sublime Porte at Constantinople, albeit in a more sophsticated manner. Whenever the Sultan decided that one of his satraps was becoming a little too independent for his liking, the offending governor or provincial ruler would be invited to reside in Constantinople. It was an offer no subject, no matter how powerful in his own region, could decline. If the Sultan wished to have the benefit of a subject's company, it was that subject's duty to present himself at the Sublime Porte at the earliest opportunity, or face the awful consequences.

Sultan Abdul Hamid II (1876–1909), 'an unhappy man and an inhuman Sultan'[1] and the last and most despotic of the great Ottoman rulers, manipulated this tactic to perfection. His rule in the closing years of the Ottoman empire depended upon maintaining a vast network of spies and informers. When it was discovered that a certain leader or family was disputing the Porte's authority, he was not above having them assassinated. When such men were either too eminent or popular in their locality, an invitation would be issued for them and their families to travel to Constantinople where they were treated with all dignity, but where it was much easier for the Sultan's spies to keep an eye on them. In this way Hussein ibn Ali, the Grand Sherif of Mecca and the great-grandfather of the present King Hussein of Jordan, spent fifteen years residing with his wife and four sons in a villa on the Bosphorus.[2] The Sultan, the architect of the plan to build the Hejaz railway between Constantinople and Mecca to consolidate his position as leader of the Muslim world (it was later to be the primary focus of the attentions of one Lawrence of Arabia), decided Hussein was far too important to leave to his own devices. Hussein was not technically held hostage in Constantinople, but nor was he exactly residing there of his own free will. Nor was the delicacy of the Grand Sherif's position lost on the rest of his subjects, which in turn made them more inclined to be respectful of the Sultan's wishes. When Hussein was finally allowed to return to his home in Mecca in 1908, it was not long before he was leading the Arab world in the revolt which helped ultimately to destroy the Ottoman empire.

Ironically, it was as a result of the other commitments Britain undertook at the time of the alliance with Hussein, during the First World War, that one of the most intractable

[1]Lord Kinross: *The Ottoman Centuries*, Jonathan Cape, 1977.
[2]Peter Mansfield: *The Arabs*, Allen Lane, 1976.

problems in the recent history of the Middle East was created, an issue which was to transform the nature of hostage-taking from a parochial concern to a matter for international diplomacy. When on November 2, 1917 Arthur Balfour, the British Foreign Secretary, issued his famous statement committing the British government to 'the establishment in Palestine of a national home for the Jewish people', few of those concerned could have anticipated the cataclysmic effect it would have on the region. Certainly, had the Foreign Office had the slightest inkling of what they were letting themselves in for, they would never have allowed Balfour to issue his historic declaration. The ultimate consequence of that declaration was the establishment of the state of Israel in 1948 and with it the displacement of hundreds of thousands of Palestinian refugees around the Levant.

Until the arrival of the Zionist settlers, Palestine had been a fairly unremarkable area of the Arab world. But the growth of Zionist aspirations in Palestine gradually brought about conflict with the indigenous Arab population, and when the British authorities, who had responsibility for keeping law and order, tried to place restrictions on the Zionists, they quickly found themselves on the receiving end of attacks by Jewish terrorist groups. Many of the newly-arrived Zionists came from central Europe where they had witnessed first hand the success extreme political groups had achieved by employing modern terrorist tactics. It was not long before Zionist terrorists, the Stern Gang and Irgun, were using bombs and carefully planned assassinations in their campaign to force the British to leave. Kidnapping was not a tactic widely employed by the Jewish underground groups, although when they did abduct someone, whether a maverick agent from their own organisation or a British policeman, the victim rarely lived to tell the tale.

If the activities of the Zionist underground in Palestine

helped to introduce modern methods of terrorism to the Levant, it was not long before Palestinian groups were emulating these tactics for their own benefit. Until the creation of the PLO in the 1960s, Palestinian 'terror' attacks mainly consisted of small groups of Palestinians attacking Israeli settlements, targets they believed to be legitimate war objectives. It was the emergence of radical Palestinian groups under the auspices of the PLO in the mid-1960s, a decade when heady revolutionary rhetoric was in plentiful supply throughout the world, that a whole new dimension was added to the simple practice of hostage-taking. It reached its apogee, perhaps, in the autumn of 1970 when groups of Palestinian terrorists belonging to the Popular Front for the Liberation of Palestine, a radical group led by Dr George Habbash, conducted a mass hijacking of several aircraft over northern Europe. As with so many Palestinian terrorist adventures, however, the master-plan, if such a thing existed, fell apart when the crew of an Israeli Boeing 707 overpowered two would-be hijackers, killing one and detaining the other, a young Palestinian woman called Leila Khaled. An argument broke out when the plane landed at London's Heathrow Airport when the Israelis at first refused to hand over Khaled, whom they wanted to take back to Israel for interrogation. Finally the authorities at Heathrow prevailed and Khaled was escorted to Ealing police station.

While the British authorities initially claimed that Khaled was being held on a legitimate criminal charge, this was not how her revolutionary comrades in the Middle East regarded the matter. They had three aircraft and some 300 civilians held hostage at a remote airstrip in Jordan, and they made it clear they would not release either planes or hostages until Khaled and six more Palestinian terrorists held in German and Swiss jails were freed. Edward Heath, the Conservative leader who had only recently been elected prime minister, was placed in a quandary over what to do with Khaled. Heath's difficulties were eased when Peter Rawlinson, the attorney-general, and Geoffrey Howe, the solicitor-general, agreed that, because Khaled's crime had taken place 'somewhere south of Clacton', and therefore not in British air space, the British authorities would have difficulty presenting a *prima facie* case against her. When the hijackers then blew up three of the hijacked jets to drive home the seriousness of their demands, Heath was quickly persuaded that the most sensible course of action would be to set Khaled free. A few days later Khaled was escorted from Ealing police station to board an RAF Comet which flew her to Beirut, making brief stopovers in Germany and Switzerland to collect six other terrorists who were freed as part of the same deal.

Never had a group of terrorists been given such first-class treatment, and never had the seizure of a group of Western hostages produced such spectacular results. The attitude of the Heath government, and indeed those in Germany and Switzerland, was that this was a Middle East problem, and not one with which they should get involved. Not everyone in London, however, was quite so sure that they had done the right thing. At the House of Commons there was general unease about the capitulation to the terrorists' demands, an unease which was most stridently articulated by a certain Margaret Thatcher, the rising star of the Conservative Party's right wing. She expressed her outrage that Britain had suffered such public humiliation to anyone who cared to listen, including the prime minister. And she made it abundantly clear that, if ever the day came when she was running the country, RAF jets would most certainly not be put at the disposal of terrorists.

The success of the PFLP operation, however, was short-lived, for Mrs Thatcher was not alone in her disdain for the hijackers' triumph. King Hussein, who had become the grudging host to all the radical Palestinian groups, decided the Palestinians would destroy Jordan if they continued as they were, and when they ignored his request to abide by the laws of the land, he had no alternative but to expel them by force. The Palestinians rebased themselves in Beirut where, in April 1975, a similar dispute with the Lebanese government over who had ultimate responsibility for the Palestinians caused the outbreak of the civil war.

Exactly who started the kidnapping at the outset of the Lebanese civil war is lost in the chaos, but the fact that the various factions were not averse to kidnapping each other whenever feasible was highlighted during the brief political crisis in 1958 which resulted in American marines making their first entry to Lebanon to restore the peace. In the five days of chaos which swept Beirut before the marines landed, Christian and Muslim factions set about kidnapping one another. A Muslim group would kidnap some Christians, torture them, then either kill or release them, and the Christians would retaliate in kind. But this did not even amount to a dress rehearsal compared with what was to follow.

Lebanese Muslims will tell you that the Christians started the kidnapping in 1975 by forcing two Muslims off a bus in Beirut, then shooting them in the back after telling them to run for it. Christians will tell you the Muslims started it with a group called the Knights of Ali. These enterprising individuals are said to have kidnapped a group of fifty Christians, and murdered them in cold blood. According to local lore, the bodies were found in a cemetery near the dividing line between the two communities, their penises neatly severed and stuffed in their mouths.[1] Whatever the claims and counter-claims, there is no doubt that within a very short space of time all

[1]Jonathan Randal: *The Tragedy of Lebanon*, Chatto & Windus, 1990.

parties involved in the Lebanese civil war became expert at kidnapping. In those early days, people were kidnapped to be killed. Each side thought that if they could kidnap sufficient numbers of the other side and mutilate them, it might discourage their enemies from continuing the war. In fact it had the opposite effect, and as soon as news reached a militia that some of their number had been kidnapped, they would set off in pursuit of their own captives, so that very quickly both sides were locked into an ever-escalating spiral of kidnap and murder.

Kidnapping soon became as commonplace in Beirut as car bombs and rocket attacks. By far the most terrifying aspect of the kidnappings was the flying checkpoints which were set up by different groups without any warning at any point in the city. With no government forces capable of maintaining order, the groups would set up a roadblock and force every man to produce his official identity card, which states each individual's religion. If someone had the misfortune to be of the wrong religion, they were taken to some remote spot and shot. Often atrocities were committed and the bodies mutilated. If a kidnap victim was a fighter with a rival militia, he would have his trigger finger, if not all his fingers, cut off. Women were rarely kidnapped, but when they were it was not unheard of for their kidnappers to cut off their breasts. One group of journalists who visited the Green Line area dividing Christian East from Muslim West Beirut returned to their hotel that evening convinced that a group of Christian militia *women* who had stopped them at a checkpoint had shown them a sack filled with male genitalia.[1]

One ritual which was established early on in the civil war was the practice of dumping the bodies of the kidnap victims

[1] *Ibid.*

at one of the main flyovers in the centre of Beirut. The flyover was too close to the Green Line to be used by ordinary civilian traffic, so every morning at dawn an unofficial ceasefire was observed while militiamen drove to the flyover in jeeps and trucks and dumped the bodies of their victims from the top of the flyover onto the road below. Relatives of people who had been kidnapped then had the gruesome task of sorting through the cadavers, most of them mutilated, to try and find their loved ones. While this macabre spectacle was taking place, it was not uncommon to see curious schoolchildren cycling up to the flyover to have a look. A few years later, after a childhood devoted to such morbid pastimes, these children provided the militias with a fresh generation of fighters.

Not everyone who was kidnapped was killed, nor were they all necessarily victims of the civil war. Sometimes, if a victim could prove he had no affiliation with any militia, he would be held for a short time and used as a bargaining chip to get other hostages released. In general, however, the militias avoided holding people hostage because of the effort involved in feeding and housing them. Not that the militias expended too much effort on the housing conditions when they did hold onto captives. The Christians in particular hit upon the idea of converting metal shipping containers into mobile prisons. Holes were made in the side of the containers, usually with a heavy machine-gun, and then up to fifty people could be squeezed into the container. This also made it relatively easy to move large numbers of hostages without too much fuss. It was simply a question of loading the container onto a lorry. In the heat of summer, however, many captives died of suffocation or dehydration inside the containers.

The chaos of war also enabled private individuals to settle old scores. A significant proportion of those kidnapped in Lebanon were taken because of a row over a business deal or a lovers' quarrel. Generally, but not invariably, those captives who were killed were shot. If the kidnappers believed their captive was deeply involved in a rival militia, or sometimes if they were just plain bored, more inventive methods were found for killing them. One of the more popular was to tie the captive to the back of a car, and speed around Beirut with the screaming victim dragged behind. The sport continued until long after the victim's death, to ensure that the spectacle reached as wide an audience as possible.

Tens of thousands of Lebanese were kidnapped during the sixteen-year civil war, a figure which puts the fate of the fifty or so foreigners kidnapped between 1982 and 1991 in its proper perspective. At least 7,000 people – some estimates put the number as high as 17,000 – were listed as missing when the war finally ended, a figure that compares favourably with the 6,000 'disappeared' victims of the rule of the generals in Argentina, and yet there was far less of an international outcry about the fate of the Lebanese, most probably because in Argentina it was fairly clear who the culprits were.

It will never be possible to assess the deep psychological damage the culture of kidnapping had on the non-combatant population. Mothers lived in perpetual fear from the moment their sons and husbands walked out of the door that they would never see them again. It was natural, therefore, for a mother to try to prevent the menfolk from leaving the safety of the house, which itself became a source of conflict, especially in the case of teenage boys. Even if the men could be persuaded to stay at home, that did not guarantee safety. Gangs of militiamen were likely to come knocking at the front door, either because they were looking for someone in particular or just because they needed to kidnap some men of a certain religious faith to keep their numbers up. One of the biggest, indiscriminate round-ups of Muslim men took place in the early autumn of 1982 when the Israeli army finally took control of West Beirut. Soon afterwards, in clear contradiction of undertakings they had given to the Americans, the Israelis allowed hundreds of Christian militiamen into West Beirut – the first time they had been able to reach the Muslim heartland since 1975 – who rapidly set about settling old scores. On one night during September 1982 – at about the same time Christian militiamen carried out the massacres of hundreds of Palestinians in the Sabra and Chatila refugee camps – 2,671 Muslims were kidnapped from their homes by Christian militiamen. Of these some were no doubt clearly targeted for their political or militia connections. The majority were taken simply because they were Muslims. When the civil war ended, only 200 had been released. Of the others, nothing was ever seen or heard again.

An insight into what happened to many of these victims came three years later when the main Phalange Christian militia released thirty-five 'prisoners'. At the same time the militia announced it had no more hostages in its possession – the first time, incidentally, the militia leaders had admitted in public that they *were* holding hostages. One of the thirty-five released was able to give a small insight into their experience. 'We were put in these containers and moved around from place to place,' the hostage recalled. 'No one spoke to us or let us know what was going to happen to us. After a while they took us to a barracks and we were held there until our release. As for the others, I got the impression they were all killed soon after they were taken.'

If the fear of kidnap had its psychological effect, this was as nothing compared with the experience of the families of victims who disappeared without trace; theirs became a limbo world in which they were expected to continue their lives irrespective of whether the victim would ever return. In the spring of 1992, a few months after the last American and British hostages had been released and Giandomenico Picco, the United Nations diplomat who assisted in the final negotiations, had returned to New York, I met a Lebanese woman who had not heard a word about her husband since he disappeared in September 1985. Like many of the American hostages, he worked at the AUB. The week before a group of men had gone to the house of her husband's brother; they kidnapped the brother, his wife, their son and the family dog. For the rest of that week the woman's husband had trailed around Beirut exploring every avenue in an attempt to make contact with the kidnappers. At one point, according to the woman, her husband received a telephone warning asking him not to interfere. Despite her protests, however, he continued to look for his brother. 'He was mad,' she told me as we sat in her small office on campus where she taught English part-time. 'He was in a terrible state. He was very close to his brother and could not bear the thought of someone doing harm to him.' One week later the woman's husband was kidnapped. In the intervening years she had to raise their two children – the son was eighteen and the daughter fourteen at the time of their father's abduction – ever mindful that a similar fate might befall her son, at the same time trying to find out what had happened to her husband. A member of Beirut's modest Greek Orthodox community, the woman tried her church, which in turn tried its own militia contacts. No information was forthcoming. 'It is a nightmare which never goes away,' said the woman, the deep pain of her experience etched in the hard lines in her otherwise attractive features. 'I have heard recently that he may be alive and I have been told many times that he is dead. But no one really knows, and this is the torture of my situation. If I knew for sure that he was dead I could cope with my grief and get on with my life. But this state of never-knowing is the worst of all.'

When the civil war finally ended, various committees were set up in an attempt to solve the problem of the missing kidnap victims. Sinan Barraj, a Lebanese Muslim lawyer who had been involved during the civil war in negotiations to get hostages freed, was appointed to run a pressure group calling itself The Committee of the Parents of the Kidnapped. The idea was that the committee would contact existing and past militia leaders to try to establish the fate of the 17,000 missing civilians. Mr Barraj thought his chances of success would be improved by the decision of the new Lebanese president, Elias Hrawi, to grant an unconditional amnesty to all militiamen for acts of violence committed during the war. His optimism was misplaced. All the militia leaders proclaimed that they were no longer holding any hostages, even though as late as December 1991, when the last Americans were released, militias were organising their own 'hostage swaps', although the numbers involved were relatively modest. One of the main reasons Mr Barraj was unable to make much progress in his humanitarian mission, however, was the disinclination of President Hrawi's government to get involved in an issue which had the potential to rip open all the wounds of war the new government was attempting to heal. More to the point, perhaps, was the fact that many former militia leaders had been appointed to senior government positions as part of the deal to stop the fighting, and asking them for information about people kidnapped by their groups could have caused great political embarrassment.

To try to alleviate the difficult circumstances of wives of kidnap victims who were still not allowed access to their husbands' financial resources – in some cases ten years had passed since the husband went missing – Mr Barraj proposed that the Lebanese government adopt a similar attitude to that taken by the French government at the end of the 1939–45 war, namely to proclaim as dead all those who had not come back. But the Lebanese government behaved as if, as far as it was concerned, the hostage crisis was a closed book. Thus when the United Nations Commission on

Human Rights, when drawing up a report for the Working Group on Enforced and Involuntary Disappearances, made a formal request to the Lebanese government in late 1991 for information on fifty-two people as part of a case study, the Lebanese government made no response. The only option left open to relatives of the missing was to place adverts in the local press. Nothing better illuminates the emotional suffering these families have endured than the pathos of announcements such as this, which appeared in Lebanon's *An-Nahar* newspaper in January 1992: 'Zuhair Khaled from the village of Karoun in south Lebanon was kidnapped in 1985. To his kidnappers we say: your conscience must wake up and you must return our son after you have called us many times and promised to release him. If you have any humanity left you should inform us immediately about his fate. Whoever knows anything about him negatively or positively, we beg you to let us know whatever information you have.'

Perhaps these intense and extended sufferings partly explain the rather unsympathetic attitude the Lebanese seemed to take with regard to the fate of the Western hostages. When the first foreigners were kidnapped in the mid-1980s – the civil war started, remember, in 1975 – many Lebanese were genuinely surprised at the amount of attention generated about the fate of a few foreigners, many of whom had no reason to be in Lebanon, and who had been frequently warned that they remained entirely at their own risk. Then when Western governments started to dance up and down to whatever tune the kidnappers happened to be playing, the Lebanese became increasingly resentful that the West only seemed interested in its own hostages. Just about everyone in Lebanon knew someone, directly or indirectly, who had been kidnapped; even if they did not, they had to live under the constant threat that they soon would. But in the absence of any central government authority, relatives of Lebanese kidnap victims had no one to work to get their loved ones freed.

Nothing the British, American, French or any other government did to secure the release of their hostages ever benefited the Lebanese, or so they believed. And as the numbers of foreigners filling the basements of radical Islamic groups in Beirut gradually increased, a general mood of apathy about their plight settled over a population which had seen it all many times before. If the Western hostages, their relatives, friends and governments expected sympathy, they had most definitely come to the wrong place.

4

TEMPTING FATE

The British troops had gone and the Americans, French and Italians were packing up when the kidnapping of foreigners began in earnest in Beirut in February 1984. Given the atmosphere of studious frenzy which had descended on the city, it is perhaps not surprising that so little attention was paid to the kidnapping of Frank Regier, Professor of Electrical Engineering at the AUB, on February 10, just two days after the last British troops left and the decision was taken for the rest of the peacekeeping force to follow.

Regier, after his release, often gave the impression that he felt somehow cheated about his kidnap experience, that he had not been given his full share of credit for being kidnapped. In interviews he made caustic comments about some of the other American hostages who he seemed to imagine had hogged the limelight at his expense. But even though he was only held for a couple of months, his experience nonetheless had its place, not just in terms of the effect captivity had on Regier as an individual, but by the very fact that his confinement was brought to a premature end in mysterious circumstances.

In many ways Regier, then in his late fifties, was a typical example of the American expatriate, who had opted to stay in West Beirut long after the majority of Americans had either fled or been evacuated. Regier and his wife, Mary, had lived in Beirut for more than twenty years. They enjoyed the lifestyle, in spite of the civil war. Mary Regier was half-Lebanese and half-Palestinian – her family was dispossessed during the creation of Israel, which probably explains the very strong pro-Arab, anti-Israeli views, bordering on the anti-Semitic, that her husband held and was not averse to expressing in public. Given his job at the AUB and his deep sympathy for the Arab cause, Regier felt very comfortable in Lebanon and, for all the difficulties the American government was causing for itself in Lebanon, did not feel particularly at risk. For Mary Regier, moreover, the attraction of life in Lebanon, even in wartime, outweighed anything else. 'Beirut was so interesting. In Lebanon it was no sin to have fun. You could have fun every day,' she later recalled when the couple had been forced to settle for life in a dull suburb of Cleveland, Ohio.

Regier's kidnapping merited no more than a couple of paragraphs in the next morning's papers among the columns of dispatches filed by the small army of foreign correspondents still based in Beirut. Regier's kidnapping was expertly executed, in almost exactly the same way as David Dodge's nearly two years previously. He was pushed to the ground with a gun at his head, bundled into the back of a car and driven off. Five days later he was joined by Christian Joubert, a forty-two-year-old French civil engineer who was similarly kidnapped in broad daylight outside the French embassy, less than half a mile from the university campus. That day the two men were brought together. At no time during their captivity were they able to talk to each other, but at least, unlike Dodge, they had the company of another human being. For the next two months they were held in a series of houses in Beirut, always blindfolded and gagged.

As with Dodge, their kidnappers never told them who was holding them or why.

People did, however, start to sit up and take notice when, three weeks later, Jeremy Levin, the fifty-two-year-old bureau chief of Cable Network News (CNN) was kidnapped as he walked to his office in the centre of Beirut on March 7. Levin cut a rather unusual figure among the crowd of macho, hard-drinking and even harder-living newsmen who were based in Beirut in the spring of 1984. When I had first arrived in December 1983, I had been rather overwhelmed by the characters who each night seemed to get into noisy and sometimes violent drunken arguments about who had got the better story or pictures that day. As the new boy in town, I was expected to sit and listen to the wild rantings of men who seemed to live for the 'fix' of the daily story, but to have no wider appreciation of the political complexities involved. The worst offenders were the cameramen and the small army of fixers and hangers-on who worked for the three major American television networks; they made it quite clear they were in Lebanon to make as much money as possible in the shortest possible time. Among this group was a smattering of people who had covered the Vietnam War and reckoned they could handle anything Lebanon threw their way. Only later did I discover that the journalistic endeavours of many of these people were sustained by the daily consumption of large amounts of cocaine. Apparently this was the only way they could summon the courage to drive up to the Chouf mountains and risk their lives filming for the news bulletins back home.

One of the more bizarre characters was a huge bear of a man who worked as a cameraman for an American network. He hailed from Texas, where he had been a policeman. When, on one of the rare occasions I managed to have a straightforward conversation with him, I inquired why a Texan policeman would want to come to Lebanon and risk his life for a few rolls of film, he lifted up his shirt to reveal a succession of deep and unpleasant scars scattered across his considerable stomach. 'Hell, I got myself shot up three times in Texas when I was a cop,' he proudly announced. 'I've been here three months and no one's shot me yet.' Lebanon was clearly a better bet than life in the lone-star state.

When Jeremy Levin arrived in Lebanon at about the same time as myself, the Commodore Hotel, situated about 100 yards from the main Hamra shopping centre in West Beirut, had become the unofficial press centre for visiting journalists. In late 1983 CNN was considered something of a joke by the high-salaried, high-profile doyens of the Beirut press corps; partly because the latter were arrogantly certain that nothing could start to challenge the supremacy of the established television networks; partly due to the unspoken apprehension that a 24-hour cable news service might ultimately usurp their privileged position – a fear subsequently borne out during the Gulf War in 1991, when CNN produced the first live television coverage of a war.

Jeremy Levin did not fit easily into this milieu; he was rather old to be taking up his first foreign assignment. A wiry, intense man, Levin had strong views on almost any subject, and from the moment he arrived decided it was his mission to provide all the support he could for the American marines in Beirut. His initial attitude was that the American forces could do no wrong; if they got themselves into difficulties, it was because they had been put in an intolerable position by the radical Muslim forces trying to drive them from the country. Levin, eager to make an impact in his new job, was not the sort of journalist who stopped to think why the Muslim militias were so intent on driving the Americans out, or even why the Americans had been sent to Beirut in the first place. The world as Levin saw it divided comfortably between us and them, the good guys and the bad guys. Many of his television colleagues shared this attitude; there were notable exceptions who knew Lebanon well, such as Charles Glass of ABC television news in New York, but they were in the minority. Yet Levin was not accepted by his colleagues. It was all right for the veterans of the Lebanese civil war to express their opinions, but not for upstart newcomers, no matter how many books they might have read on the subject.

Whatever reservations his colleagues may have had about Levin as a person, however, his kidnapping was not a matter to be taken lightly. For by abducting Levin, the kidnappers had struck at the very heart of the Beirut press corps, an area everyone thought to be inviolable, a veritable sanctuary for the world's media. The press, after all, was there to do a job, and it was in the interests of all parties to respect the freedom of the media to come and go. Surely even the Islamic fundamentalist groups, whoever they might be, had the sense to see that. The kidnappers struck as Levin was walking from the Commodore Hotel to the CNN office across the street. The CNN office was in the same building as the BBC, ITN, NBC, CBS, ABC and just about every television news service worth mentioning. Scores of Levin's colleagues working for the television companies made the same journey each day. If they could take Levin, they could take any of them.

Suddenly the telex machines in the television company offices in Beirut clattered into life. Worried executives were calling from their plush offices on New York's Fifth Avenue and the BBC's television centre in London demanding an assessment of the risks to their own staff. Was Beirut getting too dangerous? Was the story worth the risk? Most important of all, what were the rivals going to do? If all the other television companies leave, shall we hang on and scoop them all? That night in the Commodore bar some of the world's best known television journalists were to be found behaving like coy teenagers at their first dance.

'So what are you doing, Chuck? You staying put or shipping out?'

'Don't know yet, Bob. The office has been giving me heat all day to get the hell out of here, but what do they know? It's a good story but it sure is getting more difficult to function. We'll wait and see what happens. How about you?'

'I think we're going to try and stick it out, although New York is starting to get very jumpy. I hear that Johnny and his crew have chartered a plane and that they're flying out to Cyprus first thing in the morning. Perhaps we should. I dunno. Anyway I gotta get going. We got an early start in the morning. Life's a bitch. See you around.'

Gradually people would break off from one group to listen in to another noncommittal chat about what people might or might not do. Then the groups would gradually disperse, and everyone would discreetly make their way back to their offices to fill in the executives in London or New York about the latest developments. The executives, some of whom thought stepping outside the office to buy a sandwich in central Manhattan a dangerous assignment, just loved to get a 'fill' from the boys on the ground. All that detailed information of what everyone was up to thousands of miles away made them look very impressive reporting at the executives' meeting. Just to know that Chuck was paying Ahmed $6,000 to provide extra protection for the boys on the ground, or that the team were exhausted because they'd been kept awake all night by the noise of the *New Jersey* shelling the Chouf mountains, gave the executive a terrific vicarious thrill.

At times like this, everyone attempted to rationalise why they would not fall victim to the kidnappers. This rationalisation process was to become a common feature of the hostage crisis; every individual who ended up being kidnapped had managed to convince himself that it was still all right to remain in Beirut. The first big rationalisation took place after Jeremy Levin was kidnapped; it became necessary to explain that, just because Levin had been kidnapped, it did not follow that the rest of the foreign press corps was at risk. Levin had been kidnapped because he was Jewish; it was all right to stay so long as you weren't Jewish. But a fair number of American correspondents in Beirut were also Jewish, so this argument died a quick death. Levin had been kidnapped because he was new in town and inexperienced; as all the other correspondents considered themselves veterans, there was no danger of them falling into Levin's trap.

To illustrate Levin's alleged naivety, the story started to circulate of how Levin had been seen dancing on the hotel roof one night when the *New Jersey* was firing shells into the Chouf mountains. Levin was said to have been dancing up and down, punching his fist in the air and shouting: 'Go give it to them, boys.' Small wonder the Islamic fundamentalists had kidnapped him. Experienced war correspondents knew better than to get drunk and dance on the roof shouting when the *New Jersey* shelled Lebanon, so there was no reason for them to leave. This *reductio ad absurdum* was passed down the line to the executives in New York and London who discussed it and decided this was an acceptable rationalisation. If Levin had known better, he wouldn't have been kidnapped. Correspondents no longer had to worry about whether to stay or leave; they could just get on with their work. Besides, the money was good.

If people did not take full cognisance of this spate of kidnappings, it was because no one had yet grasped the significance of what was happening. There were far more pressing matters for them to contend with.

The collapse of the multinational peacekeeping effort had led to a heated and at times acrimonious trans-Atlantic debate over the value and nature of the Anglo-American relationship. It was obvious that the relationship was becoming strained when the Foreign Office stated publicly that the British government had expressed 'strong reservations' about the American decision to allow the *New Jersey* to shell the Chouf mountains; strong words indeed in the mealy-mouthed lexicon of diplomacy. At a time when the British government, against considerable domestic political opposition, had shown the depth of its commitment to Washington by approving the deployment of cruise missiles at American bases in Britain, the British establishment was starting to feel that the Americans had involved Britain too deeply in something which was essentially an American problem. Britain's sponsorship of a move to send United Nations troops to Lebanon to replace the failed multinational peacekeeping force was one way of indicating Britain's view that America should cut its losses in Lebanon while the opportunity presented itself.

But in 1984 all the tensions of the Cold War, certainly as far as the Reagan administration was concerned, were running at fever pitch and the Middle East in general, and Lebanon in particular, was regarded as the main testing ground for the battle of wills between Reaganism and the Soviets. This was at a time, it must be remembered, when there was still a long way to go before Gorbachev, *glasnost* and Reykjavik changed the face of East-West relations beyond recognition. One of the central policy goals Ronald Reagan had articulated during his election campaign in 1980 was to rebuild America's military strength and to stand up to Soviet expansionism throughout the world. With Ronald Reagan as president, the Reaganites announced, the world would be safe from any act of Soviet aggression such as the invasion of Afghanistan. From the moment he took office, Reagan filled the key foreign policy posts with ultra-conservatives, and during his first term he persuaded Congress to accept the funding of the biggest peacetime arms build-up ever in the defence budget, the cost of which, a decade later, would cripple the American economy.

With all these resources at his disposal – including the Second World War battleship *New Jersey* which had been placed in mothballs by previous, more financially prudent, administrations – and so much ideological rhetoric to live up to, Reagan was not inclined to back down over Lebanon which, far from being a remote civil war of marginal international significance, was regarded by the apostles of Reaganism as a classic confrontation between the policies of West and East. It was not so much the Lebanese who posed such a threat to Western civilisation as Lebanon's largest and most influential neighbour, Syria.

Like Lebanon, Syria had once been under French control, but after gaining full independence in 1946, Damascus – a renowned hotbed of radical Arab political activity even in Ottoman times – had been a focal point of post-colonial Arab nationalism, to the extent that in 1958 it tried to merge Egypt, Yemen and Syria into one nation called the United Arab Republic. The experiment failed because each 'member' of this new country thought itself the most important – rather like the modern-day rivalries within the European Community. But the Syrian obsession with uniting the Arab peoples into a single, powerful nation free from colonial influence resulted in the 1960s in the emergence of the Ba'ath party, a strange hybrid of traditional Arab nationalism and the trendy socialist dogmas then so much in vogue.

Not even his severest detractors have ever accused General Hafez al-Assad, a career Syrian airforce officer who rose through the ranks to become defence minister before seizing control of the country in a bloodless coup in 1970, of following the dictates of fashion, sartorial or ideological. A dour workaholic whose attitude to life is more akin to seventeenth-century puritanism than the exotic self-indulgence associated with so many of his contemporaries in the Arab world, Assad embraced the teaching of Michel Afleq, the Syrian architect of Ba'athism, because it fulfilled his own burning sense of injustice. Assad was an Alawite, an obscure offshoot of mainstream Islam which some Muslim leaders consider so esoteric as to fall outside the strict definition of Islam. Consequently the Alawites, who come from the north-west of Syria, were generally disadvantaged in terms of political patronage, and the combination of an education in the Syrian airforce and Ba'athist social doctrine resulted in Assad becoming the most powerful man in Syria.

Although Ba'athism may be roughly described as essentially socialist in outlook, it had little in common with the hardline communism then practised in the Soviet Union. And yet by the early 1980s Syria had acquired the almost automatic epithet 'pro-Soviet' whenever it was mentioned in the Western press. This strong alliance came about not because of any mutual admiration between Syrians and Soviets, but in the interests of realpolitik. The roots of the Syrian–Soviet pact go back at least as far as the 1967 Six Day War when it was generally agreed among the defeated Arabs that Israel's decisive military victory would not have been achieved without the tacit support of the United States. When, during the 1973 October war, President Nixon, under pressure from Henry Kissinger, his Jewish Secretary of State, authorised an airlift of American weapons to Tel Aviv, the decisive effect American assistance had in helping Israel to repulse what, until then, looked an odds-on Arab victory, drove the radical Arab governments to re-arm themselves with Soviet equipment.

When American marines took up their positions in Beirut in late 1982 they were less than forty miles from the nearest Syrian positions and, as far as the ideologues in Washington were concerned, that put them as close to confronting directly what Reagan called 'the evil empire' in the Middle East as they were likely to get. Standing up to the Syrians had become the *cause célèbre* for the Reagan camp in Washington. When an American airman was shot down on a reconnaissance flight over Syria in December 1983, it was by a Soviet-made Mig fighter. When Syrian troops deployed in the Bekaa Valley, they drove Soviet-built T-72 tanks. And when the Syrians rebuilt their air defences after the mauling they suffered during the Israeli invasion of Lebanon in June 1982, Soviet-made surface-to-air anti-aircraft missiles (SAM) were set up in Lebanon. And to make sure the Syrians made the most of their arsenal, some 7,000 Soviet 'advisers' were assigned to the Syrian armed forces, more than three times the number of American soldiers based in Lebanon.

So preoccupied had the Americans become that any setback to their interests in Lebanon was blamed on Syria. Even though the truck-bombs which blew up the American embassy in April 1983 and the marine barracks the following October were driven by Islamic fundamentalists funded and supported by Iran, the Americans blamed it on Syria, which had allowed the Iranians to deploy in Lebanon in the first place. And when Islamic fundamentalists started kidnapping American citizens, the blame was laid at the door of 'Syrian-backed terrorists'. The failure by the Reagan administration to understand that Islamic fundamentalist groups were pursuing an entirely different agenda to Syria was to have a profound and lasting effect on the hostage crisis.

Certainly, as preparations went ahead to withdraw the 1,450 marines still in Beirut, there was enough political activity in the Middle East to give the Reagan camp sleepless nights. On

February 8, 1984, Moscow announced it was sending a senior Politburo member to Syria on a 'brief working visit' to discuss the situation in Lebanon. This was a rare visit to Lebanon by a senior Kremlin official, and top of the agenda would be a discussion on how to replace President Gemayel with a government more acceptable to Damascus and Moscow. Clearly the Russians were taking every advantage of America's difficulties in Lebanon. By the middle of the month President Gemayel, with no more American troops to back him, announced his intention to abrogate the May 17 troop withdrawal agreement which, when it was signed by the governments of Israel and Lebanon in 1983, was seen as the high point of American influence in Lebanon.

George Shultz, US Secretary of State, had felt so confident of America's position in Lebanon that he had not even consulted the Syrians during the negotiations for the agreement which, because it set out a timetable for Israel to withdraw its army from Lebanon, had a direct bearing on Syrian interests in the region. Gemayel's decision to abandon the agreement compounded the failure of American policy in Lebanon, and confirmed the revival of Syrian influence there. By the end of the month, as the first American marines were evacuated, President Gemayel was forced to accept the inevitable and drive to Damascus to pay homage to the new master of Lebanon, President Assad of Syria.

Had this obsession with all things Syrian not been the predominant concern in Washington, it is possible that the Reagan administration might have avoided the intelligence disaster which was to shake the wider interests of the US in the Middle East to their foundations. But with so much to digest on the political front in Lebanon, neither the State Department nor the analysts at the CIA at Langley were able to foresee the consequences of the kidnapping campaign until it was too late.

William Buckley, the fifty-eight-year-old CIA station chief at the American embassy in Beirut, had been personally chosen by William Casey, the CIA director, the previous year to take charge of the US intelligence operation. Buckley, a bachelor, had enjoyed a long and distinguished career in the service, first making a name for himself in Vietnam where he helped to organise hill tribes to attack the Vietcong.

In Vietnam he experienced first-hand the horror of torture, when he came across a young American field surgeon who had been overcome with anger after treating horrendous injuries suffered by American servicemen during a particularly fierce encounter with the Vietcong. The surgeon, escorted by friends, broke into the prisoner-of-war compound and seized a young Vietcong. While his colleagues held down the screaming victim, the surgeon ripped open his ribcage and removed his heart. Buckley had filed an account of this horrendous experience back to Langley, but had been told by his superiors not to take the matter any further.[1]

From Vietnam Buckley moved on to Zaire where he was involved in the CIA-organised conspiracy to kill Patrice Lumumba, the left-wing president. A few years later he was in Rome on vacation in 1981 when Mehmet Ali Agça shot and seriously wounded the Pope. Buckley was asked to attend Agça's interrogation; he formed the view the would-be assassin had been heavily drugged, and perhaps even 'programmed', for the attack. He then returned to Egypt where he was in the process of training President Anwar Sadat's personal bodyguard when a group of soldiers turned their guns on Sadat during a military parade. The bodyguards failed to fulfil their role, and seemed more concerned with saving their own skins than that of their president. Buckley, who was on

[1]Gordon Thomas: *Journey into Madness*, Bantam Press, 1988.

the presidential podium, is said to have drawn his own revolver when he saw the soldiers break rank. When it was all over and President Sadat, who only two years previously had signed the historic peace treaty with Israel, was officially certified as dead, Buckley broke the news to his bosses at Langley: 'He's dead as a dodo,' he shouted down the phone.[1] And so was Buckley's career, or so it seemed to colleagues, who clearly believed his reputation would never recover from such a humiliating setback.

Thanks to the CIA's first major disaster in Beirut, Buckley was offered an opportunity to redeem himself. Whether by accident or design, although all indications pointed to the latter, the pick-up truck loaded with one ton of TNT which had devastated the American embassy in West Beirut on April 18, 1983 had detonated just at the time a meeting of all the CIA's senior operatives in the region was taking place on the third floor. More than a dozen CIA agents, including Robert C. Ames, the agency's senior analyst on the Middle East, and Kenneth Haas, the Beirut station chief, were among the sixty-six fatalities. At a stroke the bomb destroyed the CIA's ability to function in the region, which might go some way to explaining the serious intelligence lapses which were later to occur. William Casey took the bombing very hard. Determined not to let the attack undermine morale within the agency, he decided to select Buckley, because of his long record in covert operations, to take charge of the Beirut station and try to rebuild the intelligence operation.

Nearly a year later, on March 16, 1984, Buckley awoke as usual at 7 am in his penthouse apartment on the seafront. It was his habit to play classical music on his stereo system – he had a speaker wired through to the bathroom – while he

---

[1]Cooley, *op. cit.*

prepared himself for work. He had a busy schedule for that day. After eleven months in Beirut, Buckley had developed a healthy scepticism for the exotic characters he was obliged to meet. He had taken a crash course in Arabic and had read a collection of books in English on the history of Islam. *Islam and the Logic of Force* by Mohammed Hussein Fadlallah, the spiritual leader of Lebanon's Shia Muslim community, nestled among the European classics he always had with him: Maugham, Thackeray, Joyce – and the complete works of John le Carré.

His duties that day included meeting with Shia Muslim contacts to reassure them that the enormous car-bomb which two days previously had nearly killed Sheikh Fadlallah was not the work of the agency. Fadlallah, who escaped serious injury, had made no bones about where he thought responsibility for the attack lay. A large banner bearing the legend 'Made in the USA' had been strung across the remains of the multi-storey building destroyed by the blast. Fadlallah retaliated by ordering the closure of the American University because, in his view, its Western-style education undermined Islam. With so many American teachers still working at the campus, Buckley was anxious to ensure the university did not become the next target of a suicide truck-bomb.

Buckley filled his briefcase with the top secret briefing papers he was required to take home each evening to study. The briefcase, known by the technicians at Langley as a burn-bag, was fitted with small gas containers which, at the press of a button, instantly ignited and burned the contents. Buckley strapped the briefcase to his wrist with a small handcuff. He then took the elevator to the car-park in the basement. For some reason that has never been adequately explained, and probably never will, Buckley had dispensed with the services of his embassy driver for the day, thereby breaking the strictly enforced rule that no American embassy official travelled alone in the city. Buckley had apparently decided to drive himself that day – a trained secret agent, it was no doubt anathema for him to let anyone know what he was up to.

The lift stopped at the floor below Buckley's and a young Lebanese man with a thick beard carrying a suitcase entered. A few floors further down a Lebanese woman whom Buckley knew got in, and they exchanged pleasantries. When the elevator stopped in the basement, Buckley let the woman out first and followed her. Buckley had taken only a few steps from the elevator when he was knocked to the ground by a mighty blow to the head from the Lebanese man's suitcase, which was later found to be full of rocks. As Buckley lay groaning on the ground a white Renault came roaring up from the car-park. Two men jumped out and helped to bundle Buckley, his burn-bag still strapped to his wrist, into the back of the car which then sped off through the main entrance. The woman, who had turned round to see Buckley being bundled into the car, screamed for help. But by the time anyone took any notice, Buckley had gone.

It was 3 am in Washington when Casey was awakened with the news that Buckley had been kidnapped. Buckley's abduction was a major intelligence disaster; Buckley knew the names of every CIA agent in the Middle East and the details of all the covert operations. Buckley's kidnapping was also a major embarrassment. In less than twelve months, Casey had lost two heads of station in Lebanon, a disaster never before experienced by the agency anywhere in the world, not even at the height of the Cold War. As Oscar Wilde might have said, to lose one station chief might be regarded as a misfortune; to lose two looked like carelessness. Nor was there any doubt that the kidnappers knew exactly who they had in their possession, and would lose no time extracting every last morsel of information from the agent. Of course there would be an inquest into how someone of Buckley's importance was not provided with adequate security. What was so shocking was how easy it had all been.

Casey ordered his men to pull out all the stops to get Buckley released. Agents were sent to Israel to enlist the help of Mossad, others to Lebanon to make contact with militia groups, friendly and hostile, to see if there was any word on Buckley's whereabouts. Casey made it clear he was prepared to do anything to get Buckley released, even if it meant paying a king's ransom. Casey saw it as a personal duty to get his man freed, come what may. But the problem was knowing where to look. The first questions the experts at the CIA had to answer were, who had taken their station chief and why.

5

IN THE NAME OF ALLAH

In the Gulf emirate of Kuwait, hundreds of miles away from the scene of America's burgeoning hostage crisis in Lebanon, a solemn procession of twenty-one men was escorted into a former girls' school which had been specially converted into a courtroom. It was less than twenty-four hours after Frank Regier had been forced into the back of a car and driven off into captivity in Beirut. Kuwait, whose one million inhabitants enjoyed the world's highest living standards, had never seen a security operation like it. Heavily armed guards had sealed off the entire area, while inside the makeshift courthouse there were twice as many guards, all armed with machine-guns, as there were defendants. Military helicopters hovered overhead, acting as a look-out for any possible attack on the building, while the centre of Kuwait city was almost deserted as the population observed a self-imposed curfew to make easier the task of their hard-pressed security forces.

As the defendants were led into the specially constructed cage which was to act as the dock for the six-week trial, the young men showed no sign of being overawed by their surroundings. They wore dark-blue sweaters and baggy canvas trousers, the standard issue Kuwait prison uniform. After the opening session at which the charges were formally to be put, the trial was to be held in secret. But the defendants, according to diplomats who watched the opening formalities, treated the whole issue as a big joke. They talked to each other, smiled a lot and laughed frequently, rather like undergraduates about to be reprimanded for a student prank.[1]

The charges they faced were no laughing matter. These twenty-one men, all of them Shia Muslims (normally they would have sported full, dark beards, but prison regulations had required them to submit to the barber's razor) were to stand trial for carrying out a ninety-minute wave of explosions that had shattered the tranquil sheikhdom, killing six people and injuring more than eighty. The casualty toll, moreover, would have reached catastrophic proportions had not faulty planning narrowly averted what would have been the worst terrorist incident of the twentieth century in the Middle East. The first bomb to explode on December 12, 1983 was at the American embassy compound on the Kuwait seafront. A truck laden with forty-five large cylinders of gas connected to plastic explosives careered through the main gates and rammed into the three-storey administrative annex, reducing the L-shaped complex to rubble. Whether by accident or design, the driver missed the main chancellery building which housed most of the administrative staff, thus avoiding an even bigger casualty toll.

An hour later came the second attack when a car-bomb exploded outside the French embassy. The ambassador narrowly escaped serious injury when the force of the blast sent the large crystal chandelier above him crashing onto his desk. The blast ripped a thirty-yard hole in the embassy

[1]Robin Wright: *Sacred Rage*, André Deutsch, 1986.

wall and injured five staff. The biggest catastrophe, however, was avoided at Kuwait's Shuaiba petro-chemical plant, the main oil refinery in a nation with reserves larger than those anywhere else in the world. The suicide driver of a truck laden with 200 gas cylinders rigged to plastic explosives, either through loss of nerve or inexpertise, detonated his consignment 150 yards short of his target, the No. 2 refinery. Five months later a Western diplomat commented that, if all the bombs had gone off, 'Shuaiba would still be burning today'.[1] The bomb would also have destroyed Kuwait's water desalination plant, leaving the desert kingdom with no water. Other booby-trapped bombs exploded at the control tower at Kuwait international airport, the electricity control centre and the living quarters for American employees at the Raytheon Corporation.

The bombings surprised the Kuwaitis just as much as they did everyone else. Compared with the autocratic regimes that prevailed in other parts of the Gulf, the ruling al-Sabah family had a reputation for being liberal. Kuwait, for example, had the first democratic assembly in the Arab world and the royal family made sure that the state's fabulous oil wealth was widely distributed. Even in its relations with its neighbours, Kuwait tried to take an even-handed attitude. Under constant attack from the Saudi royal family, which considered Kuwait's domestic politics to be too liberal, and repeatedly criticised by the Iranians for not enforcing sufficient Islamic discipline, the Kuwaiti royal family had to tread a precarious diplomatic tightrope.

But it was a conflict over which they had no control, namely the bitter war between Iran and Iraq which had begun in 1980, which caused the Kuwaitis the most difficulty. Saddam

---

[1] *Ibid.*

Hussein, leader of the country which dominated Kuwait's land border, was demanding that Kuwait declare its open support for the Iraqi cause. The Iranians, on the other hand, threatened to unleash the full force of the Islamic revolution on Kuwait if it did any such thing. The bombings, it transpired, had been ordered by Teheran because, even though the Kuwaitis had said nothing in public, the Iranians suspected the Kuwaitis of siding with Saddam. It is ironic that nearly seven years later Saddam should launch his invasion of Kuwait citing the opposite argument.

It was only by a fortuitous piece of detective work that the Kuwaitis had been able to round up the twenty-one suspects. Searching through the wreckage of the truck-bomb at the American embassy, the thumb of the suicide driver was recovered, and scientists were able to match the grisly digit with the thumb-print of a well-known Shia terrorist called Raad Muftin Ajeel. The Kuwaiti authorities were able to determine that Ajeel belonged to the radical Dawa Shia Muslim group, which had recently moved its headquarters to Teheran after being driven out of Iraq by Saddam. Once this had been established, it was relatively simple to round up the defendants who were finally put on trial on February 11, 1984.

All the defendants tried in Kuwait, including four tried in absentia, were originally accused of membership of the Dawa, which had been outlawed in Kuwait. The strongest charges against them were to have been 'joining a group whose objectives aim at spreading destructive principles, and the practice of terrorism'. When the defendants appeared in court, however, the charges were considerably watered down, a response no doubt to the repeated threats broadcast on Teheran radio that Kuwait would face 'serious consequences' if the Dawa heroes were put on trial. The Kuwaitis decided to omit all reference to the true provenance of the accused.

They were charged with 'belonging to a group bent on demolishing the basic values of society through criminal means'. Terrorism was not mentioned in any of the six charges, and nor was Iran, despite repeated references to 'another state'. The defendants actually protested when their membership of the Dawa was not included among the charges, rather as an Irish gunman might if the prosecuting authorities failed to mention his membership of the IRA. Several loudly shouted their allegiance to the Dawa and demanded to be reinstated in the organisation. 'They were boasting about it, bragging, even though conviction would insure a guilty verdict and the death penalty,' commented a diplomat who witnessed the proceedings.[1]

Six weeks and forty-six witnesses later, the judges passed their verdict. Six of the accused, including three still at large, were sentenced to death, seven to life imprisonment, seven to terms of between five and fifteen years. Five were found not guilty. A total of seventeen men were taken off to Kuwait's central prison. As the trial concluded Sheikh Jaber, the ruler of Kuwait, made a televised speech in which he made it clear that he gave his wholehearted support to the court's verdict and would resist any attempt, by fair means or foul, to have the men released. 'We will not bend to these threats,' announced Sheikh Jaber. 'We will never be shaken. We will never give up our dignity in the face of terrorism and whoever stands behind it.'

Little did Frank Regier know as he lay in his Beirut cell that he had been kidnapped because two of the Dawa 17, as they were to become known, jailed in Kuwait were closely related to the men who had abducted him. The kidnappers thought that by taking Regier, and the French hostage,

[1] *Ibid.*

Joubert, they would be able to put pressure on Kuwait to release the Dawa convicts. The kidnappings were just part of a campaign of terrorism Shia Muslim fanatics would unleash across the Middle East in their attempts to get the Dawa 17 released. An assassination attempt was made on Sheikh Jaber, and Kuwait Airlines, the national carrier, was to be the victim of repeated hijacks. But the stubborn refusal of Sheikh Jaber to make any concessions in the face of the most daunting provocation ultimately defeated the terrorists' more outrageous attacks. Soon they would have no option other than to concentrate their energies on the oldest trick in the Middle East – hostage-taking.

From whatever angle one approaches the hostage crisis in Lebanon, all roads ultimately lead to the somewhat remote provincial town of Najaf in southern Iraq. Situated some 200 miles south of Baghdad close to the banks of the Euphrates River, Najaf is, together with Karbala, one of the holiest cities in Shia Islam. Its importance dates back to the earliest days of the great schism in Islam in the seventh century, following a dispute over who should succeed the Prophet Mohammed to govern the newly-created Muslim nation. When Mohammed died on June 8, 632 after a painful illness, he left no instructions as to who should succeed him. An unseemly dispute broke out between Abu Bakr, the father of Mohammed's young wife Aisha, and Ali, the husband of Mohammed's daughter Fatima, over who had the better claim. After a lengthy argument which, if nothing else, proved that neither had a legal claim as successor, Abu Bakr finally won sufficient support to be proclaimed *Khalifat rasul-Allah*, or successor to the Apostle of God, from which the term 'caliph' is derived. Ali only reluctantly submitted to this decision several months later.

Just over twenty years later, owing to the death of Abu Bakr and his successor, Ali was able to proclaim himself Caliph after beating off an attempt by Abu Bakr's widow to deprive him of the honour. One consequence of Ali's victory was that the capital of Islam moved from the Hejaz, in what is now Saudi Arabia, to the area around Basra in southern Iraq. Ali's victory, however, was short-lived. A rebel faction rose against him and met him in battle at the Syrian-Iraqi border. Just as it looked as though Ali's forces were about to win decisively, thus consolidating his position as undisputed leader of the Islamic world, his enemies hit upon the clever idea of riding into battle with copies of the Koran attached to the ends of their spears. Being devout Muslims, Ali's troops immediately halted the fighting, and it was decided to resolve Ali's claim to the caliphate by arbitration. Ali may have been a brave soldier and a good general, but he was also a poor statesman; the arbitration went against him in favour of the governor of Syria.

Ali refused to accept the decision, but his chances of doing anything about it suffered a severe setback when arguments among his own followers resulted in a significant group breaking away and setting up on their own. Ali spent the next few years languishing in southern Iraq hoping to make a come-back, until he was assassinated in January 661 by one of his former followers. Ali was buried at Najaf, quickly established as a major shrine by his friends and supporters who continued to argue that he had been cheated out of the caliphate. The followers came to be known as the Shia, or partisans, of Ali while those Muslims who accepted the status quo, irrespective of how it had been achieved, came to be known as Sunni, or orthodox, Muslims.

Out of the estimated 500 million Muslims in the world today, about one-tenth are Shias. They can be found in Iran, Iraq, the Commonwealth of Independent States, Afghanistan,

India, Pakistan, China, Turkey, Syria, the Gulf, Saudi Arabia, Yemen and Oman. Until Shia Islam became the ruling faith in Iran in the sixteenth century, the two most important centres of Shiism were southern Lebanon and southern Iraq. Because Ali and his followers effectively lost the decisive power struggle which was to decide the political, as opposed to the religious, orientation Islam was to follow for centuries, the Shias became increasingly marginalised, both politically and socially, in Arab society. As a result, the Shias came to see themselves as the dispossessed of the Middle East, the unfortunate victims of a massive conspiracy by the Sunnis to keep them in their place.

Shiism has correctly been described as a 'religion of lament'. Shia Muslims regard themselves as the true guardians of the theocratic ideals set out by the Prophet which have been usurped by the more worldly ambitions of the Sunni dynasties. Like the English puritans of the seventeenth century, their ultimate ambition is to create God's kingdom on earth as laid down in the Koran. Shia history is an endless litany of how the Shias have been oppressed and have suffered tyranny for pursuing their belief in equity and justice. This sense of grievance is reinforced by the strong tradition of martyrology which lies at the heart of Shia teaching. The leading Shia teachers, or imams, are all portrayed as having suffered death by poisoning or in battle by cruel usurpers. The young men driving their truck-bombs into American institutions around the Middle East in the 1980s were merely following the higher traditions of Shia Islam. And when Shia leaders were persecuted, whether by the Israelis or Saddam Hussein, there was no shortage of volunteers willing to wreak vengeance.[1]

---

[1]Fouad Ajami: *The Vanished Imam*, Cornell University Press, 1986. This book gives one of the most accomplished accounts of the radicalisation of Lebanon's Shia Muslims.

By the 1970s Najaf had become the world's most important centre of Shiism by virtue of the fact that Ayatollah Ruhollah Khomeini, the radical Iranian leader, had lived in the Iraqi town since being forced into exile by the Shah in 1964. Khomeini had fallen foul of the Shah for publicly criticising his decision to grant diplomatic immunity to the thousands of American military advisers and their families then working in Iran; a move which revived memories of the humiliating conditions that had been imposed on Iran by the great powers during the nineteenth century. Khomeini wrote a pamphlet, widely distributed throughout Iran, condemning the Shah's humiliating concessions to the Americans. The Shah had him arrested and sent into exile. Fifteen years later Khomeini would return in triumph to replace the Shah and put his own vehement brand of anti-Americanism into practice.

During his years of exile at Najaf, between 1965 and 1978, Khomeini formed the nucleus of what would become the Islamic government of Iran. In 1969 he published a collection of lectures he had given at Najaf and previously in Iran about his philosophy for setting up an Islamic state. The work, *Velayat-e-Faqih* (*On Islamic Government*), was to have a similar effect on the Iranian political scene in the 1980s as *Das Kapital* had in Russia at the turn of the century. He gathered around him the finest Iranian scholars, who subscribed to Khomeini's dream of an Islamic state. To ensure that Khomeini's message was made available to his followers in Iran, an elaborate network was established between the exiles and Islamic fundamentalists inside Iran. One man who played a key role in disseminating Khomeini's tracts and pamphlets in Iran was Hashemi Rafsanjani, the future president of Iran. Rafsanjani, who was born in 1946, had become a devotee of the Ayatollah when he studied under Khomeini at the Iranian holy city of Qom in the early 1960s. He later described the impact on his generation of Khomeini's political militancy:

'Mr Khomeini was in the vanguard, and struggled more firmly than many others in this cause. I, who was with him, was his student and found his approach more to my liking, drew closer to him. That year, for the first time, I began political activity.'[1] Apart from helping to disseminate Khomeini's propaganda, Rafsanjani was also the key link between Khomeini and the Muhajideen guerrillas who, by the early 1970s, had begun to undertake clandestine attacks against the Shah. One other important aspect of Khomeini's work at Najaf was to establish contacts with like-minded Islamic fundamentalist Shia groups in the Middle East.

Khomeini suffered a personal tragedy when Sanei Khomeini, one of his two sons, was killed in a road accident, prompting some of his followers to claim he had been deliberately murdered by Saddam Hussein as a warning to the Ayatollah. If Saddam did kill Khomeini's son, it was because Khomeini's presence at Najaf, no matter how studious Khomeini himself might be, was having a deleterious effect on the surrounding Shia communities. It was while Khomeini was at Najaf, for example, that radical Iraqi Shias set up *al-Dawa al-Islamiyya*, or Dawa (the Dawn). The Dawa was originally established to fight Saddam Hussein, the Iraqi leader and a Sunni, because he had violently suppressed the political aspirations of the Iraqi Shias. The Dawa was also based around Najaf. One of the reasons Saddam expelled Khomeini from Najaf in 1978 was because of his growing unease at the effect Khomeini was having on the Shia population of southern Iraq. He was to feel the full force of the Shia backlash following the defeat of his forces in Kuwait by Allied troops in 1991, when Shia insurgents tried to establish an independent Islamic republic at Basra, the capital city of southern Iraq. At the same time as he expelled

---

[1]Shaul Bakhash: *The Reign of the Ayatollahs*, Basic Books, 1986.

Khomeini from Iraq, Saddam launched a violent campaign against the Dawa, rounding up several Shia leaders and having them executed. The group was relocated to Teheran after Khomeini's triumphant return. When Iran decided to bomb Kuwait as punishment for supporting Saddam Hussein during the Iran-Iraq war, Khomeini turned to the Dawa. Of the seventeen people convicted of carrying out the bomb attacks in Kuwait in December 1983, the clear majority were Shia Muslims from southern Iraq.

More important than his ties with the Shias of southern Iraq, however, were the contacts Khomeini and his followers cultivated with the Shia community in Lebanon. Since the sixteenth century, when the Safavid dynasty imposed Shiism as the state religion in Iran, a steady stream of Lebanese clerics had travelled to Iran to spread the Shia faith. As a result Iranians, latecomers to Shiism, have always held the Jabal Amil mountain area of southern Lebanon, Lebanon's Shia heartland, in high regard. Many of the leading teachers and thinkers of modern Shiism were Lebanese, and it was not uncommon for Iranians, or Persians as they then were, to travel to Lebanon to pay their respects to Lebanese teachers and to visit holy Shia shrines. Later on many Lebanese religious leaders played an active role in opposing the policies of the Shah of Iran. And by the time Khomeini came on the scene, the whole emphasis of the Shia movement in Lebanon was, of its own accord, beginning to shift from the religious to the political arena.

When Lebanon gained independence from France in 1946, the constitution bequeathed to the new country seemed to confirm all the Shias' historic phobias about not getting their fair share. For the constitution, with the full backing of the French, gave the Christian community the presidency in perpetuity, together with many of the most important offices of state. The reason for this was that the Christians believed, even though no census was ever carried out to prove it, that they comprised the majority of the population of Lebanon, and therefore deserved a greater say in the nation's decision-making process. They further argued that, as a minority in the Arab world surrounded by millions of hostile Muslims, their survival as a community depended upon their ability to control their own destiny. The French, ever hopeful that the Christians would provide them with an entrée to the post-colonial Middle East, lent their full weight to Christian aspirations in Lebanon.

A census would have shown that the Muslims of Lebanon, Sunni and Shia, outnumbered the Christians and the underlying tensions caused by the inherent unfairness of the constitution ultimately resulted in civil war. The Christians were able to get away with this iniquitous overlordship for so long partly because traditional rivalries between the Sunni and Shia communities meant they were never able to present a united front againt the Christians. The Sunnis commanded all the power and patronage within Lebanon's Muslim community. Urbane, well-educated and generally secular in outlook, the Sunnis preferred to reach a mutually beneficial accommodation with the Christians rather than fight for a better deal for their Muslim brothers. Confined to the relatively remote, backward and impoverished area of southern Lebanon, the Shias, even though they constituted the majority of the *Muslim* population, were effectively disenfranchised.

The first serious attempt to redress the balance in favour of the Shia community was started in the late 1970s by Musa al Sadr, a charismatic Iranian teacher who had settled in Lebanon and was determined to provide the Shia with better political representation. While Lebanese leaders frequently visited Iran, the average Lebanese took a more circumspect view of Iranians, regarding them as crafty and untrustworthy, as demonstrated by the Lebanese saying: 'The Persian will slit a man's throat with a piece of cotton.' But Sadr, tall, handsome and intelligent, soon won over the doubters through his sincerity and impressive credentials. Sadr had studied with Khomeini at Qom, completing his studies at Najaf, and stayed in close contact with the Ayatollah during his own years in exile at Najaf. Sadr's cousin, Mohammed Sadr, was one of the Dawa leaders executed by Saddam Hussein in April 1980. By the mid-1970s, Sadr had sufficient support to form his own political party and militia which was called Amal (the Arabic for 'hope'; Amal was an acronym for *Afwaj al Muqawamah al Lubnanya*, the units of the Lebanese resistance). Amal, which soon became the largest Muslim militia in Lebanon, was primarily set up in July 1975 as a political gesture. Once the civil war had started in earnest, any group which wanted political clout needed its own militia. Sadr, who had befriended Yasser Arafat, the PLO leader, and visited the PLO training camps which proliferated in southern Lebanon, set up Amal to ensure the Lebanese Shia would have a voice in Lebanon's future.

One of Sadr's closest Shia allies at this time was Mohammed Hussein Fadlallah. Fadlallah, a distinguished poet, writer and thinker, was born in Najaf in 1934 and studied there with great distinction. A radical thinker who believed in the primacy of Islam, Fadlallah had become close friends with Khomeini even before he arrived in exile at Najaf. Shortly afterwards, however, Fadlallah decided to move to Beirut in the mid-1960s to help with missionary work among the impoverished Shia Muslims in the shanty towns of Beirut's southern suburbs. Fadlallah and Sadr soon established themselves as the two most important Shia leaders in Lebanon, and while working to enhance the political profile of the Shias in Lebanon, they maintained close contact with Khomeini.

In the years leading up the Iranian Revolution, they provided Khomeini with one invaluable service. Because of the increasing restrictions imposed on the activities of the Iranian exiles by the Iraqi government, it was increasingly difficult for Iranian guerrillas to receive training in preparation for the Iranian Revolution. Sadr hit upon the idea of arranging for the Iranians to travel to southern Lebanon, where they were provided with first-class training by Yasser Arafat's PLO fighters. This quickly became a popular pastime with many Iranians who were later to become senior figures in the Islamic government in Teheran. Apart from the military training, it enabled them to acquire a first-hand education about Lebanon. Among those who took advantage of the PLO's training facilities in Lebanon were Mohammed Mohtashemi, who as the Iranian ambassador in Damascus in 1982 would play a key role in the terror attacks against the West; Hadi Ghaffari, one of the founders of the Revolutionary Guards; Rafik Mohsen-Doste, another leader and later minister for the Revolutionary Guards who supervised the kidnapping of David Dodge; Mohammed Montazeri, son of Ayatollah Hussein-Ali Montazeri who was then Khomeini's designated successor. Rafsanjani himself paid a secret visit to Lebanon in 1975 to meet with members of the Islamic revolution training with the PLO. On his return to Iran, however, Rafsanjani was arrested, probably following a tip-off by the Israeli Mossad intelligence service to Savak, its Iranian counterpart. Rafsanjani was tortured at Evin prison and sentenced to seven years in jail.

After the outbreak of civil war in Lebanon in 1975, relations between Fadlallah and Sadr began to cool. Some commentators have attributed this to jealousy on the part of Fadlallah at the growing success of the more charismatic and populist Sadr. Whatever truth there is to this, it is a fact that the civil war exacerbated the considerable doctrinal differences between the two men. Even though Sadr was a religious figure of considerable influence, he took a far more relaxed view in the application of Shia ethics than did Khomeini and Fadlallah. Sadr's main goal was to achieve a better deal for the Shia through the existing Lebanese system of government. If that meant dealing with Christian leaders, so be it. Fadlallah took a far more radical view, more in line with the teachings of Khomeini at Najaf. Fadlallah's view, which hardened with the outbreak of civil war, was that the entire Lebanese system of government needed to be overthrown and replaced by an Islamic government.

Fadlallah's thinking was reinforced by his experience in 1976 when Christian militiamen seized control of the area in which he was living and drove out all the Shia Muslim families. It was at this time that Fadlallah wrote his treatise, *Islam and the Logic of Force* (the book found in William Buckley's apartment). Fadlallah later recalled he wrote the book during 'times of intermittent fighting in the part of the city where I lived . . . by candlelight, under heavy shelling'.[1] In this book he sets out the radical Shia creed which was to dictate the activities of the Shia terrorist groups of the 1980s, the suicide bombers and the kidnappers. The crux of Fadlallah's argument is that if the Lebanese Shias wanted to achieve anything, they must achieve it by force. 'Force means that the world gives you its resources and its wealth; conversely, in conditions of weakness, a man's life degenerates, his energies are wasted; he becomes subject to something that resembles suffocation and paralysis. History, the history of war and peace, of science and wealth, is the history of the strong.' To back up his argument Fadlallah quotes several Koranic verses, including: 'Allah loves those who fight for his cause in ranks as firm as a mighty edifice.' And again: 'Make war on the unbelievers and the hypocrites and deal vigorously with them.' Written

[1]Ajami, *op. cit.*

two years before the Iranian Revolution, Fadlallah's book would have a decisive impact on the course of the Lebanese civil war.

The philosophical differences between Sadr and Fadlallah would later have a major effect on the hostage crisis. Sadr's Amal militia, which had a more secular and reasonable approach, was fundamentally opposed to the kidnapping of foreigners, while Hizbollah, the radical Shia militia founded in 1982 which regarded Fadlallah as its spiritual leader, masterminded the vast majority of the kidnappings. The ideological differences between Sadr and Fadlallah would also result in the two Shia militias taking up arms against each other.

The opportunity for the two men to reconcile their differences was lost when Sadr mysteriously disappeared while on a trip to visit Colonel Muammar Gaddafi, the Libyan leader, in 1978. Gaddafi was then heavily committed to supporting the more radical Palestinian groups based in southern Lebanon such as Abu Nidal, and he is said to have been increasingly angered by Sadr's insistence that the Palestinians should not ride roughshod over the interests of the Shia population. No one knows for sure what happened, but it is said that, after a furious row between the two men, Gaddafi had Sadr abducted from his hotel in Tripoli and murdered. To cover his tracks, Gaddafi then got his agents to check Sadr's luggage on to a flight to Rome. The disappearance of Sadr perfectly suited the Lebanese Shias' persecution complex and, thus equipped with a new 'martyr', made them even more inclined to accept the more radical teachings of Fadlallah.

Iranians were not the only Shia Muslims training and taking part in guerrilla raids against Israel in the 1970s. A small percentage of Lebanese Shias was also actively involved in the Palestinian movement. The majority of Shias who wanted military training joined their own Amal militia. But a small minority felt Amal's policies were either too accommodating or pragmatic, and decided to throw in their lot with the Palestinians. One such volunteer was a short, square-set man from a remote village in the Jabal Amil mountains. Imad Mugniyeh was in his late teens when he first volunteered to fight with the Palestinians. Little is known about his early life except that he was deeply attached to the radical Shia political philosophy being preached by Khomeini at Najaf. Only five foot four inches tall, he nevertheless had a very strong physique. Quietly spoken and intelligent, he quickly developed a reputation as someone who could not be pushed around.

The Palestinian leadership was clearly very impressed with Mugniyeh, for they made him the personal bodyguard of Abu Iyad, Arafat's closest political confidant. Working so close to the small circle of Palestinian decision-makers, Mugniyeh must have picked up a great deal about how to run a sophisticated terrorist operation. Working with a group whose survival depended on secrecy, Mugniyeh also learned the importance of being able to mount clandestine operations. While working with the Palestinians, Mugniyeh made several trips to Najaf and, after the Iranian Revolution, to Teheran where he established a close working relationship with radical ayatollahs such as Hussein-Ali Montazeri and leading figures within the Revolutionary Guards. His main commitment, however, remained the Palestinians, and when Israel invaded Lebanon in the summer of 1982, Mugniyeh was wounded in the leg fighting alongside his Palestinian comrades.

The consequences of the Israeli invasion were to change Mugniyeh's life. Apart from being wounded, Mugniyeh suffered the humiliation of having his village occupied by the Israelis. Ten years after the invasion, he had still not been allowed to return to his home because of the Israeli presence.

A further setback for Mugniyeh was that the Israeli intervention in Lebanon resulted in the expulsion of the PLO, taking away his own considerable powerbase. He was not to be without gainful employment for long. Within weeks of the PLO evacuation from Lebanon, Mugniyeh had been appointed Sheikh Fadlallah's personal bodyguard and very soon was closely involved in establishing Hizbollah (Party of God), a radical Shia militia modelled on Iran's Revolutionary Guards.

Mugniyeh's PLO training, moreover, was to prove an invaluable asset a year later when Mustafa Youssef Badreddin, Mugniyeh's cousin and brother-in-law, was identified as one of three Lebanese Shias among the Dawa 17 jailed in Kuwait. Badreddin, who also came from Mugniyeh's village in southern Lebanon, was identified as the bombers' ringleader and given the death sentence. Another Lebanese prisoner sentenced to death in Kuwait was Hussein Yousef Musawi, a first cousin of Hussein Musawi, the head of the Amal militia in the Bekaa Valley. Mugniyeh, who had already proved his terrorist credentials by helping to organise the suicide truck-bombs, was in no doubt about his next move.

It was not just a matter of family honour, even though it was rumoured that Mugniyeh's wife, a sister of Badreddin, had withdrawn her husband's conjugal rights until he secured her brother's release. For Mugniyeh it was a question of principle; he and like-minded Shia Muslims were obliged to do everything in their power to get the Dawa 17 released. A campaign was to be launched to force the Kuwaiti ruling family to release the prisoners. Apart from organising a wave of aircraft hijackings, bombings and assassination attempts, Mugniyeh resolved to revert to the tried and tested formula of kidnapping. And what better target could there be than the dozens of Americans and French residing a stone's throw from his Beirut apartment.

6

MISSION CONTROL

Sunday was a normal working day at the American embassy in Teheran, and the staff were engaged in routine duties on the morning of November 4, 1979, when a noisy group of Iranian students began to gather outside the main embassy compound, chanting anti-American slogans. The staff were not unduly alarmed. The embassy, the most visible expression of American interests in the Middle East, had become a regular target of the more radical elements among the Iranian students. Only the previous Valentine's Day, the first Sunday after Ayatollah Khomeini's triumphant return to Teheran, the embassy had actually been taken over by a crowd of frenzied students, and the ambassador and his staff taken hostage. The situation had been saved by the personal intervention of Khomeini's retinue who arranged for the embassy to be protected by a ragtag collection of self-appointed Revolutionary Guards.

Much had changed, however, since those heady February days. The government of Mehdi Bazargan, which had been formed after Khomeini's return, was finding it increasingly difficult to assert its authority in the face of the constant demands for the complete Islamisation of Iranian society from Khomeini and his supporters. About the only issue upon which all parties were agreed was in their universal condemnation of the way Washington had supported the Shah during the Revolution. Thus when the Carter administration finally agreed to allow the Shah to enter the United States for medical treatment on October 20, anti-American sentiment moved into an entirely different gear. Khomeini used the presence of the Shah in America as a whipping post for the Bazargan government, which was accused of being too accommodating to the West. Khomeini's Islamic Republican Party co-ordinated an intense campaign, directed as much against the Americans for harbouring the Shah – whom the students regarded as public enemy number one – as the Bazargan government. And on November 1, the day a massive anti-American demonstration was planned, Khomeini's office issued a statement which was to have disastrous implications for the Americans: 'It is therefore up to the dear pupils, students and theological students to expand their attacks against the United States and Israel so that they may force the US to return the deposed and criminal Shah.'[1]

At 10.30 am Bruce Laingen, the American chargé d'affaires, and two assistants were at the Iranian foreign ministry for a routine meeting when the news came through that about 3,000 Iranian students had broken into the embassy compound. Following the occupation of the previous February, security at the embassy had been improved, and at the first hint of trouble the staff, in a well-practised drill, barricaded themselves behind the steel doors of the main chancery section; this was to allow the staff to hold out for between two to three hours until help arrived, as it had in February. Laingen, at the foreign ministry, was well placed to put pressure on the Iranian authorities to act

[1]Gary Sick: *All Fall Down*, I.B. Tauris and Co. Ltd., 1985.

before the situation got out of control. Laingen and Ibrahim Yazdi, the Iranian foreign minister, believed the situation had been saved when they learned that Ahmed Khomeini, the Ayatollah's son, was on his way to the embassy. It was only when news filtered back that the young Khomeini had clambered over the compound wall, losing his turban in the process, and warmly congratulated the students for their success that the realisation dawned, both in Teheran and Washington, that this time help would not be on the way.

Lebanon, therefore, was not the first country where Washington severely underestimated the ability of Islamic fundamentalists to dictate the course of events; the experience the Americans suffered when the embassy staff in Teheran were held hostage for more than a year should have given them some idea what to expect when they took on the Islamic fundamentalists in Beirut. Sheik Fadlallah, after all, played a similar role in Beirut to the one his close friend Ruhollah Khomeini played in Teheran. The Hizbollah militia, which was to become, under the guidance of Imad Mugniyeh, the most important Shia Muslim militia in Lebanon, was modelled on Iran's Revolutionary Guards. In fact the term 'hizbollah' was first heard at about the time the students were clambering over the walls of the American embassy in November 1979. Hadi Ghaffari, the founder of the Revolutionary Guards in Teheran, described himself as a 'hizbollahi' or a partisan of the party of God. In Teheran the hizbollahis were given the more appropriate nickname of *chomaqdars*, or club wielders, because of their penchant for using clubs to break up political meetings which did not meet the required Islamic standard. Their chant: 'Only one party – Hizbollah; only one leader – Ruhollah'[1] became a familiar chorus in the great drama of

[1]Bakhash, *op. cit.*

the Iranian Revolution. Nor was it long before the same cry echoed through the tenements of Beirut's southern suburbs.

Just as President Jimmy Carter's foreign policy team in the late 1970s had failed to anticipate the Shah's demise, so President Reagan's staff in the early 1980s failed to take proper cognisance of the mounting militancy of Lebanon's Shia Muslims. After Carter famously described the Shah as 'an island of stability in a turbulent corner of the world', his administration consistently discounted the doomwatchers' reports. Uri Lubrani, Israel's acting ambassador in Teheran at the time who later became his country's main hostage negotiator, was among the more prescient observers in Iran. He had predicted in July 1978 that the Shah would most probably not survive in power another two years. Lubrani's report was passed to Washington, but ignored.

Failure to accept the political realities of the Iranian Revolution also resulted in the embassy staff being taken hostage. Until the Revolutionary Guards were actually inside the embassy, Washington policymakers clung to the belief that a 'moderate' Iranian faction would emerge from within the new Islamic government, a faction with which the Americans would be able to do business. The mistake would be repeated by the next generation of Washington policymakers working for Ronald Reagan, and their misjudgement in trading arms for hostages was to be as damaging for Reagan as the Teheran embassy siege was for Carter.

There were many useful lessons the Reagan administration, and all the foreign governments which became embroiled in trying to negotiate the release of hostages in Lebanon, could have picked up from the difficulties Carter and his advisers faced. The first difficulty, once the siege had been consolidated and had Khomeini's official blessing, was to find out who ultimately had authority for the hostages. The seizure of the embassy forced Bazargan to tender his resignation, which was accepted by Khomeini, and brought Bani Sadr, Khomeini's 'devoted son', to power. But while Washington believed that Bani Sadr could now dictate the fate of the hostages, Bani Sadr merely picked up where Bazargan had left off in the power-battle between the moderates and the Islamic radicals. Bani Sadr, as would Rafsanjani when he was elected president, believed the Islamic revolution could only survive if it worked through the established government structure. The revolution would merely devour itself if each faction was allowed to arm and follow its agenda with impunity. Down that road chaos lay, but that was the direction in which the Islamic fundamentalists were prepared to take the revolution if necessary to ensure the establishment of a truly Islamic government.

With the benefit of hindsight it is clear that Khomeini's Islamic Republican Party cynically manipulated the embassy hostage crisis for political ends. Once Bani Sadr had been deposed and the IRP's supremacy confirmed in the summer of 1980, the hostages were no longer of any practical value and it then simply became a question of trying to work out a practical means to secure their release to the satisfaction of all concerned. Gary Sick, who worked as Carter's personal troubleshooter at the National Security Council during the embassy crisis, alleges that the managers of Reagan's election campaign in 1980 did a secret deal with the Iranians to delay the release of the American hostages until after the November election in order to maintain the hostage issue as an electoral liability. Had the hostages been released in October 1980, as many observers believed would happen, Carter's campaign would have received a major, and perhaps decisive, boost. His diplomacy would have been seen to have paid off, and all his gush about the late Shah forgiven.

William Casey, Reagan's campaign manager and the future head of the CIA, was greatly concerned about the impact of what he called the 'October Surprise'. According to Sick,[1] Casey, with the active assistance of George Bush, who was running for vice-president, had a series of secret meetings with leading Iranian officials in the autumn of 1980, and persuaded them to release the hostages after the election. Sick's thesis has its merits, not least because Casey, Reagan and Bush were to open up a similar dialogue with Khomeini's government when Americans were taken hostage in Lebanon. Against this, there is still the considerable problem of why Khomeini's supporters would have been in the least bit interested in facilitating the election of Ronald Reagan as the next American president, when everything he said about the type of no-nonsense, Republican government he would run if elected presaged nothing but confrontation for the Iranians. The truth of the matter, like so many of the unknowns in America's secret dealings with Iran in the 1980s, probably lies buried with William Casey, who died of a brain tumour in 1987 before the bloodhounds of Washington's Congressional committees could get their teeth into him.

Apart from the trauma suffered by the hostages, the capture of the embassy in Teheran by the Revolutionary Guards was a serious setback for US interests in the Middle East. Although the staff had got into the daily habit of shredding highly sensitive documents as a precaution against just such an eventuality, many sensitive documents, needed on a day-by-day basis, were in the building when the students burst in. The staff did the best they could by continuing to shred documents until they were finally forced to give in to the students' demands and relinquish control of the embassy. But the students, who had nothing better to do, painstakingly set out over the next few months to piece back together all the

[1]Gary Sick: *October Surprise*, Random House, 1991.

shredded documents. One reassembled document contained a list of all senior CIA operatives in the Middle East. William Buckley was one of those whose names appeared on the list.

The other major setback for the US was that, with the embassy in Teheran closed down, and the embassy in Beirut soon to be blown up together with all the CIA's top Middle East brains, American intelligence in two of the most important areas in the region were effectively knocked out of action. This partly explains why the Americans failed to note, in the wake of the Iranian Revolution, the close working relationship being built between Teheran and radical Shia leaders in Lebanon, a relationship which would ultimately result in the US facing an infinitely more difficult and traumatic hostage crisis in Lebanon.

From the moment Khomeini established himself in power in Teheran, one of the most important issues on the Iranians' agenda was to export their revolution throughout the Islamic world. The preamble to the constitution Khomeini introduced referred to the 'ideological mission' of the Iranian army and the Revolutionary Guard to 'extend the sovereignty of God's law throughout the world'. It also committed the Iranian government to strive for the political, cultural and economic unity of the Islamic world. The Iranians lost no time in trying to stir up trouble in the two regions which contained large Shia populations – southern Iraq and Lebanon. The attempts of the mullahs in Teheran to interfere in southern Iraq resulted in the outbreak of the Iran-Iraq war in the autumn of 1980; in Lebanon it resulted in Western civilians being taken hostage.

Nor were the Iranians slow to move in on Lebanon. The most obvious attempt was made in December 1979, a few weeks after the seizure of the American embassy in

Teheran, when a force of 300 'volunteers', led by Mohammed Montazeri, son of Khomeini's official successor, arrived at Damascus airport. They had arrived with the intention of joining PLO fighters in southern Lebanon in their continuous battle against Israel. The Syrian president, Hafez Assad, was given no warning of the Iranians' impending arrival, and was initially unsure what to do with them. After deciding they were a harmless enough bunch, he was quite prepared to let them travel to Lebanon until Elias Sarkis, the then Lebanese president, telephoned Assad and begged him not to let the Iranians in: 'Please, with all the Palestinians, Israelis and Syrians we have in Lebanon now, the last thing we need is for the Iranians to come in.' Assad took his point, and asked the Iranians to take themselves off to PLO training camps in Syria, out of harm's way. The Iranians, for the time being, had to contain their ambitions for Lebanon.

The Israeli invasion of Lebanon in 1982 gave the Iranians the opportunity they had been waiting for. After the Israeli airforce, as a precautionary measure, destroyed the bulk of the Syrian airforce – Assad's pride and joy – the Syrian president no longer felt disposed to keep the Iranians under control. At moments like these, Assad wanted all the friends he could get, and the Iranians were only too willing to make their contribution. Because by then the Iranians were locked in a fight to the death against Iraq, little attention was paid to the 300 Revolutionary Guards climbing aboard the American-built C-130 air transporters for the flight to Lebanon, and then the journey onto Baalbek. A British diplomat who was in Teheran at the time remembers watching on television as the Revolutionary Guards boarded the aircraft. 'They looked a bit of a rabble, really. They were shouting the usual Khomeini slogans and suchlike, but given what was going on with the war in Iraq, it was a fairly pathetic effort by comparison. Looking back I think we underestimated just how important Lebanon was to them.'

The decision to send the Revolutionary Guards to Lebanon was probably taken by one of the ad hoc committees running Iran at the time, although there is little doubt that Hashemi Rafsanjani, who was then the speaker of the Iranian majlis, or parliament, had a say in the decision. The arrival of the Iranians in Lebanon in June 1982, however, was not the only contact Teheran had with Lebanon. The arrival of Mohammed Mohtashemi in Damascus as Iranian ambassador to Syria in early 1982 was of far greater significance in terms of Iran extending its influence over Lebanon.

The Iranian embassy in Damascus was and remains Teheran's most important diplomatic mission in the Arab world. A modern, unimpressive four-storey building on the main Mezze highway leading into the centre of Damascus, the embassy has been in the vanguard of the ayatollahs' efforts to spread the Islamic revolution throughout the Middle East. From the start of the Iranian Revolution, the embassy became the cornerstone of efforts to publicise the benefits of adopting an Islamic lifestyle. The walls outside the embassy were covered with posters displaying the benign features of the most popular ayatollahs. Syrian soldiers stood outside, keeping an eye on the activities of the diplomats. The Syrian intelligence service also had its work cut out monitoring the constant communications traffic passing through the complex web of aerials and antennae on the embassy roof.

In many ways the embassy was to become the start and finish of the hostage trail. From the embassy it is about an hour's drive to the Syrian border in the ante-Lebanon mountain range. From there it is a further hour's drive to Baalbek, the ancient Roman frontier post which, with the arrival of the Revolutionary Guards in 1982, became the forward staging post of Iran's advance into Lebanon.

Situated in the heart of the Bekaa Valley, Baalbek is the capital of one of the most fertile and productive agricultural areas in the whole Levant. A wide variety of crops are grown in the valley, which also sustains a thriving wine trade that continued to produce vintage wine even through the worst years of the civil war. Château Musar, which has been acclaimed by such distinguished wine connoisseurs as Auberon Waugh, even became a regular selection for the Sainsbury's supermarket chain.

The Bekaa also has a reputation for the quality of its hashish, a drug which has been grown for hundreds of years in the region, long before it became a trendy adjunct of Western culture. The Assassins, a fanatical group of Shia Muslims from northern Syria who terrorised the Arab world and struck fear into the hearts of the Crusaders in the early Middle Ages, are said to derive their name from hashish, which is the Arabic for herbage, the plural of which is *hashishiyyin*. It is easy to see how this word could have been transliterated into assassin by the Crusades' chroniclers, most of whom were writing in Latin. The Assassins specialised in committing suicide terrorist attacks. The sect originated in Iran and spread to Lebanon. They were brought up to follow their leaders with blind obedience and total commitment to the Islamic faith. One particular leader, Hasan al Sabah, in the eleventh century, inspired a particularly loyal following. Known as the Old Man of the Mountain, Sabah raised a team of highly-trained professional killers who, armed with daggers and swords, were sent on secret missions to murder opponents of the Old Man. Often these assignments were little more than suicide missions, but there seems to have been no shortage of volunteers. It has been suggested that these young men were so willing to give up their lives because they were given hashish before their missions. The drug induced a state of euphoria and provided a 'foretaste of the delights of heaven' awaiting their success. Many years later Western intelligence analysts came to a similar conclusion, namely that the young Shia drivers of the truck-bombs were stoned out of their minds.

During the 1960s and 1970s Baalbek became accustomed to seeing strangers wandering through the narrow alleyways or lounging along the river by the Roman ruins. For the hippies and backpackers of that generation, Baalbek was top of the list of places to visit on the international dope trail. 'Lebanese black', as the produce of the Bekaa became known, was regarded as a high quality product. Thus the natives of the Bekaa, themselves partial to their own product, made a good living out of the scores of young people who spent many a happy summer in the Bekaa. Nor was there any risk of the authorities in Beirut trying to interfere. The tribes of the Bekaa were considered a law unto themselves, and far too much of a challenge for the urbane bureaucrats running the Lebanese government. The tribes in the Bekaa essentially fall into two distinct groups. The Christians generally congregate in the north where, among other occupations, they run the wine industry, one of the more endearing products of their exposure to French culture. The rest of the valley is occupied by Shia Muslims who are mainly poor farmers. Even so, these were country-dwellers who had no time for the bright lights of Beirut, preferring independence and self-sufficiency. If it was rare for someone from the Bekaa to have a job in a swanky government office in Beirut, it was even more uncommon for someone from the Bekaa to want one.

Long before the Revolutionary Guards arrived, the Iranians had worked hard at establishing contact with leading members of the Shia clans in the Bekaa. One family in particular, the Musawis, from the small village of Nabi Sheet, about fifteen miles south of Baalbek, established a close relationship with the Iranians. A religious family, the Musawis saw their alliance with the Iranians as an opportunity to increase their standing in the community. The Iranians provided them with money and a certain degree of prestige; not every Shia Muslim from the Bekaa commuted frequently to Teheran for 'consultations' with the leading figures in the Iranian government. Three members of the Musawi clan in particular were to make a reputation for their role in the hostage crisis. Hussein Musawi who, with Imad Mugniyeh, helped found the Hizbollah militia in Lebanon, was one of the principal architects of the kidnappings in Lebanon. His cousin, Abbas Musawi, was elected secretary-general of Hizbollah, a post he held until his assassination by the Israelis in February 1992. Another cousin, Hussein Yousef Musawi, was one of those sentenced to death for the bombings in Kuwait. He, together with Mugniyeh's brother-in-law, was to become the *cause célèbre* of the Lebanese kidnappers. Not surprisingly several of the Western hostages spent periods of their captivity at the Musawi clan's stronghold at Nabi Sheet.

The relationship the Iranians had built with Shia tribes in the Bekaa served them well when the time came for the Revolutionary Guards to move into Lebanon. People like Hussein Musawi made sure they were welcome and before long the 300 Iranians had been billeted with local Shia families. At about the same time Musawi, who had become the leader of the Bekaa branch of the Amal militia, fell out with Nabih Berri, who had succeeded Musa Sadr as the leader of Amal in 1980 after Sadr disappeared in Libya. Berri, an accomplished Beirut lawyer firmly committed to Sadr's policy of improving the lot of the Shia through the existing Lebanese government structure, had not been too enthused by the achievements of the Iranian Revolution, which he saw as a threat to his own aspirations in Lebanon. By the time of the Israeli invasion, Musawi was so much in the debt of the Iranians that his determination to push for the creation of an Islamic state in Lebanon resulted in a deep rift between Berri and himself.

The result was that Musawi announced in July 1982 he was leading a breakaway group from the main Amal militia, which he called Islamic Amal. Musawi's militia, the first Islamic fundamentalist militia in Lebanon's modern history, was to be the forerunner of Hizbollah in Lebanon.

Musawi's other big achievement that summer was to assist the Revolutionary Guards to take over a disused Lebanese army barracks in Baalbek. The Sheikh Abdullah barracks had been built in the 1950s as a training camp for the Lebanese army. But as the army disintegrated into the various factions at war in Lebanon, the barracks were abandoned. Musawi hit on the idea of turning the barracks into a base for the Iranian soldiers, and before long the barracks, which afford a panoramic view over Baalbek and the entire length of the Bekaa Valley, had been turned into an Iranian military base in Lebanon. The barracks soon acquired a cluster of military radio antennae which enabled the Iranians to be in direct contact with Teheran and Damascus.

Throughout this ambitious programme Musawi worked closely with Mohammed Mohtashemi, the Iranian ambassador to Damascus. Musawi was frequently seen taking the two-hour drive to the Syrian capital in a large black Mercedes with curtains shrouding the back windows, rather like a hearse. Mohtashemi, who had trained with the PLO in southern Lebanon in the 1980s, was likewise a familiar figure in Baalbek. A political appointee, he reported back directly to Ayatollah Hussein Ali Montazeri, Khomeini's designated successor and the ayatollah with primary responsibility for exporting the Iranian Revolution. Thus if Teheran was mission control, the Iranian embassy in Damascus became the forward command centre and the Sheikh Abdullah barracks in Baalbek became the forward operations post.

Keeping up with the diplomatic comings and goings at the Iranian embassy in Damascus became a full-time occupation for Western intelligence services. Since the embassy was less than 100 yards from the residence of the British ambassador and next to a large United Nations compound, it was not too difficult to keep an eye on the Iranians. 'Making sure we knew what the Iranians were up to was one of our most important tasks,' said a British diplomat based in Damascus at the time. Nor was it simply the diplomats who had a watching brief. The British monitoring station at Cyprus was also listening very carefully to the messages being passed between the Iranians. For example British intelligence intercepted and decrypted messages sent from Teheran to the Iranian embassy in Damascus which hinted that a major attack was about to take place on the multinational force in Lebanon. Officials in Teheran then transferred some $25,000 to Mohtashemi's personal account in Damascus. This was followed by requests being transmitted to the Syrians asking them to allow twelve Iranians to move through Damascus into Lebanon. A few days later a truck packed with explosives drove into the compounds of the American and French contingents of the multinational force, killing more than 300 people.

One mile away, in Beirut's southern suburbs, Imad Mugniyeh watched the simultaneous explosions send up plumes of smoke, from the rooftop of Sheikh Fadlallah's apartment block.

The impressive structure the Iranians put together in Lebanon was to act as a springboard for the second wave of the Islamic assault on the West's interests in the Middle East. For all the time and effort the Iranians expended on increasing their influence over the Lebanese Shia, however, it did not encounter universal approval. The Amal movement which, since its creation by Musa Sadr, had become the established representative body for Shia interests in Lebanon, derived its support more from the appeal of its political agenda than the desire of the Lebanese Shia to embrace Islam fully as a way of life. Khomeini may have lamented after Sadr's abduction by Colonel Gaddafi: 'I could almost say I raised him as a son', but it was Sadr who appealed to the Lebanese, not Khomeini. Lebanese Shia Muslims, like all the other Lebanese confessional groups, enjoyed a secular lifestyle and had no wish to have their lives determined by Islamic decree.

The best example I personally encountered of the resistance of ordinary Shia Muslims to the attempts of the pro-Iranian religious fanatics to impose their will on the easygoing lifestyle of West Beirut was shortly after the Muslim militias, led by Nabih Berri's Amal, had taken control of West Beirut in February 1984. Berri was determined to ensure his 5,000 militiamen acted responsibly – his political credibility depended on it. If he could show that the Shias were capable of administering their own affairs in a civilised and reasonable manner, this would undoubtedly add weight to Berri's campaign for the Shias to have their fair share of Lebanon's political cake. While Amal militiamen were constructing roadblocks and trying to impose some semblance of law and order on West Beirut, pro-Iranian militiamen appeared on the streets of West Beirut for the first time and began harassing women in Western dress and smashing up any bar that sold liquor.

The Commodore Hotel, that battered sanctuary of the world's press, was no exception. One evening soon after the militias had taken control of the city a bunch of bearded gunmen marched into the bar. The conversation came to an abrupt halt when they pointed their guns at us and ordered us to put down our drinks. We were all, bar staff included, required to keep our hands in the air while two gunmen clambered behind the bar. In the centre of the bar was a tall, round display cabinet which advertised the wide range of exotic, and somewhat dangerous, refreshments on offer. Our visitors smashed every single bottle on display with their rifle butts. Next they turned their guns on the stocks beneath the bar, breaking all the bottles which contained liquor, and emptying the cans of beer down the sink. For those among us who were seasoned travellers in the Middle East, the sight of these Islamic extremists abusing the ambience of our early evening cocktails brought back painful memories of scenes in Teheran shortly after the Iranian Revolution, when a similar fate befell the renowned wine cellars at the Intercontinental Hotel. When they had finished destroying the Commodore bar, one gunman gave a smile of satisfaction. 'No drinking, no more,' he announced. 'Drinking no good. Islam no like drinking.' Having thus put us all firmly in our place, the gunmen trooped off to wreak havoc elsewhere.

The next evening when I returned to the bar, I was surprised to see bottles of orange juice, lemonade and soda water neatly stacked in the cabinet where once had stood arak, gin, vodka and a range of bottles of varying shapes and shades which would have done any self-respecting apothecary proud. Pointing to this abstemious collection, I inquired of Mohammed, one of the regular barmen, whether the Islamic revolution in Beirut was here to stay. Even though Mohammed came from a Shia village in southern Lebanon, I knew from his own drinking habits that he did not take the teachings of the Koran too much to heart; if Mohammed was taking the strictures of the Islamic militants seriously, it might be time for the rest of us to do likewise.

'Do not worry, Mr Con. This is only for show. We have plenty of drinks down here. What would you like?' So saying, he triumphantly produced a bottle of scotch in one hand and a bottle of gin in the other. For this Shia Muslim at least, the attempt to bring the Islamic revolution to Beirut had made no impression.

During this period, Nabih Berri's Amal militia was still a very powerful force in Beirut, and Berri gave his men orders to curb the wilder activities of the pro-Iranian groups. There were actually gun battles on the streets between the two Shia groups, and inevitably it was Amal which won. Although Berri was against the American presence in Lebanon, he was totally opposed to using kidnapping as a tactic to drive foreigners out. He demonstrated this opposition by securing the release of Frank Regier and Christian Joubert within two months of their abduction.

According to the story which was published at the time, Regier and Joubert, who were being held in a cellar in West Beirut, were released after a group of schoolchildren playing football on some waste ground stumbled across the two men sitting bound and blindfolded. They ran to tell their parents, who summoned the local militiamen. They went to investigate, found the men and released them. The two men, wearing red and white pyjamas and dazed and unshaven, were ceremoniously handed over to American diplomats at Nabih Berri's home on April 15, 1984.

The truth is somewhat different. Berri, angered at the adverse effect the Islamic fundamentalists were having on his attempts to govern West Beirut, was determined to prove his influence by freeing the three Americans then held – Regier, Levin and Buckley. Apart from improving his standing in the US, he also hoped to teach the Hizbollah gunmen a lesson. His men combed the southern suburbs offering generous handouts to anyone with information about the missing Americans (at the time no one had noticed Joubert had gone missing!). Eventually Amal got the information they wanted and staged a raid on a Hizbollah stronghold in Beirut. Clearly outnumbered, the Hizbollah gunmen gave in without putting up any resistance. Regier and Joubert were set free.

After the initial sense of triumph, however, disappointment quickly set in. Berri, and the American government, had been hoping to get all the hostages released, especially Buckley. But there were no other hostages to be found and, after a ruthless interrogation by Berri's henchmen, it transpired that the Hizbollah gunmen knew next to nothing about the fate of the other Americans. Nevertheless the action showed that Berri's men were still the real power-brokers in Beirut, whatever Teheran might say. For their part the Hizbollah leaders realised they were no match for the Amal in Beirut, but they did not lose any sleep over this. If Hizbollah could not keep its hostages in Beirut, it would just have to keep them where they would not risk being inconvenienced. From now on, the Western hostages kidnapped in Beirut would be taken immediately to Baalbek, the headquarters of the Iranian Revolution in Lebanon.

Regier's release was also something of a disappointment for Ted Turner, the ebullient founder and head of CNN. Turner was said to have paid $40,000 to one of the Amal leaders to find Levin, his kidnapped bureau chief. When the news first came through that an American was to be released, Turner thought his ploy had worked. When he discovered the released American was not Levin, he demanded, and received, his money back.

7

PAWNS IN THEIR GAME

Each morning as he sat blindfolded and bound in the small room of a house on the outskirts of Baalbek, Jeremy Levin listened intently for the sounds which suggested he was not alone in his ordeal. His only contact with the world was on the rare occasions that his guards paid him a visit to bring food. The guards were surly and unfriendly, not prepared even to engage in the most cursory of conversations. The kidnappers took no chances with Levin. Not for him a rescue mission in Beirut. Soon after his abduction, he was thrown into the boot of a car and driven over the mountains to the Hizbollah stronghold in the Bekaa Valley.

His room was at the end of a corridor next to the bathroom, and every morning he would listen for the noise of a fellow hostage being escorted to the bathroom after he had completed his own ablutions. In the early days of his captivity he heard what he thought were at least two other people padding along the stone floor in their bare feet. A year later, shortly before he escaped, the number had risen to six.

Although Levin saw none of the other hostages for the entire year of his captivity, there is little doubt that his first two companions were William Buckley and Hussein Farrash, the consul at the Saudi Arabian embassy in Beirut. Farrash had been kidnapped in January because of the Saudis' attempts to resolve the deepening Lebanese political crisis through diplomacy. Although religion is enshrined in the Saudi Arabian constitution, as Sunni Muslims the Saudis were often at odds with Teheran once the ayatollahs had established their own brand of Shia fundamentalism. The rivalry between the two Islamic traditions quickly reached an intensity which brought the two countries to the brink of war. The Saudi royal family not only supported Saddam Hussein's decision to declare war on Iran, but also provided him with substantial financial support for the war effort. The enmity was reflected in the way the kidnappers treated their Saudi hostage. A proud man, Farrash would often shout orders at his guards in Arabic. Their response would be to beat him.

From the moment Buckley was kidnapped, William Casey, the CIA director, became obsessed with his case, and suffered much private torment at the thought of Buckley's ordeal. Casey, who had worked in undercover operations during the 1939–45 war, knew from first-hand experience the risks run by his agents in the field, and he was prepared to do practically anything to get Buckley back. He ordered the CIA to take extraordinary measures. Money would be authorised to pay informants, and Casey ordered that intercepts of the communications between Teheran and Baalbek be stepped up. He established a special hostage task force which had satellite photos enhanced of the Bekaa Valley in the search for clues to Buckley's whereabouts. While he was aware that neither he nor the agency could bargain for Buckley without violating Reagan's professed policy of not negotiating with terrorists, as an experienced operator Casey knew a way could always be found to circumvent such political niceties, so long as the life of one of his agents could be saved. The CIA's national intelligence officer for the Middle East sent a five-page memo to the State Department suggesting that the government took a conciliatory stance towards Iran in the hope that moderates in the Iranian government might be able to help improve relations with Washington. The memo was later to be used to justify the arms-for-hostages deals carried out during Reagan's second presidential term.

The effort made on Buckley's behalf was also designed to send a message to other CIA operatives that if they found themselves in a similar predicament, the CIA would do its best to get them out. Casey even arranged for an expert FBI team trained in locating kidnap victims to go to Beirut. But after a month exploring all the possible channels, they came up with nothing.[1]

Casey felt a deep personal responsibility for Buckley as he himself had sent him to Beirut to rebuild the CIA network after the 1983 embassy bombing. Third-hand reports that Buckley had been severely tortured deeply affected both Casey and President Reagan. Although Casey, by training a lawyer and a long-term Republican party apparatchik, was normally a cold-blooded professional, he felt a special horror and rage about Buckley, especially when he was told that Buckley had broken under pressure and divulged the agency's secrets in a lengthy confession. These reports, even though unreliable, drove Casey to distraction, which is probably just what the kidnappers intended, since he was unable to know which of his assets had been compromised, which agents needed to be pulled and protected, and how much the Soviet Union, still the main object of Casey's attention, may have learned about American operations in the Middle East.

At some point soon after his abduction Buckley was flown

---

[1]Bob Woodward: *Veil: The Secret Wars of the CIA 1981–87*, Simon and Schuster, 1987.

from a former Lebanese airforce base in the Bekaa to Teheran. After all the difficulties the Iranians had experienced with David Dodge, they were careful to avoid Damascus, although it is hard to believe the Syrians, with their sophisticated Soviet-built radar facilities, did not take note of the unusual air traffic less than a hundred miles away. Rafik Mohsen-Doste, the Revolutionary Guards official who supervised the transfer of Dodge to Iran, was in Damascus at the time of Buckley's transfer. Within days of his arrival in Teheran, Buckley was being interrogated at a Revolutionary Guards' interrogation centre in Fereshte Street, close to the Iranian state television and radio building.[1] At some point after the Guards had finished their interrogation, Buckley was shipped back to the Bekaa. His were to be one of the pairs of feet Levin would hear padding to the bathroom.

On May 7, 1984, fifty-three days after Buckley's abduction, the US embassy in Athens received a video cassette mailed in Athens and addressed to the ambassador. The tape was of a cheap East German make sold widely in the Middle East. Within hours Casey, together with senior CIA analysts, was watching a gruesome video of Buckley being tortured. The video showed Buckley naked and being beaten while clutching to his stomach a secret document, which the CIA men took as evidence that Buckley's burn-bag had failed to work. The fact that the video had no sound made the spectacle all the more perverse. The film showed signs that Buckley had been drugged, for there were puncture marks in his skin.[2] The second video arrived a month later, this time at the American embassy on Rome's Via Veneto. This video contained a soundtrack. Although the tape did not show Buckley being mistreated, it was clear from his slurred speech and dazed

[1]Cooley, *op. cit.*
[2]Thomas, *op. cit.*

look that he was not in the best of health. His hand and legs shook in spasms as he pleaded to be exchanged under a deal removing all American and Israeli influences from Lebanon.

The third and final video arrived at the American embassy in Cairo on October 1984. This again showed an emaciated Buckley. He stammered as he read a prepared statement into the camera, making defensive comments about his captors and Lebanon's right to self-determination. His statements were punctuated by screams in the background. Medical experts conducted a computer analysis of his voice patterns, eye movements and general physical appearance. They concluded that Buckley was seriously contemplating suicide. Whether the videotapes were made in Teheran or the Bekaa, it was impossible to tell. Nor could the Americans be sure that each videotape had been made shortly before its release. Throughout the hostage crisis the kidnappers would get their captives to record a videotape, but then hold onto it for several months before going public.

The delivery of these videotapes only served to intensify Casey's preoccupation with Buckley's case. Casey played the tapes to Reagan, who was deeply shocked. To drive home the importance of getting Buckley back alive, Casey ordered his staff to place two photographs of the missing agent on the wall of the main conference room at the CIA's headquarters at Langley. One was of Buckley before his kidnapping, showing his craggy good looks, cool professional eyes and the barest hint of a smile. The other was a blurry, haggard image of their colleague in the hands of his torturers. No matter what the administration's rhetoric might be, Buckley was Casey's man, and Casey was determined to get him back.

During his interrogation in Teheran, Buckley made a long and detailed confession of the work both of himself and the CIA in the Middle East. A copy of the confession was eventually passed to the Americans several years later, after a copy was obtained by an American agent. The confession is a tribute to Buckley's professionalism. Confronted with the most appalling psychological, medical and physical torture, Buckley was still able to tell his kidnappers everything they wanted to hear without giving away anything of great significance about the CIA's operations in the Middle East. In the confession, Buckley portrays himself as being essentially a 'trainer and instructor', posted to Lebanon to assist the Lebanese government in establishing its own intelligence network. He admits to having had a regular weekly briefing session with Colonel Simon Cassis, then head of President Gemayel's intelligence service. Given Buckley's position, however, there was nothing surprising about that. By divulging this and other information which was fairly obvious, Buckley, as far as it is possible to tell from the barely legible copy of the confession in the CIA's possession, was able to conceal whatever real secrets the CIA had left in the Middle East.

The effort to recover Buckley highlighted the deep inadequacies of US intelligence operations in Lebanon. For all the warning signs that had been forthcoming about the rise of Islamic fundamentalism in Lebanon since the Israeli invasion in 1982, Washington had little understanding of what was going on. This was partly because too many Washington policy-makers tended to view Lebanon from the Christian-tinted viewpoint of President Amin Gemayel. What dealings the Americans did have with the Muslim community tended to be with the more plausible Sunni business figures and Shia leaders like Nabih Berri, sophisticated Lebanese who spoke American-accented English and dressed in elegant Western suits. When it came to Muslims who wore traditional

Arab dress and only spoke Arabic, the Americans were less surefooted.

The lack of good intelligence contacts in Lebanon also resulted in the CIA authorising some operations it would probably now prefer to forget. One tactic employed early on in trying to locate Buckley was to put the word around the Beirut streets that the Americans were prepared to pay well for any information about his whereabouts. When Fadlallah got to hear of this – it was inevitable that he would – he immediately issued a stern warning against accepting such offers. Not everyone heeded the warning, however, and a few days later two boys, one aged eleven and the other aged twelve, were picked up by Hizbollah militiamen as they crossed the Green Line from Christian East into Muslim West Beirut. The militiamen, most of whom were themselves only teenagers, became suspicious when they discovered the boys had a considerable amount of money on them. They beat the boys severely with their rifle butts, until the boys admitted they had been given the money in return for providing information about the American hostages. On hearing this, the militiamen shot the boys in the back of the head.

A year later, in March 1985, the CIA was involved in another incident in Beirut which only served to put those Americans still in Lebanon in even greater danger. During a lunch Casey had at the residence of Prince Bandar, the Saudi Arabian ambassador to Washington who was already helping to finance the Reagan administration's illegal support for the Nicaraguan resistance movement, the two men agreed that a dramatic blow against the terrorists would serve the interests of both the US and Saudi Arabia, and decided to assassinate Sheikh Fadlallah, whom they believed to be personally responsible for the suicide truck-bomb attacks against the Americans in Beirut and the kidnapping of the Saudi diplomat. On orders from Prince Bandar, the Saudis hired a former British SAS commando who knew his way around the Middle East and was a specialist bomb-maker.[1]

Casey was happy to let the Saudis handle the whole operation so as not to offend the CIA bureaucracy, which was growing more and more resistant to active anti-terrorist measures. The SAS man established operational compartments to carry out separate parts of the assassination plan; none had any communication with the others except through him. One operative was detailed to obtain the explosives, another to find a car. On March 8 a car packed with explosives was driven into the Beirut suburb of Bir el-Abed, a predominantly Shia area. The car exploded about fifty yards from Fadlallah's high-rise residence. The force of the blast caused widespread devastation, causing several buildings in the area to collapse and killing eighty innocent people, many of them women and children, who were in the street when the car exploded. Fadlallah escaped with only slight injuries, but his supporters were in no doubt where responsibility for the car-bomb lay, and a massive anti-American demonstration swiftly followed.

For all the Americans' efforts to come to terms with the rising tide of Islamic fundamentalism in Beirut, and perhaps even to defeat the mullahs at their own game, Hizbollah continued to highlight the impotence of the US by kidnapping American citizens at will. While the CIA was expending all its efforts to rescue Buckley, the kidnappers struck again on Tuesday May 8, 1984. This time their target was an American Presbyterian minister who had devoted his life to helping the deprived of Lebanon.

Benjamin Weir and his wife, Carol, were walking from their apartment in West Beirut for a meeting at the Near East School of Theology, a seminary which trained priests for

---

[1]Thomas, *op. cit.*

missionary work all over the Middle East. Weir had worked in Lebanon for thirty-one years and had developed a deep sympathy for the plight of the Shia Muslims. His main task that morning was to try and persuade the president of the seminary to change his mind about wanting to leave Lebanon. The Weirs had been very happy in Lebanon, both because it was a beautiful place to live and because they felt they were doing something worthwhile. Not even the horrors of the civil war had affected their deep sense of mission. When West Beirut fell under the control of the Muslim militias, the Weirs never thought for a moment they were at risk. Unlike the official American presence in the country, the Weirs had devoted their lives to working for the Lebanese. The Lebanese knew exactly who they were and what they were doing, and they would ensure that no harm came to them. The Weirs quickly learned that the kidnappers made no attempt to distinguish between 'good' and 'bad' Americans.

They had walked only a few yards when a car pulled up behind them and two men got out. One of the men said something, which Weir did not understand. 'What do you want?' he asked.

He could hardly understand the response: 'We want you.'

With that one of them grabbed Weir's arm and started to pull him towards the car. Mrs Weir started screaming while her husband yelled for help. But no help was forthcoming, and as Weir continued to resist, one of the men grabbed him by his tie, making his eyes almost bulge out of their sockets, and dragged him into the back of the car. One of the gunmen followed him in and put an automatic pistol to his head. As the car sped off, Weir was forced onto the floor and a sack placed over him. For the next fifteen minutes the car raced through Beirut towards the southern suburbs, an area Weir knew well from all the missionary work he had done with the Shia communities there. Gradually the kidnappers began to relax and talk amongst themselves in Arabic. As they neared their destination, the driver turned round and called to Weir: 'Hey, man, how are you? You OK?'

Weir's initial response to his abduction, once he recovered from the shock, was anger and indignation. 'What right have they to take me from Carol and my work?' he thought to himself. 'Kidnapping is a violation of human rights and against the religion of Islam. I have served the personal and social needs of hundreds of Lebanese people during the past thirty-one years in this beloved country. How dare they consider me the enemy? I will say nothing in response to his question. I will be stubbornly silent. My muteness will be my resistance.'[1] That may have been how Weir saw his presence in Lebanon, but for the kidnappers he was just another pawn they could use to heap further embarrassment on the American government.

When the car came to a halt the driver had lost his breezy familiarity. 'Be quiet. Don't make any noise, or I'll kill you.' Weir was helped out of the car and a plastic bag was placed over his head, nearly suffocating him. He was led to a large warehouse and made to lie face down on a bed. The kidnappers began to search through his pockets, and were disappointed when they could not find his passport, which Weir had given to his wife for safe keeping. He then became aware of another man entering the room who seemed to be held in respect by his kidnappers, who left the room. The new arrival was short and stocky. His name was Imad Mugniyeh and he came straight to the point. 'Who are you?' he asked Weir.

'I'm Benjamin Weir, an American. I am a pastor.'

'What church?'

---

[1]Ben and Carol Weir: *Hostage Bound, Hostage Free*, Lutterworth Press, 1987.

'The National Evangelical Synod of Syria and Lebanon.'

'You work with with Lebanese churches?'

'No, I'm a pastor. A Protestant pastor. Protestant.'

'You Maronite?'

'No. Not American University, Near East School of Theology. Teach of God.'

This farcical conversation merely confirmed the gulf between Weir's concept of what he was doing in Lebanon and the kidnappers' total lack of interest or understanding about what a middle-aged American from the Mid West was doing in their country. Mugniyeh and his colleagues, though native Lebanese, had clearly never heard of the Near East School of Theology. Nor was the fact that Weir was a pastor, or priest, of much significance. The fact that Weir was an American was all they wanted to know.

Carol Weir had a similar experience when she tried to report her husband's kidnapping to the Lebanese police force. There was probably no more pathetic an institution in Lebanon during the civil war than the once-proud gendarmerie. After the militias seized control of the country, the police were reduced to a state of complete impotence. Even though the most horrific crimes were being committed daily all around them, they were never allowed to intervene. To do so would probably have meant a bullet in the head for the investigating officer, if not a car-bomb parked outside the police station. And yet Lebanon's policemen did not desert, but stayed at their posts, patiently waiting for the day when they would be allowed to fulfil their proper role. Their main function during the war was to keep an official score-card of the fatalities. Whenever there was an Israeli air raid, or a car-bombing, or the militias had a particularly ferocious shoot-out, the police would be monitoring the situation and would release an official statement at the end of the day along the lines of: 'Forty-seven people were killed and 200 injured during intense fighting in Sidon.' Occasionally, during a lull in the fighting, the gendarmes would venture out in their immaculately-pressed uniforms and attempt to direct Beirut's chaotic traffic. They even handed out parking tickets, an exercise in utter futility because no one ever paid them. Once, during a lull in fighting during which several highly-publicised atrocities had occurred, I tracked down the chief of detectives in West Beirut at his office. A cold wind was blowing in from the Mediterranean through a hole in the wall which had been caused by a direct hit from a tank round. The wind was blowing all his neatly stacked crime reports over the floor. While we were talking he would pick them up and put them back on his desk.

'Why do you bother?' I asked. 'Will you ever get the chance to solve these crimes?'

'Who knows?' the detective replied with a shrug. 'Perhaps one day, when the war is over. We have to do our job as best we can and just hope that justice will win in the end.'

Carol Weir's instinct after seeing her husband kidnapped in broad daylight was to run to the nearest police station.

'Help! They've kidnapped my husband! Please go after the car, a white car!' she pleaded. The policemen on duty were sitting around smoking and drinking coffee. They looked at her as though she were mad. She tried to explain in Arabic, but that made no difference. Eventually someone hit upon the idea of introducing her to the station chief. She was taken into his office. 'Please help me. Go after the car!' implored Mrs Weir.

The police chief tried to calm her down. 'Don't worry, we will get your husband back soon. We will alert our men at all the roadblocks. We will stop the getaway car.'

It all sounded very reassuring, but then that was the one department in which the Lebanese police had a great deal of experience. They had not solved a major crime in years, nor were they now in a position to help Ben Weir. There were

The kidnappers. Imad Mugniyeh *(above left)* became the most wanted man in Lebanon after forming Islamic Jihad. He worked closely with Hussein Musawi *(above right)*, who broke away from the Amal militia. The hostage crisis suffered a further complication when Mohammed Hamadi *(right)* was arrested at Frankfurt Airport in January 1987. *(Photo of Hussein Musawi: Popperfoto)*

(Left) David Dodge became the first American hostage when he was kidnapped in June 1982. *(Popperfoto/UPI)*

(Above) Britain's contribution to the multinational force in Lebanon marking their first anniversary in Beirut in February 1984. Two days later they were evacuated. *(Below)* David Miers, the British ambassador, narrowly escaped serious injury during a Lebanese suicide truck-bomb attack against the American embassy in Beirut in October 1984. He was meeting the American ambassador when the bomber struck.

(Above) Hizbollah's main Fathallah barracks in Beirut's southern suburbs after being occupied by Syrian troops. Most of the Western hostages spent their first few days in captivity at the barracks. *(Lena Kara)* Alec Collett *(below right)*, a British journalist working for the United Nations, was kidnapped by Abu Nidal's breakaway Palestinian group in March 1985. He was hanged in retaliation for Britain's involvement in the American bombing raid on Libya a year later *(below left)*.

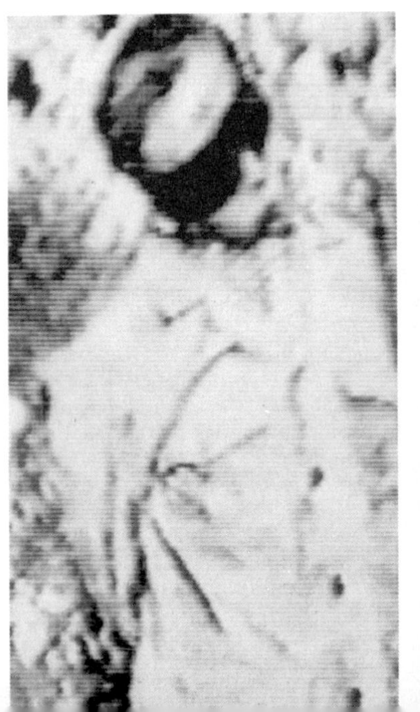

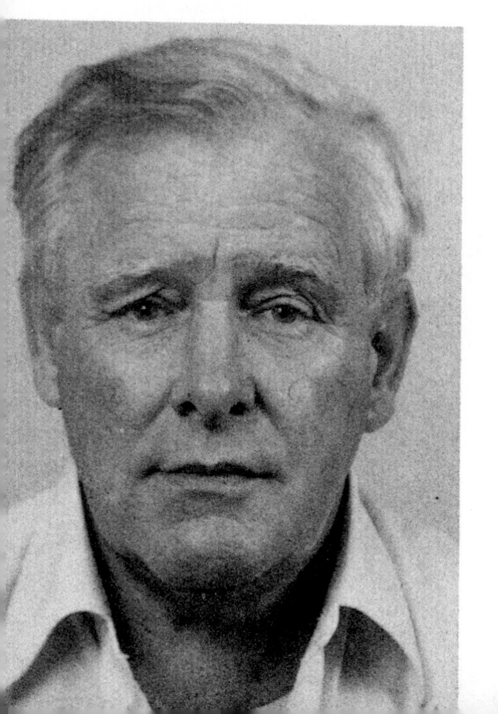

Lucky escapes. Jonathan Wright *(above left)* was kidnapped by Abu Nidal, but managed to escape. Brian Levick *(above right)* and Geoffrey Nash *(left)* were kidnapped by Islamic Jihad in March 1985, but were released after ten days. *(Photo of Wright: Associated Press/Topham; Levick & Nash: Reuters/Bettmann)*

(Above) Terry Waite's Lebanon hostage mission in late 1985 was conducted amid a fanfare of publicity. His press conferences in Beirut attracted intense media interest. *(Lena Kara)* *(Below)* Terry Waite posed for this photograph while trapped at the Commodore Hotel in November 1985. The rocket-propelled grenade launcher was left by a group of Druze militiamen. *(Lena Kara)*

(Above) Hazel Moss and Amanda McGrath were kidnapped for pursuing dangerous liaisons with Lebanese militiamen. *(Reuters/Bettmann)*

Leigh Douglas *(left)* and Philip Padfield *(right)* were kidnapped on Good Friday 1986 after a night out on the town in Beirut. Their bodies were recovered three weeks later.

Brian Keenan *(inset)* swapped a dead-end job in Belfast for an exotic lifestyle in Beirut. He lived in this house *(above)* for six months. While in Beirut he became close friends with Hazel Moss *(below)* but ignored her warnings for him to leave. *(Photo of Keenan's house: Lena Kara)*

(Above) Oliver North's commitment to freeing the American hostages in Lebanon was equal to his enthusiasm for his fund-raising activities on behalf of the Nicaraguan Contras.

(Left) North was spotted at Larnaca Airport in November 1986 shortly before the release of David Jacobsen – the Iran-Contra scandal broke two days later.

no police roadblocks, there were no men to be informed. All the policemen on duty were safely tucked up inside the police station and had no intention of venturing out, certainly not for a hysterical American woman whose husband had just been kidnapped. What did she expect? Hadn't there been enough warnings?

Carol Weir was asked to fill in a crime report. Name – maiden name – husband's name – mother's maiden name – husband's occupation?

'He's a Protestant pastor,' replied Mrs Weir.

'And what is that?'

She tried to explain. No one at the police station, to Mrs Weir's increasing frustration, knew anything about the Protestant church. 'A priest,' someone offered. 'No . . . yes, a priest,' Mrs Weir finally agreed. 'Like a priest.'

'Ah, like a priest, but not a priest,' replied the police chief pleasantly. 'I understand. Do not worry, Mrs Weir. We will have your husband back with you tonight.'

Mrs Weir received a far less friendly reception when she travelled across the Green Line later that day to report her tale of woe to the American embassy. Being an American diplomat in Beirut was becoming an increasingly fraught business. With one American embassy already a bombed-out shell, the new compound resembled a high-security fortress. Apart from the constant risk of being kidnapped or assassinated themselves, the diplomats' workload was becoming more onerous as a succession of Americans were gradually joining the ranks of the hostages. Frank Regier, Jeremy Levin, William Buckley, and now Benjamin Weir.

'What did you expect?' the American Deputy Chief of Mission snapped at Carol Weir. 'Hasn't the embassy suggested that all non-essential Americans leave? We can't keep our own personnel safe from kidnapping.'

'The kidnapping of Americans is a response to our foreign

policy,' Mrs Weir ventured, which provoked the diplomat to deliver a stinging rebuke.

'You don't expect us to change our foreign policy for you, do you?'

Nor was it just the diplomats who were starting to feel the heat as the number of Americans being kidnapped continued to increase. By the spring of 1984 Ronald Reagan was well into his campaign for election to a second term. In many respects he stood a good chance of beating off the challenge from Walter Mondale, Jimmy Carter's vice-president and the Democrat nominee. The economy was bouncing back with a low inflation rate while record numbers of Americans held jobs. At home Reagan's position was unassailable.

In foreign affairs Reagan had also refuted critics who had predicted his hard-line policies would result in his being a trigger-happy warmonger. Reagan and his team were determined not to allow the humiliating setbacks foreign policy had suffered in Lebanon to undermine the campaign. Reagan, who in 1980 had made much political capital out of Carter's embarrassment in Iran, was determined not to allow Lebanon to become a similar electoral liability. Reagan had been nicknamed the Teflon president by the wits in Washington, because no matter how much trouble his policies caused, none of the blame ever stuck to him. To avoid getting caught up in a Lebanon hostage crisis in the run-up to the presidential election, Reagan needed to draw deeply on his Teflon reserves. As usual, he depended heavily on the good judgement of his aides to protect him. At one point in the campaign, Reagan could not resist taking a swipe at Carter's humiliation at the hands of the Iranians. In a televised address he boasted about a 'new patriotism' that 'began . . . when after 444 days our hostages came home from Iran to breathe American freedom again'. With a new generation of Americans being taken hostage by Iranian-sponsored terrorists in Lebanon, however,

White House officials were sensitive about placing too much emphasis on Carter's misfortune. Later on in the campaign a television commercial was made which showed rabid-looking Iranians shredding the American flag to emphasise how far the US had come under Reagan's presidency. But James Baker, the White House chief of staff, quietly had the advertisement withdrawn.[1] He was well aware that in trying to score a cheap political point, the campaign managers were playing with fire. Knowing how sensitive Reagan was to human suffering, his close aides protected him from most of the details of what was going on in Lebanon. That way he would not have to worry about it. Apart from all the attention that was paid, with Reagan's knowledge, to getting Buckley released, the administration behaved as though none of the other hostages existed.

The day after Ben Weir's kidnapping, May 9, 1984, a group calling itself Islamic Jihad made its first public announcement, to the effect that it had kidnapped Buckley, Levin and Weir. The concept of jihad, which is Arabic for a holy war, lies at the very heart of Islam. The call to jihad is made when the survival of Islam is said to be at stake, although it had often been proclaimed for purely political reasons. The Ottoman rulers called for a jihad to be waged against the British in the First World War. More recently Saddam Hussein called for a jihad against the Western forces sent to liberate Kuwait. But as Saddam has always been more at home in a Baghdad nightclub than the mosque, few Muslims took him too seriously. By invoking the name Jihad, the kidnappers were clearly trying to give the impression that they were in the vanguard of a wider crusade against Western interests in Lebanon. In fact Islamic Jihad was a small group of fundamentalists within the

[1]Jane Mayer and Doyle McManus: *Landslide: The Unmaking of the President 1984–88*, Houghton Mifflin, 1988.

Hizbollah militia who had a separate agenda of their own to follow, namely to secure the release of the seventeen prisoners held in Kuwait. The group was run by Imad Mugniyeh whose desire to secure the release of his brother-in-law gave him a personal interest. As Sheikh Fadlallah's personal bodyguard, Mugniyeh was in a good position to know what was going on in Lebanon, and to assess likely targets for kidnapping at the most opportune moment. Given his good relations with the Revolutionary Guards based in the Bekaa Valley, and the financial support he was receiving from Teheran, Mugniyeh was perfectly placed to hold the West to ransom.

The growing success Islamic Jihad was enjoying through its kidnapping policy was not lost on other radical groups in Lebanon with a grievance against the West, as Jonathan Wright, a thirty-year-old British journalist with the Reuters news agency discovered in late August. Wright, an Oxford-educated Arabist who knew Lebanon well, having covered the Israeli invasion two years previously, was driving by himself through the Bekaa to inspect the damage caused to a Lebanese village by an Israeli air raid. At this time only Americans had been kidnapped, and the few British residents left felt they had nothing to fear. Wright had made similar journeys on several occasions, and preferred to travel alone because he found it easier to work that way. Once he got into the Bekaa, however, he was unable to find the location of the air raid. He stopped at a checkpoint manned by Palestinians, a common enough occurrence in that area, and asked for directions. One of the Palestinians disappeared into a house at the side of the road. When he returned ten minutes later he asked Wright if he would like to step inside for a cup of coffee. The moment Wright entered the house, he was seized by the guards and thrown into a room which had once been the kitchen but had been stripped bare, save for a sink and a single tap. So much for Palestinian hospitality. The only window was boarded up.

There were two mattresses in the room, and on one sat a young Lebanese man. Wright began to bang on the door, shouting: 'You can't do this to me, I'm a journalist.' The guards took no notice.

Wright had been kidnapped by Abu Nidal, one of the most notorious and feared Palestinian groups which was involved in some of the most horrific attacks against civilians, all carried out in the name, so they claimed, of the Palestinian cause. But few Palestinians approved of Abu Nidal's tactics. The guards told Wright very little during the first ten days of his captivity, visiting him just three times a day to deliver food – dry bread and processed cheese. When someone did arrive to talk to Wright, he was almost apologetic.

'We know who you are,' explained a middle-aged Palestinian guerrilla in olive-green battle fatigues. 'We have nothing against you personally. But we have an argument with Mrs Thatcher. When we have sorted it out, we will let you go.'

He then told Wright something which gave him the first clue as to the group's identity. His interviewer, in order to identify his group, boasted that they had killed Kenneth Whitty, a forty-four-year-old first secretary at the British embassy in Athens, who was shot dead in March 1984 as he drove home to lunch. The murder was carried out by Abu Nidal to put pressure on the British government to release two Arabs jailed for the attempted murder of the Israeli ambassador in London in June 1982. Although he was not killed, the ambassador never fully recovered after being shot several times in the head, and was reduced to a human vegetable. Israel invaded Lebanon in retaliation for the attack. Wright, a well-informed journalist, knew all about the Whitty murder, and realised at once what they wanted in return for his release. A few days later a group calling itself the Organisation of Revolutionary Socialist Muslims contacted the

British government and repeated its demands for the release of Arab prisoners held in British jails.

Wright saved the British authorities the trouble of having to act on his behalf. From the moment he was kidnapped, he began plotting his escape. During the next two months he was moved several times. On the last move he was placed in a large room with an air shaft built into one of the walls. Over several days, Wright explored the possibility of escaping through the air shaft. He had to work out whether it would be possible to remove the metal grill, and then whether it would be possible to squeeze his body through so small a space. He was able to remove the grill with a spoon, and decided he could just about squeeze his spare frame through the vent. His only remaining concern was how big a drop there would be from the vent to the ground. At 2 am on the day he chose to put the escape plan into action, he arranged his bed frame so that he could reach the vent, then wriggled his way through. He need not have worried about the drop; as he poked his head through the end of the shaft, he discovered he was only a couple of feet from the ground. He dropped down and made his way to freedom.

The first moments of freedom were the worst. He had no money and only a vague idea of where he was. He walked along a road leading down a mountain and after half a mile he came across a checkpoint. He decided to take a chance and went up to the guards, who turned out to be members of Walid Jumblatt's Druze militia. When he identified himself, they knew exactly who he was, and immediately placed him in their guardhouse out of harm's way. Any suspicions Wright entertained that his guards had allowed him to escape were laid to rest the next morning when his guards asked him to accompany them, disguised in a Druze militia uniform, back up the mountain road to identify his abductors. They drove back up to the house, and when they drove past there was clearly a great commotion going on. Later that day the Druze told him the local commander had been to visit the Palestinians who had been detailed to hold Wright. He gave the guards a very hard time for their lapse in allowing him to escape. For the next couple of days Wright stayed in the guardhouse while the Druze organised his release, a frustrating experience. 'They saw me as something of a curiosity,' he recalled. 'They laughed and joked about my experience. They seemed to think that being kidnapped was an occupational hazard in Lebanon.' Eventually they drove him down to Beirut in a Range Rover and delivered him to his office.

Jonathan Wright's ordeal was over. But his guards would not repeat the mistake that had allowed him to escape. The next Briton to be kidnapped by Abu Nidal would never see freedom again.

8

INTRODUCING TERRY WAITE

Terry Waite's humble beginnings as the son of a village policeman in Styal, Cheshire, did not exactly herald a glittering career as an international troubleshooter, the man called to the rescue when the combined talents of some of the finest diplomatic brains in the world were unable to resolve a crisis. Not for him an education of privilege at Winchester and Balliol, Eton and Christ Church; not for him the effortless rise to positions of power and influence on the strength of old school connections or long-established family tradition. The young Waite received his religious education, one of the most important influences in his life, in the upstairs room of the local Ship Inn public house.

The closest the young Waite came even to touching the hallowed portals of the British establishment elite was when, at the age of sixteen, he left school to join the Grenadier Guards, the first regiment of the Household Infantry, not as an officer, but as a simple soldier. At six foot eight inches, Waite would have made an imposing guardsman. But even this was not to be. Shortly after joining the army, he was taken ill with a mystery virus which manifested itself in a nasty rash which covered his body. He was carted off to hospital where the ailment cleared quickly. He returned to his regiment believing himself cured, only for the rash to reappear. An exhaustive series of tests revealed he suffered from an allergy to the dye in the khaki uniform. His army career was at an end. His extreme sensitivity to allergies, moreover, was to have far more severe repercussions many years later.

Frustrated in his attempts to be a soldier of the Crown, Waite decided to become a soldier of the Church. The Church Army is a peculiarly English institution of whose existence people are vaguely aware but, when challenged to explain precisely what it is, do not have the foggiest notion. Everyone has heard of the Salvation Army, with its distinctive uniform and brass bands. The Church Army fulfils a similar function, but without ever having quite managed to reach the same level of publicity. Members of the Church Army wear uniforms and conduct drill, rather like glorified boy scouts, and the quaint concept of discipline, where senior members of the Church are addressed as 'sir' and saluted at all times, had a certain attraction for the Cheshire policeman's son. He was also attracted by the sense of mission, the sense of doing something useful, of helping the community and his fellow man. Were it not for his military predisposition, Waite would have been perfectly suited to a career in social work.

Waite made the most of his new start in the Church Army. He was never interested in being ordained – he preferred the personal liberty of being a lay person. But his practical approach and deep sense of humanity impressed his superiors, and he was able to make the most of the opportunities on offer. After working as an adviser to the Bishop of Bristol on adult education, which was in effect a form of social work, Waite discovered his metier when he moved with his wife and young family to Uganda.

Post-colonial Uganda was not the most attractive of regimes, and few people were interested in working as an assistant to the first African archbishop, Eric Sabiti. But Waite, his sense of adventure aroused, considered it an opportunity not to be missed. With Idi Amin in power, Waite was soon in the thick of a major crisis. During one of the regular purges Amin inflicted on his fellow countrymen, he arrested Yona Okoth, the chief administrator of the Church of Uganda. Waite was asked to intervene on Okoth's behalf. He visited the Ugandan in his prison cell and said communion for him while all around lay the unconscious bodies of others who had been dealt with by the Ugandan army. Using his contacts with the Church of England, Waite was able to put pressure on Amin to release Okoth, which he duly did. Many years later Waite returned to Uganda for the enthronement of Okoth as the new Archbishop of Uganda, and was fêted like a national hero. It was at about this time that Waite confessed to having once had a 'biblical dream', in which he had witnessed the death of an African. The following day, Ugandan Archbishop Janani Luwum had been assassinated.[1]

From Uganda Waite moved to a plum job in Rome, working for a Catholic teaching order. At the Vatican Waite spent an enjoyable seven years at the heart of one of the most powerful and influential institutions in the world. On the deliberations of the bishops and ecumenical councils at the Vatican rests the fate of millions throughout the world. Waite was able to watch all the machiavellian intrigue of a classic Italian city state at work. At the time Waite was in Rome, the Vatican was moving very much on the offensive to reassert the conservative orthodoxy of the Catholic catechism which was in danger of being subsumed by the doctrinal chaos caused by the

[1] *Daily Telegraph*, February 1, 1984.

conflicting claims of liberation theology revolutionaries and Opus Dei reactionaries. Moreover in the Pope, the Vatican had a figure who had the power to shape the destiny of peoples at the drop of an encyclical.

By the time Terry Waite was invited to join the staff of the newly-elected Archbishop of Canterbury, Robert Runcie, he had a highly developed sense of the important role the Church should play in world affairs. In many respects he was well-suited to working with Runcie who interpreted his position at the See of Canterbury in a far wider context than many of his predecessors. Runcie saw himself not only as head of the Church of England, but as head of the Anglican Communion, the sixty-five-million-strong network of communities and congregations scattered throughout the world which look to Canterbury for practical leadership and spiritual guidance.

'I thought by paying more attention to the Anglican Communion this would help to refresh and renew the Church of England which would see itself not so much as the custodian of English culture but as a truly international church,' is how Runcie explained his vision of the Church during his tenure as Archbishop when I met him following his retirement. 'I did not think it right that a parish church should be regarded as a village preservation society.' Runcie, who was steeped in the Anglo-Catholic tradition of the Church of England, saw his international role as being consistent with his desire for greater ecumenical understanding. Indeed Runcie's appointment in 1980 as the 102nd Archbishop of Canterbury was supposed to herald a dynamic new era in the Church of England. When he accepted the appointment, Runcie made it clear he did not see himself as a 'talking ornament' and did not want to become a 'platitude machine'.

Runcie cherished a vision of a more energetic and decisive involvement in the issues confronting the Church at home and abroad, and it was in this context that Waite, with his field experience in Uganda and education in Rome, was seen as an ideal candidate to work as the Archbishop's Assistant for Anglican Communion Affairs. One aspect of Waite's job would be to act as Runcie's advance man, to work out the schedule for Runcie's travel abroad. 'I picked Terry because of his experience in Africa and because he had learned how an international church operated during his time at Rome,' said Runcie. Although a lot of African churches were trying to distance themselves from their former colonial identity, whenever they found themselves in trouble they turned to Lambeth for help. When Idi Amin terrorised the Ugandan Church, Lambeth was able to come to its aid. When President Numieri of Sudan imposed Islamic law, Runcie contacted the Sudanese high commissioner in London and asked him to respect the rights of the Sudanese Church, which he did. Waite's job was to assist Runcie in supporting Anglican churches around the world and to maintain an active dialogue between Lambeth Palace and the Anglican Communion.

When Runcie hired Waite he did not foresee his new assistant spending much time in the Middle East. The entire Middle East, despite the fact that it contains all the holy shrines of Christendom, constituted just one province among a total of twenty-eight in the Anglican Communion, the largest proportion of them being in Africa, Australia and the US. These were the areas where Runcie envisaged Waite would spend most time.

One of Waite's first tasks was to arrange a three-week visit of the Archbishop to the United States. Waite is mainly remembered from that trip for the expertise with which he handled the demands of the American media, never an easy task. Waite also made a number of important contacts with the Episcopal Church, an institution which, had it not been for a certain Declaration of Independence in 1776, would have remained the Church of England in America.

If Waite dreamed of helping the Archbishop to fulfil a similar international role to that of the globe-trotting Pope John Paul II, his ambitions were frustrated by practical difficulties. Unlike the Vatican with its vast wealth and resources, Waite found to his dismay that the Church of England was simply not in the same financial league. When the Runcies moved into Lambeth Palace in 1980 they were appalled at the building's ramshackle condition, the result of years of systematic parsimony on the part of the Church Commissioners. On a winter's night the Palace looked more like a derelict prison than the headquarters of the Anglican Church. Children climbed over the walls for horse chestnuts by day and by night tramps slept in the gardens. Inside the conditions were little better. Lambeth was underfunded, understaffed, overworked and isolated from the world of which it had to be a part. When Runcie started work at Lambeth, he was shocked at the primitive conditions in which he and his staff were required to work. For example, there was no kitchen to make coffee and no lavatory for the secretaries; the only one was next to Terry Waite's office. There were no word processors or electric typewriters. There was no effective internal telephone system. There was not even any Tipp-Ex, as Runcie's secretary discovered when she wanted to correct some official correspondence. 'Oh, no,' the other secretaries told her, 'they won't let us have it.'[1] Lambeth as an institution was as poor as the proverbial church mouse. If Terry Waite had big ideas, Lambeth Palace most certainly did not have the resources to finance them.

The other major difficulty, which was to have a direct

[1]Jonathan Mantle: *Archbishop: The Life and Times of Robert Runcie*, Sinclair-Stevenson, 1991.

bearing on Waite's involvement in the hostage crisis, concerned the rather ambivalent relationship between the Church of England and the state. In many respects, the fact that the Church of England is the nation's established church frequently causes difficulties on both sides of the ecclesiastical divide. Because it is always aware of the deep responsibility and loyalty it owes to both the Crown and the government, the Church often finds itself in a moral quandary when it is obliged to pass comment on the great issues of the day. Thus when Margaret Thatcher led Britain in the victorious recovery of the Falkland Islands, Archbishop Runcie was required to conduct the service of thanksgiving at Westminster Abbey. According to the hierarchy of British public life, the prime minister ranks below the Archbishop, so that responsibility for organisation of the service was laid primarily at Runcie's door, although he did consult with Thatcher's office. Thatcher expressed her dismay when she discovered that Runcie planned to read the Lord's Prayer in Spanish as well as English, and that a recent sermon preached by the Pope at Coventry Cathedral against nuclear weapons would be repeated. Runcie, anxious not to upset the prime minister, decided to drop these ideas. He need not have bothered. The sermon Runcie delivered, which took as its theme 'Blessed are the peacemakers for they shall be called the Sons of God', drove Thatcher into an apoplectic fit. As Denis, her husband, commented memorably when asked what his wife thought about the service: 'The boss is livid.' The *Sun* newspaper, among others, went big on the story the following day. 'War Hero who Hates War', it trumpeted, referring to Runcie's distinguished war record, while the *Daily Telegraph* used more measured tones to put across the same point. 'Dr Runcie Angers Tories,' said the front-page story.

The Palace of Lambeth may be just across the Thames

from the Palace of Westminster, but nothing so clearly demonstrated the modern gulf in understanding between the two institutions than the rift between Runcie and Thatcher over the Falklands sermon. It is a dispute which has been unresolved since the infamous battle of wills between Henry VIII and Sir Thomas More, and the difference of opinion between Thatcher and Runcie was to affect the relationship between Downing Street and Lambeth for the duration of both incumbents. The rift between Thatcher and Runcie went back to their Oxford days when the then Margaret Roberts, a chemistry undergraduate at Somerville, had Runcie dropped from the university Conservative Association because of his 'excessive frivolity'. (By a quirk of fate and for entirely different reasons, both Thatcher and Runcie resigned from office in the autumn of 1990.) Thatcher thought *her* Archbishop should back her policies to the hilt, while Runcie believed it was his duty to seek a higher moral ground than that afforded by the grubby, underhand world of Westminster politics. As a result the two leaders were constantly at odds. Thatcher believed that in Runcie she had a fifth columnist in her midst, and viewed all the activities undertaken by Lambeth Palace with deep suspicion.

'Mrs Thatcher had an almost religious conviction in what she was doing, and I think it genuinely distressed her that the Church of England did not see the world as she saw it,' said Runcie. 'To her mind, the Church was simply "not one of us".'

It was against this unpromising political backdrop that Dr Runcie received a request for Terry Waite to intervene on behalf of the hostage Benjamin Weir. The decision to seek Waite's help was in many respects a reflection of the deep frustration the relatives of the American hostages felt about the performance of their own government. Carol Weir was not alone in feeling that the American diplomatic service, and the government for that matter, considered securing the release of her husband a low priority. Sis Levin, Jeremy Levin's wife, had encountered a similarly cold reception when she had started to do the rounds in Washington in search of information about what the government was doing on her husband's behalf. There was some irony in the fact that William Buckley, the man on whose behalf the Reagan administration was making the most strenuous efforts, was a bachelor and had no immediate family to worry on his behalf.

Washington's apparent lack of interest in the hostages came as a severe shock to people such as the Weirs and Levins who were imbued with the notion that the great American government machine always acted for the benefit of its citizens. 'We were brought up to believe that wherever Americans ventured, the government of the United States was there behind them,' Jeremy Levin explained once his ordeal had ended. 'There was this belief that if you somehow got yourself into trouble, the cavalry would be there to help you out. This just did not happen as far as we were concerned.'

Sis Levin, frustrated with the apathetic attitude of the government and the reluctance of her husband's television company to do anything which did not bear Washington's stamp of approval, embarked on her own campaign to secure her husband's release. At the time of his abduction, she knew next to nothing about the complicated political background to the Middle East, but she gradually built a network of contacts in Washington and elsewhere of people who knew the region and were prepared to advise and help her. As a result, she was able to make a private visit to Damascus where she managed to schedule a meeting with Farouk al-Sharaa, the Syrian foreign minister. She believes that it was as a direct result of this meeting that her husband gained his freedom a few weeks later.

After such a discouraging opening encounter with the

embassy in Beirut, Carol Weir resolved to do as much as she could to rescue her husband. To begin with she decided to remain in Beirut. The kidnappers might have broken one Islamic code by kidnapping her husband, but they generally drew the line at kidnapping women. She made the rounds of the local Lebanese press and television stations, giving them a full account of her husband's missionary work in Lebanon, which was duly published, in the hope of persuading the kidnappers to release her husband. Her message certainly got through, for during one round of interrogation the kidnappers made reference to something they had read in the press. 'You have been in Lebanon a long time. From 1935,' one of the kidnappers proudly announced. Weir corrected him politely, saying he'd been there since 1953. But it made no difference. The kidnappers knew that Weir visited the American embassy – to get his passport renewed – and for them that confirmed he was working for the CIA.

As well as exploring all obvious avenues in Beirut, Carol Weir fell back on the institutional support of the Presbyterian Church in the US. Presbyterians are by nature suspicious of large government bureaucracies and prefer to maintain a proper distance. In spite of this reticence, however, the Church certainly had a better understanding of how the American government system worked than a woman who had spent most of her adult life as a missionary in a country thousands of miles away, and so Carol Weir asked the Church to help her. At first the Church was unable to make much progress. Fred Wilson, an associate director at the Church's headquarters in New York, was given responsibility for liaising with the US government on Weir's case. His first efforts met with little success. Whether it was because a high percentage of the Washington elite are practising Anglicans, or simply because they felt there was nothing more they could do for the hostages, Wilson's request for Mrs Weir to meet George

Shultz, the US Secretary of State, was turned down. They were able to meet with some lower-ranking officials, but they only reinforced what Mrs Weir had heard at the embassy in Beirut. They had no information about where Benjamin Weir and the other hostages were being held, nor did they know who was responsible. They would do the best they could, but they could make no promises.

At about this time, in late 1984, when Mrs Weir was beginning to despair of seeing her husband again, someone at the Church had an idea which could possibly lead to a breakthrough in the deadlock. An official at the Presbyterian Church in New York happened to mention to Fred Wilson that he had heard of someone who worked at the Archbishop of Canterbury's office in London who had done some work on hostage crises in other parts of the Middle East. This person seemed to fit the bill perfectly. He had intervened in similar situations, and he had managed to bring hostages home unharmed. Even more impressively, he had achieved these considerable feats without offending the principles or policies of any of the parties involved. Every time his services had been called upon, he had won applause and plaudits all round. Fred Wilson resolved to contact this miracle-worker at once. If anyone could help get the hostages freed, it was this man. The next day he telephoned Lambeth Palace and asked to speak with Terry Waite.

After Fred Wilson had ascertained that Waite was prepared to help out, an official request was made to Dr Runcie. The Presbyterian Church in the US asked the Episcopal Church to ask Dr Runcie, as head of the Anglican Communion, if they could have the benefit of Waite's services. The Americans would, of course, pay all Waite's expenses while he was working on their behalf. Runcie was not immediately acquiescent to the request, which annoyed Waite intensely. Runcie felt Waite was getting into something potentially very dangerous, and which would also mean that Waite could not fulfil his duties at Lambeth Palace.

Waite's reputation had spread to the other side of the Atlantic following the success he had achieved in the first few months of his career at Lambeth Palace. Soon after the Revolutionary Guards seized the American embassy in Teheran, they turned their attentions on the small community of Anglicans in Iran. A British woman, Jean Waddell, the secretary to Bishop Dehqani-Tafti of Teheran, was shot and seriously wounded while revolutionaries killed the Bishop's only son. In the ensuing mayhem allegations of spying were made against Mrs Waddell and two other members of the Anglican Church, John and Audrey Coleman, which resulted in the Iranians refusing to allow them to leave the country. With the British embassy also under pressure, there was little the British government could do on behalf of the trapped churchmen. The Bishop, however, was allowed to leave, and when he arrived in London he appealed to Dr Runcie to intervene as head of the Anglican Communion.

It was at this juncture that Runcie made his first contact with Ayatollah Khomeini. He wrote to Teheran appealing as one man of God to another for the hostages to be freed. Although he received no reply, Waite, never one to pass up a travel opportunity, applied for an Iranian visa which, to everyone's surprise, materialised just before Christmas 1980. Waite had been asked by Runcie to handle the Teheran problem, and when the idea arose of sending a representative of the Anglican Church to the court of Khomeini, Waite originally suggested that Runcie send a bishop. But Runcie, impressed by the work Waite had put into the affair, decided that Waite should go, thereby conferring upon Waite the powers of an envoy for the first time.

Waite flew to Teheran on Christmas Day 1980 amid a fanfare of publicity. It was the first time Waite had come to public prominence, and he revelled in it. For several days he was kept waiting by the Revolutionary Guards, during which he happily posed for the television cameras and the photographers. At a quiet time of year for news, he gained the maximum publicity, even though he did not achieve very much. His reward for hanging around Teheran was to have a brief meeting with Waddell and the Colemans, at which he delivered a message of support from their Bishop, and then he returned to London. A few days after Waite's return, Khomeini finally ordered the release of the American embassy hostages. As the Americans were freed, a new visa was granted to Waite. He flew to Teheran, and this time the Iranians presented him with the three Britons.

Waite flew back to London in triumph to be fêted like a hero. The joyous scenes at the airport were broadcast all over the world. Waite had become a household name, an idol for listeners of BBC Radio Four who showered the station's news programmes with letters singing Waite's praises. Waite was proposed for 'man of the year', for the Nobel peace prize, as the next secretary-general of the United Nations. He was awarded the MBE, which he received from Buckingham Palace later that year. Waite was finally fulfilling the ambition that had begun all those years ago when he applied to join the Grenadier Guards of being accepted by the British establishment. Lambeth Palace, Buckingham Palace, the BBC, the MBE; Waite was in his element.

Waite went out of his way to court the media. There was even a subtle change in his title to make him more media-friendly. His official title, 'the Archbishop of Canterbury's Assistant for Anglican Communion Affairs', was fairly hard to digest, even for those who knew what it meant. So Waite became 'the Archbishop of Canterbury's special envoy',[1] a far easier title for the press to cope with and one that suggested an importance at Lambeth which far exceeded Waite's actual job description. When Runcie sent Waite to Teheran, he did so in the expectation that this was a one-off event, not to be repeated during his time as Archbishop. In Runcie's view, the powers of an envoy were conferred on Waite solely for the Teheran mission. Runcie had no desire for Waite to be his envoy on a permanent basis, a job for which Waite had neither the qualifications nor the experience. 'It was never my intention for Terry to be my envoy,' said Runcie. 'I wanted Terry to be my assistant and maintain contact with the Anglican Communion. Terry rather assumed the role of envoy, but this had nothing to do with the job I had employed him to carry out.'

At the time Runcie had more pressing matters on his mind. This was about the time that the General Synod, for example, was debating 'Homosexual relationships: a Contribution to Discussion', and Runcie was keen to prevent the Lesbian and Gay Christian Movement from making further inroads into the Church. Anyway, it was not Runcie's style to fuss over precise job definitions. Waite seemed to be doing a good job which helped to raise Lambeth's profile. Waite's success in Iran even occasioned a rare morsel of praise from Mrs Thatcher.

'What a brave man your Terry Waite is,' Mrs Thatcher remarked to the Archbishop when they met at a function after the Iranian hostages had been freed. 'He must have a lot of courage.'

Not everyone in the Thatcher cabinet, however, viewed Waite through rose-tinted spectacles. Willie Whitelaw, Thatcher's aide-de-camp in the Conservative Party and one

[1]Mantle, *op. cit.*

of the shrewder political minds of her circle, remained sceptical about Waite's activities. Runcie recalls conversations with Whitelaw in which he articulated his reservations about Waite. 'Willie used to huff and puff and ask what Terry was really up to,' said Runcie. 'I had to tell him I didn't really know, but that I trusted Terry's integrity entirely.'

William Whitelaw's suspicions were not entirely without foundation, and might have been prompted by the daily reports he received from British intelligence in his capacity as Home Secretary. Had closer scrutiny been given to events in Iran after the release of the three British hostages, perhaps more attention would have been paid, for example, to the arrival of a consignment of machine-guns and light weapons at the Iranian port of Bandar Abbas a few days later. The arms were sent to Iran by Michael Aspin, an arms dealer from Norfolk. Aspin later claimed he was working on behalf of British intelligence, and that the arms were sent to Iran as part of a deal to secure the release of the three Britons. A Scandinavian diplomat who worked as an intermediary confirmed elements of Aspin's story, which was met with stony silence at Whitehall. Aspin was jailed for six years at the Old Bailey in 1988 for another arms-running deal to Iran. On this occasion Aspin claimed to have been working on behalf of Lieutenant-Colonel Oliver North of the US National Security Council, a claim which he was unable to verify at his trial. Waite was also assisted in his mission by the decision of the British government to return the body of an Iranian terrorist who had blown himself up after a bomb exploded at the Queen's Garden Hotel in London the previous May. There was also a promise that Britain would equip the Iranian army with spare parts for its Chieftain tanks, a crucial issue for the Iranians who were now at war with Iraq. Waite gave no indication at the time or subsequently that he had any idea of the deals going on behind his back, but the fact that there were several other dimensions to Waite's humanitarian activities was sufficient for eyebrows to be raised in certain quarters. Clearly there was a lot more to the avuncular Mr Waite than met the eye of his adoring British public.

When the American Church asked Waite to help in Lebanon, Carol Weir was told nothing could be done until Waite had finished a mission he was undertaking to rescue four Britons held hostage in Libya. The diplomatic crisis which broke out in late 1984 between Libya and Britain was in many respects tailor-made for Waite. Relations between the two countries had steadily deteriorated since April 1984 when a young policewoman, Yvonne Fletcher, was accidentally shot dead by an enraged Libyan diplomat who had opened fire from inside the Libyan embassy in London at a crowd of anti-Gaddafi demonstrators outside. The ensuing political row and tit-for-tat diplomatic expulsions reached a climax when Gaddafi, exasperated that no one seemed to be taking him seriously, seized four Britons working in Libya on trumped-up spying charges. The result was a classic diplomatic stalemate. Margaret Thatcher, the Iron Lady, was not going to concede anything to someone she considered one of the prime architects of modern terrorism, and Gaddafi was not prepared to bow down before what he considered the neo-colonial dictates of the British government. And yet for all the public rhetoric, both governments realised they had got themselves into an impossible fix over a few Britons who had done nothing wrong.

The impasse was broken by Terry Waite. Even though there was only the most tenuous connection between the four Britons in Libya and the Church of England – one of them had played the church organ – Waite was eager to become involved when the relatives sought Lambeth's assistance. 'We were stretching a point really,' said Runcie, 'but I didn't think there was any harm in Terry having a go at getting them released.'

As with Teneran, Waite's visit to Libya was carefully organised to obtain the maximum publicity. Waite arranged to fly to Tripoli for Christmas 1984, the second Christmas in four years he had sacrificed being with his wife and four children at their modest semi-detached house in Blackheath. Waite arrived bearing a Christmas gift for Gaddafi, *Aristotle and the Arabs*, which he handed to the Libyan leader when the two met in a bedouin tent constructed in the middle of the main military barracks. There is nothing Gaddafi, who once trained at Sandhurst, likes more than to have dignitaries visit him, flatter him and seek his assistance in solving their problems. Unfortunately for Gaddafi, however, the number of international dignitaries willing to travel to Tripoli to humour the Libyan leader in his tent are but few. With Waite, however, Gaddafi felt in his element. Waite was good at making Third World leaders feel important and Waite listened attentively while Gaddafi went into his usual nonsensical ramblings about the destiny of the Arabs and the relationship between Islam and Christianity. When it was over Gaddafi handed Waite a signed copy of the Koran bearing the inscription: 'My greetings and congratulations for the new year, hoping it will be a year of blessing for humanity.' He also promised Waite he would try to free the British prisoners.

Waite was delighted. After his session in the tent he announced to the waiting press that Gaddafi had promised to release the men 'out of respect for the Church and my mission'. It was during the Libya trip that Waite perfected his relationship with the media. In particular he struck up a good working relationship with British television reporters. Terry Waite was, in media parlance, 'good television'. His distinctive height and beard made him instantly recognisable to the British public, and he never turned down a request for an interview. Waite, moreover, appreciated the importance of television in projecting his image. The symbiosis of Waite with the media was the cornerstone of his popularity.

The meeting with Gaddafi, however, did not produce immediate results. He returned to London empty-handed. Together with Runcie he posed outside Lambeth Palace with a copy of the Koran. He then visited a group of Libyans being held on remand at Durham prison for causing explosions on mainland Britain. They were all subsequently convicted and given lengthy prison terms. Then he returned to Libya to address a meeting of Gaddafi's People's Congress held inside a circus ring. Waite made a short speech in which he said: 'Politics is made by men. Mercy, justice and compassion come from God. The way to deal with the enemy is not by the gun or the bullet. The way to deal with the enemy is by superior moral and spiritual strength.' The speech made a favourable impression on Gaddafi's apparatchiks, and within days Waite and the four Britons were flying home in triumph.

On arrival at Gatwick Waite was exposed to an orgy of triumphalism by the British media. The press, almost without exception, was effusive in its praise. Waite was blessed with 'a commanding presence' wrote one columnist, while the leader writer at the *Daily Telegraph* commented: 'He is gaining the reputation of taking on impossible missions and succeeding.' Margaret Thatcher once more set aside her deep antipathy towards anything associated with Lambeth Palace and publicly praised Waite's 'patience and skill'. Sir Charles Powell, the former diplomat who became Thatcher's *éminence grise* on foreign affairs at No. 10, remembers that the attitude of Downing Street to Waite was one of 'grudging respect' after his involvement in Libya. 'He hadn't done anything wrong, he hadn't compromised any of our principles. And he managed to pull it off. In the circumstances you had to give him some credit,' said Powell. More awards followed Waite's Libya trip. Waite was voted 'man of the year' by listeners to

Radio Four's Today programme (Mrs Thatcher was a frequent recipient of the female honour). He was given a cluster of honorary degrees and awarded the £2,000 Templeton Prize for humanitarian work, which he donated to two local charities.

As with the Iran mission, however, the suspicion remained that the dead hand of the Foreign Office had been involved behind the scenes in a deal to get the Britons released. Before handing over the four men, the Libyans had set a series of preconditions. In particular the Libyans were concerned at the continuing activities of dissident groups in Britain, and wanted the British government to take action to ensure that the dissidents discontinued the anti-Gaddafi propaganda. They also wanted guarantees that Libyans in Britain would not be persecuted by the British authorities. In effect the Libyans, after the trauma of a deep rift in diplomatic relations with London, were looking for reassurance from the British authorities which, according to many officials both in Britain and abroad, the Foreign Office duly provided.

In the circumstances, however, all parties involved were content to let Waite take the credit. The Libyans did not want the world to know they had been intimidated by Britain's diplomatic bullying, and the British government did not particularly want it known that, for all its public pronouncements, it was capable of assisting the Libyans if they were prepared to play ball. Certainly if Waite knew anything about the quiet diplomacy which had smoothed the path for his success, he made no reference to it. Flushed with his latest triumph and riding a wave of personal popularity, Waite was setting his sights on an entirely different challenge, one which would consolidate his reputation as a humanitarian intermediary *par excellence*. He would attempt to resolve the hostage crisis in Lebanon.

Waite's determination to tackle this problem was the beginning of a rift between himself and Runcie which would steadily widen as Waite became more and more obsessed with Lebanon. From the outset Runcie was against Waite getting involved; he believed that to do so would be to venture well beyond the clearly-stated parameters within which the previous two missions had been conducted. Before Waite travelled to Teheran and Tripoli, Runcie had been in direct contact with Khomeini and Gaddafi. On both occasions he was able to establish the ground rules for Waite's visit, which were vital to the success of Waite's mission.

'On both occasions I was able to tell them that Terry was coming,' said Runcie. 'In return they agreed to accept full responsibility for his well-being while he was there. They would supply a visa, they would meet him at the airport and treat him as they would any visiting dignitary. While he was there they would provide him with all the necessary facilities. They also agreed to pay his bills. Having satisfied myself that it was safe for Terry to travel, I was happy for him to proceed.

'But Lebanon was a different matter altogether. There was no government and we had no idea who we were dealing with. It was shadows chasing shadows. If Terry went to Lebanon, there was no way of guaranteeing his safety. And besides, none of the Americans in Beirut was the responsibility of the Church of England as far as I could see,' said Runcie. 'I could understand Terry's humanitarian concern for the hostages, but I felt we were getting into an area well beyond our capabilities.'

Waite was determined to go to Lebanon, and went out of his way to persuade Runcie to grant him permission. At one point he brought a delegation to Lambeth Palace to persuade Runcie of the validity of the Lebanon mission. The group was led by Fred Wilson of the Presbyterian Church, and Runcie only learned many years later that the delegation included Lieutenant-Colonel Oliver North, who said very little but seemed to take a keen interest in the discussion. As a result of this meeting, Runcie reluctantly agreed to allow Waite to help them.

'But I was rather devious about it,' said Runcie. 'I did a deal with the Episcopal Church in the US whereby I agreed to second Terry to them and they would pay all his bills, as Lambeth Palace simply did not have the financial resources for a mission like this. Our involvement in Iran and Libya had only been possible because of the financial help we received from the Iranians and Libyans. And I made it clear that I didn't want Terry to be away too long because I did not want the Anglican Communion to be neglected.'

Although Waite was grateful to Runcie for allowing him to display his talents on the American stage, he harboured a deep resentment towards the Archbishop for putting up so many obstacles in the first place. From now on Waite would display a less than Christian attitude towards his employer, especially in his dealings with the media. He would frequently offer the opinion that Runcie was 'indecisive' and 'a silly old fool', and whenever anyone asked him what Runcie thought about his mission, Waite would reply, 'He doesn't think anything because he doesn't know anything. I doubt if he even knows which country I'm in.' Waite did not say that the reason Runcie knew so little was because the 'special envoy' preferred to provide his Archbishop with as little information as possible.

9

THE HOSTAGE HARVEST

Terry Waite could not have chosen a more inauspicious moment to embark upon his adventure into the labyrinthine complexities of the hostage crisis. The longer lawlessness prevailed in Lebanon, the more the terrorist groups grew in confidence and struck with impunity whenever it suited them.

The campaign by Islamic Jihad to win the release of the Dawa 17 was run in tandem with an effort to destroy every remaining vestige of the West's presence in Lebanon. As in Iran, the Islamic fundamentalists intended to fulfil their dream of establishing an Islamic republic in Lebanon free from any outside interference, be it Soviet or American. After Ben Weir's abduction in May 1984, there was a brief respite from the kidnappings as the terror gangs concentrated on more eye-catching targets. On September 20 a re-run of the disastrous 1983 attack on the American embassy in Lebanon was narrowly avoided when Islamic Jihad organised a suicide truck-bomb attack on the new embassy compound in East Beirut. David Miers, the British ambassador in Lebanon, had just finished a meeting with his American counterpart, Reginald Bartholomew, when a large station-wagon bearing diplomatic licence plates careered into the heavily-fortified compound. The truck was laden with half a ton of explosives, plus four Soviet-made Grad missiles. Fortunately one of Miers's SAS-trained bodyguards saw what was happening and shot the driver dead before he could reach his target. Even so, the blast caused severe damage to the embassy, killing several people. When the rescue teams finally reached the ambassador's office on the fourth floor, they found Miers with blood streaming from a head wound. Seeing that help had arrived, Miers stopped digging through the rubble to help free his American colleague who was trapped beneath.

'If you're looking for your ambassador, he's buried under that lot,' Miers remarked to the American rescue team with all the aplomb one would expect of a Foreign Office training. Miraculously, Bartholomew sustained only superficial cuts and bruises.

A fainthearted attempt was made at Lausanne to persuade the rival Lebanese factions to reconcile their differences. But within hours of the talks commencing, the meeting broke up amid the usual flurry of accusation and counter-accusation, and all parties returned to Lebanon intent on pursuing the civil war to the bitter end. The complete absence of government authority meant the terrorist groups could do as they pleased. So proficient had they become that even the mighty Israeli army was on the retreat. After several key Israeli bases in southern Lebanon were destroyed by truck-bombs, Israeli prime minister Shimon Peres decided the Israelis should leave Lebanon. In the ensuing retreat the proud Israeli armed forces, which only two years previously had swept victoriously into Lebanon to be welcomed with rice and rose-water, were reduced to a ragged, nervous rabble as the soldiers gave up their hard-won positions and headed for home as fast as their trucks and tanks could carry them. The success of the Shia Muslim militias in driving the Israelis out of Lebanon, coming hot on the heels of driving the multinational force out of the country, gave the militiamen untold confidence. It also meant that there was virtually no one to stand up against them.

Nor were their activities confined to Lebanon. The most spectacular foreign escapade occurred in December 1984 when Terry Waite was still planning his trip to Libya. A Kuwait Airways flight from Dubai to Karachi, Pakistan, a shuttle service for Pakistani labourers, was hijacked in mid-air by four Lebanese who had joined the aircraft at Dubai and who ordered the British pilot, John Clark, to head for Teheran. At first the Iranians were reluctant to allow the aircraft to land, but they relented when the hijackers threatened to blow it up in mid-air. The passengers were herded into the economy section and their passports and identification papers confiscated. Soon after the plane landed, shooting was heard and the half-dead body of one of the passengers was thrown onto the tarmac. The hijackers continued to fire at the lifeless figure, to make sure he did not survive. He was later identified as Charles Hegna, an American working for the American Agency for International Development in Pakistan. He had been murdered because he was American and because the kidnappers wanted to underline that they were serious about their demands. They wanted the seventeen prisoners in Kuwait released.

For the next six days the world was horrified by the spectacle of a succession of similar atrocities as the hijackers, getting increasingly desperate, tried to force the Kuwaiti government to capitulate. But despite several crisis cabinet meetings, the Kuwaitis remained firm. The al-Sabahs reasoned that if they gave in to such brazen intimidation, they might as well wave goodbye to their rule over their emirate. The situation was saved, to the genuine disbelief of most foreign observers, by the Iranians. Many people in London, Washington and Kuwait thought the Iranians were behind the hijacking in the first place; the action taken by the Iranians seemed to prove them wrong. In a well-executed operation, a group of Iranian soldiers, dressed as cleaners, broke into the aircraft and overpowered the four hijackers, who were escorted off the plane and taken to Evin prison. The surviving American and Kuwaiti hostages were released.

The hijackers, it materialised, were all members of the Lebanese Hizbollah militia, but this time they had overstepped the mark. Sheikh Fadlallah, the militia's spiritual leader, ruled that the hijacking was 'unIslamic', and by ending the hijacking forcibly, the Iranians were clearly sending a message to their Shia accomplices in Beirut that, from now on, hijackings were out. For those still determined to get the Dawa 17 released, that meant there was nothing for it other than to escalate the kidnappings, which they did with a vengeance. The year ended with the kidnapping of Peter Kilburn, a confirmed bachelor who worked as the librarian at the AUB.

If 1984 had been a bad year for US interests in Lebanon, the only fact that prevented 1985 from being worse was that there were fewer targets for the extremists to hit. In terms of kidnapping foreigners, however, 1985 was the year the kidnappers reached the high-water mark. On January 3 Eric Wehril, the Swiss chargé d'affaires, was kidnapped. The Swiss embassy was next to the French embassy, and the kidnappers probably mistook him for a Frenchman. Luckily for him, the kidnappers could think of no use for a Swiss diplomat, so he was released four days later. The next day they made up for their generosity by kidnapping Lawrence Jenco, an American Roman Catholic priest who ran a centre which helped refugees and other victims of the civil war. Jenco's kidnapping was almost a copybook re-run of Weir's abduction. He was taken early in the morning as he walked to his office at the Catholic Relief Centre. A mild-mannered, softly-spoken man who believed passionately in the inherent goodness of man, it had never occurred to Jenco that he might be a target, because he believed all Lebanese appreciated the value of his missionary work.

The only bright spot came in mid-February when Jeremy Levin managed to escape from his makeshift prison in the Bekaa Valley. Like all the hostages, Levin had thought many times about escaping, but he considered the prospect of an opportunity presenting itself to be exceedingly remote. From the start of 1985, however, one of his guards began to adopt an altogether more friendly attitude, and Levin's conditions improved slightly. He was given a longer chain – a major improvement in the circumstances – which allowed him easy access to the room's only window. Once Levin had accustomed himself to this uncharacteristic latitude, it was not long before he was able to free himself from his chains. He then knotted his blankets into a rope, climbed through the window to a balcony, tied one end of the blankets to a railing, and lowered himself to the ground one floor below.

Whether Levin was allowed to escape on purpose because of his wife's visit to Syria, or whether he simply took advantage of an opportunity is difficult to judge. Levin, with commendable honesty, said of himself: 'I'm no macho man. It was all very scary.' But as the opportunity to escape was almost laid on a plate for him, Levin could not ignore it. 'I was convinced Hizbollah wanted me to escape. Otherwise I would have stayed with the others,' he said. Certainly it is possible that the Syrians, possibly in response to Sis Levin's visit to Damascus, but more probably because President Assad considered it to be in his interests to curry favour with Washington, decided to free one of the Americans. It would be a relatively simple matter for the Syrians to bribe one of the guards. Judging by the response from the other guards once they discovered Levin's escape, however, not everyone was in on the secret. The first Ben Weir knew one of the hostages had escaped was when he was awoken by the guards shouting. He heard a lot of noise and angry exchanges in the next-door cell where he knew there was another hostage; clearly that hostage was no longer present. Within hours Weir was bound, blindfolded and bundled into the back of a car. The next day, as he settled into a new cell, rapidly contructed from planks and chipboard, Weir summoned the courage to make contact with the hostage on the other side of the partition.

'My name is Ben Weir, a Protestant pastor. Who are you?' he hissed in a whisper.

'Lawrence Martin Jenco, a Catholic priest,' came the whispered response. It was the first contact Weir had made with a fellow hostage in nine months of captivity, and he immediately began to pray for his new companion.

Levin's euphoria at being free was short-lived. After his escape he was picked up by a Syrian patrol which almost seemed to have been expecting him. He was then driven to Damascus where he was handed over to the American embassy with a surprising degree of ostentation on the part of the Syrians. After a good meal and a bath and an emotional reunion with his wife, Levin was led to a room for his debriefing by the American counter-terrorism specialists. At the time Levin escaped, there were some five or six people making the morning trek to the bathroom, and once he learned that other Americans were being held hostage (he heard no news about the outside world during his year in captivity), it was not difficult to deduce that Buckley, Weir and Jenco had been among Levin's fellow hostages.

For Levin, the thought that, less than a two-hour drive from his current, luxurious residence, fellow Americans were suffering the ordeal from which he had just escaped was almost unbearable. Now he had passed on his precious intelligence, he expected his debriefers to lead an immediate raid on the Bekaa Valley to free the others. He found it difficult to accept that the Americans just quietly digested the momentous news he had given them, and went away to think it over.

Some of the points Levin made about his abductors led the debriefing team to conclude that he was suffering from a classic case of Stockholm syndrome, when a hostage starts to believe in the cause of his tormentors. Certainly Levin's behaviour on his return to the US raised more than a few eyebrows. Levin told anyone who cared to listen how grateful he was to the kidnappers for giving him a new direction in life. One of his first acts was to convert from Judaism to Christianity. It is probably no more than coincidence that Levin spent most of his captivity close by the road to Damascus; the more likely explanation for his conversion was that his kidnappers opened his eyes to all the alleged atrocities committed against the Shia Muslims by the state of Israel, the Jewish homeland. As a consequence Levin could not bear to be identified with the Israelis, even though he conceded that 'culturally and ethnically' he was still a Jew. Moreover, upon his return to the US, Levin embarked on a one-man crusade to bring home to the American people the fact that the Shia Muslims had a just cause; the same Shia Muslims, that is, who had blown up two American embassies, one marine barracks and terrorised scores of innocent Americans. It was not long before Levin was being vilified in Washington as anti-American and a self-hating Jew, and parting company with his employers, CNN. If Levin was naive when he arrived in Lebanon, he was none the wiser when he left.

No matter how much Washington gleaned about Lebanese attitudes towards the US through its attempts to resolve the deepening hostage crisis, there was no change in the way the US tackled the problem of Lebanon. One of the more vivid examples of the wide gulf in understanding between the Levant and the US was provided when, just two days after Levin's escape, Mohammed Ali, the former world heavyweight boxing champion, arrived in Beirut to use his considerable presence to free the remaining Western hostages. Ali had converted to Islam many years previously, changing his name from Cassius Clay, and believed his association with the more radical, ethnically-orientated pressure groups in the US would give him a degree of credibility in Beirut. His advisers arranged for him to visit the Bir-al-Abed mosque in Beirut's southern suburbs where Sheikh Fadlallah regularly preached against the infidel West, exhorting the faithful to kidnap foreigners. After Levin's escape, the hostages were thought to have been moved to a hiding place not a stone's throw from Fadlallah's home. When Ali arrived at the mosque, however, he was greeted by a chanting crowd of demonstrators waving placards which read: 'Down with America, down with Israel. God is Great.' It may have been because his advisers were unable to provide an adequate translation, or because Ali's illness from Parkinson's disease impaired his judgement, but Ali responded to the chanting by giving the crowd a clenched fist salute, the symbol of the American black power movement, under the mistaken impression that the crowd was chanting in his favour.

A development which was to have far more serious consequences for those Americans still in Beirut was the attitude of the Reagan administration to a United Nations resolution condemning Israeli policies in southern Lebanon. Although many Middle East specialists at the State Department in Washington believed Israel's involvement in Lebanon had severely damaged American interests in the region, the White House still refused to countenance any action which was in any way critical of Israel. While many countries who were not concerned either way about the fate of the Shia Muslims abstained from the vote, the US delegation actually went so far as to veto it. A few days later a prominent Hizbollah leader held a news conference on behalf of the militia at which he declared: 'Americans must leave Lebanon for good.'

One of the journalists listening attentively and making copious notes was Terry Anderson, the Middle East bureau chief of the Associated Press. As the most widely read news service in the US, the AP played a crucial role in relaying news about all developments in Lebanon. Anderson, a stocky, no-nonsense former marine who had served in Vietnam, took his job as a journalist very seriously. Having arrived at the height of the Israeli assault on Beirut in the summer of 1982, Anderson had developed the hard-arsed, mean-what-you-say attitude to the war that one would expect of a former marine. Before working in Lebanon, Anderson had been the AP man in South Africa where, like so many American journalists who attach a sense of mission to their work, he had come to believe it was his duty to highlight the plight of the oppressed – the South African blacks – and expose the hypocrisy of the oppressors – the South African whites.

Anderson took a similar approach in his coverage of the Lebanese civil war. To his mind, the oppressors were the Israelis who had caused the whole mess in the first place, and the oppressed were the poor Shia Muslim peasants, struggling to liberate their land from the Israeli occupiers. If American marines got blown to pieces by Shia terrorists, Washington was to blame for siding with Israel. Anderson also took an almost macho pride in being the first journalist to get to the scene of a particularly gruesome car-bomb, or the aftermath of a ferocious artillery duel. He would sift through the wreckage with complete professional detachment, taking down every detail in his notebook, before running to the nearest phone to get his story back to New York. The sheer weight of his factual accuracy – exact numbers of dead and wounded, amount and type of explosives used – combined with the force of his personality, made him a formidable opponent for any journalist assigned to cover the Middle East.

He worked closely with Robert Fisk, the Middle East correspondent of *The Times* of London. They made an odd couple: Fisk, the frenetic fidget, forever arranging his spectacles and eyebrows in contrasting directions, who, the moment he heard the distant crackle of gunfire, would lapse into a stream-of-consciousness rant about anything that came into his head, from the bombing of Dresden to imagined conversations between senior executives at *The Times*; and Anderson, the muscular Vietnam veteran whose favourite line when confronted with a Lebanese checkpoint was to scream *sahafi*, the Arabic for press, at the bemused sentry as though this gave him the right to travel wherever he desired with impunity.

Among the small band of journalists who remained in Beirut when the majority packed and left were those, like Anderson and Fisk, who suffered from an addiction to the story they were covering. Journalists can experience a dangerous sense of self-importance when they perceive themselves to be on the side of David as he confronts the bully-boy Goliath, whether it be villagers fighting to save a treasured wood from destruction to make way for a new road, or bands of Shia Muslims fighting to liberate their country from foreign occupation. What Anderson and his kind failed to understand was that, to the young fundamentalists rallying to the call of Islam in the southern suburbs, they were almost as unwelcome in Lebanon as the Israeli soldiers. Young fanatics such as these, who had been brought up to revile the corrupt teachings and lifestyle of the West, were not impressed when these privileged foreigners acquired a smattering of colloquial Arabic which, like colonials of past generations, they spoke as a means of humouring the natives. However noble their motives for remaining in Beirut, the majority of foreigners continued to enjoy a lifestyle which consisted of dining out every night and sipping the finest Château Musar wines at sunset from their well-appointed balconies overlooking the Mediterranean. It was beyond the comprehension of a Shia Muslim, moreover, that someone like Anderson could abandon his wife and child in the States in order to work in Lebanon, and set himself up with a Lebanese mistress.

No matter how bad the security situation, Fisk and Anderson would travel all over the country in pursuit of a story. In October 1983, they travelled together to Baalbek to interview Hussein Musawi, one of the founders of Hizbollah and a man destined to be one of the kidnappers' ringleaders. As they left Musawi's house, one of the guards asked to see Anderson's passport. He took the passport to an adjoining room where he photocopied Anderson's details – name, age, date of birth and address. The passport was then returned to Anderson.[1]

This disquieting incident had probably escaped Anderson's memory on the morning of Saturday March 16, 1985, when he rose early at his apartment on the corniche in West Beirut and left his pregnant girlfriend Madeleine, whom he had met a year previously when she was working as a fixer at an American television network. Saturday was generally a quiet news day, and Anderson had arranged a game of tennis with Don Mell, a young photographer with AP. The previous night I had seen Anderson at the Commodore. He was in good spirits, sitting in his favourite seat at the bar with Madeleine at his side, engaging in heated argument with journalistic colleagues about the merits of a particular story. When he was in full flow, Anderson, with his short-cropped hair, jutting chin and heavy pebble glasses, was very much the king of the press castle, and heaven help anyone who dared contradict his point of view.

[1]Robert Fisk: *Pity the Nation*, André Deutsch, 1990.

There was, however, an element of bravado about Anderson's bonhomie that night. A couple of days previously Anderson had been driving alone to his office when four Lebanese in a Mercedes tried to head him off the road. He managed to avoid them by turning sharp left. He decided not to tell Madeleine, so as not to alarm her unduly. But he told his good friend Fisk, and the two had a long conversation about what they would do in the event of someone trying to kidnap them. Fisk took the view that it was better to fight than to give in. Anderson, as usual, had his own ideas. 'You're out of your mind,' he informed his colleague. 'These guys have guns. You don't have a chance . . . If they come, it's better to let them take you . . . Almost all the people who've been kidnapped have been set free after a while. It's always sorted out in the end.'[1] That same day Anderson had also travelled to the southern suburbs to interview Sheikh Fadlallah. He wanted to know what Fadlallah thought about the kidnappings. Fadlallah was courteous but unyielding. If Americans insisted on remaining in Lebanon, they were making themselves targets. If all the Americans left Lebanon, there would be no more kidnapping, said Fadlallah. Anderson as ever took copious notes of what the Sheikh said, but he paid little attention to what he meant.

Anderson played his usual vigorous game of tennis until, exhausted and covered with sweat, he and Mell decided to call it a day. The tennis courts were about a half-mile drive from Anderson's apartment. Don Mell's flat was on the way, and Anderson offered to give him a lift home. As they pulled up outside the flat, they were intercepted by a green Mercedes containing three bearded Lebanese militiamen. Mell had noticed the car cruising outside the

[1] *Ibid.*

tennis court, but had not paid it much attention. The men jumped out of the Mercedes, pulled Mell from the car and pinned him against a nearby wall, a gun pointed at his head. Anderson was then pulled out of his car and dragged into the Mercedes. The three men jumped into the Mercedes and sped off, leaving Mell in a state of complete shock.

Anderson's friends and colleagues in Beirut made a determined effort to rescue him. Fisk travelled to the local mosque to ask if anyone knew where Anderson was. An Irish diplomat, one of the few Western diplomats still living in West Beirut, offered his services. Anderson's colleagues at the AP had photographs of Anderson copied and distributed among all the militias. The AP, mindful that Amal had managed to free Frank Regier the year previously, contacted leaders of the militia to see if they could intervene again. Unfortunately, Amal did not exert the same influence over Hizbollah extremists in the spring of 1985 as they had in the spring of 1984, and were unable to help. Not that this dampened Fisk's optimism. That evening he telephoned Anderson's sister, Peggy Say, at her home in Florida to break the news of Anderson's abduction. 'Peggy, this will be over within twenty-four hours,' Fisk informed her.[1] He could not have been more wrong.

I had only been in Lebanon a few days when Anderson was kidnapped, and the thought that someone I had been drinking with the previous night was now part of the ever-growing band of hostages filled me with a distinct sense of unease. There were those, like Fisk, whom wild horses would not drag from Beirut. I did not share his confidence. Because all the telephone lines were down, the only way of communicating with London was to telex from the Commodore lobby. Once I learned of Anderson's abduction, I filed the story to the

[1]Peggy Say: *Forgotten*, Simon and Schuster, 1991.

Sunday Telegraph. Unsure of whether I should stay or go, I ended my dispatch with a message to the foreign editor, written in the distinctive telex idiom used worldwide before the advent of computers and fax machines made the trusty telex obsolete: ATTENTION FOREIGN DESK TELEGRAPH LONDON INFORMATIVELY STOP SITUATION IN BEIRUT VERY DANGEROUS DUE INCREASED KIDNAP ACTIVITY STOP INTEND REMAIN WEST BEIRUT FOR PRESENT STOP APPRECIATE CONTACT STOP COUGHLIN

The editors in London responded immediately. After a few check phone calls had been made to senior executives at the *Telegraph*, I received a telex reply a few hours later from Peter Eastwood, the *Telegraph*'s managing editor. It was marked: URGENTLY FOR CON COUGHLIN ROOM 621 COMMODORE HOTEL. When I opened it I was in left in no doubt as to what to do: VIEW DEVELOPING SITUATION INSIST YOU LEAVE BEIRUT SOONEST STOP SUGGEST YOU CYPRUSWARD NO LATER THAN TOMORROW AND THEN MAKE YOUR WAY TO ISRAEL STOP ADVISE STOP EASTWOOD. I could have done without the direct reference to Israel on an open telex line in the heart of Islamic West Beirut, but at least I no longer had to worry about staying behind and putting myself at risk. I got the first plane to Cyprus.

Throughout the first year of the kidnapping of foreigners in Lebanon, Islamic Jihad, Mugniyeh's cover name for the main Shia kidnap gang, mainly concentrated on Americans. On the rare occasions when other Westerners were picked up, such as the Swiss diplomat, they were quickly released. Occasionally Mugniyeh targeted Arab victims, such as the Saudi Arabian consul. But most victims were Americans, taken both to put pressure on Washington not to interfere in Lebanon's internal politics and as part of the general campaign to secure the release of the Dawa 17. From their headquarters at the Sheikh Abdullah barracks at Baalbek, Mugniyeh and his cohorts believed they could persuade Washington to apply pressure on Kuwait to release the prisoners.

From the spring of 1985, however, the kidnappers began to expand their horizons. Two days before Anderson's abduction, Geoffrey Nash, a sixty-year-old British metallurgist working for the Lebanese Industry Institute, was kidnapped as he left his house for work. The next day Brian Levick, the fifty-eight-year-old British general manager of the Coral Oil Company, was kidnapped by five gunmen as he left his office in West Beirut. The news spread like a bush-fire through the British community in West Beirut. With the exception of Jonathan Wright – and word had quickly spread that he had been taken by Palestinians, not Islamic fundamentalists – the 100 or so British in West Beirut had been untouched by the mounting wave of terrorism. Shortly after the abduction of Nash and Levick, a statement issued by Islamic Jihad, claiming responsibility for the abduction of the two Britons and Anderson, should have left no one in any doubt as to how the Islamic fundamentalists viewed those foreigners still in West Beirut.

'We are convinced that Islamic West Beirut is full of agents from all sides and accordingly we are working day and night to purge our region of any subversive element,' the statement read. 'We address a final warning to foreign nationals residing in our Islamic region to respect our hospitality and not to exploit their presence among us to undertake subversive activities against us. Assuming the profession of a journalist, merchant, industrialist, scientist and religious man will from now on be of no avail to spies staying amongst us.'

The British residents who chose to remain in the face of such clear-cut paranoia were by then a fairly mixed bunch. Some were journalists; some were elderly British couples such as Jackie and Sunnie Mann who ran an English-style pub and had nowhere else to go; and there was a cluster of teachers, some academics, others teaching English as a foreign language. The latter group was divided between those who sought adventure and those who had discovered they were either unemployable in Britain, or only qualified for the more menial posts, and preferred to take advantage of the AUB's exotic environs, no matter how great the risk.

By the spring of 1985, this maverick group of expatriates had become expert at interpreting every aspect of the Lebanese civil war, and could provide a whole range of reasons why they could remain in Beirut, despite the repeated advice of the British embassy for them to leave. The Foreign Office, moreover, knew what it was talking about. During the Iranian Revolution, it was mere chance that the staff at the British embassy had not suffered the same fate as the Americans. Besides, since Ronald Reagan's election as president, the close working and ideological relationship he had struck up with Margaret Thatcher made the Iranians view Britain as the 'little Satan' compared with the American 'great Satan'. Looked at objectively, if the same forces which had persecuted Americans and Britons in Iran were now operative in Beirut, there was no logical reason why the Iranian-backed militias should not target British subjects in the same way that they were targeting Americans. The Foreign Office certainly saw the abduction of Nash and Levick as the start of a new chapter in the hostage crisis, and took the precaution of closing the British embassy's visa section in West Beirut. The small British diplomatic community was now re-established in Christian East Beirut, where the threat of kidnapping was minimal.

On the day of his abduction, Brian Levick had popped home to his apartment on the corniche to pick up his bathing costume before driving to the golf club to join his wife for lunch. Levick had spent a lifetime working in dangerous and exotic places as an executive for Shell oil. He had been in Aden at the height of the troubles, and had worked in Brunei during the rebellion.

After retiring from Shell, he accepted the job of running a small Lebanese oil company. 'I knew there were dangers when I took the job,' recalled Levick, who later settled in the more tranquil environs of Thames Ditton, Surrey. 'But it was the price you paid for doing an interesting job and living in an interesting place.'

As Levick pulled up outside his apartment, a group of armed men surrounded him. Within minutes he was lying on the floor of a car as the kidnappers sped to their hideout. He was taken to the underground car-park of an unfinished building somewhere close to the southern suburbs where he was subjected to an intensely hostile interrogation.

'It was clear from the questions they kept asking that they thought I was an American,' said Levick. 'The interrogation went on for some considerable time, and it was not very pleasant. At various times they put a pistol to my head and carried out mock executions. They made constant allegations that I worked for an intelligence agency.'

Despite his protestations of innocence, the kidnappers eventually took him to a building which looked like a barracks, where he was put in a cell. The cell, furnished with a mattress, was so small he could hardly stand up. For much of the time it was in complete darkness. Although he was held in solitary confinement, he thought he could catch, from time to time, the faint strains of French being spoken further along the corridor. At the time Levick held out little hope that he would ever see his wife and children again.

'I thought there was a 90 per cent probability that they would kill me,' said Levick. 'Having taken me in the first place, I just understood that, from the point of view of the kidnappers, there was no point in letting me go.' Levick nevertheless undertook a daily fitness routine, which lasted several hours. Apart from the three meals brought to him each day and a daily visit to the bathroom, Levick's only contact with the world was when his captors came to conduct the daily interrogation. Although the kidnappers now adopted a more relaxed attitude when they spoke to Levick, they were still convinced that he was an American, and kept accusing him of being a spy.

After about ten days, however, Levick's protestations that he was British finally seemed to get through, and the attitude towards him began to change remarkably. When one kidnapper told Levick: 'Tomorrow, you go home,' he was inclined not to believe it. But the next day a guard appeared with a bottle of Head and Shoulders shampoo and took Levick to the bathroom to clean himself up, the first time he had been able to have a proper wash since his abduction. The kidnappers, the same group which had abducted American and French citizens, apparently had no quarrel with the British authorities, and therefore decided they had no reason to hold Levick. He was handed back his clothes, blindfolded, and driven back into the city centre. The car drew to a halt, and the kidnappers helped Levick out of the car. He was told to stand with his back to the car, keeping his blindfold over his eyes until the kidnappers had driven off. Levick still fully expected to be shot at any minute, but to his surprise the car drove off as promised. When he finally plucked up the courage to remove the blindfold, he found he was standing less than 500 yards from his home. Later that day he was taken to the British embassy to explain his story to David Miers and other British officials. It was while he was there that he met up with Geoffrey Nash who, it transpired, had been held in the same place as Levick and had suffered an almost identical experience. Like Levick, Nash had a British passport, and the kidnappers simply were not interested in British hostages. A year later it would be a very different story.

There was considerable surprise, not to mention relief, among the British community when Nash and Levick were set free. Their release was regarded as a vindication of the British expatriates' argument that Islamic fundamentalist groups were not interested in kidnapping them. This was not to say, however, that Beirut was in any sense a safer place to live, a fact that was driven home by the abduction of a third Briton, Alec Collett, who was taken while Nash and Levick were still being interrogated by Islamic Jihad.

Collett, a sixty-three-year-old journalist working for the United Nations, was no stranger either to working in foreign countries or to getting himself into scrapes with authority. At the end of the 1939–45 war, Collett had set up as a freelance journalist in the newly-liberated republic of Czechoslovakia. He quickly established himself as the *Daily Telegraph*'s correspondent in Prague, but his promising career in central Europe came to an abrupt end once the Soviet communist machine began to make its presence felt. In a scene reminiscent of *The Third Man*, Collett was summoned to the aliens section of the Prague police headquarters in April 1948 and handed an expulsion order to take effect with seven days. The Czech authorities said he was being required to leave because his presence in the country might constitute 'a threat to public peace, order, or the safety of the State'. On his return to Britain, Collett worked for a variety of Fleet Street newspapers, before moving to New York to report on the United Nations.

From the early 1980s, Collett received regular commissions from the UN department which specialises in running the Palestinian refugee camps in Lebanon and elsewhere, to travel around the Middle East and write a series of articles about them. The articles were inevitably biased in favour of the Palestinians, but Collett liked the travel and enjoyed the Middle East. When the UN asked him to go back to Beirut in early 1985, Collett was happy to accept the assignment, although his wife, Elaine, expressed reservations and wanted him to remain in New York. 'I didn't like the idea of him going back to Lebanon,' recalled Mrs Collett. 'Every time

I turned on the television there was something going on in Beirut. People were being kidnapped, and it didn't seem like a good idea to me. But Alec wanted to go and said he would be safe with the UN.'

The first six weeks of Collett's assignment passed without incident. He telephoned Elaine in New York regularly and told her what he had been up to and about his plans for the next stage. In mid-March he told her he was going to southern Lebanon and would be out of touch for a few days, as the international communications from that part of the world were non-existent. Collett set off for a brief tour of the Palestinian refugee camps around the south Lebanese ports of Tyre and Sidon. Since the Israeli invasion of 1982, most of the mainstream PLO fighters had been expelled from the camps. But a hard core of Palestinian groups, such as the Abu Nidal organisation, had filled the vacuum. Collett was driven around the camps in a jeep covered with the distinct white and blue markings of the UN, and, with his Austrian driver constantly at his side, did not feel in any danger.

A few days later, when Collett finished his research, he and his driver set off back to Beirut. The journey passed uneventfully until they reached the outskirts of the city. There they came across a checkpoint apparently manned by Palestinians. As Collett's jeep stopped, a group of militiamen surrounded it, demanding to see Collett's passport. As he produced it, one of the guards snatched it and began to study it carefully. A note of triumph entering his voice, the militiaman called to his colleagues to look at something he had found. Suddenly the mood of the militiamen began to darken. Returning to the car, they drew Collett's attention to a small, rectangular customs stamp. It contained the mark of the State of Israel, the sworn enemy of the men who were now surrounding Collett's jeep in a state of considerable agitation. It was not uncommon for journalists working in the Middle East to travel between Arab countries and Israel, but it was a cardinal rule of all who knew the region to ensure that they carried no evidence that they had visited Israel when travelling in a hostile Arab country.

One of the gunmen put a gun to the head of Collett's driver. At the same time the other gunmen dragged Collett out of the jeep and into a car. They then drove off in the direction of southern Lebanon. A few hours later they issued a statement claiming responsibility for Collett's kidnapping in the name of the Revolutionary Organisation of Socialist Muslims, the same group which had kidnapped Jonathan Wright seven months previously and murdered British diplomat Kenneth Whitty in Athens.

By the time Terry Waite had taken a rest following his exertions in Libya and was ready to turn his attention to Lebanon, there was a great deal more for him to contend with there than merely securing the release of a lone American Presbyterian pastor. The spate of kidnappings had reached epidemic proportions, and Waite now faced a challenge infinitely greater and more dangerous than anything he had previously experienced in his colourful career as a self-styled international troubleshooter.

10

FULL HOUSE

From the moment he touched down in New York, Terry Waite had no difficulty in assisting his American audience to understand his rightful place in world affairs. When asked about the precise nature of his job, one of Waite's favoured replies was 'I'm the Henry Kissinger of the Church of England, if you like.' The very notion, of course, that Waite was in the same league as the former US Secretary of State was ludicrous. The analogy had first been made by one of the more excitable British tabloid newspapers, and Waite had been flattered by the concept. There was a world of difference, however, between Kissinger's achievements and those of Terry Waite, the most crucial being that Kissinger had the full weight of the White House behind him wheresoever he roamed, whereas Waite had nothing more than a limited reserve of good will upon which to draw.

Waite's direct involvement in the hostage crisis began on May 10, 1985, when he stopped off in New York en route back from Australia. There he had his first meeting with Carol Weir at the headquarters of the Episcopal Church in Manhattan. In his opening discussions with Carol Weir and other members of the Presbyterian Church, Waite described himself as 'an independent humanitarian', yet another description he had coined for himself and one which was to be his calling card for the Lebanon mission.

Precisely what was meant by this description, only Waite could tell. The role he envisaged for himself went much further than his mundane job at Lambeth Palace. Many people had been employed on behalf of the Anglican Communion before Terry Waite, but none of them had seen fit to take on the role of international troubleshooter. Waite, moreover, was increasingly aware that he was operating in an area far beyond the jurisdiction of the Church of England, but that at the same time he still needed Lambeth as his reference point. He was not working for the British government, nor the American government, nor even an independent, international body such as the United Nations. Terry Waite was essentially unique, a one-off, someone who through the sheer force of his personality could operate in areas where established governments and organisations feared to tread. The very fact that he owed no allegiance or loyalty to any particular government or organisation was the underlying key to his success. His only loyalty was to some vague, humanitarian concept in which he interpreted his role as being to assist mankind in solving its difficulties, especially when it involved travel abroad.

While this may all have been very appealing in theory, putting it into practice was a different matter. Waite conceded that, with the best will in the world, even he could not do everything on his own. On occasions, in order to resolve a problem, he might have to allow himself to be used by one or other of the parties involved. If, for instance, he gave Colonel Gaddafi the impression that he thought the West was unfairly ganging up on him, where was the harm in that? There were always two sides to a story, and Waite's job was to try to bridge the chasm of misunderstanding between the parties in dispute. For the Lebanon mission, Waite would need a wide range of practical support. He needed someone to explain to him the problems he would face once he arrived, and he needed to learn what action was already being taken on behalf of the American hostages. He needed to make a careful assessment of how best to go about getting them released, and how his talents might best be employed.

One of Waite's few contacts in the US was Canon Samir Habiby, who worked for the Episcopal Church in New York as director of its fund for disaster relief. Born in what was then Palestine, Habiby had come to the US as a student and stayed on. In the 1960s Habiby had been a chaplain in the US marines and received the purple heart after being wounded in a combat zone in Vietnam. Like many immigrants, Habiby professed a loyalty for his adopted home more fierce than that of many native Americans. He espoused strong Republican views, and through family ties had developed good connections throughout the Middle East. He had known Waite long before he had become a public figure, and helped to arrange the meeting with Gaddafi in 1984. An enormous bundle of energy who could be ruthlessly singleminded when the mood took him, Habiby had spent the better part of ten years attempting to turn the modest resources of the presiding bishop's fund into a major international charity. He had travelled all over the world raising funds and initiating projects. Now the fund was to be used to finance Waite's Lebanon mission, even though the Episcopal Church was not directly concerned with the hostage problem. Habiby was delighted at the prospect of working with Waite with whom he shared a love of travel and adventure. Like Waite, Habiby took great care over the contacts he cultivated in the American establishment.

Even though the Episcopal Church was founded by the pilgrim fathers in Virginia in 1603 (Francis Drake is said to have celebrated the first Anglican liturgy in San Francisco), it is among one of the smaller churches in the US with a membership of just under three million. Since the 1960s the church has often been the despair of its more conventional members as it became the battleground of radical Christian groups. In the 1960s black militants seized control of the platform during the annual convention, while in the 1980s the church suffered a wounding split over questions such as whether homosexuals could marry in church. In spite of the efforts of the lunatic fringe, the Episcopal Church, especially under Ronald Reagan, was still regarded by most Americans as the church of the establishment, and in the 1980s many of the most senior officials in the Reagan administration were practising Episcopalians, including George Bush, Reagan's vice-president, Robert McFarlane, head of the National Security Council, his deputy, John Poindexter, and Lieutenant-Colonel Oliver North, who worked at the NSC on counter-terrorism. It was through the Episcopal Church that Waite flew down to Washington from New York for a meeting with Vice-President Bush.

When Waite began the laborious process of making introductions in the US, the Reagan administration was still in a quandary about the growing number of Americans being taken hostage in Lebanon. Since he had won a landslide victory against Walter Mondale in the presidential election in November 1984, the hostage problem did not now pose the same political dangers for Reagan. Nonetheless, Reagan had difficulty in coming to terms with the issue. His Lebanon policy had provided the most spectacular failure of his first term, and he was determined not to repeat the performance. The few attempts which had been made to do something about the hostages had got nowhere. On the recommendation of CIA director William Casey, North had arranged the transfer of some $200,000 in late 1984 to the Bekaa Valley to two

American Drug Enforcement Agency (DEA) agents working undercover. The money had been provided by H. Ross Perot, the right-wing millionaire champion of patriotic causes. The DEA agents paid the money to a Lebanese middleman who promised to deliver two American hostages. Neither the middleman nor the money was seen again, and no hostages were released.

Embarrassing failures such as this only reinforced the opinion of the more hawkish members of the administration such as George Shultz, the Secretary of State, that there was absolutely no point in even attempting to strike a deal with the kidnappers. Islamic Jihad had issued several messages, both through videotapes of hostages reading prepared statements and by notes delivered anonymously to news agencies, in which they made their demands abundantly clear. The hostages would be released if the Americans put pressure on Kuwait to release the seventeen prisoners. Some senior officials, William Casey among them, wanted Reagan to do just this. But Shultz stood firm, and insisted that Washington would only be playing into the hands of the kidnappers. Shultz set out his position squarely and somewhat forcibly when he met Carol Weir who had started a nationwide campaign to whip up support for the hostages. When Mrs Weir suggested the American government should either talk directly to the kidnappers or put pressure on Kuwait, Shultz became angry and banged the table. 'The American government is not in the business of negotiating with a bunch of lunatics, Mrs Weir,' he announced, bringing the meeting to a speedy conclusion.

To complicate matters even further, a mysterious package was delivered one morning in May at the New York home of Elaine Collett. The postmark showed that the package had been sent from Switzerland. It contained a video-cassette. She phoned the British consulate on Third Avenue, and a senior official came round within minutes. He then escorted

Mrs Collett back to the consulate to watch the video. As she expected, it showed her husband Alec reading a prepared statement. He was dressed in a jogging suit and was smoking a cigarette, something he had not done for many years, as he read the kidnappers' message. At first Mrs Collett felt relieved, as this was the first news she had received that her husband was still alive in the six weeks since his kidnap. But relief quickly turned to apprehension when she heard what the kidnappers wanted. As with Jonathan Wright, Collett's kidnappers, who were Palestinian rather than Lebanese, were demanding that the British government release the Arab terrorists jailed for the attempted murder of the Israeli ambassador in London. The British officials said they would look into it.

Through the UN, Mrs Collett learned that Terry Waite was in New York and arranged to see him at the Episcopal Church centre. Waite was very pleasant, and reassured Mrs Collett that he would do everything he could. In reality, Waite was not in a position to do anything on behalf of Collett, even though he was a British citizen. Waite was now tied up with the Americans to work for the release of the American hostages who were held by a completely different group to the one holding Collett. Waite had his work cut out trying to make progress on behalf of the Americans; Collett's case only complicated matters, and Waite could ill afford that.

During his stay in the US, Waite initially had a discouraging time. Officials at the State Department gave the strong impression that they did not take Waite very seriously. In their attempts to locate the hostages, these officials were required to deal with a whole range of strange characters and do-gooders who promised much, but delivered little. Waite seemed to fit this category and, had he not presented himself as a personal emissary of the Archbishop of Canterbury, he would most probably have been shown the door. Through his meeting with George Bush, who was in charge of counter-terrorism policy at the White House, Waite was encouraged to arrange a meeting with Lieutenant-Colonel Oliver North, which duly took place in New York on May 18, 1985.

Even though North and Waite were approaching the hostage issue from completely opposite angles, they had far more in common than either could ever appreciate. For a start North was a devout Christian and regular churchgoer. When he first met Mrs Weir he announced: 'I'm a born-again Christian. I have accepted Jesus Christ as my Lord and Saviour.' Besides, where Waite had managed to build upon a fairly unremarkable job at Lambeth and turn himself into an international figure, North was embarking on a similar path from his job as a relatively junior member of the National Security Council in Washington. The NSC was very much the poor relation of the US foreign policy-making machine. The NSC was supposed to be the main instrument for policy co-ordination and management, but it had been systematically weakened and filled with people whose skills were not equal to their antagonists' in other departments. The NSC generally occupied a position of power within the Washington political structure when the president took a close interest in foreign policy. Foreign policy, however, was Ronald Reagan's blind spot, as his policy towards Lebanon had shown, with the result that he saw a succession of NSC directors quit because they could no longer tolerate the constant infighting and squabbling over policy between the CIA, the State Department, the Pentagon and the White House, with the NSC usually caught up in the crossfire.

Robert 'Bud' McFarlane, head of the NSC since late 1983 and North's immediate boss, much admired the skills of his most distinguished predecessor, Dr Henry Kissinger, but, unlike Waite, never sought to compare himself with the accomplished exponent of shuttle diplomacy. On the contrary, McFarlane, a former marine with a deep sense of duty, was only too well aware that he was ill-equipped for the post. 'This job is way beyond me,' he told a friend in a moment of doubt. 'They should have gotten somebody better, like Kissinger.'[1] McFarlane had only been appointed because the cabinet could not agree on a more suitable successor to William P. Clark, who had resigned because of continual infighting at the White House. James Baker, the future Secretary of State, was the first candidate proposed, but was rejected because he was considered too moderate. Jeane Kirkpatrick, the hawkish and prickly ambassador at the UN, was rejected because she was considered too right-wing. McFarlane was a compromise candidate. As Clark's number two, he knew how the NSC worked, was immensely loyal and did not pose a threat to the preening egos of William Casey at the CIA, Caspar Weinberger at the Pentagon, George Shultz at the State Department and Donald Regan, White House chief of staff.

Apart from being plagued by doubts about his ability to do the job, McFarlane, whose whole career had been in public service, felt uncomfortable amidst the ostentatious wealth of the Reagan crowd. His modesty and sincerity, however, found an unexpected admirer; Nancy Reagan liked the McFarlanes and often invited them to sit at the presidential table at official functions, a singular honour. She even went so far as to praise McFarlane's ballroom dancing, proof indeed of his popularity.

North's official title at the NSC was deputy director for political-military affairs, but in essence his job was to ensure that Reagan's ideological rhetoric on foreign affairs was put into action. Reagan's strong personal commitment to

[1]Mayer and McManus, *op. cit.*

the Contras, the Nicaraguan resistance fighters seeking to overthrow the left-wing Sandinista regime, resulted in North devoting a large percentage of his working day to finding ways to provide the resistance with military and financial support. When the Marxist regime of Maurice Bishop was overthrown on the tiny Caribbean island of Grenada in an ideological putsch, North organised the American invasion to re-establish a democratic government. What made North's achievements all the more remarkable was that they were achieved with so few resources. North worked from a small office in the Old Executive Building, next to the White House. Thanks to a sophisticated computer system, North could access the Pentagon's data banks, which provided information such as the flight paths and refuelling stops of military aircraft. Apart from his computer, however, the only resources at North's disposal were a couple of assistants, the good will of the White House and his own formidable personality. In more ways than one, North was Waite's alter ego.

North was always bristling with ideas, such as hiring British mercenaries to train the Contras in special operations, or to sail the Contra leaders on a cruise ship to Philadelphia to unveil a Nicaraguan declaration of independence. He was a rabid self-publicist and a spellbinding storyteller, stories which invariably put him at the centre of events. He liked to give the impression that he was a close confidant of Ronald Reagan, although the two never actually met alone. And while North liked to portray himself as the architect of operations such as the Grenada invasion, he had in effect been the link man between the military establishment and the White House, relaying orders and information between the commander-in-chief, the President, and the military top brass.

North arrived for his meeting with Waite and Habiby in New York wearing a leather bomber jacket. Despite his casual attire, the two churchmen were deeply impressed by

North who presented himself as being at the apex of power in Washington. After all the snubs he had received from the Washington bureaucracy, Waite was relieved to have made contact with someone important. North went through his usual routine of telling Waite and Habiby how he had masterminded the Grenada operation, strange behaviour indeed for someone in such a highly sensitive job. North gave Waite his telephone number at the Old Executive Building and told him to keep in touch. Whenever Waite or Habiby subsequently phoned North in Washington, North always gave the impression he was running the American government. He would tell Waite to hold on while he took a call from William Casey. The call might have been from the CIA, but it seems unlikely that the head of the world's largest intelligence organisation had nothing better to do than to be constantly on the phone to North. As one of North's colleagues at the NSC later commented: 'Ollie was thirty to fifty per cent bullshit. He was notorious for constantly exaggerating his role in things. He was always "coming from a meeting with the vice-president". We checked once, and he hadn't been in to see the vice-president at all.' This was the man with whom Waite was fated to work closely on the Lebanon mission.

Even at that early stage in their relationship, there was a striking divergence in their approach to the hostage issue. Waite and Habiby dreamed up a quaint scheme under which the relatives of those killed by the terrorist attacks in Kuwait would be paid compensation, or blood money, in return for the release of the prisoners in Lebanon. This scheme was perfectly acceptable under the teaching of Islam, which allows for prisoners to be released if the victims' relatives are prepared to forgive them. Waite had already raised the idea in Washington, and been given short shrift by the professional foreign policy advisers who thought it seemed no different to paying a ransom. North was more encouraging and, clearly hoping to humour Waite, told him to work on the project. North himself had a far more daring proposal in mind. After the $200,000 payment to the middleman in the Bekaa had produced nothing, he hit on the idea of launching an American operation to break into Kuwait's top security prison, capture the 17, remove them from Kuwait, and trade them for the hostages. If the Americans were smart enough, they might even be able to trick Islamic Jihad into releasing the hostages, then pull a double cross and send the prisoners back to Kuwait. Such was the fantasy world in which North operated.

While Waite and North were airing their ideas in the US, the need to act became more pressing every day, as the number of Westerners held hostage in Lebanon continued to grow. In an attempt to increase the pressure on the Kuwaiti authorities, the kidnappers turned their attentions to the French. Marcel Carton and Marcel Fontaine, who both worked at the French embassy in West Beirut, were kidnapped on March 22. The next day Gilles Peyrolles, head of the French cultural centre in the north Lebanese port of Tripoli, was kidnapped. On May 22, Jean-Paul Kauffmann, a French television journalist, and Michel Seurat, a French academic, were kidnapped as they drove from the airport into Beirut. At the same time Islamic Jihad allowed the American hostages to write letters to their families in which, in their own words, they could set out the kidnappers' demands. The families of Ben Weir and Lawrence Jenco received letters reiterating the kidnappers' demands for the 17 to be released. 'As long as they are being held, I am held,' wrote Jenco. Almost anticipating Oliver North's wilder schemes, Jenco concluded his note somewhat plaintively: 'Any military intervention on my behalf will not be good for me.'

On May 25 Islamic Jihad again turned its attention to Kuwait. As the motorcade of Sheikh Jaber, the ruler of Kuwait, sped towards Spif Palace, a car pulled out from a sidestreet. With split-second timing, it rammed into the lead vehicle of the royal entourage. Two bodyguards, a passerby and the suicide driver were killed instantly in the explosion which shattered the city. Sheikh Jaber miraculously escaped serious injury because the suicide driver hit the wrong car. Within hours an anonymous caller was on the phone to a news agency issuing a statement on behalf of Islamic Jihad: 'The Emir has received our message. We ask him again to liberate our comrades held in Kuwaiti jails. Otherwise all the thrones of the gulf will be targeted.' The assassination attempt failed to weaken the Emir's resolve not to make any concessions over the Dawa 17; on the contrary it strengthened it.

Back in Beirut David Jacobsen, a fifty-four-year-old American in charge of running the American University Hospital, was continuing with his normal daily routine in spite of the fact that a growing number of his fellow countrymen were joining the ranks of the hostages. Jacobsen had spent most of his working life as a hospital administrator in California, but after a particularly messy divorce had decided to take a job in Beirut where he could make a fresh start and earn a good, tax-free salary which would make up for what he had lost financially in the divorce settlement. As news of each kidnapping filtered through the close-knit expatriate community, Jacobsen worked out his own reasons why he was not at risk. He was not unduly alarmed that Levin and Anderson had been kidnapped; journalists put themselves at risk because their articles often caused offence. Nor was he alarmed when Weir and Jenco were abducted; clerics were required to travel in the most dangerous areas of the city, so it was not surprising they had been kidnapped (Weir and Jenco were seized less than half a mile from Jacobsen's apartment). Because Jacobsen was working with Lebanese at the sharp end of the civil war, caring for the victims of the fighting, he believed he was fulfilling a worthwhile function which was appreciated by the Lebanese.

Jacobsen remembers the morning of May 28 as a beautiful, sunny day. He was sucking a tangerine after his early morning jog, as a doctor friend drove him to work. Having parked at the back entrance to the hospital, the two men set off towards the main entrance. As they neared the building, Jacobsen noticed a young man running towards him, but took little notice until the man stopped suddenly, pulled out a 9mm pistol and pointed it at Jacobsen's head. The man yelled at Jacobsen to get in a van which had screeched to a halt in the middle of the road. Not speaking Arabic, Jacobsen at first did not understand. Before he had a chance to work it out, he was bundled into the van. For a few heroic seconds Jacobsen, a fitness fanatic, wrestled frantically to get free. His resistance ended when a sharp blow was delivered to the back of his head with the butt of a gun. Jacobsen slumped forward, vaguely aware of blood dripping down his neck and onto his shirt.[1] Yet another American who thought himself immune had been taken hostage.

The following day, May 29, the British residents of West Beirut were shocked out of their complacency when the body of Dennis Hill was discovered a short distance from his residence at the American University. Hill, who was fifty-three, had only arrived in Lebanon the previous October to work at an intensive English language programme designed for Lebanese students who wanted to study at the university, but failed to meet the language requirements. His colleagues knew little about Hill's background, other than that he had left behind a broken marriage in Britain and liked to drink. One of his favourite haunts was the Pickwick bar at the Mayflower Hotel, an English-style pub run by Jackie Mann, a retired commercial airline pilot with Lebanon's national carrier,

---

[1]David Jacobsen: *Hostage: My Nightmare in Beirut*, Donald I. Fine, 1991.

Middle East Airlines, who had distinguished himself with the Royal Air Force during the Battle of Britain. With its tartan wallpaper, prints depicting scenes of English country life and well-polished oak bar, the Pickwick was the archetypal home counties country pub, except that it was in the heart of West Beirut. When he was not teaching, Hill was usually to be found perched on a stool at the Pickwick, escaping the heat of the Mediterranean sun and quaffing considerable quantities of imported British keg beer.

Hill had another appetite, which was to cost him his life. Although he was grossly overweight and had the looks of someone who drank far more than was good for him, he had an eye for the girls, especially the pouting teenage femmes fatales who attended his classes on the English language. Lebanese women have always had an advanced fashion sense, a relic of their French colonial heritage which, combined with their natural good looks and dark hair, makes them extremely eye-catching. Exactly how far Hill pursued his infatuation with the Lebanese girls in his care has never been established, but his behaviour certainly aroused the resentment either of the young men who also attended his classes, or the parents of the young women. Many students at the AUB were directly or indirectly involved in the militias active in Beirut. Thus if a student felt a grievance against Hill for the attention he was paying the female students, merited or not, it was quite a simple matter for them to do something about it.

Hill was abducted from the campus on the morning of May 27 as he left his apartment to take a lesson. His body was found two days later dumped in a street close to the university. A single bullet had been fired into the back of his head. A statement was issued later that day in the name of Islamic Jihad claiming that Hill had been shot while trying to escape. Officials from the British embassy drove to the university and did their best to work out the motive for his kidnap and murder, if a motive existed. During their inquiries they learned about Hill's sexual harassment, and many of the Lebanese students they interviewed confirmed the story. Details of the real reason for Hill's murder were soon circulating throughout the British community. It was just what they wanted to hear. Had Hill been kidnapped and murdered as part of the widening campaign by Islamic fundamentalists to drive Westerners out of the city, there would have been genuine cause for concern. But once it emerged that Hill had effectively brought about his demise through his unfortunate behaviour, the British breathed a collective sigh of relief. There was no reason for them to leave, so long as they did not harass Lebanese women.

While the kidnappings and mounting attacks on foreign interests in Lebanon were the primary concerns of the outside world, there was much else besides going on in the country which made it an extremely dangerous place to be. The Israeli armed forces completed their withdrawal from Lebanon in the spring of 1985, but as they withdrew they opened up a hornets' nest of unresolved rivalries and scores still to be settled between the rival militias. A succession of bitter and bloody skirmishes between Christians and Palestinians; Palestinians and Shia Muslims; Druze, Shia and Palestinian fighters against the Christians erupted throughout the country. There was also the question of the Syrians to take into consideration. President Assad had no intention of seeing Lebanon slip out of Syria's sphere of influence as the Israelis withdrew, and whenever one or other of the Lebanese militias looked like overreaching themselves, Assad would dispatch a few battalions to put them back in their place. In addition the Shia Amal militia continued to harry the Israeli forces as they withdrew to the Israeli border, staging guerrilla attacks and planting roadside bombs, while the more fanatical members of

Hizbollah continued to launch suicide attacks against Israeli positions.

Sixteen-year-old girls were among those who volunteered to drive vehicles packed with explosives at Israeli positions. Before carrying out the attack, it was customary for the would-be martyr to make a video to be shown once the mission had been accomplished. After Sana Mahaidali, a sixteen-year-old Shia Muslim from Sidon, had driven a Peugeot 504 packed with explosives at an Israeli convoy, killing herself and two Israeli soldiers in the process, a video she recorded shortly before her death was broadcast on Lebanese television. Dressed in a red beret and a smart two-piece suit, Mahaidali calmly explained the purpose of her mission.

'I am very relaxed as I go to do this operation which I have chosen because I am carrying out my duty to my people. I am from the group that decided on self-sacrifice and martyrdom for the sake of the liberation of the land and people. I hope our souls will form an explosive mixture that will blow up an earthquake on the heads of the enemy.' Such was the force of Shia sentiment in Lebanon.

The general effect of the non-stop battles between Lebanese groups did little to improve the general security situation. Disputes between rival militiamen over the most inane problems all too often resulted in a shoot-out. One day at the Hamra shopping district, just a few yards from the Commodore Hotel, an argument broke out between a Syrian soldier and a Druze militiaman over a bag of cement. The Syrian had helped himself to the cement which the Druze militiaman had himself stolen some weeks previously. As the Syrian turned to walk away, he was challenged by the Druze and accused of theft. The Syrian retorted that the Druze had no right to accuse him of stealing as the cement had already been stolen. The Druze disagreed, arguing that as he had been the first to steal it, the cement was his.

Whereupon both men produced pistols and shot each other dead.

On June 9, 1985, Thomas Sutherland completed the kidnappers' tally of American hostages. Sutherland knew as much as anyone about the dangers of living in Beirut, but his cavalier attitude to returning to the city even though David Jacobsen had been kidnapped less than two weeks previously was typical of the man. Sutherland was raised in rural Scotland, where he studied agriculture before moving to the US in the 1950s to continue his education. A fanatical soccer fan and a nippy winger, Sutherland had once been on the books of Glasgow Rangers Football Club, but just failed to make the grade as a professional. For many years Sutherland was dean of agriculture at Colorado State University, but in 1983 he applied for leave of absence to head a similar department at the AUB, where his wife Jean would teach English.

Many years later Sutherland admitted he had been thoroughly naive to fly back from Denver. When Sutherland had heard about Jacobsen's kidnap, he had phoned the AUB headquarters in New York to check out the situation on the ground in Lebanon. He was told that Jacobsen's kidnap had been a mistake, that he would soon be released, and that there was no threat to the staff at the AUB. 'If anything happened to me, I reckoned the AUB would be able to get me out,' Sutherland explained. 'I didn't realise how dangerous the situation in Lebanon had become. To be honest I didn't follow it very closely. I found it difficult to understand. I just trusted that my judgement was sufficiently good that I would not be kidnapped.' Sutherland's determination to fulfil his commitment to the AUB remained strong despite the fact that the number of Americans working at the university had declined from about fifty when he had first arrived in 1983 to just seven. Nor was he prepared to take any notice of the repeated requests from the American embassy for him to leave. 'There were thousands of people going about their business every day, and I had an important job to do. I did not see any reason not to go back.'

After Terry Anderson, Sutherland would spend the longest period in captivity of all the American hostages – nearly seven years. It was a terrible price to pay for a simple error of judgement.

The basement shelters in Beirut's southern suburbs where the kidnappers now kept the hostages in their miserable confinement were filling up. There were seven Americans held captive: Buckley, Weir, Kilburn, Jenco, Anderson, Jacobsen and Sutherland. In addition there were at least four Frenchmen and an assortment of other prisoners. It was now the task of Terry Waite and Oliver North to set them free.

11

AMERICA AWAKES

When Tom Sutherland was driven off to the southern suburbs, the kidnappers had perfected their routine to such a fine art that new arrivals went through a rigorous assessment process, similar to the way inmates are handled on arrival at a penal institution. The kidnappers' task was easier now there was no longer any need to put their captives in the boot of a car and drive them over the mountains to the Bekaa Valley. Hizbollah had now consolidated its hold over the southern suburbs to the extent that all the Shia Muslims were effectively card-carrying members of Hizbollah. This meant that the kidnappers could go about their business without interference from those, such as the Syrians, who had a vested interest in getting a piece of the hostage action.

Immediately after being seized, the new hostage would be taken to an empty warehouse. There he would be thoroughly searched and interrogated by about three guards. Imad Mugniyeh, with his distinctive high-pitched voice, was usually somewhere in the background, although he let his accomplices do most of the talking.

The kidnappers displayed a high degree of paranoia. The

slightest irregularity raised their suspicions. When they went through David Jacobsen's wallet, for example, they found a list of numbers on a scrap of paper.

'What are these numbers? Is this some kind of code?' one of the guards demanded.

Jacobsen didn't know what they were talking about and asked to see the paper. It was a list of the numbers of videos he had selected from a local catalogue. He tried to explain this to the kidnappers, but they were disinclined to believe him.

More often than not the interrogation would deteriorate to an infantile level.

'What is your name?'

'David Jacobsen.'

'You are CIA. Don't lie.'

'No, I am not CIA.'

'You travel much out of Lebanon. Why is this?'

'I do not travel much outside Lebanon.'

'Jacobsen. That is a Jewish name. You are an Israeli spy.'

'My name is Scandinavian and I'm not Jewish. I am not an Israeli spy.'

And so on, until the kidnappers either became bored or resigned to the fact that they did not have another CIA station chief in their possession. When Jacobsen's interrogation was over, Imad Mugniyeh announced in his squeaky voice: 'Now we will tell the world, no, the universe, that we hold David Jacobsen!'

Thomas Sutherland got into trouble because the kidnappers found an article called 'Islam Today' which his wife had slipped into his briefcase before he left Colorado, had forgotten to tell her husband, so that Sutherland was genuinely nonplussed when challenged about it.

'What is this article? Why do you have it?'

'I don't know, I've never seen it before.'

'It was in your briefcase. Why do you want to know about Islam? You are a spy.'

'I am not a spy. I am interested in Islam. I live in Lebanon.'

'Only spies want to live in Lebanon. You are a spy.'

Sutherland's little problem over the 'Islam Today' article was to bother him for months. Whenever the kidnappers were displeased with him, they would call him a spy and remind him of the article. However trivial all this might have seemed, it had very serious consequences for Sutherland. One of the reasons the kidnappers held him for so long while others were freed was because they never completely overcame the suspicion that he was a spy.

From the warehouse most of the hostages were taken to the main Hizbollah barracks in the southern suburbs. The Fathallah barracks, as they were known, were situated in the Basta area, close to the Green Line, and contained two floors of underground cells. The cells were tiny – nine feet long, six feet wide and about six feet in height – and fitted with heavy metal doors. The complex was not far from Sheikh Fadlallah's residence, and on occasions the hostages saw the guards listening intently to one of Fadlallah's Friday prayer sermons. Each cell was equipped with a mattress and a couple of blankets. Many hostages placed their mattress diagonally on the floor to make the most of the floor space. Each cell was also fitted with a small air-conditioning vent. Hostages were required to wear a blindfold every time a guard appeared. Most of the time the hostages were held alone. It was only when they were moved to 'dispersal centres', apartments rented by the kidnappers to hide the hostages, that they were put together.

Once the kidnappers felt it was safe to hold the hostages in the city, they would be taken to an apartment or house no more than a fifteen-minute drive from the barracks. The building would no doubt belong to the family of one of the kidnappers, who were paid for its use as a makeshift prison. Before a hostage was brought in, the guards would construct a pen of chipboard and timber, such as had been made for Weir and Jenco when they were transferred from the Bekaa Valley following Levin's escape. A few days after his interrogation Jacobsen was moved to a house in the southern suburbs, and was chained up in his underwear and put in his pen. From what he could hear, he gathered there were hostages either side of him. On one side was Terry Anderson and on the other William Buckley. In other parts of the house were Jenco and Weir, and the four Frenchmen. The only American hostage never accounted for was Peter Kilburn, the AUB librarian.

One of the more distressing aspects of the early captivity of both Jacobsen and Anderson was listening to the terrible coughing fits coming from William Buckley's quarters. Jacobsen, who had spent his life working in hospitals, recognised his fellow hostage was very sick and asked the guards to help. At one point Jacobsen heard Buckley say to one of the guards: 'I don't know what has happened to my body. Thirty days ago I was so strong.'

On another occasion Buckley, obviously in a state of delirium, was heard to say, 'I'll have my hot cakes with blueberry syrup now.'[1]

The general deterioration in Buckley's health had probably been caused by his living conditions rather than systematic torture. Once he had been brought back to the Bekaa from Teheran, Buckley spent the next year of his captivity in close proximity with other American hostages, and none of them ever heard him being tortured. Even the guards noticed that Buckley was in a bad way, and asked Jacobsen for advice. He

[1]Jacobsen, *op. cit.*

told them Buckley needed to be taken to a hospital as soon as possible, otherwise they would have a dead hostage on their hands. The guards seemed to take Jacobsen's advice on board, but then did nothing about it. At about 10 pm one night in early June 1985, while the guards were watching television in their quarters down the hall and debating what to do with Jacobsen's advice, Buckley's condition deteriorated to the extent that he even ceased his incessant mumbling. Jacobsen, lying a few feet away the other side of the partition, heard what he later described as 'an ominous gurgling', the distinct noises of a man in his death throes.[1] Then silence fell. After a few minutes Jacobsen heard a thud, then feet shuffling as though weighed down by a heavy object. The kidnappers were removing Buckley's body. When the blindfolded Jenco asked the guards what they were doing, they replied they were taking Buckley to the hospital. Later they told Jacobsen that Buckley was 'in a wonderful place where the sun is shining and the birds are chirping,' the Koranic view of paradise.

Buckley's death actually benefited those hostages still living. The kidnappers appeared to be genuinely shocked that one of their captives had died; they needed the hostages alive if they were to get their colleagues released from jail in Kuwait. Mugniyeh made one of his rare appearances and ordered the guards to undertake a massive clean-up. They hosed down the makeshift cells and actually got down on their hands and knees to scrub the floors and walls. New mats and bedding were provided, and the guards even provided a doctor to examine the hostages. The doctor was Elie Hallak, a Lebanese Jew who had been kidnapped a few months previously, and probably one of the most tragic figures of the whole sorry

[1] *Ibid.* Jacobsen is the only hostage to have provided a detailed account of Buckley's death, which he believes occurred on the night of June 3, 1985.

hostage episode. Dr Hallak was never required to wear a blindfold; all the others were ordered to wear theirs in front of the guards on pain of death. But Dr Hallak was allowed to travel between the different hideouts, and could readily identify them. There was a reason why the kidnappers did not require Dr Hallak to wear a blindfold, a reason which led the French to nickname him Dr Death. The kidnappers had no intention of ever releasing the Jewish doctor. When he had fulfilled his usefulness for them, they would kill him. It did not matter how much the doctor found out, because he was not going to live to make use of the information.

The kidnappers may have had their cells filled with hostages, but they were still no closer to getting their comrades released from Kuwait. Despite the constant demands sent to Washington, every time President Reagan referred to the Middle East and the hostages he reiterated his policy of not doing deals with terrorists. Nor were the relatives of the hostages in the US enjoying much success in trying to pressure their government to act. Peggy Say had embarked on a one-woman campaign to get her kid brother released, but her initial contact with Washington was disappointing. 'They didn't even want to acknowledge they had a hostage problem,' she later commented. With the Kuwaiti government standing firm on its policy of making the Dawa prisoners serve their sentences in full, the fate of the hostages was deadlocked. It required a major change of policy on the part of one of the parties involved to break the stalemate, and that change was finally forthcoming when a group of Shia terrorists seized control of TWA flight 847 from Athens to Rome and forced the pilot to fly to Beirut with 145 passengers and the crew of nine.

At first the hijackers seemed confused about what they wanted. They took the plane on a tour of the Mediterranean, releasing selected groups of passengers along the way. The passengers were particularly bemused when, on the frequent occasions the hijackers became overwrought, they ran up and down the aisle screaming, 'New Jersey, New Jersey.' What, thought the puzzled passengers, could the hijackers possibly have against the state of New Jersey? Later they found out the hijackers had nothing against the state, but everything against the battleship named after it which had caused untold damage to their country thanks to Reagan's gunboat diplomacy a year previously.

By the time the aircraft arrived at Beirut, the number of passengers had been reduced dramatically and most still held had American passports. Once in Beirut the hijackers, who identified themselves as members of Islamic Jihad, seemed to rediscover their confidence and issued demands, which mainly consisted of the release of Shia prisoners in Israel. To make it clear they meant business, they shot dead an American passenger, Robert Stethem, and threw his body on the runway. As the hijackers liaised with their fellow conspirators on the tarmac, it became clear that a Hizbollah official by the name of Mohammed Hamadi was running the operation. Like Mugniyeh, Hamadi was a Shia Muslim from a southern Lebanese village now under Israeli occupation. Hamadi shared Mugniyeh's hatred of the West and Israel, and the hijacking of the TWA aircraft was conceived as the only means of persuading the Israelis to free the hundreds of Shia Muslims from southern Lebanon who were being detained without trial. Hamadi was well-placed to organise the hijack. Apart from being a close confidant of Mugniyeh, his elder brother, Abdul Hadi Hamadi, was head of security of Hizbollah, a job description which was really a contradiction in terms given the high profile role Hizbollah was playing in terrorist attacks throughout the Middle East.

The hijack plunged the Reagan administration into a major crisis. It was Reagan's nightmare come true. After all the political capital he had made at Jimmy Carter's expense over the hostages in Iran, Reagan was now faced with wall-to-wall television coverage of his own hostage crisis in Beirut. When it came to the crunch, moreover, the real Reagan came to the fore. For all his rhetoric over five years about not doing deals with terrorists, the first question Reagan asked at the NSC meeting called to discuss the crisis was, what needed to be done to get the hostages freed. If the kidnappers wanted their prisoners freed from Israel, then Washington should put pressure on the Israelis to deliver. Reagan's attitude dumbfounded George Shultz, who could not believe the President was prepared to ditch all his principles to get the hostages back.

The need to do something, however, became more urgent every day, as the situation on the ground became daily more complicated. Nabih Berri's Amal militia, still, in terms of numbers, the most important Shia militia, was nominally responsible for airport security at Beirut. Initially Berri's men had tried to prevent the TWA jet from landing, only granting permission after the hijackers threatened to blow up the plane in the sky. The hijackers, meanwhile, claimed to be members of Islamic Jihad, which was generally regarded to be an off-shoot of Hizbollah, the rival Shia militia. The hijacking resulted in the most public stand-off between the two Shia groups, the culmination of tensions that had been gradually building up since the pro-Iranian Hizbollah militia emerged in Lebanon in 1982. In order to ensure no further harm came to the thirty-nine American passengers and crew, Amal gunmen removed them from the plane and placed them in safe houses around West Beirut. This tactic was only partially successful, however, as the hijackers, determined that their demands should not be overlooked, held onto six Americans who had either Jewish-sounding names or US government passports. The crisis had effectively become a test of wills between

Amal and Hizbollah to see who had the most influence in West Beirut.

As the US explored ways of getting the TWA hostages released, Reagan was gradually made to realise that he was faced not with one hostage crisis, but two. For as the relatives of the TWA hostages clamoured for the President to act, the relatives of the seven 'forgotten' hostages (Buckley was still thought to be alive) held by Islamic Jihad began to insist that they be included in any deal. One of Reagan's most bruising encounters occurred in Chicago when the TWA hostage crisis was into its second week. The White House had arranged for Reagan to travel to Chicago to meet with the relatives of the TWA hostages, and somehow John Jenco, the brother of Lawrence, got himself invited. He immediately wanted to know why the President was paying so much attention to the TWA captives when he had shown virtually no interest in the fate of the other hostages. Reagan was deeply moved by his conversation with Jenco, which lasted some thirty minutes. By the time it was over, Reagan had resolved to get all the hostages out of Beirut, come what may. As he remarked to Bud McFarlane, who had travelled with him to Chicago, 'It's an awful thing these parents and loved ones have to live with.' Reagan was an old sentimentalist at heart, and from now, as far as the hostage crisis was concerned, his heart would rule his head.

The White House was not the only place where the TWA hijack was regarded as a watershed. Nabih Berri's Amal movement had always been vehemently opposed to Hizbollah's kidnapping campaign. How could the Shia Muslims ever hope to be taken seriously as a political force so long as they were held responsible for such unacceptable behaviour? Berri, an accomplished lawyer and politician, saw the TWA hijack as a golden opportunity to reassert Amal's authority in Beirut. Berri also had his contacts in Teheran, and before long he had persuaded none other than Hashemi Rafsanjani, one of Khomeini's closest aides and the speaker of the Iranian parliament, an extremely powerful political position in Teheran, to travel to Damascus to help resolve the crisis. If proof was wanted of Teheran's influence over the kidnap groups, this was it. Rafsanjani travelled to Damascus with a powerful delegation which included Mohammed Mohtashemi, the former Iranian ambassador to Damascus who had now been promoted Iran's Interior Minister, and Rafik Mohsen-Doste, the Revolutionary Guards' Minister. Soon after their arrival in Damascus they were joined by Sheikh Fadlallah, the self-styled 'spiritual' leader of Hizbollah, who was in almost daily contact with Imad Mugniyeh and knew exactly where all the hostages were being held.

Within days of Rafsanjani's intervention, all thirty-nine TWA hostages were on their way home. Berri was triumphant, and the scenes as the hostages were released had almost a carnival atmosphere about them. The hostages were showered with rose petals and given personal copies of the Koran. The only drawback, and it seemed to have been overlooked amidst all the euphoria, was that there was no mention of the seven Americans and four Frenchmen still held hostage. Rafsanjani, it seemed, could put pressure on Hizbollah to go so far, but he could not make them go all the way. Rafsanjani's efforts, however, did not go unnoticed in Washington. Reagan sent a personal note of thanks for his help in resolving the TWA dispute, which was relayed by Yasuhiro Nakasone, the Japanese prime minister, in early July.

From his cell in the southern suburbs, Jacobsen witnessed the determination of Amal to secure the release of *all* the hostages. One day while on patrol ostensibly looking for Palestinian fighters, a group of Amal militiamen happened upon the house in which the American hostages were being held. Jacobsen did not speak any Arabic, but he could tell the conversation between the Amal and the kidnappers was becoming heated when he heard his guards arming their weapons. After the argument had lasted several minutes, silence suddenly fell, and Jacobsen heard the guards uncock their guns. Later one of the guards admitted to Jacobsen that 'Amal security forces' had been looking for the hostages. 'It's lucky for you that they didn't find you because if they did, we would have been forced to kill you.'[1]

The next day the hostages were moved to another hideout, as a precaution against Amal attempting to release them as they had freed Regier and Joubert. In the next house, also in the southern suburbs, the hostages were held in pairs; Jacobsen with Anderson, Jenco with Weir. Sutherland had yet to arrive. The attitude of the guards continued to improve, so that within a few days the four Americans were allowed to talk to each other. They were all still required to wear blindfolds, and were chained up for large parts of the day, but they could talk to one another. Occasionally they could remove their blindfolds so long as the guards were nowhere to be seen. The attitude of the guards almost led them to expect they would soon be going home.

In the few months that they had been held, both Anderson and Jacobsen had rediscovered religion, and before long Jenco and Weir were taking it in turn to conduct daily religious services. The hostages nicknamed their congregation The Church of the Locked Door.

By the end of June, Sutherland was brought from the prison complex to join the others. The first person Sutherland saw was David Jacobsen, the man whom he had been told by the AUB in New York would soon be released.

'Hi, Tom,' said Jacobsen. 'Am I glad to see you.' Then he

---

[1] *Ibid.*

quickly corrected himself: 'Oh no I'm not, because if I can see you that means you've been kidnapped.' Sutherland merely smiled to himself and sat down on the mattress which was to be his home for the next few months. The five would remain together while Oliver North and Terry Waite embarked on their ambitious plans to get them released.

The TWA hostages returned to the US at the end of June 1985, and on July 3, Reagan chaired a special meeting of the National Security Planning Group at the White House Situation Room to review how the administration had handled the crisis. Reagan expressed frustration that America's intelligence resources seemed so thin on the ground. He made it clear he wanted more information on the terrorists still holding hostages, and asked his officials to seek all the help they could from their allies. Bud McFarlane took the President's comments almost as a personal rebuke, and left the meeting determined to find a plan.

The fact that McFarlane was continually racked by feelings of insecurity in his dealings with the White House did not prevent him from dreaming of pulling off a major diplomatic coup to enhance his reputation. One area which particularly fascinated him was Iran. Although America had bitter memories of its recent involvement there, McFarlane realised that Iran remained of crucial strategic importance to the oil fields in the Gulf. With the Soviet Union breathing down Teheran's neck, McFarlane believed Iran too important to be ignored. Thus when Michael Ledeen, a freelance counter-terrorism expert with excellent contacts with the Israeli intelligence establishment, suggested to McFarlane that there were 'moderate' factions within the Iranian hierarchy who took a more accommodating view of the West than the Islamic zealots, McFarlane seized on the information.

This was precisely the type of diplomatic initiative McFarlane had been seeking, and he was soon drawing parallels between

Kissinger's diplomatic breakthrough with the People's Republic of China and his own more modest effort with Iran. Ledeen's argument, backed up by David Kimche, the erudite director-general of the Israeli foreign ministry, was that the moderate factions in Teheran would be prepared to help secure the release of the American hostages in Lebanon – much as Rafsanjani had helped over the TWA hostages – in return for military spare parts. A large percentage of the Iranian armed forces' equipment – especially tanks and jet fighters – were American-made, and without spare parts Iran was at a distinct disadvantage in its war against Iraq. The key to the deal was Manucher Ghorbanifar, a corpulent Iranian arms dealer who operated from a luxurious apartment in Paris. Ghorbanifar, who had worked for the Shah's Savak intelligence service, had been forced to flee during the Revolution. Even so, he had maintained contact with the Iranians who had hired him to get the spare parts. Ghorbanifar approached the Israelis, with whom he had built up a good relationship when Israel maintained an embassy in Teheran. Ghorbanifar indicated that if Israel shipped 500 TOW US-made anti-tank missiles to Teheran, the American hostages in Lebanon would be released.

The idea of doing a deal through Ghorbanifar received greater support when Graham Fuller, a Middle East expert with the CIA, submitted a report to McFarlane in which he made the gloomy prediction that Iran would more than likely turn towards Moscow when Khomeini died, unless the Americans were prepared to do something. One course of action the Americans could take, he concluded, would be to encourage friendly countries, such as Israel, to sell arms to Iran. Like McFarlane, Casey was preoccupied with the Soviet menace and, given his obsession with getting William Buckley released, was prepared to give the Ghorbanifar deal a try. With both McFarlane and Casey backing the initiative, a powerful lobby was emerging in Washington in favour of making an opening to Iran. Shultz, who had only found out about McFarlane's intentions by accident, was the one dissenting voice. Opening 'back channels' would get Washington nowhere, he argued. But Shultz had only sketchy details of what was planned, and was forced to back down. All that was left was to secure the President's approval.

It was not the most opportune moment to trouble Reagan with such a complicated package. In early July a polyp, or small cancerous growth, had been found in Reagan's lower intestine, and emergency surgery was carried out. Reagan was recovering at Bethesda Naval Hospital on July 18 when McFarlane was finally able to see him. The first question Reagan asked was: 'How are the hostages doing?' and McFarlane had to concede that not much progress had been made. In a ten-minute conversation, McFarlane outlined the Ghorbanifar plan of getting the Israelis to ship missiles to Teheran in return for the release of the hostages. The US would then replenish Israel's stocks. Reagan approved the plan. 'Gee, that sounds pretty good,' he commented, and thus was born the American arms-for-hostages deal with Iran.

The fact that the deal was technically illegal did not seem to cause too much concern. Congress had passed legislation banning the sale of American weapons to countries accused of sponsoring international terrorism. This legislation also banned 'friendly' countries such as Israel, which purchased American military hardware, from passing it on to enemy states. But McFarlane believed he had the President's tacit approval for the plan, and therefore such matters were of little consequence.

Even though Oliver North played only a peripheral role in the initial arms deal, his relationship with both Casey and McFarlane made it inevitable that he would become involved at some stage. North had already effectively been 'adopted' by Casey because of the work he was doing on behalf of the Contra resistance fighters in Nicaragua. A close bond had developed between North and McFarlane as they had both served as marines in Vietnam. McFarlane admired North's energy, sincerity and general 'can-do' attitude, which, given the NSC's limited resources, was worth its weight in gold. So long as there was someone like McFarlane to keep a close watch over North's more hare-brained schemes, North was considered very much an asset at the NSC. As far as the Ghorbanifar deal was concerned, North was given the brief of making the arrangements for getting the hostages released: transport, debriefing, press conferences, etc.

While Washington was concentrating all its energies towards Iran, Terry Waite was still working out how he could be of practical use in Lebanon. By July the Kuwaiti authorities had made it clear to Waite that they were not interested in his 'blood money' idea. Even if all the relatives of the people injured in the 1983 terrorist attacks could be tracked down – and the Kuwaitis doubted it, as many of those injured were Pakistani labourers and had long since returned home – the Kuwaitis were reluctant to make any concessions regarding the Dawa 17. Undeterred, Waite and Habiby soldiered on, and came up with another idea, which was essentially a re-working of the deal negotiated for the release of the TWA hostages. In return for allowing the passengers and crew to go free, Nabih Berri had persuaded Washington to pressure Israel to release a group of Shia prisoners held in Israeli detention camps in southern Lebanon. There were still some 700 Shia prisoners held by the Israelis, however, and Waite and Habiby contacted North to see if he was interested in the idea. To their surprise North caught the next flight to London, and met Waite and Habiby the following morning at a hotel near Heathrow. At this meeting, which took place in mid-July 1985, North was still in the dark about the impending arms deals He gave Waite and Habiby every encouragement, however, and suggested that Waite visit Israel.

The first arms shipment left Tel Aviv airport on the night of August 20, 1985 and contained 96 TOW missiles made by Hughes Missile Systems in California. The DC-8 aircraft landed at Mehrabad Airport on the outskirts of Teheran and unloaded the cargo. North, who had been issued with a passport in the name of William P. Goode, was waiting in Washington for news of the hostages being released so that he could activate his contingency plan. But owing to a misunderstanding, no American hostages were released, and the plane returned to Tel Aviv empty. Ghorbanifar was blamed for the failure of the operation. His excuse was that the 'wrong' Iranians had seized the missiles. If a further consignment could be sent, he was sure the hostages would be released. Reagan and McFarlane reluctantly agreed to give it one more try. On September 14 the operation was repeated, only this time 408 TOWs were sent to Iran. This time the aircraft flew to the city of Tabriz to ensure the missiles were delivered to the Iranian army, and not the Revolutionary Guards.

Within hours the Israelis were calling up Washington. There was good news and there was bad news. The bad news was that only one American hostage would be released; the good news was that McFarlane could name the hostage to be freed. McFarlane was placed in an agonising predicament. 'I was being asked to play God,' he said later. In fact the choice was never in any doubt. William Buckley was the longest-held American hostage, and he was also the most important. McFarlane named Buckley.

Little did McFarlane realise as he fretted over his decision that thousands of miles away in their basement cell the hostages had already been asked to undertake a similar exercise. Towards the end of July, one of the guards announced to the five Americans that they had decided to set one of them free to make sure that the kidnappers' message got through to Washington.

The decision to release one captive reflected the mounting frustration among the kidnappers that, no matter how many hostages they acquired and how many messages they released, no one seemed to be taking them seriously. It is highly unlikely that the kidnappers at this stage knew anything about the arms deals that were being negotiated between Washington and Teheran. As the kidnappers had made abundantly clear, their primary objective was to secure the release of the Dawa 17, not to assist Iran's war effort. This fundamental conflict of interest between Iran and the kidnappers in Beirut poses intriguing questions about the nature of the relationship between 'mission control' and the operatives in the field. That there were close links between the two is not in dispute; Hizbollah, and therefore Islamic Jihad, was totally dependent on Iranian support, financial and political, for its existence and, in general terms, agreed with the policies of the Iranian Revolution. But Islamic Jihad also had its own agenda to fulfil. It all seems far too convenient for Iran that the kidnappers should decide it was in *their* interests to release an American hostage at precisely the moment that the Iranians wanted an American released so that they could get their hands on some badly-needed American supplies. Was this mere coincidence, or had the Iranians and the kidnappers worked out a compromise solution? Or had the Iranians suggested to the kidnappers that they release a hostage without telling them what the Iranians hoped to gain from the deal? If the latter case were true, then there would seem to be some truth in the age-old Lebanese view of Iranians as 'crafty Persians'.

Having announced that one of the five would be released, the guard really put the cat among the pigeons by telling the hostages to decide among themselves who should be the one to go. Whatever attempts the hostages had made to maintain some semblance of civility to one another evaporated as they all got involved – the two clerics included – in an unseemly and self-centred series of arguments, with everyone advancing a persuasive case why he should be the one set free. The only way to resolve the dispute was to conduct a series of secret ballots, which would result in two candidates remaining in the contest. After a series of votes Terry Anderson and David Jacobsen emerged as the front-runners, and in the final ballot Anderson won by a 3–2 majority.

Neither McFarlane nor the hostages should have believed that such a decision was in their gift, and when, in September 1985, a hostage was finally released, the guards arbitrarily chose Ben Weir. There was some reasoning behind their decision. Buckley was dead, and releasing his body would not do the kidnappers any favours in Washington. After Buckley, Weir was the longest-held hostage and, as a clergyman, could be relied upon to present the kidnappers' case fairly. In so much as there was ever any rationale to the kidnappers' behaviour, this was it. Needless to say, the decision prompted a near riot among the hostages. Anderson was outraged that the guards would not accept the democratic verdict of the hostages.

'No, no!' shouted Anderson, close to tears. 'It's me that's supposed to be going home. I was the one elected.'

Mugniyeh refused to change the decision. 'No. You are a bad man. You will stay.'

Anderson appealed to Jacobsen, as the runner-up, to plead on his behalf. Jacobsen made a half-hearted attempt, but realised the guards had already made up their minds. When the kidnappers left the room, a furious row broke out between Anderson and Jacobsen, which would have resulted in violence had not both men been chained to a wall.

'Fuck it, Dave,' Anderson screamed. 'You didn't do a

fucking thing to defend me. Why didn't you fight for me, you arsehole.'

'Screw you Anderson,' Jacobsen retorted hotly. 'You wouldn't listen to me when I said they would choose who they wanted, not us. You're just like a fucking kid who can't stand to be told what he wants. I want to go home just as much as you. But it's going to be their decision every fucking time.'

Before releasing Weir, one of the guards, who had been a barber in his pre-militia life, gave Weir a haircut and trimmed his beard and then allowed him the luxury of a long, hot shower. The kidnappers wanted to ensure their hostage looked his best when he was presented to the world. Before Weir took his final leave, all the hostages sat in a circle and prayed together. It was a sobering moment. All the bitterness of the earlier exchanges had abated. Now the four who were to be left behind – Anderson, Sutherland, Jenco and Jacobsen – looked at Weir with a mixture of awe and hope. In a few hours Weir would be free from all this misery and squalor, and in him resided their hope that one day soon they would all make a similar journey to freedom.

If McFarlane was surprised when Weir was released, he was even more surprised when he got to meet the Presbyterian minister. Weir was taken by helicopter to Cyprus, then flown to a naval base in Norfolk, Virginia. News of Weir's release was delayed for four days in the hope that more hostages would be released. When it became clear there would be no others, Reagan personally announced Weir's release to a cheering crowd at Concord, New Hampshire. During those four days, however, while Weir had been held at Norfolk, relations between Weir and his debriefers deteriorated to such a level that the Americans openly referred to him as the Reverend Weird. All the blame for the administration's disastrous handling of Weir's release was put down to Oliver

North, the man assigned to arrange the release schedule. From the moment Weir arrived in the US, his only interest was in being reunited with his wife. In his desire to debrief Weir, however, North tried to prevent him leaving the base, hardly a realistic attitude to take towards someone who has just been locked up for seventeen months.

Weir was appalled at the naivety of the questions North and the other debriefers asked him. 'What was the food like?' 'What were the health conditions like?' And when North pulled out satellite photographs of the Beirut area and asked Weir if he could identify any of the places where he had been held, Weir's co-operation came to an abrupt halt. Fearing that North and his colleagues might be considering a military raid to release the hostages, Weir refused point blank to answer any more questions, fearing that to do so would endanger the lives of the hostages he had left behind. Weir simply repeated the message he had been asked to pass on by the kidnappers, the same message that he relayed directly to Ronald Reagan. 'My captors told me they expect you to put pressure on Kuwait to release the seventeen men being held there. Second, they want me to tell you that they have released me as a sign of their good intention to resolve this issue.' Weir's refusal to co-operate any further infuriated North and the team which had worked on the first arms-for-hostages deal. Michael Ledeen, the architect of the whole affair, said he even went so far as to contact Ghorbanifar and, only half in jest, ask him 'if it was possible for the Iranians to take Weir back, and send us a patriotic American instead.'[1]

The fact that Weir was able to confirm conclusively that at least four of the American hostages were alive gave their relatives a field day in their campaigns to get the American

---

[1]Michael Ledeen: *Perilous Statecraft*, Charles Scribner's Sons, 1988.

government to take action. Since the TWA crisis in the summer, Reagan had come under increasing pressure from the Jenco family and Peggy Say to act. Reagan hated being caught up in an emotional issue like this, not least because he genuinely sympathised with the plight of the families. When he proudly announced Weir's release, he believed this would give him some breathing space from the other relatives. Far from it. Weir's release resulted in a succession of own goals for the administration, starting with North's treatment of Weir and culminating in a heated clash between Peggy Say and Vice-President George Bush at the White House. Disappointed that Terry Anderson, her brother, had not been released with Weir, she exploded at Bush for not showing more concern.

'How can you accuse me of not caring?' the Vice-President countered. 'I'm a Christian man.'

'You'll have to excuse me,' Mrs Say replied evenly, 'but don't tell me you're a Christian, show me.'

Faced with this public relations disaster, North had only one trick left up his sleeve. He telephoned Terry Waite at Lambeth Palace and asked if he would like to come to Washington to meet Ben Weir. Waite jumped at the chance. The last few months had been very frustrating for him; he had made no progress on the Lebanese hostage crisis. The Kuwaitis were not interested in the ideas he had put together with Habiby, and the Syrians, even though the Archbishop of Canterbury had personally written to President Assad, had refused to grant Waite a visa to visit Damascus.

Throughout the summer North had been talking to colleagues about Waite almost as if he owned him. He had boasted how Waite was an ideal 'magnet' for the press and that North would be able to 'manage' him in the right way whenever the occasion required. With Weir refusing to have anything further to do with North, the moment had arrived to send for Terry Waite and, as usual, Waite was happy to oblige.

A week after Weir's release, Waite arrived in New York and held a joint press conference with the freed hostage. Waite was once more in his element. Posing for the cameras with a smiling Ben Weir, he gave the definite impression that he had played a central role in securing Weir's release. Maybe he genuinely believed that his ineffectual efforts to open a dialogue with the Kuwaitis – who had nothing to do with the kidnappers – had in some obscure way helped in the release of Benjamin Weir. But Waite had made no contact either with the Iranians or the kidnappers. It is highly unlikely that Oliver North, given his attitude to Waite, would have told him anything about the complicated arms deal behind Weir's release. But given all the experience Waite had acquired as an 'independent humanitarian', it is surprising he did not feel a certain unease at so publicly taking credit for something in which, at best, he could only have played a marginal role. Michael Ledeen, who set up the whole Weir release, is in no doubt about the role Waite played in the exercise. 'He was window-dressing, pure and simple,' said Ledeen. 'Ollie wanted somebody to take the heat off him and stop the questions about what had really gone on to get Weir out. Waite solved a lot of Ollie's headaches.'

Certainly that was not the impression Waite gave at the Weir press conference, or subsequently. When the British press proudly trumpeted that the Archbishop of Canterbury's special envoy was the secret negotiator behind the release of an American hostage in Lebanon, Waite did nothing to correct this blatant misrepresentation of the truth. Those who worked in North's office said Waite was encouraged to take the credit in order 'to strengthen his role as a mediator'. But Waite was playing a dangerous game. The kidnappers wanted to deal with somebody who could deliver tangible results, not someone who was merely proficient at posing for the cameras. If they ever found out that Waite was not everything he made himself out to be, he would be in serious trouble.

12

FACE TO FACE

There was an unmistakeable buzz of excitement as the camera crews and reporters settled into their seats in the first-class compartment of the Middle East Airlines flight from London to Beirut. Much of the attention was focused on the six-foot-eight-inch frame of Terry Waite who had organised himself a seat in the front row, where he was guaranteed extra leg room. For those of us who had been to Lebanon before, there was the added anticipation of returning to a city fraught with danger.

It was Wednesday November 13, 1985, and Waite was on his way to Beirut at the start of his mission to free the hostages. Many of the television journalists on the flight had worked with Waite during his Libya mission, and an easy familiarity marked the relations between the newsmen and their subject.

'Here we go again, eh, Terry,' remarked Brent Sadler, the effervescent ITN reporter. 'This is going to be the big one,' he predicted with evident relish at all the good stories Waite's visit to Lebanon would bring him.

'I wouldn't say that,' Waite replied with a self-deprecating chuckle. 'But I do think it will be a very interesting trip.'

'You bet. How about a one-to-one on the visit and what you are hoping to achieve?' continued Sadler, using the idiom favoured by television journalists when referring to an interview.

'With pleasure, Brent. Once we have taken off and everyone's settled,' Waite replied affably. 'How long do you want?'

'Oh, just five minutes will do it. Then we can shoot it straight back to London when we touch down for the News at Ten,' said Sadler.

'That's wonderful, Brent. I don't know how you television chaps do it,' said Waite.

'Genius, pure genius,' Sadler replied with a grin, giving Waite a friendly pat on the back.

'Magic guy to work with,' Sadler later confided to me as we made ourselves comfortable for the five-hour flight. 'Ask him anything, and he'll always give you something. Never says no to an interview. Goes out of his way to help. Can't ask much more than that.' Sadler had become close personal friends with Waite since the Libya mission the previous year, to the extent that he had asked the Anglican envoy to assist at his wedding, an invitation Waite readily accepted.

For those of us who had had no previous dealings with Terry Waite, his accessibility to the media was a revelation. Whenever I had previously attempted to make contact with an official on a secret diplomatic mission in the Middle East, the most I had achieved was a brusque 'No comment', and then only on those rare occasions when I had succeeded in tracking the elusive official down. In the Middle East, knowledge is power, and people involved in any form of negotiation prefer to keep their own counsel, so as to maintain the maximum advantage. Terry Waite was the opposite. Once the aircraft was airborne, Waite busied himself making the acquaintance of all the journalists on board, giving numerous interviews and reassuring them individually that they could count on his fullest co-operation.

'The *Daily Telegraph*, a fine newspaper,' said Waite after I had introduced myself. 'That Bill Deedes, he's a fine fellow. How can he spend all his time playing golf with Denis Thatcher and edit the newspaper at the same time?' W.F. Deedes was then the editor of the *Telegraph*, and had achieved a measure of immortality through a column in the satirical magazine *Private Eye*, in which a letter purportedly written by Thatcher to Deedes was a regular item. There were frequent references to golfing expeditions in the 'Dear Bill' feature, but I had to inform Waite I was not privy to my editor's domestic arrangements. I was more interested in what Waite thought of the dangers his mission posed.

'I don't think there is anything in Beirut to worry about,' said Waite. 'I've been in some sticky situations in the past myself, you know, and this is all part of my job. The hostages are my top priority.'

Shortly before leaving London, the Archbishop of Canterbury had received a letter written by four of the American hostages – Jacobsen, Anderson, Sutherland and Jenco – asking for his assistance. According to Waite, the letter contained a statement he considered to be helpful, and it also contained a threat. I wondered why Waite, who appeared to be travelling to Beirut on behalf of the Archbishop of Canterbury, was concentrating on the American hostages, and not on Alec Collett, the Briton who had been abducted the previous May. Collett, of course, was being held by a Palestinian group, while the Americans were held by Lebanese. Even so, I was surprised that Collett was not a priority in Waite's plans. He had got British hostages released from Iran and Libya, why not Lebanon?

Waite replied that he was responding to a direct request from the kidnappers to work for the Americans, but if the discussions went well, it was possible that Collett 'might enter the frame'. This surprised me even more. Was it possible that Lebanese kidnappers could persuade a Palestinian group to release a hostage? It seemed highly unlikely, but I assumed there were hidden dimensions to Waite's mission of which I knew nothing. I then asked what would happen if the kidnappers decided to take him hostage, a genuine possibility given the unpredictable nature of the groups operating in Lebanon.

'I have left strict instructions at Lambeth Palace that in the event of my kidnap, no ransom is to be paid,' Waite announced firmly. Even so, I was struck by how relaxed Waite appeared. He wore a smart, well-tailored three-piece suit and a gold watch-chain dangled across his waistcoat. His thick, black beard was neatly trimmed and pomaded. His demeanour was more that of an Edwardian gentleman on his way to lunch at the Athenaeum than of a man about to enter one of the most god-forsaken cities in the history of the late twentieth century.

Little did I or any of the other journalists on the MEA flight know that the reason our flight had been delayed for a few minutes was that Oliver North had turned up at Heathrow demanding to see Waite before he left for Lebanon. North had a picture of Imad Mugniyeh that he wanted to show Waite. While conceding that Washington knew very little about Mugniyeh, North said he would be very interested in any information Waite could bring back about the man he described as 'the world's most wanted terrorist'. North also advised Waite that he could make a 'humanitarian gesture' about the Kuwait prisoners. Had any of us known that this meeting had taken place, we would have been less inclined to take Waite's claim that he was going to Lebanon as 'a free agent' at face value.

I had been back to Lebanon several times since my hurried

departure on the day of Terry Anderson's abduction. After the immediate panic had died down, journalists began to return piecemeal to cover the stories that continued to grab the headlines, such as the TWA affair. But every time I went back I had a deeper sense of foreboding. The security situation showed no sign of improvement, in spite of the repeated efforts of different Lebanese factions and the Syrians. Walid Jumblatt, the Druze militia leader, had fallen out with Nabih Berri, his erstwhile ally, over their approach to a final settlement of the civil war and Berri's treatment of the Palestinians. And the more the different factions fell out, the stronger became Hizbollah's power-base, with all its implications for the Westerners still in West Beirut. Only a few weeks before Waite embarked on his mission, in October 1985, the kidnap gangs had surpassed themselves by kidnapping two British women and four Soviet diplomats.

Hazel Moss and Amanda McGrath were taken from their West Beirut apartment in late September. Moss, who was in her late thirties and originally came from Manchester, was a well-known figure in the dwindling expatriate community. She had come to Beirut in the early 1970s to work as a secretary for one of the big oil companies. A glamorous blonde, she had no shortage of admirers among the city's wealthy hedonists. She was invited to all the best restaurants and nightclubs, and, as she recalled years later, 'I was part of the world's biggest non-stop party', until the civil war brought the party to an abrupt halt. In spite of the war, Hazel Moss remained in Beirut, becoming an increasingly sad figure as she hopped from one job to another, managing one restaurant after another, until Jackie Mann employed her to run his Pickwick bar.

Hazel, who remained a redoubtable character, befriended a young English teacher called Amanda McGrath who had come to work in Beirut in the summer of 1985. Amanda was introduced to Hazel Moss by Dennis Hill, the British teacher, shortly before he was murdered, when he brought her into the Pickwick for a drink. Amanda, who was twenty-eight, arrived in Beirut with the intention of enjoying herself to the full, and had no difficulty making the acquaintance of Muslim militiamen who were not averse to frequenting bars and enjoying the company of Western women. Amanda had little understanding of or interest in Beirut's sectarian rivalries, and saw nothing wrong in dating a Christian militiaman in East Beirut at the same time as socialising with Druze militiamen in West Beirut. Nor did she see anything wrong in showing the Druze militiamen, who by then had spent ten years engaged in bitter conflict with their Christian adversaries, pictures of her with her Christian boyfriend.

The Druze gunmen were distinctly unimpressed, and a few days later militiamen hammered on the door of Hazel Moss's apartment which she shared with Amanda. When she opened the door, the gunmen grabbed her and dragged her down the stairs. They then went into the apartment and seized Amanda. The women were taken to a derelict house close to the Green Line where they were thrown into a filthy, rat-infested room and, in Hazel's words, 'left to rot' for ten days. Fortunately, their abductors had taken them merely to teach them a lesson. It is a cardinal rule of the Islamic code not to harm women, and once the gunmen felt the women had learned the error of their ways, they set them free. Amanda, suitably chastened, fled the country, never to return. Hazel, who had lived in Beirut without any problems before she met Amanda, decided to remain in a city where she could still count upon her close friends to look after her.

The case of the four Soviet diplomats showed what could be done when a government was still in a position to exercise some influence in Lebanon. Although the Soviet Union maintained strong ties with both the Syrians and some of the

Lebanese Muslim militias, their influence was deeply resented by the Islamic fundamentalists who regarded all foreign interference in Lebanon as pernicious. While most of the other diplomatic missions in West Beirut had either been closed or had their staff reduced to the bare minimum, the Soviets still maintained a full-size diplomatic presence, confident that their close relations with Damascus would guarantee their diplomats' safety. On the morning of September 30 a group of Muslim gunmen changed all that when they kidnapped four Soviet diplomats. Two days later the bullet-riddled body of one of them was found dumped on a Beirut street.

The kidnappings brought the Soviet diplomatic presence in West Beirut to an immediate end. The next day three buses carrying the remaining diplomats and their families beat a hasty exit across the Green Line, escorted by Mr Jumblatt's Druze militiamen. The Soviets, however, applied all their diplomatic muscle to get the three released. With the Druze acting on their behalf, it was not long before the Soviets were set free. The Druze tactic was simple but highly effective; they discovered who was holding the Soviets, and responded by abducting the brother of one of the kidnappers. The next day his family received one of his fingers in an envelope, followed by another finger the next day. Forty-eight hours later, the three Soviets were released unharmed. The Soviets had proved what could be achieved by maintaining good relations with Beirut's militia leaders. An embellished version of this story became an established part of Lebanon's hostage folklore, in which the fingers are replaced by a more sensitive part of the anatomy.

A general mood of anarchy prevailed. Security in West Beirut was supposed to be in the hands of Amal and Druze militias but, due to the mounting political rivalry between Nabih Berri and Walid Jumblatt, the city was effectively broken up into small pockets, with each militia controlling an area varying in size between a few apartment blocks to several streets. Some militiamen had signed up because they genuinely believed in the cause; others, particularly the Druze, signed up because of family tradition. But within the ranks of the 5,000 militiamen operating in Beirut at any given moment, there were many who had taken up arms simply because they loved the macho image, loved dressing up in quasi-military uniforms and indulging in Lebanon's infamous gun culture. Pity the militiaman who could not tell an M-16 from a Kalashnikov (pity the journalist, for that matter). Officially a militiaman was paid between £20 and £50 a month, a pittance even by Third World standards – and Lebanon, though areas of Beirut were beginning to look like downtown Lagos on a good day, still did not consider itself a Third World country.

To supplement their income, some militiamen undertook other activities. Some insisted that shops and businesses paid protection money, others made a good living by providing families with cheap electricity from generators parked in the street (the Christians controlled the electricity supply, with the result that West Beirut went for long periods of the day disconnected from the national grid). One or two groups of militiamen, blessed with a social conscience, formed the Lebanese equivalent of neighbourhood watch schemes. Apart from ensuring that residents in their care were protected from attack by rival militias, they fulfilled a range of social functions, such as maintaining the public utilities. If a sink became blocked, you called for a militiaman to unblock it. If the telephone packed up, you called a militiaman to fix it.

Many more militiamen, alas, were engaged in far less scrupulous undertakings, such as running prostitution or gambling rackets. Often street battles would erupt between rival groups over who had the right to control a brothel or a casino. Like the Chicago mobsters of the 1930s, the militia gangs were intensely jealous about anyone attempting to move onto their turf.

With the collapse of the central banking system (the Lebanese currency remained remarkably strong for the first ten years of the war, but collapsed after February 1984), Lebanon became a militia economy. The militias had all the power and finance, and a young man could improve his family status immeasurably by signing up with a militia. Each militia had its independent source of finance. Both Amal and the Druze received money at different times from the Syrians, depending on who was in favour. The Druze, mainly because of Walid Jumblatt's radical political outlook, received occasional donations from both Moscow and Gaddafi in Libya.

The general atmosphere of lawlessness made virtually any activity in Beirut hazardous. Phoning for an ambulance was dangerous because, rather than use their sirens to clear a path through the traffic, the gunmen would fire their guns in the air. On several occasions curious citizens peeped over their balconies to see what was going on in the street below, only to be shot by an ambulanceman, who would then have to make a return trip to collect his own victim. Going to the cinema was dangerous because the only movies shown were Rambo-style war films. When the film reached a moment that particularly appealed to the militiamen, they would fire their guns into the ceiling in appreciation, causing a small avalanche of masonry and plaster. No one in their right mind asked for a circle seat. Even going for a swim was dangerous, as the fishermen had long ago given up the tiresome task of using nets. They found it much easier to throw sticks of dynamite into the sea, and collect the stunned fish as they floated to the surface. If you saw a fishing boat coming your way, you swam for your life.

The fact that the other militias became gradually more corrupt and out of control played into the hands of Hizbollah. From its humble beginnings in the Bekaa Valley in 1982, Hizbollah had developed into a major force in Lebanon. While the other militias squabbled among themselves, Hizbollah strengthened its position both through the purity of its message and its impressive track record of attacks against the Israelis. The more Israelis were killed by Hizbollah, the more Shia Muslims wanted to sign up. With money provided by Iran, Hizbollah had constructed an impressive infrastructure both in Beirut and the Bekaa Valley. Money was not given away, but carefully invested. If a Shia family wanted to add an extra room to their house, they went to the local mullah and, providing they could make a case, would receive a loan at a good interest rate. Hizbollah built hospitals and schools for the needy in the southern suburbs. In the area around Sheikh Fadlallah's residence in the Bir al-Abed quarter, a whole range of social utilities – housing, hospitals, and schools – was constructed.

The money for all this came from several sources. Some of it came from the 'martyrs' foundation', a charity set up in Iran to raise funds for the relatives of young Shia men and women who had sacrificed their lives in the fight against Israel. The money raised far exceeded the requirements of the relatives concerned, and was used to help other needy Shia families in Lebanon. This was supplemented by direct grants from Iran. Western intelligence estimated that about £10 million ($18 million) was transferred from Teheran to Lebanon each month, money which could go a long way in Lebanon's bankrupt economy, but which constituted only a tiny fraction of Iran's annual oil revenue. Such philanthropy contrasted sharply with the lawlessness of Hizbollah's main rival, Amal, so that Hizbollah had no difficulty attracting new followers. Hizbollah militiamen were paid no more than members of other militias, but they had a more clearly defined purpose.

As Hizbollah grew in strength, so it grew in confidence. In 1985, Hizbollah issued a political manifesto setting out its commitment to establishing Islamic rule in Lebanon. The manifesto was issued by Sheikh Subhi Tufayli, a radical Shia cleric based at Baalbek; it pinpointed the main enemies of Hizbollah as being Israel, America, France and the Lebanese Christians. Britain was not mentioned anywhere in this document, either as friend or foe. Britain, as far as Hizbollah was concerned, simply did not count.

Hizbollah had also developed a sophisticated political leadership. Because Hizbollah was primarily a guerrilla group, its activities were rooted in secrecy. The organisation was led by Sheikh Tufayli who, from 1984, served as Hizbollah's secretary-general. Tufayli headed the Hizbollah politburo, a group of individuals each with special responsibility for a specific department. One member would be responsible for the social development programme, another in charge of the guerrilla campaign against Israel. And from early 1984 Imad Mugniyeh was the politburo member in charge of Islamic Jihad, the section of Hizbollah responsible for holding the Western hostages.

One of the more remarkable aspects of the activities of the kidnappers in Lebanon was their ability to conduct their activities in total secrecy. Despite the intense efforts made by a variety of groups to infiltrate them – Western intelligence as much as Syrian intelligence – no one ever succeeded in breaking into Hizbollah. The secret to Mugniyeh's success was that the number of people directly involved in the kidnappings was very small. Only about fifty people at most were involved throughout an eight-year period. The kidnappers came from a variety of backgrounds. Some had studied at the AUB and spoke perfect English (one of the kidnappers attended English lectures given by Tom Sutherland's wife Jean at the AUB in between guarding the hostages!), while others were relatives of the leaders of the kidnap gangs who were commandeered for guard duty or to provide 'safe houses' in which the hostages could be held. The fact that Hizbollah had succeeded in turning the southern suburbs into an impregnable stronghold was also very much to the benefit of the kidnappers.

The inexorable rise of Hizbollah to a position of power and influence in Lebanon was greatly assisted by the awe in which the organisation was held by the West. To the ordinary Lebanese who knew the members of Hizbollah, they were nothing more than a bunch of gangsters dressed up in the rags of Khomeini's ideology. 'They were nobodies until the West made them important,' explained a Shia Muslim who was a senior official in the Amal movement at the time. 'The big mistake of the US and the West was to make Hizbollah more important than it was. All the envoys and missionaries who came to Beirut, making deals here and making deals there, made the Hizbollah leaders feel really big. We did not take them seriously ourselves. Instead of making such a fuss about the hostage issue, the West should have ignored it, and then the hostages would have been useless to Hizbollah. They would all have been freed sooner or later.'

This was not a point of view shared by Terry Waite. Such a view would have destroyed the whole *raison d'être* of his role as an 'independent humanitarian'.

Beirut was not the only focus of terrorist activity in the Middle East when Terry Waite set off on his mission. In late September a group of PLO gunmen murdered three Israelis in Larnaca harbour who were alleged to be Mossad agents. One of the gunmen, Ian Davison, turned out to be a reformed skinhead from Newcastle who had joined the PLO having discovered the Palestinian cause. The Israelis responded by bombing the PLO's headquarters in Tunis, killing more than thirty people. The next day Islamic Jihad issued a statement claiming it had 'executed' William Buckley after he had been found guilty of being a CIA spy. No one knew that Buckley had died of pneumonia the previous June, and Islamic Jihad's statement was taken as an indication that Buckley had been killed in retaliation for the Israeli raid.

The next terrorist incident in the Middle East helped to consolidate Oliver North's position as the star of the NSC. A group of Palestinian terrorists hijacked an Italian cruise ship called the *Achille Lauro*. Their original intention had been to stow away on board the ship which was bound for the Israeli port of Haifa. Once in Israel, they intended to kidnap some Israelis and hold them hostage in return for the release of Palestinian prisoners held in Israel. But while the ship was still cruising in the Mediterranean, the terrorists were discovered. Brandishing their guns, they then took control of the liner, together with 400 passengers. For the next forty-eight hours the ship made a crazy zig-zag pattern across the eastern Mediterranean as the hijackers tried to work out their next move. At one point their frustration got the better of them and they murdered an elderly, wheelchair-bound Jewish American called Leon Klinghoffer and dumped his body overboard. Eventually President Mubarak of Egypt was able to persuade the kidnappers to bring the ship to Port Said and abandon the hijack. In return he guaranteed the hijackers safe passage out of the country.

At this point, Oliver North made his mark. At first the Egyptians said they had allowed the four Palestinian terrorists to leave the country as promised, claiming they did not realise the terrorists had killed an American citizen. North, who had been asked to work on the case by McFarlane, was outraged, but was on the point of accepting the Egyptian version of events when he received a call from a contact at the Israeli embassy in Washington telling him the Palestinians were still in Cairo, but would be flown to Tunisia later that day. North then had the brainwave of getting American warplanes to intercept the terrorists in mid-air as they were flying to safety. He put the proposal to Reagan, who liked the idea and gave it his approval. That evening, when the four Palestinians took off in a civilian Air Egypt airliner, F-14 Tomcat fighters were dispatched from the aircraft carrier *Saratoga* to intercept it. The Egyptian aircraft was forced to land in southern Italy.

That was where North's ambitious plan fell apart. Believing he could not trust the Italian government to keep a secret, he did not inform Rome of the operation until the Tomcats were escorting the terrorists to Italy. As a consequence, when the aircraft landed, there was an embarrassing stand-off between the American and Italian troops which came within a whisker of shots being fired. Reluctantly the Americans were forced to back down and hand the Palestinians over to the Italians, thus depriving North of the publicity coup of having the terrorists brought to America to stand trial. Nor did North win many friends in Cairo. President Mubarak, one of Washington's closest Arab allies, was livid when he heard what had happened, and seriously considered breaking diplomatic relations with the US. North appeared totally untroubled by the diplomatic fall-out his efforts had caused.

As North admitted candidly in his autobiography,[1] the whole operation had been run by the seat of its pants. North's job was to get things done, and to hell with the diplomatic fall-out. George Shultz protested loudly about the damage North's mission had done to Washington's relations with both Rome and Cairo. When he next met North, he commented icily: 'So here's the man who brought down the Italian government.' North simply smiled and replied, 'Good morning, Mr Secretary.' North was more concerned with the banner headlines in the American tabloid press the

[1]Oliver L. North: *Under Fire*, HarperCollins, 1991.

next morning. 'We bag the bums,' wrote the *New York Daily News*, while the *New York Post* went one better and suggested a phrase for Reagan to use when he spoke publicly about the operation. 'You can run, but you can't hide,' Reagan duly declared on the evening news, and the *Post* had its front-page headline.

North's involvement in the *Achille Lauro* affair raised his standing considerably within the White House. North did not suffer any fall-out from the unfortunate handling of Ben Weir's release; North's view was that if Weir would not co-operate, there was nothing much anyone could do about it, and somehow he got all his superiors to agree with him. Apart from having the personal backing of McFarlane, his immediate boss, North had also been taken under the wing of William Casey, who was impressed by North's enthusiasm and commitment to the Nicaragua guerrillas. Add to North's list of admirers President Reagan, and it was clear that North was becoming increasingly powerful in the small circle of White House advisers. North's problem, however, was that he needed to be kept on a tight leash. McFarlane recognised this, but was becoming increasingly disenchanted with the continual infighting among the key members of Reagan's cabinet. He therefore was not paying sufficient attention to his subordinate's activities, with the result that North became a loose cannon pitching across the deck of the White House.

Following the partially successful arms swap which resulted in Ben Weir's release, North was given a wider brief to undertake further contacts with Iran, using the Israelis as intermediaries, with a view to getting the remaining American hostages out. By the time Waite had embarked on his mission amid the usual publicity, North was quietly working on another arms shipment to Iran. Since the summer of 1985 he had developed a close working relationship with Amiram Nir, Israeli prime minister Shimon Peres's personal counter-terrorism expert. In fact Nir was no such thing. A handsome television journalist who specialised in defence matters and who had married the daughter of the owner of Israel's largest tabloid newspaper, Nir knew no more about counter-terrorism than most journalists. His brash manner quickly resulted in his being ostracised from the mainstream Mossad intelligence establishment, rather in the way North was regarded with a fair measure of scepticism by career intelligence officers at the CIA. North and Nir quickly reached a mutual understanding whereby they could make significant contributions to each other's careers by working closely together. The arms deals to Iran were the perfect vehicle for enhancing both their reputations, so that when Ghorbanifar said more American hostages would be released if North could arrange for a batch of Hawk anti-aircraft missiles to be shipped to Iran, both Nir and North were willing to oblige.

No sooner had Terry Waite's plane touched down at Beirut airport than he found himself at the centre of a classic example of the inter-militia rivalry that had made life for the ordinary citizen in Beirut unbearable. Both the Druze and Amal militias had sent bodyguards to meet Waite to guarantee his safety. Angry scuffles broke out while Waite was still waiting to collect his bags, and it was only out of deference to Waite that the whole affair did not immediately deteriorate into a shoot-out.

Eventually it was agreed that Amal should guard him, as the Commodore Hotel, where Waite was initially staying, was in an Amal-controlled area. Waite seemed remarkably unfazed by it all, and was soon taking the short ride into town along the road on which Thomas Sutherland had been kidnapped five months previously. Once he had settled at the hotel,

Waite held an impromptu press conference at which he said it would be 'necessary for me to drop out of sight for a while'. He was going to attempt to make contact with the kidnappers and begged the press not to try to follow him, 'as lives are at risk'. It was a classic Waite ploy, to whet the appetite of the press and leave them asking for more.

One of Oliver North's more constructive contributions to Waite's Lebanon mission before he left London had been to introduce him to an undercover agent who had worked in Lebanon for both British and American intelligence. North called the man 'Spiro', but Waite, hardly stretching the bounds of his imagination, preferred to call him 'John Smith'. Ian Stuart Spiro was born into a family of north London Jews in 1945. After a privileged education at Carmel College, Britain's only exclusive Jewish public school, the young Spiro left at the age of sixteen to make his fortune. He started work as a property developer, taking advantage of London's property boom in the early 1970s. According to close friends, he made a considerable fortune. But like so many of his contemporaries, he lost it as quickly as it was made. Moreover, in Spiro's case, the collapse of his business left him with a mountain of debt and under investigation for fraud. Spiro's response was to abandon his wife and two young children and move to the Middle East to make a new start.

Exactly how Spiro became involved in working for Western intelligence will probably never be known. But in the Byzantine world of the Middle East, foreign businessmen, especially those involved in selling arms, inevitably develop contacts with those involved in the shadier side of international diplomacy. Certainly by the late 1970s, Spiro was deeply involved in selling arms to Iran. He worked closely with Cyrus Hashemi, a London-based Iranian exile. Hashemi later died in mysterious circumstances in the summer of 1986 in London. Together the two men made a good living selling arms to Iran after the outbreak of the Iran-Iraq war. Spiro's contacts with the mullahs in Teheran, furthermore, led him to be introduced to Islamic fundamentalist leaders in Lebanon. Like the opportunist he was, Spiro was not slow to appreciate the value of such contacts at a time when Western interests were being driven out of Beirut. And when American citizens started to be kidnapped in Lebanon, it was not long before the CIA and other intelligence agencies were offering to pay Spiro considerable sums for any information which might lead to their release.

By far Spiro's biggest achievement was to obtain a copy of William Buckley's confession. He did this through his contacts in Iran. Thus when Waite was preparing to go to Beirut, it was only logical that William Casey, the CIA director and North's mentor, should pass on Spiro's name. At North's request, Spiro contacted Waite at Lambeth Palace to offer his services. Waite invited Spiro to London and the two men met in Waite's office. Spiro claimed to have contact with Islamic Jihad and offered to set up a meeting for Waite. In fact his main contact was with Dr Adnan Mroueh, a Shia Muslim gynaecologist and occasional politician. Spiro's second wife Gail, a physiotherapist from Cumbria, worked as a nurse at the American University Hospital, and it was through her that Spiro had met Mroueh. Apart from pursuing his medical practice, Mroueh also harboured political ambitions, and had served as a junior minister in a Lebanese cabinet. In order to further his political career, Mroueh had cultivated good relations with the emerging Shia leaders such as Sheikh Fadlallah. There was also a professional dimension to Mroueh's relationship with Fadlallah, in that he had often treated Fadlallah's wife. When Waite announced his decision to visit Beirut, Mroueh was perfectly placed to arrange a meeting between the Anglican intermediary and Islamic Jihad.

For all the fuss Waite made about going to a 'secret

hideout', he travelled less than a mile from the Commodore to Terry Anderson's vacant apartment on the Corniche. It was such an obvious choice that within hours television crews had gathered outside the apartment to film Waite going to meet the kidnappers. Waite got angry and said the camera crews threatened to ruin his mission, but what did he expect? The media attention he had deliberately cultivated was not something he could turn on and off at will.

Waite's first task was to make contact with the kidnappers. The letter which the hostages had written to the Archbishop of Canterbury before Waite left London included details of how Waite could contact the kidnappers on two short-wave channels. Waite had brought a short-wave radio from London, and as soon as he had settled into the apartment, he called up the kidnap groups. The kidnappers had devised this method of contact because they knew every telephone Waite touched would be bugged; a short-wave radio, however, would make it far more difficult for unwanted parties to interfere. After a couple of days at Anderson's apartment, a man claiming to represent the kidnappers contacted Waite and told him he wanted to meet him to discuss the hostages. At first Waite was suspicious, and wanted the man to verify himself. He asked him to find out the name of Robert Fisk's Scandinavian girlfriend, a name Waite knew could be obtained from Terry Anderson (Fisk had appointed himself Waite's personal media adviser). Within minutes the contact came back with the correct name. Waite then agreed to go to Dr Mroueh's clinic near the American Hospital. Once Waite arrived, a group of Hizbollah members appeared and asked Waite to go with them. Waite was still uncertain, and produced a Polaroid camera and a recent edition of *The Times*. The Hizbollah representatives disappeared, and half an hour later returned with pictures of Anderson, Sutherland, Jacobsen and

Jenco with the newspaper. Waite was now ready to meet the kidnappers.

In their cramped apartment, the sudden appearance of a copy of *The Times* and a Polaroid camera had a dramatic effect on the spirits of both the guards and the captives. For several weeks the hostages' hopes had been raised that they could be home for Christmas. At some point in November, an Iranian calling himself Ali had introduced to himself to them. Ali spoke good English and oozed self-confidence, and it was clear that the Lebanese guards did not like him. When he was not there they would make comments about the 'Persian' and joke about the way he dressed and spoke. But once he appeared, the Lebanese treated him with grudging respect. The Iranian was clearly a man of considerable influence, and the kidnappers were required to do whatever he said. Ali said he wanted the hostages to help him. 'We want you to write a letter to President Reagan and the Archbishop of Canterbury.' It was these letters which had resulted in Waite's trip.

The appearance of Ali resulted in a marked improvement in the hostages' conditions. They were no longer required to wear chains all the time, and were kept together in a small room where they did their best to humour each other, keeping themselves fit by doing push-ups and exercises, and conducting a brief prayer service twice a day. The guards were also instructed to provide them with a shortwave radio, which they listened to eagerly for news of the outside world. For a few days the guards, who seemed to bear no personal grievance against the hostages, became positively friendly towards them, promising them they would be home for Christmas. Mugniyeh also paid the hostages a brief visit to discuss Waite's mission. Mugniyeh never appeared at the same time as the Iranian, but the hostages assumed he was in contact. Mugniyeh, however, did not seem as optimistic about Waite's mission as the Iranian. Mugniyeh wanted to talk to Waite, but the enterprise would be dangerous. People would try to follow them, and if they did, it could result in everyone, hostages and kidnappers alike, being killed.

There is no doubt that Waite's decision to put himself at the mercy of unknown Lebanese gunmen on the night of November 15 was the bravest act he had ever been required to undertake in his career as a mediator. Not only had no foreign intermediary previously had any contact with the kidnappers, but the combined resources of the West's most sophisticated intelligence services had failed to produce even the faintest clue as to where the hostages were being held. The people Waite was going to see, moreover, had been directly involved in the terrorist attacks against Western interests in Lebanon, which had resulted in the deaths of some 300 foreigners.

As the gunmen blindfolded him and gently pushed a gun barrel into the small of his back, Waite must have wondered if he was about to make the same one-way trip as the hostages he had come to save. But as far as the gunmen were concerned, the precautions were necessary. Waite was being taken to see Imad Mugniyeh, and they could not take any chances. Waite later confessed to his friends that he had found the whole experience 'absolutely terrifying'. According to the account Waite later gave of his face-to-face meeting with Mugniyeh, the two men had a business-like discussion about what was required for the hostages to be released. Waite's opening tack was to ask Mugniyeh if he wanted money, which served only to enrage Mugniyeh. No, he screeched, the kidnappers did not want money. They were devout Muslims. Why couldn't the West understand that they were not a bunch of bandits? They wanted the release of their friends in Kuwait, and that was the end of the matter. Waite said he was confident something could be done for the Dawa 17. He promised to travel to Kuwait and deliver letters on behalf of the kidnappers to their jailed relatives. Then the meeting broke up. As Waite left the room, Mugniyeh seemed almost to issue a threat. Time was at a premium, said Mugniyeh. Something needed to be done, and it needed to be done soon. Waite was driven back to Mroueh's surgery, from where he returned to Terry Anderson's apartment.

The next day a triumphant Waite gave a press conference at the Commodore at which he announced, 'There is absolutely no doubt at all that I have got through to the right people and that a measure of trust has been established.' Waite was jubilant, but whether the kidnappers, who regarded publicity as an unnecessary vanity, shared Waite's enthusiasm for trumpeting his every achievement to the world was another matter. Even so, the successful meeting with Mugniyeh was undoubtedly the high point of Terry Waite's career as an independent humanitarian. He had shown that, simply by virtue of his good will, sincerity and sheer guts, it was possible for him to open doors which were closed to others. The big challenge now was to see what Waite could do with the opportunity he had been given.

13

NO WAY OUT

Champagne was served in the first-class compartment, almost as if the hostages' release was already assured, when Terry Waite took the next flight back to London. On arrival at Heathrow he was told by his office at Lambeth Palace that Oliver North was waiting to see him at the nearby Penta Hotel. An American official who had been sent by the State Department 'to keep an eye on Ollie' was taken aback at how well Waite and North seemed to know each other. 'It was as though they were both playing some kind of big game,' the official recalled. 'You could tell they were both very excited. Waite seemed to enjoy the game he was playing, all the daring-do and playing hide-and-seek with the press. He was having a ball.'

The official was also surprised by the inane questions North asked Waite. When Waite said he had embraced the kidnappers, North asked him: 'How did they smell?' North was also keen to know if Waite's radio had worked properly. The two men talked for an hour, during which North pressed Waite for as many details as possible about his trip. North was still exploring the possibility of launching a rescue operation to recover the hostages, something he had not confided to Waite.

Nor did North confide that the Americans were well advanced in their second plan to get the Israelis to send another shipment of arms to Teheran. This time the Iranians wanted Hawk anti-aircraft missiles to shoot down the Iraqi jets which were nightly laying waste to Iran. The arms shipment was due to arrive in Teheran on November 22, and Ghorbanifar promised more American hostages would be released. North told Waite he wanted him to go back to Beirut for the hostage release. This must have come as a surprise to Waite, who had just left Beirut having been told by Mugniyeh that it was up to Waite whether the hostages would be released. There were specific requirements for the release of further hostages, and Waite had not even started to deal with them. Foremost among the requirements was that Waite should go to Kuwait. Given North's persuasive nature, it is possible he could have led Waite to understand a hostage release was on the cards because of his own historic meeting with the kidnappers. Waite was still on such a high he was not in the mood to dispute anything North told him. Waite agreed to get the next flight back. Before he left, North presented him with a belt with a tracking device fitted to it. The belt could be used to locate Waite if he got into difficulties. It could also be used to lead North and his friends to the kidnappers' hideout, if they should agree to another meeting. Waite categorically denies he ever wore the belt, but some of the officials who were with North believe that Waite, who had a fascination for electronic gadgets, found it impossible to ignore North's intriguing offer.

Waite returned to Beirut on November 18, four days before the arms shipment was due to take place. This time the militias had worked out a deal between themselves, so there were no unseemly scenes at the airport. From now on Waite would be guarded by Druze bodyguards personally selected by Walid Jumblatt. And whatever reservations Waite may have harboured about returning to Lebanon so soon, they were not apparent at the press conference he gave on his return. His mood was upbeat. He said he was 'pleased to be back' and 'optimistic' of getting the hostages freed. He would return to his 'secret hideout' – Terry Anderson's apartment – to resume contact with Islamic Jihad. He said the kidnappers realised he was on a 'religious and humanitarian' mission, and he was greatly encouraged by this. 'I would like to thank the captors of the four American hostages for placing their trust in me. They took the risk and they should know I will honour their trust.'

Nor was Waite in any doubt about the importance of his mission compared with developments taking place in other parts of the world. On November 16, two days before Waite's return to Beirut, President Reagan had flown to Geneva for the breakthrough summit with Mikhail Gorbachev, leader of the Soviet Union. Waite saw his mission to Lebanon as being on an equal footing with the momentous events unfolding in Geneva. 'The eyes of the world are focused on two places, Geneva and Beirut,' declared Waite. There could be 'no better opportunity for the dignity and honour of Islam to be shown to the whole world than now' – by the release of the hostages.

Whether the kidnappers shared Waite's grand vision was another matter. It is more than likely his premature return only served to arouse their suspicions. Only a few days previously, Waite had left Lebanon promising to go to Kuwait. Now here he was back in Beirut, having been nowhere near Kuwait. And it must have seemed to the kidnappers that Waite was talking in riddles. 'I believe that last time was a good step forward. I think now it's possible to take another step forward,' said Waite. The appearance of the Iranian in their midst must also have unnerved the kidnappers. As far as the hostages could tell, the kidnappers were being persuaded to open a dialogue with Waite by the Iranian. It is doubtful whether the Iranian told the kidnappers about the arms shipments. The kidnappers were not interested in Iran's problems; their only concern was the Kuwait prisoners, and it is unlikely that Mugniyeh would have allowed a single hostage to be released had he known the real reason for the Iranian's insistence that he talk to Waite. When the Iranian government said it did not control the kidnap groups in Lebanon, but had 'influence' over them, this was the kind of relationship they were talking about.

Waite went to Anderson's apartment and waited for the kidnappers to make contact on the shortwave radio. Mugniyeh was not going to risk another face-to-face meeting; to do so would have jeopardised the whole hostage programme. Thus when the kidnappers called up Waite, it was to express their surprise that he had returned so soon without even attempting to explore their demands. Waite replied that the Americans had said they would support his application to go to Kuwait. The kidnappers were bemused. What did the Americans have to do with Waite's visit to Kuwait? If he wanted to go to Kuwait, he should ask the Kuwaitis, not the Americans. Time, they reminded Waite, was running short. This was not a game. Lives were at risk, and it would be better for all concerned if Waite paid attention to the demands they had set out at their first meeting.

Waite called back to North, who had returned to Washington to supervise the latest arms transfer. He told him the kidnappers did not seem to be in the mood to release hostages. To Waite's surprise, North said his assessment was probably right. North's inadequate organisational skills had struck again; this time the arms shipment had gone badly wrong. After a series of delays, the anti-aircraft missiles had arrived in Iran, only for the Iranians to discover that they were the wrong kind. More to the point, they were covered in Israel's national symbol, the Star of David. The Iranians were furious and thought they had been cheated. Ghorbanifar phoned up North in a highly emotional state to tell him no hostages would be released. North had also directly ignored an order from McFarlane that no weapons should be delivered to Iran before the hostages had been released.

There was no option but for Waite to return to London and get on with fulfilling the promises he had made to the kidnappers. Waite went to the Associated Press building, across the street from the Commodore Hotel, to prepare for a final press conference before flying home. His return to Beirut, far from living up to the lurid expectations he had raised on his arrival, had achieved very little. The kidnappers had refused to grant another meeting, even though Waite requested one, and told him they would not see him until progress had been made on their conditions. At the AP office, however, Waite continued to give the impression that everything was proceeding according to plan. He made his usual round of phone calls which, to the journalists working in an adjoining room, made Waite look impressive. There were several calls to Washington, one to Samir Habiby in New York and one to Lambeth Palace. Waite was clearly a very busy man at the centre of a very important assignment. As the time for the press conference neared, all the journalists who had travelled to Lebanon to cover Waite's mission were gathering in the hotel lobby when, without warning, pandemonium erupted.

Because Waite had become the primary focus of attention, no one had taken much notice of the ominous signs that trouble was brewing. After so many years of civil war, the inhabitants of Beirut had developed a sixth sense that told them when the fighting was about to recommence (one of the reasons why so many civilians survived the fearful battering the city suffered). With hardly a word being spoken, streets would clear and offices empty while shopkeepers pulled down their iron shutters. Within minutes streets that had been filled with the bustle of city life were deserted. Journalists covering the war adhered strictly to the maxim that the moment they found themselves in an empty street, they were in deep trouble. In the few minutes that we had been gathering for Waite's press conference, the street outside the Commodore had quietly emptied.

At about the time Waite should have been walking across to the hotel, a battered old Morris 1100 came chugging along the deserted street. Inside was a middle-aged Lebanese man, his wife and sister-in-law, all dressed in black, returning from the funeral of the man's sister. A few yards after they passed the hotel lobby, the car indicated to turn right, and as it did so the deafening roar of a heavy machine-gun being fired at close range filled the air. Bullets ripped into the Morris's windscreen hitting the driver in the head and killing him instantly. The car careered out of control and crashed into a shop, shuddering to a halt, with the two hysterical women trapped inside with the dead driver. As the journalists rushed outside to see what was happening, I witnessed the most remarkable act of personal bravery I have ever seen. While the majority of us, with bullets still flying all over the place, stood rooted to the spot by the sheer horror of what was happening, two young Turkish photographers ran into the street and waved their arms frantically at the gunners to cease firing. There was a brief lull while the photographers ran to the driver's door and dragged the body into the street. But as they tried to help the two women out of the car, the gunmen, their suspicions aroused, started firing again. With bullets crashing into masonry all around them, the photographers managed to yank the women out of the car and brought them to the safety of the hotel lobby.

The flag war, as it was to become known, was just one among many pointless skirmishes between the rival militias which simply added to the general atmosphere of lawlessness that had overtaken Beirut. The violence, which was to keep Terry Waite trapped in Beirut for forty-eight hours, began when Amal militiamen attempted to raise the Lebanese national flag on the roof of the television station to mark the country's independence day celebrations. For all the havoc they had wreaked on their country, the Amal militiamen still harboured strong feelings of patriotism. They looked forward to the day when the civil war was over and Shia Muslims would be given their rightful positions of power within the existing Lebanese constitutional framework. This position was rigorously opposed by Walid Jumblatt and his Druze followers. They were convinced the Lebanese constitution would always favour their bitter enemies, the Christians, and argued that the only way the Muslims would ever get a fair deal would be to defeat the Christians and frame a new constitution. To the Druze, the Lebanese flag represented the supremacy of the Christians, while for Amal the flag represented their aspirations for the future. Relations between the two militias, which only eighteen months previously had combined to take control of the city, were now so bad that when the Druze attempted to prevent the Amal gunmen from raising the flag, another miserable chapter in Lebanon's interminable conflict was opened.

For those of us trapped at the Commodore, it was like February 1984 all over again. The shooting of the elderly man in the Morris 1100 turned out to be the opening round of a bloody street battle between Amal and Druze which continued unabated for two days, with the Commodore the centre of the battleground. Not that the fighting was simply over a matter of principle. The area around the Commodore had become a centre for the illegal gambling dens which were a lucrative source of income for the militias – one had even been opened in the hotel basement. The profits from the casinos, which had no overheads to speak of, were such that men, especially militiamen, were prepared to die rather than let them fall into rival hands.

As was usually the case in the Lebanese civil war, however, it was rarely the militiamen who died, but the civilians caught in the crossfire. With so many journalists trapped in the hotel, the militiamen were more image-conscious than ever. Soon after the fighting started, a group of Amal gunmen had positioned themselves outside the hotel, and were firing machine-guns, automatic rifles and rocket-propelled grenades in the general direction of the Druze. For the camera crews, who had been required to subsist on a diet of endless Terry Waite press conferences, the fighting was a heaven-sent opportunity to do something different. A rapport was quickly established between the crews and the gunmen. At a given signal, the militiaman would run into the street and empty a magazine of bullets in the vague direction of the enemy. If the crew were not satisfied with the shot, the militiamen were quite happy to do a re-run. The whole scenario resembled a Hollywood film set, except these gunmen were firing live ammunition, and scores of people, most of them civilians, were being killed and wounded. But it made great television.

Terry Waite was in no way intimidated by the chaos unfolding all around him. On the contrary, he seemed to revel in it; the whole world would now understand fully how much of a risk he was taking by coming to Lebanon. Far from going into hiding, Waite was happy to accommodate the requirements of the press. At the AP office, he posed for a photograph lying on the floor, telephone in hand. The picture was duly published in the British newspapers the following morning, together with stories about how the Anglican churchman was continuing his mission in spite of the fighting raging all around. Even more audacious was an interview Waite conducted with Brent Sadler of ITN, who discovered that from the Commodore bedrooms he could look into the AP office.

Sadler telephoned Waite at AP and asked him to go to a certain window where the ITN cameras could film him. Waite obliged and, while the cameras filmed him smiling and waving, Sadler conducted an interview by telephone. The interview was scarely audible for the noise of weapons being fired in the street below, but when he was able to make himself heard above the din, Waite told Sadler the fighting was 'an inconvenience', but that it would not affect his mission which 'was continuing'. Asked what he had been doing during the fighting, Waite replied he had taken a shower and was relaxing by reading a book. Sadler's interview made great television and was given the prime spot on the News at Ten. The pictures were also shown on Lebanese television that evening, and were presumably watched by the kidnappers. Sadler received a telex from the ITN editors in London congratulating him on his fine work.

Whatever Waite said in public about his mission, the truth was that he had made barely any progress. He was constantly on the phone to various parts of the world, but many of the calls were for an idle chat with contacts to see what was going on. Very little of substance was discussed, because Waite had very little to say. At one point during the fighting, an official at the Episcopal Church centre in New York was asked by Samir Habiby to listen in on an important conference call he was about to arrange between himself, Terry Waite in Beirut, and an 'American official' – Oliver North – in Washington. The church official thought he was being invited to listen to something which would give him an insight as to what Waite was doing in Beirut. He was to be disappointed.

When Waite came on the line, the sound of gunfire was clearly discernible in the background.

'Howya doing, Terry?' inquired North. 'Christ, it sounds like the days when I was out in Vietnam.'

'Everything's just fine, Ollie,' replied Waite. 'Just a little local difficulty. Nothing to get too excited about.'

'I hope you're keeping your head down. We can't afford for anything to happen to you, Terry,' said North.

'Don't worry, Ollie,' said Waite. 'I'm being well looked after by my friends here. I'll be perfectly OK. As soon as it's all over I'll be flying back to London.'

'That sounds like a good idea to me, Terry,' said North. 'No need to hang around any longer than necessary. Lebanon can get to be a mighty dangerous place.'

And so the conversation went on for a few more minutes, before the line went dead. As the church official remarked to a colleague, it was hardly worth the effort of making the call.

On the second day of the fighting, the warring militias actually agreed on a temporary ceasefire to allow Waite to move from the AP office to the Commodore. Waite was provided with a flak jacket and, flanked by a militia escort which barely reached above his waist in height, made a quick twenty-yard dash into the hotel. The appearance of Waite in a flak jacket and tin helmet provoked a near riot from the cameramen as they jostled for the best position from which to photograph the beaming churchman. Waite took it all in his stride and, after announcing that he was going to catch up on his sleep and listen to Schumann on his Walkman, he took the lift to his suite on the seventh floor.

While Waite was resting upstairs, by far the most bizarre incident of the flag war occurred. A group of journalists had gathered at the bar which, because it was surrounded on three sides by brick walls, was considered one of the safest places in the hotel. From the bar, they could look out across the swimming pool. On the far side of the patio, the pool was shaded by cypress trees. Occasionally the branches would shake as they were raked by bullets fired along the street outside. To see the trees moving was a reassuring sight, because it meant the fighters were firing along the street and away from the hotel. At first nobody took much notice when the trees began to shake more violently. It was only when about twelve militiamen, their heads covered by balaclavas and carrying rocket-propelled grenade launchers on their backs, dropped from the trees and began to run straight towards the bar that the impromptu drinking session came to halt.

The Amal gunmen who had done such sterling work for the cameras were apparently on the retreat, and our new companions, it transpired, were Druze militiamen who were going to protect the hotel and make sure no harm came to Terry Waite. As if to prove their point, and sensitive of the fact the cameras were again trained on them, one militiaman ran out into the street and fired a rocket-propelled grenade, a highly destructive anti-tank round, at the first building that came into his sights. Again this totally unnecessary act of violence made great television but the militiaman was so preoccupied with performing to camera that he omitted to adopt the correct firing position. The shock caused by firing the weapon travelled through his body into his testicles, so that our hero doubled up with the most intense pain. Oblivious to his audience, he staggered back into the hotel and made his way to the bar where he screamed at the barman to give him a glass of cold water. He ripped open his trousers and poured the soothing liquid over his inflamed genitalia.

Later that evening Waite, looking refreshed after a good sleep and a bath, joined us at the bar. The fighting was beginning to subside, and Waite had been told by senior militia officials that he would be free to leave the next morning. For all the stress of the previous two days, Waite looked remarkably relaxed and wanted to hear all about the militiaman's painful experience. It was the first time I had been given the opportunity to talk to Waite since our flight from London.

'How's everything going with you?' he asked. 'Have you managed to get everything back to the *Telegraph* OK?' I replied that the Commodore telex machines had again served me admirably.

'And what are they doing with my story?' he asked. My story? I was slightly bemused. Most of what I had written had focused on the fighting between the militias and the sixty people who had been killed. I was writing about the Lebanese civil war. Terry Waite had simply suffered the misfortune of being caught in Beirut when the fighting resumed. The fighting was nothing to do with him personally. I said I had no idea how the story was being presented in London, because I had not seen any British newspapers for several days. I became increasingly more irritated as, having established how the *Daily Telegraph* was handling the 'Waite story', he proceeded to seek out the correspondents of ITN and BBC news to see what coverage they were giving him. It made me wonder about the real reason for Waite's mission to Lebanon. Why did he have this obsession with his own publicity? Why was he being so accommodating to the international media while engaged on a mission of the most profound delicacy and secrecy?

Not all members of the international media were as tolerant of Waite as the British. Scores of American journalists had returned to Beirut for the Waite mission, the first time they had ventured into Lebanon for many months. They felt particularly vulnerable because they were the most visible Americans in Beirut, and considered themselves prime kidnapping material. One American television journalist, who had covered the Middle East for many years, confronted Waite directly when he discovered him socialising at the bar.

'I don't know what the fuck you're doing here,' said the

American, 'but we're putting our goddam lives on the line for you, and if you're not careful, someone's going to get killed.'

'But my dear fellow,' countered Waite, trying to calm the American down, 'nobody is forcing you to be here. You can go any time you like. I have to be here for my mission, but that does not mean to say other people must risk their lives in Beirut.'

'Don't give me that shit,' the American replied, working himself into even more of a temper. 'So long as you're here, the American television companies want pictures of you, and that means we've got to be here to take them. So every day longer you stay here, the longer we have to stay, and the more we have to put our lives on the line.'

That night the militia leaders arranged yet another ceasefire which managed to halt the fighting. The next morning we were able to move outside the hotel for the first time in three days, and Waite decided to make the most of the lull and leave the country. After breakfast he appeared wearing the bullet-proof vest, climbed into the back of a Mercedes and headed off for the airport, smiling and waving for the cameras. He was driven at breakneck speed through the city, past the burnt-out wrecks of buildings and cars. At the airport he described the journey as an 'invigorating experience' and said he would return to Beirut once he had flown to the US for talks with Reagan administration officials.

As Waite flew back to Europe to resume his international troubleshooting, the war-weary Lebanese began the soul-destroying business of clearing up the mess. By far the saddest discovery made by the rescue teams as they combed the rubble for dead and injured were the bodies of fifteen children who had sought refuge in an apartment block which had suffered a direct hit from a rocket-propelled grenade.

To restore some semblance of law and order, the Amal and

Druze militiamen attempted to form joint vigilante patrols, with the intention of bringing renegade militiamen into line. Summary executions were carried out of militiamen who refused to obey orders, but it had little effect. Law and order in Beirut was rapidly becoming a lost cause, and a few more deaths were not going to make much difference.

Somewhere in the southern suburbs, no more than a mile from the main airport terminal buildings, four Americans were nervously twiddling the dials of their shortwave radio, hoping against hope that the next time they heard Terry Waite was returning to Lebanon he would not leave without them.

A few days after Waite left Beirut, I met two of the most important political figures in Lebanon, Walid Jumblatt and Sheikh Fadlallah. In their different ways, both had a direct bearing on Waite's mission and its chances of success. Jumblatt was responsible for Waite's security in Beirut while Fadlallah was in direct contact with the kidnappers. As the spiritual figurehead of the Islamic fundamentalist movement in Lebanon, no one exercised as much influence over the activities of Mugniyeh and his gang as Fadlallah.

For the first meeting I drove to the Chouf mountains with a Dutch colleague to have lunch with Walid Jumblatt at his castle at Mukhtara. I wanted to talk to him about the behaviour of his fighters in Beirut, and to inquire why he could not patch up his political differences with the other Shia leaders rather than tolerate the appalling consequences of inter-militia squabbling such as I had recently witnessed. I also wanted to know what the chances were for the release of the hostages. The two-hour journey from Beirut was like driving into another world. After the smouldering, semi-derelict city I found the imposing mountain landscape of the Chouf had remained untouched by twentieth-century technology. Druze elders still padded about in baggy trousers with their heads adorned by short, fez-like hats. As the undisputed head of the 200,000 members of the Druze tribes, Jumblatt's mornings were spent attending to his feudal responsibilities, whether settling an argument over land rights, or helping to arrange a marriage. When I arrived, Jumblatt, who was then thirty-six years old, was in an ante-room concluding the morning's business. I was shown into a large banqueting hall bedecked with family and Islamic insignia. It was rumoured that Jumblatt had acquired an impressive collection of Nazi memorabilia which he kept in the castle dungeons, but that, for some inexplicable reason, the collection had somehow perished when the Israelis invaded Lebanon.

Apart from administering the Chouf mountains, Jumblatt was highly successful at pursuing his own international diplomacy. A committed socialist who had helped to bring a hint of 1960s revolutionary fervour to the normally conservative campus of the AUB, Jumblatt had recently concluded his own co-operation treaty with Moscow, in return for which he had received a consignment of Soviet T-72 tanks. Jumblatt liked to boast that none of his recent ancestors had died in their beds. His grandfather had been hanged by the Turks, while his father, Kamal, one of the most sophisticated socialist thinkers in the Middle East, was killed by a Syrian car-bomb in 1976. Perhaps the fact that Jumblatt did not take his own longevity for granted explained his relaxed attitude to life. Though his long, hooked nose and bulbous eyes hardly qualified him for *Playgirl* pin-up of the month, he had something of a reputation as a playboy, and often spent riotous weekends in Rome with a racy crowd of Italian friends. He was also said to have a penchant for the indigenous hashish crop, which accounted for his more outlandish political statements and decisions.

Jumblatt was a charming host as we sat down to lunch in the banqueting hall with militia friends of his from Beirut.

Liveried attendants served vintage claret while Jumblatt, dressed in jeans, tee-shirt and tennis pumps, outlined his political philosophy for Lebanon. (Many years later I was surprised to find him dining at the Travellers' in London's Pall Mall dressed in a smart, two-piece Savile Row suit.) The reason for all the problems in Beirut, Jumblatt explained, was that Druze fighters hated leaving the Chouf. The Druze were a mountain people, happy only in the mountains. But they had been forced to go to Beirut because they were the best fighters, and they were needed to keep law and order. But many good Druze men had been corrupted in the city and lost their way. He had forty of his own fighters locked up in the castle because they had 'misbehaved' in the city. Some of the worst offenders had even been executed. Such doctrinaire behaviour hardly squared with Jumblatt's socialist beliefs, I observed. 'Ah yes,' he countered, 'but you have to understand that first I am a Druze leader, and then I am a socialist.'

He told me that he had not met Terry Waite, but that he was happy for his men to act as his bodyguards. 'It's better for them to look after Waite than run brothels and casinos,' he said with a sardonic chuckle. But did he think Waite would be successful in getting the hostages released? 'He will need to have a lot of luck. There are thousands of hostages in Lebanon, so why make such a fuss about a few foreigners? In a perfect world all the hostages in Lebanon would be released, but Lebanon is not a perfect world.' As we enjoyed a lazy, Mediterranean afternoon of relaxed conversation and good wine, I could not help feeling a sense of unease that the safety of a senior official of the Church of England had been placed in the hands of this eccentric, if engaging, feudal chieftain.

My second meeting was conducted in far less convivial surroundings and at considerably more risk to myself. A couple of days after lunching with Jumblatt, I drove into the southern suburbs to meet Sheikh Mohammed Hussein Fadlallah, who was in almost daily contact with the kidnappers. I drove with a Lebanese friend who was going to act as translator because Fadlallah refused to speak English, even though he knew the language. From the moment we entered the suburbs I felt as if the eyes of every bearded militiaman were focused upon me. As we pulled up outside Fadlallah's apartment, our car was immediately surrounded by Hizbollah guards, guns at the ready, who asked to see all my documents before even allowing me out of the car. Once they had confirmed my identity, I was escorted through a series of security gates, and taken by lift to Fadlallah's apartment on the fifth floor.

The apartment, in a newly-built residential block, was fairly unremarkable. There was the usual arrangement of oriental sofas and coffee tables with dishes of sweets. Fadlallah was sitting in a high-backed reading chair. Behind him a portrait of Ayatollah Khomeini hung on the wall. Fadlallah's thick, grey beard nestled on his black cleric's tunic, and as I introduced myself he merely nodded his acknowledgement, as though he had far more pressing matters on his mind. I had come to ask him about the hostages and what could be done to secure their release, but before I could ask any questions, he launched into a lengthy monologue, rather in the manner of a teacher delivering a lecture, about the guilt the West had to bear for what was happening to Lebanon. The fighting between the Lebanese militias was all part of a conspiracy between the Western intelligence services to destroy Lebanon. It was the West that made the militias fight each other. Left to themselves, they would be able to work together. Everywhere he looked he saw the hand of foreign intelligence agents – Mossad, MI6, CIA, KGB. They were responsible for the ruination of Lebanon. And what could a small country like Lebanon do against the great superpowers? Lebanon could not fight the US by conventional means, so the Lebanese had to find their own methods to defeat the Americans.

Clearly Fadlallah's paranoia knew no bounds. Eventually I was allowed to ask a question. What does the Sheikh think of Mr Waite's mission to Lebanon? I asked when the monologue had come to end. Fadlallah was noncommittal.

'I have not met Mr Waite so I have not had a chance to evaluate him. He is a man of God so he should be treated as such. I would like to have the hostage problem solved because they are only the victims of US policy. I have made efforts myself to have the hostages freed, but I have met with no success.' If Fadlallah could not get the hostages released, what chance did Terry Waite stand? Having said his piece, Fadlallah concluded the interview with a bow of his head. He padded off to his private quarters in an old pair of slippers. As I left, a distinct chill ran down my spine as I felt so many keen pairs of Hizbollah eyes taking in my every move.

Having accomplished the dangerous part of his mission – meeting the kidnappers – Terry Waite now had to deal with the difficult part, trying to get the hostages released. Waite had promised the kidnappers that, at the very least, he would travel to Kuwait and visit the Dawa 17 prisoners. Waite had done something similar when negotiating with Libya for the release of the four Britons the previous year. He had visited Durham jail to see four Libyans held on remand for terrorist offences. But going to Kuwait was a more complicated proposition. The Kuwaitis had already demonstrated their resolve not to capitulate over the Dawa 17, even when faced with the systematic terrorist campaign waged against them by Islamic Jihad. The Kuwaitis were anxious, moreover, that no link be established between the hostages in Lebanon and the prisoners in Kuwait. If Waite, who had just met with the kidnappers amid a blaze of international publicity, was to visit Kuwait for the sole purpose of meeting the Dawa 17, such a link would be clearly established. The Kuwaitis therefore had no hesitation in refusing Waite a visa to enter their country. Announcing the decision, an official at the Kuwaiti embassy in London commented: 'Mr Waite would be welcomed here as a tourist, but this is not a tourist country.'

The Kuwaiti decision constituted a considerable setback to Waite, and placed his conduct of the Lebanon mission in a new light. Had he gone to Lebanon without all the attendant publicity and met with the kidnappers secretly, it might have been possible for the Kuwaitis to allow him to make a similarly secretive visit to Kuwait. But shunning publicity was not the way Waite operated. He believed his credentials as an 'independent humanitarian' depended upon achieving maximum publicity for his missions. That way, all parties concerned could see that he had nothing to hide. The problem with the Waite philosophy was that, at the same time as achieving maximum publicity, he was also attempting to conceal vital information. In Beirut Waite repeatedly said he had confidential information that he was not at liberty to divulge. By the very act of saying this, however, he was both whetting people's appetites for more information, and giving the distinct impression that the key to the successful resolution of the problem lay in Terry Waite. Waite was giving a performance of consummate showmanship; but as with every circus act, the greatest disappointment occurs when the illusion can no longer be sustained.

There were many areas of Waite's activities outside Lebanon that he preferred to keep to himself. After leaving Lebanon for the second time, he flew directly to New York for a meeting with Oliver North. North expressed his regret that no more hostages had been released, but told Waite nothing about the failure of the second arms shipment to Iran. Sitting in the apartment of the Presiding Bishop of the Episcopal Church in Manhattan, Waite and North listened as Samir Habiby translated the letters the kidnappers had written to their relatives jailed in Kuwait. The letters were in Arabic, and North wanted to see if they contained clues or secret codes; no one seemed to consider the morality of opening private correspondence which had been handed to Waite in sealed envelopes on the explicit understanding that he would respect their confidentiality.

Waite believed that the more his stature as an international figure increased, the less the Kuwaitis would be able to resist his request for a visa. But as Islamic Jihad had found when carrying out their terrorist campaign, the more pressure was applied on the Kuwaitis, the more obstinate they became. Waite and North agreed that a meeting with a senior American government official in Washington would show the Kuwaitis that he had the full backing of the United States. Waite wanted to see President Reagan, but he was out of the country. George Bush, the Vice-President, however, was an Episcopalian, and John Allen, the Presiding Bishop, offered to arrange a meeting. On November 26 Waite flew down to Washington to see Bush at the White House. Waite's appearance put the American government in a quandary. The official policy of the Reagan administration was to support Kuwait's refusal to release the prisoners, so that when Waite told Bush that he wanted to visit Kuwait to discuss the issue of the prisoners, Bush said there was little he could do to help. The only purpose of the meeting, which Oliver North attended, was to raise Waite's profile as someone the American government was taking seriously. When the meeting ended, Waite gave an interview on the White House lawn in which he repeated his desire to have a meeting with the Kuwaiti authorities. Waite's appeal was nothing more than a glorified publicity stunt, and the Kuwaitis saw it as such. No visa was forthcoming.

Waite might have been frustrated by his lack of progress, but this was not the impression he gave as he commuted between New York and London. His performance in Lebanon, especially when he was caught up in the fighting at the Commodore Hotel, had turned him into a national figure in the US. Every time he flew into New York, the television cameras were waiting to record his every move. Waite was taking America by storm. At the Episcopal Church headquarters in Manhattan, a buzz of excitement filled the normally drab office every time Waite entered. Waite spent most of his time working with Samir Habiby, and the two deliberately added to the aura surrounding Terry Waite by refusing to divulge what they were up to. Lord Runcie remembers feeling slightly uncomfortable about Waite's activities in America from about this time.

'There was always something a bit grandiose about Terry. He would phone me up at Canterbury at strange times of the day and night and say, "Hello, Robert, I'm phoning you from the White House, so I can't say much." It made me wonder why he had phoned in the first place.' The staff at Lambeth Palace, including Runcie, had only a vague idea of where Waite was and what he was doing. Runcie himself was far more preoccupied with the doctrinal concerns of the Church of England. While Waite was travelling the world, Runcie was overseeing the publication of one of the most important documents of his primacy, *Faith in the City*, which would provide a damning indictment of government policy in Britain's inner city areas.

Waite refused to accept the Kuwait rejection, and following intensive behind-the-scenes lobbying by Habiby and his contacts in the Middle East, the Kuwaitis finally agreed to meet Waite at a neutral location, so long as there was no publicity and the Kuwaitis could claim, if asked, that no such meeting had taken place. Habiby worked out the details, and on December 18 Waite flew to Geneva. Before he left, he could not resist the temptation to confide in Brent Sadler, his friend at ITN, what he was up to. Habiby was furious when he found out, and made Waite change rooms as soon as he arrived in Geneva, so as to stop Sadler pestering them. Word quickly spread, however, that Waite was in Geneva, and suddenly Waite was besieged with press inquiries about what he was up to. For once Waite was angered by the press interest and actually told one inquirer, 'I don't want to speak, I'm not here.' Habiby had arranged a meeting with the Kuwaiti ambassador to the United Nations at his residence in Geneva, and Waite was to be Habiby's guest.

Waite and Habiby experienced the full force of the Kuwaitis' determination not to concede an inch as far as the Dawa prisoners were concerned. Waite said he wanted to improve contacts between the prisoners and their relatives in Lebanon, and asked whether the Kuwaitis would allow him to deliver the letters he had been given in Beirut. The ambassador expressed surprise that the prisoners should be singled out for special treatment. They were being treated perfectly adequately, and if their relatives wanted to write to them they should use the postal service, the same as everyone else. Waite pleaded with him that 'lives were at stake', a familiar Waite refrain. The ambassador replied that the Red Cross was the proper channel through which humanitarian work should be conducted, and that Kuwait was reluctant to grant Waite permission to visit the prisoners because to do so would be to link them directly to 'another country'.

The Kuwaitis' suspicions about the dangers of dealing with Terry Waite were confirmed the next day when a Gulf newspaper carried a report of Waite's meeting with Kuwaiti 'officials' in Geneva. It was simply not possible to have dealings with Waite and expect them to remain secret, and given the sensitivity of the subject, the Kuwaitis resolved to have no further dealings with the Anglican churchman. It was a bitter blow for Waite's mission, but Waite remained optimistic. He gave such an upbeat report of the meeting to Oliver North that North later wrote in his diary: 'December 19th. Waite called. Reports friendly meeting with Kuwaitis.'

Waite had one last trick up his sleeve, a trick that had served him well in the past. He would go to Lebanon and ask the kidnappers to give him a hostage for Christmas. In 1980 in Iran and in 1984 in Libya, Waite had made Christmas visits which had resulted in hostages being released; why not Lebanon? On December 20 Waite flew back to Beirut. This time few journalists accompanied him. After the chaos of the last mission, journalists who knew the Middle East could see little point in risking their lives to follow Waite to Lebanon if the Kuwaitis were refusing to do business with him. The kidnappers had made it perfectly clear during a terrorist campaign that had lasted nearly two years that they had one immutable condition for the release of the hostages, the release of the Kuwait prisoners. Christmas, with all its association with Western decadence and the hated Christian militiamen on the other side of the Green Line, simply did not enter into their calculations.

Thus when Waite arrived in Beirut and, at his first press conference, tried to invoke the spirit of Christmas, he received short shrift from the kidnappers. Furious that Waite had betrayed their trust in him, and that he had even dared to return without fulfilling his promise to go to Kuwait, they contacted him by shortwave radio. There was absolutely no question of the kidnappers having another meeting with Waite, they told him. As Waite later told officials in the US, the kidnappers were 'upset' that he had nothing more concrete to offer them than the season's greetings. They told him he had twenty-four hours to leave Lebanon, or he would be a dead man. Waite got the next plane back to London and arrived in time to spend Christmas at home in Blackheath, a rare treat for Waite's wife and four children.

The news that Terry Waite had made a third visit to Lebanon and had still returned home emptyhanded was received with stunned disbelief by the four American hostages. For nearly a month, every time they tuned into the BBC World Service they had heard about Waite's mission, which led them to believe they would be free by Christmas. The realisation that they were no nearer to freedom plunged them into the depths of depression. So great was their despair that even their guards took pity on them. After Father Jenco had led the small group in a short religious celebration of Christmas, the guards came into their cell and told them to raise their blindfolds. As they did so, they saw that a small birthday cake, covered in burning candles, had been placed on the cell floor. 'Happy birthday, Jesus,' sang the guards in their heavily accented English.

A few days later when the guards brought the hostages food, Tom Sutherland asked when they thought Terry Waite would be coming back.

'Terry Waite will not be coming back,' said the guard. 'Terry Waite is a very bad man. Terry Waite has promised us many things, but he has done nothing. We told Terry Waite to leave, otherwise we will kill him. He will not come back. We do not want him to come back to Lebanon ever again.'

While the Americans had to come to terms with the fact that Waite's mission had failed, the French hostages who were being held in the same block had to live with a far more traumatic challenge. Since the summer of 1985 the condition of Michel Seurat, the young writer and academic who had been kidnapped the previous May, had steadily declined. Elie Hallak, or Dr Death as the French had named him, diagnosed that Seurat was suffering from a form of viral hepatitis, and prescribed a strict diet and lots of mineral water. But Seurat was in need of constant professional medical care which the guards were not able to provide. Clearly feeling an element of guilt about Seurat's worsening condition, in August 1985 the guards had allowed Seurat to visit his wife and daughter for a day. After that, however, Seurat's condition deteriorated rapidly. His skin turned yellow and he started to cough. Hallak visited him regularly, and on one occasion when he was treating the delirious Seurat, he confided to the other Frenchmen – Marcel Carton, Marcel Fontaine and Jean-Paul Kauffmann – that he feared for his life because the guards never blindfolded him. 'It's a bad sign,' said the doctor. 'It means they're going to give me the chop.'

Seurat was found to have a red corpuscle deficiency in his blood, and one of the kidnappers donated blood which was given to Seurat by a crude method of transfusion. One of the guards joked about the grisly operation which Hallak performed each night. 'Seurat, you are becoming a Shia,' said the guard. 'You have the same blood as us now.' Just before Christmas, however, the guards tired of Hallak's efforts, and he was no longer allowed to treat Seurat. The guards later admitted they had 'executed' the Jewish medic because he was a 'bad doctor'. Hallak was blamed for not curing Seurat. Hallak's few possessions were handed to the Frenchmen. They included his diary. Every day the doctor had written to his wife: 'Darling, the 239th day of captivity . . .'

Without proper medical attention, the thirty-eight-year-old Seurat realised he would not survive. 'I'm going to die here,' he announced to his colleagues one evening, and then asked to be moved to his own cell where he could die with dignity. For the next three months the three Frenchmen listened to the agonised coughing fits of their countryman through the walls as he slowly succumbed to his illness. Then one day in March 1986, in the early afternoon, the guards took away the Frenchmen's radio. Seurat had died, and they did not want them to hear the news. The kidnappers issued a statement saying Seurat had been 'executed' for being a secret agent.

14

MAD DOGS AND IRISHMEN

They called themselves the Daring Diners, a group of British friends who, in conscious defiance of the militia anarchy, would once a week arrange to meet at one of Beirut's few remaining restaurants. In any other part of the world, there would be nothing exceptional about a group of friends organising a night out. But in Beirut it had become a necessity. No one in the city dared to go out alone. The level of lawlessness had reached such a level that no one was safe from the risk of robbery, attack, kidnapping or worse. While the militias vainly tried to maintain order, the collapse of the Lebanese economy had resulted in crime reaching epidemic proportions. Armed gangs roamed the streets looking for likely targets. Anyone who looked as though they might have even the most modest amount of money was liable to be kidnapped, not to hold a Western government to ransom, but simply to get their friends or relatives to pay a few hundred dollars to secure their release.

The Daring Diners came into existence when they realised their only chance of leading anything approaching a normal life was to go out in large groups. The kidnappers were quite capable of kidnapping two or three people at one go, but to round up twelve or fourteen required a degree of organisation that was beyond the ordinary Lebanese street gangs. Most of them were teachers working either at the AUB or the numerous language schools which taught English to young Lebanese who dreamed of a new life abroad. In spite of the interminable fighting between the militias, the anarchy and the escalating kidnapping campaign, and in spite of repeated warnings from the Foreign Office for them to leave, seventy or so British subjects continued to live in West Beirut.

Most of them had been in Beirut for several years. Most of them were single, and did not have to worry about exposing their families to the everyday violence. Although the salaries were modest, they could live like kings. For a few hundred dollars a month it was possible to rent a beautiful apartment within walking distance of the Mediterranean. For less than a thousand dollars it was possible to buy a second-hand Mercedes, which could be used at weekends for driving to the exotic Lebanese beach resorts. The work was pleasant and not too demanding, and for a few dollars it was possible to dine out at the best restaurants in town. Even with the uncertainty caused by the civil war, life as a teacher in Beirut in the spring of 1986 was still a marked improvement on working for some god-forsaken polytechnic in the north of England. And even as the security situation in the city continued to deteriorate, the British community was able to reassure itself that, in the main, the kidnappers were not interested in British hostages; they were content keeping their basements filled with Americans and French.

Philip Padfield and Leigh Douglas, friends who had lived in West Beirut for several years, were two of the founding members of the Daring Diners. Padfield, who had just turned forty, had lived in Beirut since the early 1970s. From a family of farmers in Bideford, Devon, Padfield had arrived in Beirut to work for International House, a worldwide language school. Over the years he had worked his way up to being made director of the International Language School on Hamra Street. Padfield was a keen reader and film buff, and was always talking about the latest novel he had read. He was also renowned for his sense of humour and love of practical jokes. In many respects he was the antithesis of Douglas, although the two were the closest of friends. Douglas, who was thirty-four, originally came from a village in the Norfolk Broads. After studying Arabic at Lancaster University and the School of Oriental and African Studies in London, Douglas had spent a couple of years in Yemen completing his doctorate. A studious academic who derived great intellectual satisfaction from his work in the Middle East, Douglas accepted a research post at the AUB in the late 1970s. Padfield and Douglas, both bachelors, lived in apartments just a few minutes from each other. As two of the few single male expatriates still in Beirut, they were much in demand as escorts for the small group of women teachers.

Thursday March 27, 1986, was Maundy Thursday, and staff at the AUB were given a four-day break to celebrate Easter, a throwback to the days when the university was a Protestant college. To get the weekend off to the right start, Padfield and Douglas arranged to meet friends for dinner at the Spaghetteria restaurant on the seafront. By the time they sat down to dinner, about ten people, evenly divided between men and women, had arrived. As the group ordered Château Musar and food, the conversation moved from the usual gossip, such as who was dating whom, to the altogether more serious subject of the deteriorating security situation. Kidnapping by 'freelance' gangs was reaching epidemic proportions, to the extent that no nationality was safe. The indiscriminate nature of the kidnappings was reflected in the recent targets selected. Since the start of the year, these had included the Spanish ambassador and two of his Cuban employees, the second secretary at the South Korean embassy and a four-man French television crew. Moreover, one of the group at the Spaghetteria had been told by a Lebanese friend that the gangs were combing West Beirut trying to find out where the remaining foreigners were living. Peter Kemp, a close friend of both Padfield and Douglas, who combined his work as a teacher with freelance journalism, had learned that his building was being watched by unfriendly-looking militiamen, and had decided to cross the Green Line to East Beirut the next morning, just to be on the safe side.

This conversation added a rather sombre note to the evening, and in order to raise their spirits when the meal ended, several diners, including Padfield and Douglas, decided to move on to the Backstreet nightclub for a nightcap. The Backstreet, situated about 100 yards from the main AUB campus, was about the only Western-style bar still operating in West Beirut. With its dark interior decor and the constant beat of loud disco music, it was a popular haunt among expatriates. Backstreet was also well-known among the militias as the place where the *ajnabis*, the foreigners, went to enjoy themselves.

It was about 2 am when Padfield and Douglas said farewell to the small group of friends still propping up the bar. Someone had offered them a lift home, but as yet another round of drinks was ordered, the two decided they did not want to wait any longer. So they set off to walk the short distance to their apartments. It was a beautiful, starry night, and as they made their way through the rubble-strewn streets they could see the reflection of the new moon glistening on the waves of the Mediterranean below. It was a view they would never see again.

The next four days were a holiday, so the alarm was not raised until the next Tuesday when neither Padfield nor Douglas turned up for their classes. Friends had tried to phone them over the weekend, but assumed they had gone away somewhere when there was no reply. As soon as Peter Kemp was told that neither of them had turned up for work, he jumped in his car and drove to their apartments. He hammered on Padfield's door, but there was no reply. Then he went to Douglas's apartment. He could hear Douglas's pet dog howling inside. After banging on the door for several minutes, Kemp broke in. He found no trace of his friend. His bed had not been slept in, and the dog, judging by the mess it had made in the kitchen and its frenetic state, had been abandoned for several days. As other friends continued the search in other parts of the city, the bitter truth emerged that Padfield and Douglas had never made it home in the early hours of Good Friday morning. They had fallen victim to the kidnap gangs.

The abduction of Leigh Douglas and Philip Padfield meant there were three Britons now missing in Lebanon. The last that had been heard of Alec Collett, who had just marked his first year in captivity when Douglas and Padfield were taken, was the previous Christmas when Terry Waite was making the third and final visit of his 1985 mission to Beirut. While Waite was concentrating on getting the Americans released, the group holding Collett had issued another video to coincide with Waite's return to Lebanon, although Waite was too preoccupied to pay it much attention. The video showed Collett looking haggard, although he remained coherent. In the video, delivered to a Lebanese national newspaper office in Beirut, Collett said that 'in spite of the harsh conditions, I am enduring.' He appealed to Mrs Thatcher to respond to the kidnappers' demand, namely the release of two Arabs jailed in Britain for the attempted assassination of the Israeli ambassador. The fact that a second Collett video had been released was greeted with relief in Whitehall, as some officials were beginning to fear the worst as nothing had been heard about Collett for six months. The fact that the kidnappers indicated that they wanted 'a quiet end' to the Collett kidnapping was also taken as a promising sign.

But the Foreign Office, prompted no doubt by Downing Street, lost no time in restating the British government's policy of not doing deals with terrorists. The Foreign Office did, however, give the kidnappers a modicum of encouragement, asking them to get in touch directly with the British government. The British government would not do a deal, but it was quite prepared to talk. And, as every diplomat knows, once a dialogue has been established, what the outcome will be is anyone's guess.

A few weeks later, in January 1986, John Gray, who had recently taken over from David Miers as British ambassador in Lebanon, was contacted by Mustafa Saad, a leading Sunni Muslim from Sidon. Saad had played an active role in the Lebanese resistance against the Israeli occupation, and had been blinded by a letter-bomb sent to his home by the Israelis. After Beirut, Sidon had the largest concentration of Palestinian refugees in Lebanon and, in the wake of the Israeli invasion, the refugee camps had become hotbeds of radical Palestinian activism. Breakaway terrorist groups, such as Abu Nidal, were well-supported in the camps. Saad, as the leading Lebanese political figure in Sidon, had close links with the Palestinians, and contacted Gray to tell him that the kidnappers were prepared to release Collett if the British government would provide twelve kidney dialysis machines.

Gray was intrigued. He travelled to Sidon, a highly risky undertaking for a British ambassador given the security situation, to see Saad. Saad told him he was convinced that the people who had contacted him were genuine and were holding Collett. The kidney dialysis machines were wanted for the hospitals in the Palestinian refugee camps. The kidnappers had apparently thought of the idea after hearing that Collett's wife Elaine had undergone kidney treatment in New York.

The demand certainly constituted an improvement on the group's previous demands, which had allowed the British government no room for manoeuvre. No British government was going to allow the release of convicted terrorists from its jails. But a humanitarian gesture such as providing necessary medical equipment was another matter. Arrangements could be made for a charity like Oxfam to provide the equipment in return for Collett's release. That would not be a deal between the British government and the kidnappers as such, more an understanding. It was the kind of arrangement in which the Foreign Office was well versed, and Gray devoted the next few weeks to a vain attempt to keep the dialogue open.

'The problem was getting them to accept that the British government was not going to pay for the release,' Gray explained. 'They could not accept our logic. They could not accept that we were not going to do a deal.' This brief window of opportunity closed as quickly as it had opened. As soon as the British authorities responded to the initial approach, the kidnappers began to add more demands to their initial request for medical equipment. They had made the opening offer simply to get the British interested. Once the British had indicated they were prepared to listen, the kidnappers proceeded to increase their demands until they were back to the position set out in the videotapes – Collett in return for Arab prisoners in British jails.

'It quickly became a dialogue of the deaf,' recalls Gray. 'We simply could not convince them about our position. They wanted us to do something in exchange. We were on to a trail for a few weeks, but then it went cold again.'

In April 1986 I drove to Sidon to see Mustafa Saad, having learnt through the Beirut grapevine that he had been having secret talks with the British government. At that time, Beirut had become so dangerous that I looked forward to the two-hour drive to Sidon, even though it passed through the desolate landscape of southern Lebanon created in the aftermath of the Israeli invasion. I arrived at Saad's house, an unremarkable villa on the outskirts of the town, at about 2 pm on a Sunday. To my surprise, I was told by his guards that he was still asleep, and that I would have to wait until he awoke. About an hour later I was shown into Saad's living room where he sat in a chair, still wearing his pyjamas. His face was covered with ugly scars, the result of the Israeli letter-bomb he had received two years previously, and he wore dark sunglasses to cover his mutilated eyes.

Sweet Arabic tea was served, and I asked Saad the reason for his talks with the British government. He was quite frank, and said he was trying to negotiate the release of Alec Collett. The Palestinian group holding Collett had been in touch with him and, because they trusted him, had asked him to make contact with the British government. But Saad was disappointed by the British government's response. 'The British government must understand that it will have to do a lot more if it is to secure the release of Mr Collett,' Saad explained. 'But Mrs Thatcher behaves as though she does not want to help. It is an attitude the kidnappers find very hard to understand.' Because of Mrs Thatcher's intransigence, therefore, there was no prospect of Collett being released.

The brief contact established between the kidnappers and the British government over Alec Collett was nevertheless of interest, because it demonstrated that British diplomats did have room to manoeuvre once direct contact had been established. Had the kidney machines been the only request, and had an independent charity arranged to deliver the equipment in return for Collett's release, the Foreign Office could have said with its hand on its heart that it had not done a deal for Collett's release. If news had leaked about the delivery of the kidney machines, the British government could have indicated its disapproval, while at the same time accepting the plaudits for securing the hostage's release. The action undertaken by John Gray in the spring of 1986, which was done quietly and without publicity, also rather undermined the theory that only an 'independent humanitarian' such as Terry Waite could operate in such circumstances. The Foreign Office has a long track record of resolving difficult disputes in the most bizarre circumstances which only come to light when the public records are released many years later. Despite Waite's public involvement in Beirut, the Foreign Office made no approach to Waite to see if he would be interested in helping out with the Collett case.

'There really didn't seem to be much point,' explained Gray. 'He made it quite clear that he was not particularly interested in Collett.'

The kidnapping of Padfield and Douglas came as a terrible shock to the small British community. This abduction meant that Britons could no longer delude themselves; they were just as likely to be kidnapped as French or Americans. For the first few days after the kidnapping, those who remained behind, like Kemp, clung to the hope that it was all a big mistake and that the teachers would be released as soon as their kidnappers realised they were British. But the longer time passed with no news forthcoming, the more those still at liberty woke up to the fact that they must leave Beirut.

The one exception to the general mood of despair in the British community was a thirty-six-year-old Ulsterman by the name of Brian Keenan. Keenan was something of a maverick in that, despite being a Protestant from the north of Ireland, he travelled on an Irish passport. Ever since the partition of Ireland, the Irish government had offered the right of nationality to any citizen living north of the border, but rare indeed was the Ulster Protestant who accepted this offer. Keenan, who held pronounced left-wing views, had made no secret of his pro-Republican sympathies when he worked as a teacher in Belfast in the 1970s and early 1980s, when 'the troubles' were at their height, and, as one former colleague remembers, 'he knew a lot of people in the Falls Road'. Keenan's political activism never reached the point where he was brought to the attention of the security forces, although he liked to imply he had been. But his uncompromising attitude did inhibit his career prospects, and his chances of advancing up the teaching ladder were severely limited. By his own admission, he eventually found himself in a rut, both professionally and socially, in Belfast which he longed to escape.

The opportunity to escape appeared in the form of an advertisement in the appointments section of the *Guardian*'s education supplement for teachers to go to Beirut to teach English to Lebanese students. The post offered a reasonable tax-free salary and subsidised living accommodation. Jean Sutherland, the wife of American hostage Tom Sutherland, was closely involved in the teaching programme which had been set up by Rafiq Hariri, the Lebanese philanthropist. The Hariri Foundation was an annex of the American University, and its primary function was to raise the standard of English of Lebanese students to the required level for entrance to the AUB. In spite of the abduction of her husband, Mrs Sutherland believed passionately in the AUB, and realised the importance of keeping the Hariri Foundation running if standards at the university were to be maintained. Following the abduction of so many American teachers, however, recruitment was becoming increasingly more difficult. In order to get more teachers, Mrs Sutherland toured the unemployment blackspots of the British Isles – Glasgow, Liverpool, Cardiff and Belfast – to interview respondents to the advertisement.

As a result of Mrs Sutherland's visit, five teachers, two Irish and three English, arrived in Beirut in November 1985 to start work at the Hariri Foundation. Keenan's job, to teach English to Lebanese students aged between fifteen and twenty, had been vacant since the murder of Dennis Hill the previous May. The first the Irish embassy in Beirut knew of Keenan's arrival with another Irishman was when they presented themselves to register their names.

'I couldn't believe my eyes,' recalled John Rowan, who was first secretary at the Irish embassy. 'People were being kidnapped almost daily, and out of the blue these two turned up at the embassy saying they had taken jobs at the university.' Rowan strongly advised both men to take the first plane back to Dublin. He was particularly concerned about Keenan, who was under the impression that because he was travelling on an Irish passport he would be immune from the kidnappers.

'I told him that he was not fooling anyone by carrying an Irish passport,' said Rowan. 'He was born in Belfast and came from a Protestant family and was also a British citizen. I didn't think the kidnappers would worry too much about Keenan having an Irish passport if he got himself into trouble.' But Keenan was not prepared to listen to Rowan's advice, and insisted on his right to remain in Beirut.

Keenan settled easily into the expatriate community. He would teach from 8 am to 2 pm, and had the rest of the day to himself. Together with the four other teachers who had travelled with him to Beirut, he found an apartment just a short walk from the AUB campus. The fact the apartment was in the heart of a Hizbollah-controlled area did not seem to worry Keenan. He joked to his friends that having lived in Belfast, a few militiamen with beards and guns were not going to frighten him. When he was not teaching, Keenan was usually to be found with other teachers in one of the bars close to the campus. It was in a bar that Keenan met Hazel Moss, the manageress of the Pickwick bar, who had been kidnapped the previous September. Keenan and Moss became close friends, and often went dancing and drinking together until the early hours.

Drink was a constant feature of Keenan's life in Beirut. According to a contemporary, 'Keenan was pissed half the time.' Hazel Moss recalls that sometimes Keenan would become belligerent in drink. 'He could get very angry and rude in pubs, after a glass or two,' said Moss. 'But he'd always apologise the next day if he could remember who he had been rude to.' Keenan also continued to display a cavalier attitude in the face of the worsening security situation in Beirut. He would often be found wandering the streets in the middle of the night in a state of inebriation when more sensible souls were safely tucked up in bed. On one occasion he was surrounded by four militiamen who wanted to know what he was doing walking the streets at such a late hour.

'He got out of a potentially dangerous situation by bluffing the guards that he was a very dangerous person.' said Moss. 'He eyeballed them for half-an-hour until they let him go.'

Apart from his relationship with Hazel Moss, Keenan also courted the affections of some of his female colleagues, with limited success. On one occasion Keenan became so drunk and abusive at a United Nations function that Irish officials had to escort him quietly off the premises. Compared with his Irish teaching colleague, however, Keenan was generally well-behaved. The Irish embassy was required to escort Keenan's colleague out of the country after he acquired the habit of getting drunk, climbing trees on campus and screaming at the top of his voice: 'We'll get the IRA to sort you Hizbollah bastards out.'

Following the abduction of Padfield and Douglas, Hazel Moss became so concerned for Keenan's safety that the couple had several arguments over whether Keenan should leave. 'Brian loved his pint,' Moss remembers, 'and we'd often end up arguing loudly about why he was in Beirut.

He was aware of the dangers of staying, but wouldn't be driven out because of them.' Moss would break down in tears and recount her own horrific experience when she was kidnapped, but Keenan refused to consider leaving. 'He kept repeating he had his Irish passport, and that Hizbollah had no argument with the Irish government,' recalled Moss. 'We had some fairly big arguments, but he would not change his mind, not even after the two teachers were taken. They were British, whereas Brian was Irish.'

Keenan was kidnapped at 8 am on Friday April 11, 1986, as he left his apartment for work. According to eye-witnesses, Hizbollah gunmen had been hanging around the apartment since about 5 am. No one had thought this in any way unusual because Keenan lived in a Hizbollah-controlled area. Whether the gunmen were waiting for Keenan specifically, or any one of the teachers, is unclear. Certainly the gunmen did not hesitate the moment Keenan appeared at the door. As he set off down the street, one of the gunmen put a gun to his head. Keenan was then forced into the back of a car and driven off. And no one took the slightest interest in his Irish passport.

Ever since April 1984 when a crazed gunman at the Libyan People's Bureau in London's St James's Square had opened fire with a machine-gun at anti-Gaddafi demonstrators and killed Yvonne Fletcher, a policewoman on routine guard duty outside, the Thatcher government had been seeking ways to put Gaddafi in his place. The People's Bureau had been closed, but Gaddafi, citing diplomatic immunity, had refused to surrender the official to stand trial in London. Although counter-terrorism experts generally agreed that Gaddafi was a relatively minor figure compared with the terrorist capabilities of the Syrians and Iran, he continued to be a constant source of irritation to the British government, especially in the support, both military and political, he provided to the IRA. Gaddafi had fallen further in Thatcher's estimation at Christmas 1985 when Palestinian terrorists had launched simultaneous attacks against the El Al desks at Rome and Vienna airports in which nineteen civilians, five of them Americans, were killed. Gaddafi had described the attacks as 'honourable'.

When President Reagan had first mooted the idea of taking retaliatory action against Gaddafi, whom he had denounced as a 'mad dog' in early 1986, Mrs Thatcher had cautioned against the use of illegal measures to counter international terrorism. 'I do not believe in retaliatory strikes that are against international law,' she proclaimed. 'Once you start to go across borders, then I do not see an end to it. I uphold international law very firmly.' By April, Mrs Thatcher seemed to have reversed her position. On April 5 a bomb had exploded at a West German nightclub frequented by American servicemen. Two Americans and a Turkish woman had been killed, and American intelligence said there was conclusive proof the Libyans were responsible. The Americans claimed to have intercepted a message of congratulation sent by Gaddafi to the bombers. Reagan contacted Thatcher and said that he had decided to launch a bombing raid against Libya in retaliation. He was not consulting Thatcher; he was informing her. Although the attack would go ahead anyway, Reagan said it would be rendered easier and also more precise in its targetry if F-111 bombers based in Britain could be deployed. Carrier-based aircraft, standing off the Libyan coast, could be used, but they would be at greater risk and would also cause more civilian damage. Reagan, in other words, wanted British permission to commit what the British prime minister already seemed to have described as a breach of international law.

Reagan's decision to bomb Libya posed a variety of difficulties for Thatcher. Thatcher's instinct was always to stand by the US in times of adversity, and the British government had plenty of reasons for wishing to see Libya cut down to size. Against this, the British government needed to weigh very carefully the likely impact support for such an attack would have on British interests in the Middle East. Thatcher also needed to overcome stiff resistance from senior members of the cabinet who were opposed to the attack.[1] The three senior ministers consulted about the decision all had reservations. William Whitelaw, the Leader of the House, wanted to make a clear distinction between acceding to a request from an ally and enthusing about every action the ally proposed to take. George Younger, the defence secretary, voiced similar reservations on Scottish radio, while Geoffrey Howe, the foreign secretary, was worried about the likely repercussions such a raid would have on the Middle East.

At Howe's request, the Foreign Office undertook a detailed analysis of the likely impact on British interests in the region if Britain were associated with the attack on Libya. The report was put together by David Miers, who had taken charge of the Middle East department in London after leaving Beirut. The Foreign Office painted a bleak picture, raising the possibility of reprisals being taken against the thousands of British oil workers based in Libya. It also forecast attacks on British embassies and institutions throughout the Middle East. And last, but by no means least, the Foreign Office spelt out the likely fate of the three British hostages – Padfield, Douglas and Collett – and Brian Keenan, who had joint nationality. If the US was allowed to use its bases in Britain, there was a strong likelihood that the hostages would be harmed as a consequence.

In Beirut John Gray, the British ambassador, pursued every possible avenue to get the two British teachers released. 'We

[1]Hugo Young: *One of Us*, Macmillan, 1991.

worked on the basis that the first few days of any kidnapping are crucial,' said Gray. 'If you could find out who had them right at the start, it was sometimes possible to get them released quickly. But once a few weeks had passed, the earth almost seemed to close over them and then it became a far more difficult task.' Gray, like the Foreign Office, was initially irritated at having to devote so much time to locating two British citizens who had been given countless warnings to leave. He also thought the teachers had acted in a thoroughly irresponsible manner by deciding to walk home from a nightclub in the early hours. 'They were not exactly behaving sensibly,' commented Gray. It was rumoured that Padfield and Douglas had been picked up by freelance kidnappers who were trying to sell them on to another militia. The British embassy put out its contacts to see exactly how much the kidnappers were asking, but got no reply. After Keenan was kidnapped, the British and Irish governments came to an understanding that Dublin would handle efforts to get Keenan released, in the hope that Ireland's less pronounced diplomatic profile in the Middle East might assist Keenan's chances. In the event it made no difference.

While the Foreign Office was lobbying behind the scenes against an attack on Libya, Mrs Thatcher was consulting closely with Charles Powell, her private secretary. Powell was a career diplomat who in 1984 was seconded by the Foreign Office to work at Downing Street. As part of a long-standing tradition, the Foreign Office assigned one of its rising stars to work in the prime minister's office, normally for about four years. The main function of the private secretary was to act as a link between the Foreign Office and the prime minister and to provide advice on day-to-day issues involving foreign affairs. What was unusual about Powell, a man of great ability and industry, was that he had gradually forged a close personal rapport with Mrs Thatcher. He had been her principal adviser during the Westland affair, even though the issue was technically not a Foreign Office matter. Like Thatcher's press secretary, Bernard Ingham, Powell had become a member of the prime minister's inner circle; it was even said that, intellectually and half emotionally, Powell was the son Thatcher never had. Increasingly Thatcher came to place more credence in Powell's advice on key foreign policy issues than that of her foreign secretary, a fact which ultimately resulted in Howe's removal from the Foreign Office.

According to Powell, the fate of the three British hostages in Lebanon was discussed 'at length' by Mrs Thatcher and her close advisers when considering whether to allow Reagan to use American air bases in Britain for the raid on Libya. Powell dismissed the Foreign Office warnings about the likely repercussions in the Middle East as being over-exaggerated. 'There is an institutional tendency to cry wolf at the Foreign Office when faced with a difficult decision,' explained Powell, who took a well-paid job with a leading merchant bank following Mrs Thatcher's resignation as prime minister. 'The Foreign Office was very much against Mrs Thatcher's policy towards South Africa, claiming that it would turn black Africa against us. It never happened. It was the same sort of thing with the Middle East.'

The crux of the matter as far as Powell and Thatcher were concerned was to take a decision which was in Britain's best interests. 'There was a feeling that we must stand up to dictators and terrorists, whatever the consequences,' said Powell. 'We were well aware of what might happen to the British hostages in Lebanon, but this was not a consideration that we could allow to shackle our policy.' According to Powell, Mrs Thatcher agonised a great deal over the decision; not so much over the policy itself, but over the human consequences. Even Geoffrey Howe was persuaded that allowing the Americans to use their British bases would be the right decision. For him it was a question of the British government standing by its principles. Gaddafi had long been a source of irritation, and Britain was perfectly within its rights to grant Washington permission to launch its attack on Libya from Britain.

President Reagan was telephoned by Margaret Thatcher and told that the Americans could use the F-111 fighter-bombers based in Britain for the bombing raid. As for the hostages in Lebanon, they would be left to their fate.

15

GADDAFI'S REVENGE

On the evening of Monday April 14, 1986, John McCarthy and I experienced a distinct feeling of unease as we sat in the coffee shop of the Commodore Hotel discussing what our next move should be. An eerie silence had fallen over the Commodore, which even in the darkest days of the civil war had been a hive of activity, with journalists rushing backwards and forwards to the telex machine and the noisy chatter of people exhausted from their day's labours relaxing at the bar. Now the hotel was virtually deserted. The few journalists who had stayed on in Beirut had all departed for Libya in the firm expectation that President Reagan would honour his threat to bomb Colonel Gaddafi. My newspaper was alone in deciding that its correspondent's talents were better employed in Beirut, so John McCarthy and I were the only two British journalists still there.

Over the previous two to three weeks McCarthy and I had established the kind of casual acquaintanceship one would expect of two people who were from the same age group, shared the same nationality, did a similar kind of job and found themselves washed up in the same dangerous, but nevertheless hospitable, country. I had returned three weeks previously to investigate why the kidnappers had started taking British teachers, in retrospect not the wisest decision I've ever taken. When I checked into the Commodore, I was introduced to McCarthy, who had arrived at the beginning of March and was filling in for the regular correspondent for World Television News (WTN), who was on a two-month break. WTN is an international television news agency. The job of the Beirut bureau then was to provide film of the news story of the day. The film, some of which contained a commentary from the correspondent, was shipped back to London where it was then sold around the world. As most of the big television companies had either left Lebanon or reduced their staff to a skeleton, the WTN bureau was crucial in bringing news to the outside world from Lebanon.

By the time I met McCarthy, he had found his feet and was enjoying his assignment immensely. It was his first overseas posting, and he was clearly determined to make the most of the opportunity and impress his bosses in London. What he lacked in experience and knowledge of Lebanon, he more than compensated for through his unceasing enthusiasm and boundless energy for the job. One minute he would be driving around with a camera looking for interesting shots, the next he would be back at the studio editing the film for transmission to London. Sometimes he would write his own script, giving his editors in London a complete package to sell to their subscribers. There was no job McCarthy couldn't do, from making the coffee to interviewing the Lebanese prime minister.

When he wasn't working hard, McCarthy was playing hard. There were still a few Western television journalists in Beirut, most of them freelancers drawn to the perennial threat of danger. Had they not been in Beirut, they would have been in Central America or some equally life-threatening location.

McCarthy became quite good friends with a small group of these freelancers. One of them, Nigel, who worked as a cameraman for an American company, was a particularly outrageous character. Tall and handsome and from a classic Home Counties English background, Nigel was a particularly promiscuous homosexual who entertained his friends with graphic accounts of his conquest, or more usually conquests, of the night before. Like so many gays of that generation, Nigel contracted Aids and died an emaciated wreck at the family home later that summer. In spite of his homosexuality, Nigel enjoyed the company of women and, together with McCarthy and other friends, was constantly organising nights out at nightclubs and restaurants, no matter how bad the security situation.

Even after Padfield and Douglas had been kidnapped, McCarthy's crowd continued to paint the town red. I joined them on a couple of occasions, but I felt rather uncomfortable in the midst of so much frivolity. Every time I returned to the Commodore, Lebanon seemed to take a significant turn for the worse. A year previously I had been at the Commodore only a few days when Terry Anderson was kidnapped. The previous autumn I had been trapped in the hotel with Terry Waite when the hotel was taken over by Druze militiamen. This time the gunmen were kidnapping British teachers. All in all, there did not seem to be much to smile about in Beirut, and just being in the city made me distinctly ill-at-ease. When Brian Keenan was kidnapped less than half a mile from the hotel, it made me think seriously that the time was rapidly approaching when I should pack my bags.

As we sat in the hotel coffee shop that evening, McCarthy and I discussed the likelihood of the Americans bombing Libya and the consequences if they did. Judging by the plethora of news reports circulating in Lebanon, there did not seem to be any doubt that the Americans were about to take action of one form or another. And from the comments being made by the more radical elements, any action would not be well received in Beirut. With three Britons kidnapped in less than three weeks (we all regarded Keenan as British), there was a real possibility that the kidnappers would make further inroads against the British community. But neither of us knew for sure what the Americans were planning. We parted company with a sense of foreboding and headed for our rooms for an early night, little knowing that as we did so American F-111s were streaking across the Mediterranean towards the Libyan coast.

The first I knew about the bombing raid was the following morning when I turned on my radio to listen to the news on the BBC World Service. At first, in my semi-conscious state, it was difficult, hearing the clipped and unflappable tones of the BBC, to take in the import of what the announcer was saying. At 2 am local time, about thirty American airforce and navy bombers had attacked Libya's two largest cities, Tripoli and Benghazi. In addition nine F-111 bombers had flown from a United States airforce base in Suffolk to drop laser-guided bombs on Gaddafi's headquarters in the centre of Tripoli. Some seventy Libyans had been killed, including a two-year-old child Gaddafi claimed was his adopted daughter. The news was followed by comments from President Reagan in Washington and Mrs Thatcher in London justifying the raid. As I listened to Mrs Thatcher three thousand miles away explaining why she had allowed the Americans to use their bases in England, I realised with growing alarm that the one place the full force of Arab anger would be made manifest was on the streets of Beirut. The time had come for me to leave, and the sooner the better. If the kidnappers wanted to find more Westerners, the Commodore would be the obvious place to look.

The first problem I faced was how to get out of the hotel

without being noticed. With so few people around, I would be highly conspicuous if I simply went to the front desk with my bags and checked out. That seemed the easiest way to ensure the kidnappers had a reception committee waiting when I drove to the airport, by far the most hazardous part of the journey out. I phoned Lena Kara, a Lebanese photographer friend who worked for one of the Western news agencies. I explained my predicament, which she readily understood.

'Just get in a taxi and drive over to the office. Don't tell anyone where you're going. Leave all your things at the hotel as if you'll be coming back later.' She reeled off the orders as though getting foreigners out of Beirut was a daily part of her routine.

I did just as she said. I drove over to the news agency with a Lebanese driver called Abed, who had worked for me for more than two years and whom I trusted implicitly. He had driven me on several dangerous missions, and had never once let me down. In return I had always made sure he was well paid (like all Lebanese, he had a large family to support), something which did not always endear me to the *Telegraph*'s accounts department. Once at the agency, I met up with some Lebanese journalist friends who were all insistent that I get out of the country as soon as possible. There was a flight leaving for Cyprus later that morning. Making a booking in my name was out of the question – a foreign name could easily be picked up by someone with the wrong intentions. The booking would be made under a pseudonym, and we'd take a chance that I could get on the flight. I sent Abed back to the hotel with my credit card to collect my bags and pay the bill. If anyone asked, he was to tell them I had crossed the Green Line into East Beirut.

While Abed was sorting out my affairs, I telephoned McCarthy at the WTN office. 'Christ, what a story,' was his opening remark when I got through. Clearly in a state of great excitement about the events in Libya, he told me he had been out since the crack of dawn getting reaction from the Lebanese to the bombing raid. He had just returned from the Shia Muslim heartland in the southern suburbs, filming the demonstrations which had been taking place since news of the raid first reached Beirut. 'I've got some great pictures. London will love it,' he remarked. McCarthy was clearly a braver man than I. In this climate, the southern suburbs, where more than a dozen foreigners were known to be held in miserable confinement, was the last place I wanted to be. Judging from McCarthy's reaction, I was concerned that he might not realise how dangerous Beirut had become.

'You want to be careful where you go,' I advised.

'Don't worry about me. What are you doing?'

I knew that McCarthy worked in an office where a lot of Lebanese wandered in and out, and that not all the visitors were people whose company I would choose. If I was going to take a chance and drive through the southern suburbs to the airport, I wanted as few people as possible to know about my movements.

'I'm thinking of pulling out,' I said. 'Things are getting fairly dodgy around here. But I'm not sure about the best way to go. How about you?'

'I think I'll hang around for a few more days,' replied McCarthy. 'I've only got another ten days to go before my assignment is up, so I might as well see it through to the end.'

'Are you sure, John? I think the mood is going to get fairly ugly around here. I think a lot of people will be pulling out.' I felt in the circumstances it was the strongest advice I could give. I was only leaving because I had a hunch, which seemed to be confirmed by my Lebanese friends, that Beirut was not a good place for a British journalist. And besides, I now had a big story to cover in Libya, if I could get there.

'No, I'll be all right,' replied McCarthy, 'there's plenty for me to do here, and the guys will look after me.'

When Abed returned, I still had a couple of hours to kill before leaving for the airport. I sent a telex to my London office informing them of my movements. I then asked Abed to take me to a shop where I could buy a few things I would need for the trip to Libya. Even though the shop was around the corner, we took the car because I did not want to walk the streets of Beirut. With someone like Abed at the wheel, who knew every street and short-cut in the city, I felt safe. I was in the process of making my purchases when I heard the words every foreigner in West Beirut that morning dreaded hearing: 'You, English. Kidnap.' So saying, the young Lebanese militiaman stuck the barrel of his AK-47 in my stomach.

For all the dangers I had encountered covering the Lebanese civil war, nothing had provoked such abject fear as those three words. In my mind's eye I had conjured all kinds of fantastic images as to what I would do if ever anyone tried to kidnap me. I would leap over walls, speed away in a stolen car, wrestle my abductors to the ground and disarm them. I would do anything and everything, but they wouldn't take me hostage. It was, of course, a different matter when it actually happened. When a fully primed automatic rifle is pressed into your abdomen and an intensely agitated seventeen-year-old militiaman is pressing the trigger, all thoughts of heroism quickly evaporate.

The gunman had been passing the shop and had heard someone speaking an unfamiliar language. Venturing in to investigate, he had struck gold. There could not have been a militiaman in Beirut that morning who was not looking for an American or Briton to kidnap, and having found me, the militiaman was in no doubt as to his next move. 'Stand back, I am going to kidnap the foreigner.'

While everyone, shopkeeper and customer alike, froze on

the spot, the situation was saved by Abed, who had watched the incident develop from the car outside. He walked casually into the shop and asked the gunman what he was doing. The gunman replied that he was going to kidnap me because I was English, and all English were 'bad'. To my alarm, this did not make much of an impression on Abed.

'Take him, take him if you want,' said Abed, waving his hands towards the door. I was about to interject that this was not the kind of response I expected when Abed revealed his comments were laced with irony.

'And where will you take him when you leave here? Where is your car? Where is your house?' Gradually the gunman seemed to get the point. He had hit upon the idea of kidnapping me, but he was working alone. If he abducted me, it might cause him a lot of problems. If he could not kidnap me, perhaps it would be better if he shot me. As this new idea dawned, he cocked his weapon and aimed it at me with renewed interest. Fortunately this act galvanised everyone else in the shop into action. The shopkeeper and Abed started shouting at the gunman and waving their arms. How dare the gunman behave like this, they shouted. The shopkeeper paid good protection money to the local militia, and he did not expect gunmen to come into his shop and shoot the customers. Faced with this barrage of abuse, the gunman finally relented.

'OK, I will leave him. But he must leave now. He is English and English are bad.' So saying, the militiaman departed in a decidedly bad humour. Fearing that it would not be long before he returned with reinforcements, I quickly settled my account and left.

Having survived this unpleasant encounter, I was determined to get to the airport as quickly as possible. The journey posed many dangers, but I was anxious to get it over with rather than make the acquaintance of any other militiamen.

Lena Kara offered to accompany me in the car. She would sit in the front seat next to Abed, and would wear a veil over her head in the custom of Shia women. I would sit behind and keep my head down, and with a bit of luck we would get to the airport before anyone noticed there was a foreigner in the back of Abed's battered old Mercedes.

The drive passed through some of the most desolate areas of the city. From the more salubrious suburbs of West Beirut, the road passed the Palestinian refugee camps of Sabra and Chatila. It then took a sharp left and passed along the side of the southern suburbs. Halfway along the three-mile drive the road passed a brand new mosque which had been built with money donated by Iran. The mosque was always covered with posters of Ayatollah Khomeini and quotes from the Koran. Because of its rounded shape, the structure was known as the 'champagne mosque' by the less devout. This was the most dangerous part of the journey. Tom Sutherland had been kidnapped within sight of the mosque, as had the four-man French television crew, who were on their way back to Beirut from an interview with Sheikh Fadlallah. As we passed the mosque the car approached a Hizbollah checkpoint. It was the moment I had been dreading. After my encounter with a lone gunman, I was in no mood to be challenged by professionals.

As the car pulled up, Abed said a few curt words in Arabic. The Hizbollah gunmen looked at me sitting uncomfortably in the back and studied me closely. One of them spoke a few words to Abed, then shouted 'Good luck' to me and waved us through. I was bemused. We had sailed through the most hazardous part of the journey unscathed, and the airport and freedom now beckoned. I asked Abed what he had said.

'I told them you were in a hurry because you had an exclusive interview with Colonel Gaddafi and that you were going to tell the world how terrible the Americans and British were for bombing Libya,' said Abed. Abed, through bold-faced lying, had once more saved the day.

At his modest semi-detached home in the Norfolk village of Stalham, Edgar 'Doug' Douglas, a retired security guard whose son Leigh had been missing for nearly three weeks, was making the early morning tea when he heard the news about the Libya bombing raid. From the moment he heard that the Americans had used their British bases for the raid, Douglas was in no doubt as to his son's fate. He put the teapot, milk, sugar and two teacups on a tray and went upstairs to take his wife Freda her early morning cuppa.

'That's it, love, Leigh's a goner,' said Douglas in his matter-of-fact Yorkshire accent.

'Oh Doug,' said Freda, 'whatever can you mean?'

'The Yanks have bombed Libya, and they've done it from Britain,' said Doug. 'And I reckon that means our Leigh will not be coming home.'

Ever since her son had been reported missing at Easter, Mrs Douglas had worried herself sick wondering what had happened to him. The Foreign Office in London had been in almost daily contact with both the Douglas and Padfield families. 'A nice lady used to phone me up every morning, and we'd have a nice little chat,' recalled Mrs Douglas. 'She told me the British government was doing its best to find Leigh, and that I should not worry.' But Mrs Douglas was the worrying kind. She worried that her son might be mistreated in captivity; she worried about the book he was hoping to write on the Yemen and whether it would ever be finished; she even worried that Leigh's dog was being properly cared for in his absence.

Doug and Freda Douglas knew very little about the Middle East. When their son had announced he was going to live in Beirut, they had not stood in his way because they knew he had a deep affection for the region. On the rare occasions he returned to Britain for a holiday, Mrs Douglas tried to suggest that there were safer places to live than Beirut. 'But he would always reassure me that he was perfectly safe in Beirut and that he had lots of good Lebanese friends who looked after him.' The Douglases had paid very little attention to the diplomatic build-up to the bombing raid. As far as they were concerned, Gaddafi and Libya were a long way from Lebanon and had nothing to do with their son's captivity. It was only when they heard that the bases in Britain had been used that they began to fear the worst.

Two days after the bombing raid, the bodies of three men were found in the Druze-controlled area of the Chouf mountains at the side of the main Damascus highway. Each had his hands tied behind his back and had been killed by a single bullet fired into the brain from just behind the left ear. The bodies were brought down to the American University Hospital and placed in the mortuary. All the indications were that two of the bodies were those of Padfield and Douglas, although no one was sure about the third, which was the body of someone many years older. John Rowan, the Irish diplomat who had tried unsuccessfully to persuade Brian Keenan to leave Beirut, was asked if he would come to the mortuary to make a positive identification. He was one of the few Western diplomats still resident in West Beirut and knew Padfield and Douglas from social functions. There was also the possibility that the third body might be that of Brian Keenan, although from the brief description he had been given over the telephone he thought it unlikely.

Rowan was able to provide a positive identification of Padfield and Douglas. He was unable to identify the third body. At first he thought it might be Alec Collett, who was about the same age as the dead man, but a brief examination of the body's hands knocked down that theory. Alec Collett had the top of one finger missing, whereas all the fingers on the body were intact. Rowan suggested to the hospital staff that the body might be that of an American hostage, and proposed they try to find an American to make an identification. The only American the staff could lay their hands on was Joseph Cicippio, an accounts controller at the AUB. Cicippio identified the dead man as Peter Kilburn, the sixty-one-year-old university librarian who had been missing since December 1984.

The discovery of Kilburn's body came as a surprise to the American embassy in Beirut. Not one claim had been made about him since his abduction. From time to time, one of the kidnap groups would issue a statement, together with pictures of the hostages, but Kilburn was never among them. Throughout the sixteen months he was held captive, he was never sighted by any of the other hostages. And yet for some reason, the kidnappers had taken the trouble of keeping him alive, feeding him, sheltering him, clearly hoping that one day he might be of use to them.

A group calling itself the Arab Commando Cell issued a statement saying it had killed the three men in retaliation for the Libya bombing raid. Whatever the name used by the group, however, there was little doubt that the killings were the work of Abu Nidal's radical Palestinian group. It later emerged that large sums of money had changed hands to enable Abu Nidal to take possession of the two Britons and one American. According to militia officials I interviewed in Beirut several years later, a group of 'freelance' kidnappers were paid $25,000 to abduct Padfield and Douglas. 'They just happened to be available, and there was a market for Western hostages,' explained the official. After the Libya raid, the two Britons became even more valuable, and were sold on to Abu Nidal, whose organisation was primarily financed by Gaddafi. Abu Nidal was also able to purchase Peter Kilburn, possibly from one of the Lebanese Shia groups. It later transpired that, among others, Oliver North learned that it might be possible to purchase Kilburn's freedom, and organised a typically hare-brained scheme to pay three million dollars for the American, only the money would be counterfeit and designed to disintegrate as soon as he was freed. Officials at the State Department later conceded they had lost the race to buy Kilburn's freedom. 'Gaddafi got in first with a bigger bid,' said an official.

Gaddafi apparently also made a bid for the four Americans still held by Islamic Jihad. One day not long after the bombing raid, one of the guards informed David Jacobsen that he was worth precisely seven and a half million dollars. Jacobsen was confused. How had the guard calculated he was worth so much? The Libyans had bid a total of $30 million for the four hostages, which the kidnappers had rejected out of hand.

When Doug Douglas received the apologetic phone call from the Foreign Office to tell him his son was dead, he was in absolutely no doubt as to where the blame for Leigh's death lay.

'I blame Mrs Thatcher,' Mr Douglas announced to the camera crews which had gathered on his doorstep to film the family's reaction to the loss of their only son. 'I am just disgusted that the planes were allowed to go from Britain. But for that I believe my son would still be alive and none of this would have happened.'

Nor did the Douglas family feel any better disposed to the British government when a personal letter from Mrs Thatcher dropped through their letter-box the following morning. The letter was dated April 18, 1986, and was written the day after the bodies of Padfield and Douglas had been positively identified in Beirut.

Dear Mr and Mrs Douglas,
I was deeply saddened by the news of the murder of your son in Lebanon yesterday coming on top of the anguish of his kidnapping.

As a parent myself, I can understand your grief and your feeling that your son was a victim of a war against terrorism in which he wished no part. I know that he loved Lebanon and its people which only makes the outrage which one feels at his murder the worse.

My thoughts are with you at this terrible time. I hope you will accept my heartfelt sympathy.

The above portion of the letter had been neatly typed by a Downing Street secretary. When the letter was placed in front of her to sign, Thatcher had added in her own hand: 'I know and *understand* your feelings.' The word 'understand' had two thick lines drawn beneath it. 'Yours sincerely, Margaret Thatcher.'

Mrs Thatcher's 'heartfelt sympathy' made little difference to the Douglas family. Their son had not gone to Lebanon to fight the war against terrorism, and would most probably still have been alive had it not been for Thatcher's decision to back the Americans. 'You can bet your life that if it had been Mark Thatcher [Mrs Thatcher's son] locked up in a Beirut basement, she would never have allowed the British bases to be used,' is how Doug Douglas reacted. Several weeks later, the Douglases received a small urn from Beirut containing the ashes of their beloved son. The authorities in Lebanon had advised them it would be too difficult and expensive to ship his body home in a coffin, as they would have liked, and so the body was cremated in East Beirut. They also received a few of Leigh's personal effects, including a diary he had kept of his life at the AUB. One entry for June 1985 read: 'Tom Sutherland kidnapped from the AUB today. I wonder who'll be next.'

The Douglas family were not the only ones to criticise Mrs Thatcher for supporting the Libya raid. A storm of protest greeted Mrs Thatcher when she appeared for prime minister's question time at the House of Commons on the afternoon after the raid, and not all of it came from the opposition benches. Even the most faithful Conservative columnists withheld their support. Ferdinand Mount, who had run Mrs Thatcher's policy unit for two years, wrote an article in the *Daily Telegraph* ridiculing the operation. He even suggested that Thatcher's policy might cost the Conservative Party the next general election. Max Hastings, the newly-appointed editor of the *Daily Telegraph*, himself wrote a leader which was highly critical of the raid.

The pressure increased on Thatcher when a few days later the Revolutionary Organisation of Socialist Muslims, another name favoured by Abu Nidal, claimed they had 'executed' the British journalist Alec Collett. A grisly videotape was delivered to the Lebanese newspaper *An Nahar*, which purported to show Collett being hanged from scaffolding. The video certainly showed a picture of a European-looking male of about Collett's age swinging from a makeshift gallows. But because the victim's head was covered with a large blindfold, it was impossible to identify the body. It was also impossible to ascertain whether the man had died from hanging, or of other causes, either violent or natural, before being strung up. The Foreign Office sent the video to be analysed by experts in an attempt to authenticate it. In particular the technicians tried to enhance the image in order to examine the hands, to see if the top of one finger was missing. Try as they might, the experts were unable to make a definitive identification.

The video was shown to Collett's two grown-up children, David and Suzie, who lived in London. After examining it several times, they came to the reluctant conclusion that the body was that of their father. They accepted that he had died in captivity and arranged for a memorial service to be held in London. On the other side of the Atlantic, however, their stepmother Elaine also saw the video, but refused to accept that it featured her husband. She resolved to continue her campaign to have him released.

The deaths of the three British hostages in Lebanon constituted a major embarrassment for the British government. Compared with countries such as France and the US, Britain had only recently become involved in the hostage problem. But whereas other countries eventually managed to secure the release of their subjects, even if it took years, within the space of a week three British hostages had been killed, a disastrous record. It was neither a record of which Mrs Thatcher was proud nor one about which she wanted to be reminded. Once the dust had settled and the British political agenda had moved on to new areas, the Thatcher government did its best never again to be reminded of the terrible price three innocent British citizens had paid as a consequence of the policies of their prime minister.

Soon after news of the Libyan raid reached London, Robert Burke, McCarthy's boss at WTN in London, called his correspondent and ordered him to get out of Lebanon as soon as possible. Burke, who had cut his teeth as a journalist before moving on to the management side of television, had felt no qualms about sending McCarthy to Beirut on his first foreign assignment. 'We all have to start somewhere,' Burke explained. 'John was keen and bright and was only too happy to take on an assignment overseas.'

In the next few days, Burke had reason to regret not having sent a more experienced correspondent. At first McCarthy did not seem to take his boss's words to heart, and continued working on a story he thought would help increase his standing at the company. When I spoke to him before I left for the airport, he gave no indication that he was considering leaving. The following day, when McCarthy phoned to tell Burke about his plans for the day, he received the full force of his employer's ire.

'John,' said Burke, 'I don't want to have any conversation with you while you are still in Beirut. I've told you to leave once, and the next time I talk to you I want you to be out of there.'

Even in the face of such an explicit order, McCarthy continued to prevaricate. There were two options open: he could cross the Green Line to East Beirut and take a ferry to Cyprus, which was probably the safer as he did not know his way around Lebanon. The other was to brave the airport road and fly home. Later that afternoon McCarthy went to conduct an interview with John Gray, the British ambassador, still at his residence in West Beirut. When the interview was over, Gray expressed his surprise that McCarthy was still in the city.

'You really shouldn't be here, you know,' said Gray.

'I know. But I'm leaving in the next couple of days,' McCarthy explained.

Gray asked how he intended to leave the country, and was alarmed when McCarthy told him he was going to the airport.

'I tried to persuade him against that,' said Gray. 'The airport was a notoriously bad place to be. There were lots of different checkpoints, and you could never be sure who you were dealing with or who you were going to meet next. In the circumstances they would have had any British or American citizen travelling on that road for breakfast.' When Gray told me this several years later, I was too ashamed of my own folly to admit I had taken precisely that route.

Gray wanted McCarthy to cross the Green Line, catch the

daily ferry to Cyprus and fly to London from Larnaca. 'It would only have taken him another twenty-four hours. Instead he went to the airport, and it took him a lot longer to get home.' In fact McCarthy was tempted to take Gray's advice, and said as much to his Lebanese friends. But his colleagues at his office insisted that they would take him to the airport. They would even provide him with a bodyguard.

The bureaux of foreign television companies in Beirut had always attracted an odd assortment of hangers-on. Some were there simply because they liked the image of being associated with an international television company, others for more mercenary reasons. With the collapse of the Lebanese economy, these companies were one of the few remaining sources of foreign currency. They paid in dollars and in cash for a whole variety of services, from hiring cars to paying for satellite transmissions, and a veritable army of fixers and their shady associates were always to be found at their offices, hoping to get a cut of the action. Some of these people, if not criminals themselves, had close contacts with Lebanon's criminal underclass. Certainly it became common knowledge that the reason McCarthy's Lebanese staff were so insistent that he left by the airport was that they had already made alternative plans for him.

One of the drivers at WTN had a brother who was a senior official in Hizbollah. It is said that, for a fee, he told his relation when McCarthy would be leaving and the precise route he would be taking. Those involved in making the arrangements seemed to make a conscious effort to look conspicuous. Two cars were hired for the drive, one for McCarthy and his gear, the other for 'bodyguards'. The little procession set off from outside the Commodore Hotel amidst much honking of horns. No sooner had the convoy reached the stretch of road outside the champagne mosque, than it was intercepted by Hizbollah militiamen. They knew exactly what they wanted. They went straight to the car in which McCarthy was sitting, climbed in and told the driver to head for the southern suburbs. The so-called bodyguards in the other car never fired a bullet.

The operation was carefully planned and executed. McCarthy never stood a chance of getting to the airport. He was sold to Hizbollah, reputedly for $100,000, by one of his own men. Many years later the driver was still working for a television company in Beirut, and while he has always denied any involvement in McCarthy's abduction, he has been ostracised by all his former colleagues. When I returned to Beirut in the spring of 1992, I tried to find the driver to interview him, but I was warned off by Lebanese friends who said that even though he might not be able to kidnap me, he was quite capable of killing me.

So close was the co-operation between the kidnappers and the driver that the day after McCarthy's abduction the company received a phone call from one of the kidnappers with information about where the car could be picked up. The next day they received a further call from the apologetic kidnappers. They had forgotten to return the ignition key. If a driver would like to go to a certain address, he could collect the key.

The murders of Padfield, Douglas and Collett finally persuaded the last remaining Britons in West Beirut to leave. John Gray got the staff at the embassy to contact all British citizens to tell them a convoy was being organised to take them from West Beirut to East. This time hardly anyone declined the offer. All the teachers from the AUB and the other language schools handed in their notice. The small group of journalists who had stayed to the bitter end decided to redeploy to Cyprus. All in all, about forty people joined the convoy which was escorted across the Green Line with a great deal of show by Druze militiamen. The only ones who refused to leave were a few elderly British residents, like Jackie and

Sunnie Mann, who had nowhere else to go. Embassy officials tried to persuade the Manns that they would be well looked after by the social services in Britain. But even though they were hard-up, they were too proud to accept charity, and besides, Beirut was their home. As both of them were in their early seventies, they could not see the point in anyone wanting to kidnap them.

One of the more intriguing mysteries of the hostage crisis was why Lebanon's Shia Muslims suddenly decided to concentrate on taking British hostages in the spring of 1986. Only a year previously, two British businessmen, Brian Levick and Geoffrey Nash, had been released after being held for ten days by Islamic Jihad once the kidnappers established that they were British. In March 1985 Islamic Jihad did not want British hostages. The only other British hostage held at that time, Alec Collett, was held by Palestinians, whose agenda was very different to that of Islamic Jihad. And yet a year later Islamic Jihad was making a concerted effort to kidnap British citizens. Padfield and Douglas were kidnapped by freelancers who then sold them to Gaddafi's henchmen. But McCarthy and Keenan were both kidnapped by the group which was holding the American and French hostages. This time Islamic Jihad was not going to let them go once they had ascertained their new arrivals had British passports.

It was said at the time that Keenan and McCarthy were kidnapped in retaliation for the Libyan raid, but there is a serious flaw to that argument. There was no love lost between the Shia Muslims of Lebanon and Colonel Gaddafi. As has already been shown in Chapter 5, Lebanon's Shia Muslims had nourished a deep hatred for Gaddafi ever since their inspirational leader, Musa al Sadr, disappeared while on a visit to Libya in 1978. Lebanon's Shia community to this day believe Gaddafi murdered Sadr, and they have never forgiven him. If the Americans wanted to bomb Gaddafi, that was their affair. The Lebanese Shia did not care one way or the other, and when Gaddafi offered them $30 million for the American hostages, they flatly refused to do a deal. Another explanation, which was given to me by several militia leaders during my research in 1992, was that the kidnappers took British hostages simply 'because they were there'. All the Americans and French had long since departed, and in order to keep the momentum going, the kidnappers had no alternative than to start taking British and Irish subjects.

Another explanation worthy of examination, however, is whether the failure of Terry Waite's mission contributed to the decision to take British hostages. Before Waite went to Lebanon in November 1985 for his meeting with Islamic Jihad, the kidnappers had shown no interest in Britons. All the statements and manifestos issued by Hizbollah made plenty of references to their hatred of America, France and Israel, but Britain was never mentioned. Lebanon was simply not in Britain's sphere of influence in the Middle East, and was considered of little consequence. Before Waite arrived on the scene, when Islamic Jihad kidnapped British subjects they released them because they were of no value.

If nothing else, Waite's appearance in Lebanon forced the kidnappers to take Britain into consideration. As Ben Weir had told Waite when he was preparing for his Lebanon mission, the kidnappers' understanding of the West was rudimentary. The mere fact that Weir had gone to the American embassy to renew his passport was sufficient to arouse their suspicions. They would find it difficult to understand that the Church of England was not a branch of the British government. When Waite had made his last visit to Lebanon in December 1985 on his 'hostage for Christmas' mission, he had upset the kidnappers to the extent that they had threatened to kill him if he did not leave. From then on the kidnappers referred to Waite as 'a bad man' and, given their limited understanding of the West, if Waite was bad, that made the British government a legitimate target.

The promises Waite had made about going to Kuwait, which he was unable to fulfil, may also have raised in the minds of the kidnappers the fact that Britain enjoyed a long-standing and historic relationship with Kuwait. In fact Kuwait owed its very existence to Britain. If the Americans could not influence the Kuwaitis to release the 17, perhaps the British could. Whatever their reasoning, the plain fact is that before Waite went to Lebanon, the leaders of the Lebanese kidnap gangs had no use for British hostages; after the failure of Waite's mission in December 1985, British hostages were very much on the kidnappers' agenda.

16

SCOOP!

Hassan Sabra, the editor of the Lebanese weekly magazine *Ash-Shiraa*, was sitting in his office on Monday October 27, 1986, reading through the morning papers when he received a call from his secretary telling him that a group of Iranian gentlemen had arrived in the lobby and were asking to see him. Sabra, a portly left-wing Lebanese journalist in his mid-forties who enjoyed life's comforts too much to have much truck with Islamic fundamentalism, was at first reluctant to meet the men. In his experience, Iranians only spelt one word for a Lebanese journalist – trouble. 'It was not my custom to meet with Iranians,' Sabra explained. 'Iranians always caused me problems.' He asked his secretary to tell the Iranians that he was busy and to make an appointment for another time, a classic Lebanese method of fobbing someone off. But the Iranians insisted they would not leave until they had seen Sabra in person. They had travelled all the way from Iran, and they had some very important information to give him. In the face of such persistence, Sabra had no alternative but to grant their request.

Some years previously, when Ayatollah Khomeini had been

living in Paris, Sabra had flown to France to interview him. During that visit Sabra had met many of Khomeini's close advisers, and when the men walked into his office in Beirut, he quickly recognised them as members of Khomeini's inner circle from his Paris days. Sabra opened the conversation by asking about the fate of Mehdi Hashemi, a leading Iranian radical who had been arrested on the order of Rafsanjani, the speaker of the Iranian parliament, the previous week. Hashemi in many respects typified the problems the more pragmatic members of the Iranian government faced in trying to impose order and responsibility on the chaos of the Islamic revolution. When the Shah was in power, Hashemi had worked as an undercover agent, murdering Iranians suspected of working for the secret police. He had eventually fled to join Khomeini in Paris. Related by marriage to Ayatollah Montazeri, Khomeini's heir apparent, Hashemi was one of several revolutionary leaders who were able to run their own private armies from Teheran with impunity. Hashemi ran an organisation called the Islamic Liberation Movement which was dedicated to exporting the Iranian Revolution. He had fought with the resistance in Afghanistan, and was closely connected to the kidnap groups in Lebanon. Wherever there was trouble in the Middle East, Hashemi would be in on the action. Hashemi's close relationship with Ayatollah Montazeri was a constant source of irritation to Rafsanjani. While Rafsanjani and his circle were trying to impose a measure of legitimacy on the Iranian government, Montazeri and his followers argued that Rafsanjani's policies would destroy the purity of the Iranian Revolution, and resisted Rafsanjani's initiatives at every turn. While Montazeri still carried considerable spiritual influence, Rafsanjani was a more sophisticated political operator, with the result that he was gradually expanding his powerbase within the Majlis, the Iranian parliament. His decision to have Mehdi Hashemi arrested and tried for treason was a manifestation of Rafsanjani's seemingly irresistible rise to power.

The Iranians informed Sabra that the arrest of Mehdi Hashemi was the reason for their visit. Sabra was slightly confused by this. Iran had close links with Lebanon, that he knew. But what could the internal political wranglings in Teheran possibly have to do with Lebanon? And why had they come to *Ash-Shiraa* (the Arabic for sail), a small, left-wing Lebanese weekly magazine which barely survived with its modest readership? The Iranians explained they liked the magazine's anti-establishment line, and the story they had to tell was essentially anti-establishment.

The Iranians proceeded to tell Sabra a story so incredible that the longer they continued the less inclined he was to believe it. The story concerned a peculiar incident at Teheran international airport the previous May, the month after the kidnap of Keenan and McCarthy and the murder of Padfield, Douglas, Kilburn and Collett. Robert McFarlane, the former US National Security Adviser, had tiptoed into Iran equipped with an iced cake and a Bible. The cake, which was decorated with a brass key, had apparently been conceived to symbolise the unlocking of the door to improved relations between the US and Iran. The Bible, which bore a personal inscription by President Reagan, was intended to highlight the historical relationship between Christianity and Islam. The American party all travelled on false Irish passports, and they also carried a brace of gift-wrapped .357 pistols which they intended to offer as personal presents to the ayatollahs. And just in case the Iranians were in any doubt about the Americans' sincerity, they arrived in an Israeli Boeing 707 filled with vital spare parts for Iran's war effort against Iraq.

The Iranians, according to the account given to Sabra, had been distinctly unimpressed by the Americans' surprise arrival. The young Revolutionary Guards at the airport had apparently eaten the cake before it got anywhere near the superiors it was meant to charm. Nor did the Bible and the pistols make any impact. Khomeini personally forbade any of his ministers to meet the American delegation, who were kept waiting unceremoniously at the airport for several hours before being ordered out. Before leaving, McFarlane had given the Iranians a piece of his mind.

'You're nuts,' he was reported to have said. 'If I went to Russia to buy furs, Gorbachev would come to see me three times a day.'

Sabra listened very carefully. Although he confessed himself fascinated by the Iranians' story, he found it difficult to believe. He knew his visitors were friends of Mehdi Hashemi, who was currently languishing in Teheran's Evin prison on treason charges, and he correctly deduced that their purpose in coming to see him with this fantastic tale was to discredit Rafsanjani, the man responsible for Hashemi's arrest. The visitors made it quite plain that the Americans had arrived in Teheran at Rafsanjani's personal invitation, and that the mission had failed because Rafsanjani had been overruled by Khomeini. The clear implication was that Rafsanjani had been caught out trying to undermine the purity of the Islamic revolution by doing a deal with 'the Great Satan', but had been upstaged by Khomeini. The Iranian visitors clearly hoped that publication of this story would greatly embarrass Rafsanjani, leading to his overthrow and the release of Hashemi. They wanted it to be published in Beirut, moveover, so that no one in Teheran would be able to trace the source of the story to themselves.

Sabra was intrigued by the story more because of what it said about the power struggle taking place in Teheran between Rafsanjani's pragmatists and Montazeri's radicals than the involvement of the Americans, the details about whom seemed rather far-fetched. President Reagan had stated publicly and repeatedly that the US would not negotiate any deal for the release of its hostages. Even so, the story was too good not to receive a wider circulation, and so Sabra wrote a long article, almost in the 'a funny thing happened to me on the way to the office' style, and while the article contained all the details provided by his visitors, he left his readers in no doubt that the claims should be treated with a healthy degree of scepticism. As Sabra himself later explained, 'My story was littered with exclamation marks.'

When the 25,000 copies of the magazine went to press, Sabra had no idea of the reaction it would provoke throughout the world. 'I thought it might stir things up in Teheran,' said Sabra, 'but if I am perfectly honest, I had no idea it was going to be a big international scoop.'

The story had a dramatic impact; not because of what it said about the power struggle in Teheran, but because the outlandish tale about McFarlane's visit turned out, more or less, to be true. Sabra's Iranians were seeking to expose a network of contacts which had been established between the American and Iranian governments. It had started as a straightforward exercise by the Americans to get their hostages released from Lebanon, but had developed into a far more serious dialogue in which the ultimate goal on both sides was to effect a diplomatic rapprochement. By exposing this diplomatic initiative, however, the Iranians inadvertently brought to light the biggest political scandal to hit Washington since the Watergate tapes forced the resignation of President Richard Nixon.

In the same way that Terry Waite had used Lambeth Palace as a platform from which to launch his international career, Oliver North had used his modest position at the National Security Council to pursue his own foreign policy initiative, much of which ran contrary to the officially-designated foreign policy goals of the American government. Many of North's activities bordered on the criminal. As with Waite, the reason North had been able to manoeuvre himself into such a position was because his superiors had paid insufficient attention to what he was up to. Bud McFarlane had been well aware that North's irrationality could get the better of him if he was not properly supervised, and had even recommended that North be transferred out of the White House because he was 'too emotionally strung out'. But McFarlane had resigned as National Security Adviser in November 1985, unable to cope with the perpetual in-fighting in the Reagan administration and the perpetual rumour-mongering that he was having an extra-marital affair with a television journalist. He was replaced by his deputy, Admiral John Poindexter, who was so preoccupied with his new responsibilities that he had no time to supervise North.

North had taken his first step on the road to ruin in November 1985 when Waite was in Lebanon. When the shipment of Hawk anti-aircraft missiles North had sent to Teheran in late November ran into difficulties, North got his friends at the CIA to help out. Because he was unable to use an Israeli 707 to carry the missiles, North had got the CIA to provide one of its own aircraft, registered in the name of St Lucia Airways, to deliver the missiles to Teheran. In so doing, however, the CIA had broken a golden rule which had been established following the covert operations scandals of the 1970s; namely, that the CIA should not undertake any covert operations without the express permission of the President. North had got the CIA to help out without bothering to get a presidential finding, or order, giving his approval. To cover their tracks, the CIA lawyers drafted a retrospective finding, which Reagan duly signed. The finding made it quite clear that the purpose of the arms shipment had been to secure the release of the hostages. It also absolved the CIA of its statutory duty to notify the congressional intelligence committees of the operation. Had the congressional leaders been informed of North's arms deals at this early stage, there is no doubt that the whole operation would have been brought to an immediate halt.

Encouraged by his skill at circumventing the rigorous checks and balances of the Washington bureaucracy, North's first task after Poindexter's appointment had been to draw up a long memo proposing a third arms-for-hostages deal. To add a sense of urgency to the proposal, North added that if a further arms shipment was not forthcoming, the hostages would probably be killed. Waite had also reinforced the point that 'lives were at risk' during his mission to Lebanon, although neither North nor Waite had any firm evidence that the kidnappers meant to harm the hostages. North's plan, which was given the code-name Operation Recovery, aimed to resolve the crisis once and for all. A shipment of 3,300 TOW anti-tank missiles would be sent to Teheran in return for the release of all the American hostages. Although the plan itself was not discussed at cabinet level, the notion of trying to establish a dialogue with Iran was discussed at a meeting chaired by Reagan in December, at which both George Shultz and Caspar Weinberger expressed strong opposition to the idea of trading arms for hostages. Reagan himself, however, remained obsessed about getting the hostages freed, and gave his approval to North's memo.

A thousand TOWs were shipped to Teheran in February 1986, but no hostages were forthcoming. Despite this setback, North remained optimistic. When the Iranian intermediary in London suggested that the Iranians would secure the release of all hostages if the Americans agreed to travel to Iran for a meeting with the Iranian leadership, North readily accepted the invitation. As details of the meeting were being finalised, the Iranians suggested it would be helpful if the Americans brought a shipment of Hawk spare parts with them. Ghorbanifar, who arranged the meeting, promised the Americans they would meet the top figures in the Iranian leadership, including Hashemi Rafsanjani. To give the American delegation some credence, McFarlane, for whom opening a channel with 'moderate' Iranians had been a constant obsession during his tenure at the NSC, was invited out of retirement to lead the American team. McFarlane was genuinely excited about going to Teheran, and privately compared the mission to Henry Kissinger's meeting with Chou En-lai at the start of the rapprochement between the US and China in the 1970s. North, however, was more interested in selling arms to the Iranians.

From the beginning of 1986, North had a vested interest in the arms sales to Iran. Apart from trying to get the hostages released, North's other major responsibility was to find ways of assisting the Nicaraguan resistance. North had been to Honduras on fund-raising visits, and was determined to explore any avenue to keep the Contras well-equipped and properly funded. But the restrictions placed by Congress on American aid to the Contras was making it increasingly difficult for North to maintain the level of support the Contras required to sustain a credible resistance. It was during one of many meetings North had at the Churchill Hotel in London, where he discussed the technical arrangements for the arms shipments with Ghorbanifar, the Iranian arms merchant, and Amiram Nir, the Israeli counter-terrorism official, that what North later described as 'a neat idea' took shape.

Ghorbanifar made no attempt to conceal that he was helping to sell arms to Iran primarily for the financial reward. From one transaction alone he could make seven million dollars. During one meeting when North expressed reservations about continuing with the deals, Ghorbanifar took him into the bathroom and offered him a share of the profits. North was outraged. As a dedicated servant of the state, North found the whole idea of bribes repugnant. Not put off by this rebuff,

Ghorbanifar came up with another idea. If North did not want a share, perhaps the profit from the arms sales could be channelled towards the Nicaraguan resistance that North was so fond of talking about. North was immediately struck by the idea, and within a few weeks secret bank accounts had been set up to divert the profits from the arms sales to the Contras. In order to maximise the profits, moreover, North and Ghorbanifar agreed to overcharge the Iranians for all future arms shipments. From early 1986, every arms shipment North sent to Iran meant more money for the Nicaraguan resistance.

When McFarlane's party touched down at Teheran airport on May 25, 1986, the reception they received was not quite what they had expected. There were no senior officials at the airport to meet them as Ghorbanifar had promised, and the party was escorted to the Teheran Hilton, which had the peculiar distinction of being situated at the back of the notorious Evin prison. In his autobiography, *Under Fire*, North says the cake was not taken as a present for the ayatollahs, but for Ghorbanifar's mother. They had purchased the cake at a Jewish delicatessen in Tel Aviv before they set off on the flight to Iran. The cake was placed near the sink in the hold for the flight, and when one of the crew got up to make coffee, a brass key fell from a cupboard and embedded itself in the layers of chocolate. Rather than mess the cake up and remove the key, North rearranged the cake to make it look like a decoration. If Mrs Ghorbanifar asked what the key meant, North said he would tell her, 'This is the key to our hearts.' Mrs Ghorbanifar, if she ever existed, never got to see the cake because it was eaten by hungry Revolutionary Guards when they unloaded the Hawk spare parts.

In every respect McFarlane's visit to Teheran was a failure. Ghorbanifar had promised far more than he could deliver and, as North and McFarlane waited at the Hilton, it became increasingly clear that they were not going to meet any senior members of the government. McFarlane's dream of a Kissinger-like breakthrough was scuppered. It also quickly became apparent that the Iranians McFarlane and North were allowed to meet were unable to fulfil Ghorbanifar's promise for all the hostages to be released. For two days the American team was involved in a tiring round of negotiations with low-level Iranian government officials. McFarlane was insistent that no more arms would be handed over until the hostages were released. The Iranians said this was not possible, and offered to release two hostages after the arms were delivered. Finally McFarlane was so exasperated by the whole proceedings that he ordered the delegation to pack their bags and head for the airport.

Desperate not to return empty handed, North went so far as to go behind McFarlane's back and order a second 707 loaded with Hawk parts to leave Israel and fly to Iran, against the latter's express order. He thought the offer of two hostages in return for a further shipment too good to miss. After all, North stood to make a seven-million-dollar profit for his beloved Contras if the deal went through. When McFarlane found out what North had done, he hit the roof and ordered North to cancel the delivery, forcing the aircraft to turn around in mid-flight. When the delegation returned to Washington, McFarlane was so disturbed by North's behaviour that he actually wrote to Admiral Poindexter recommending that North be given psychiatric help: 'In Ollie's interest I would get him transferred or sent to Bethesda for disability review board.' Bethesda was the naval hospital where North had been treated for emotional stress in 1974 after serving in Vietnam.

While North was busy constructing the network of covert operations that would bring about his spectacular fall, Waite still believed he could be of some use in securing the release of the American hostages. In many respects Waite would have been better advised to have abandoned his efforts. The kidnappers had made it quite clear to him that they wanted no further dealings with him. Furthermore, the frantic dealings he had experienced with Oliver North should have told him that, if this was the way the Americans went about getting their hostages released, they were best left alone to get on with it. Dr Runcie had already made it plain that he did not like the idea of Waite working in Lebanon and was anxious for him to continue with his work for the Anglican Communion at Lambeth. If Waite had simply admitted that he had tried his best to no avail, and that he could not pursue the matter any further, no one would have held it against him. But Waite was not prepared to accept defeat: he felt a genuine, personal commitment. Waite also had Oliver North constantly telling him that his role was crucial to the successful conclusion of the hostage crisis.

Although Waite and North were working more closely together, they had very different ideas about the precise nature of Waite's role. After his failure to obtain a Kuwaiti visa, Waite tried a new tack. If he could not free the Dawa 17, perhaps he could compensate by securing the release of Shia Muslims held by Israel in southern Lebanon. North thought he could get his friend Amiram Nir to facilitate a visit to Israel. Waite arranged to see North at Lambeth Palace on January 22. North told Waite he was going to be in London that day 'on business'. What he did not say was that he would first be going to the Churchill Hotel for another meeting with Ghorbanifar to arrange the February arms shipment to Teheran.

North arrived at Lambeth Palace with Amiram Nir. Waite met them at the main entrance by Lambeth Bridge and escorted them along the Great Corridor into the pink drawing room where the Archbishop on occasions received his guests. Waite was clearly uneasy about the meeting, and many months later attempted to deny any such meeting ever took place. Nor did he derive much satisfaction from it. North informed him that it would not be possible for him to go to southern Lebanon because the Israelis could not guarantee his safety. This was palpable nonsense. Foreign visitors were constantly being invited to tour Israel's security zone in southern Lebanon. North did not want Waite to go because it might have revealed Nir's activities to his superiors in the Israeli military establishment, something which Nir was anxious to avoid. Waite refused to be put off, however, and the next day he travelled to Rome with Samir Habiby to see his old friends from the time when Waite worked for the Catholic Church and to enlist the support of the Vatican for his Lebanon mission.

North perservered with Waite, even though his contact with the kidnappers had all but ceased, because North still believed Waite could be of use to him. North had not forgotten how Waite had helped him out of his public relations jam after Ben Weir's release, and he wanted to be able to count on Waite's availability in the event of further hostage releases. Indeed, North dreamt up several fantastic scenarios for Waite which thankfully never came to fruition. One involved fitting Waite up with a tracking device and sending him back to Lebanon to see the kidnappers. Once the location of the kidnappers had been established, North would send in a team of special forces to rescue the hostages. North also thought of using Waite when the Americans were planning their bombing raid against Libya. His idea then was to get Waite to go to Tripoli to see Gaddafi, with whom he had struck up a good relationship when he secured the release of the four British hostages in 1984. As soon as Waite left the meeting, the Americans would bomb the building in which Gaddafi had given the interview.

When North was planning McFarlane's trip to Teheran, he initially wanted Waite to travel with the party. North envisaged Waite looking after the released hostages in Teheran while the arms deal was completed. In the event, when

McFarlane's delegation left for Teheran, Waite was flown by North to the American embassy in East Beirut. After his experience the previous Christmas, Waite could not risk crossing into Muslim West Beirut. Before Waite left for Lebanon, North told him that further hostage releases were likely. When the McFarlane visit collapsed, Waite flew back to London empty handed.

By allowing North to dictate his movements in this manner, Waite was seriously compromising his status as an independent humanitarian, a fact which Habiby was quick to seize upon when he learned of Waite's secret trip to Lebanon. Habiby was concerned that a mission which was supposed to be carried out on behalf of the Church was becoming too closely identified with the White House, and flew down to Washington to see North at the Old Executive Building to seek assurances that North would respect the independence of the Church. Waite has never given an adequate explanation as to why he allowed himself to be used in this fashion. As an 'independent humanitarian', Waite appreciated that he needed the assistance of other agencies to facilitate his mission. But the effort to release the American hostages was no longer Waite's mission; it was being run by Oliver North. Waite had been given a specific agenda by the kidnappers, but had failed to deliver. Waite must have known that, as in the release of Benjamin Weir, nothing he had achieved personally had resulted in the release of a hostage from Lebanon, yet when Oliver North offered him the opportunity to take all the credit for a hostage release, Waite jumped at the opportunity. It was to prove a serious error of judgement.

Nor had Thatcher's support for the American raid on Libya done much to assist Waite's mission. Apart from putting West Beirut out of bounds to any British or American citizen, no matter how humanitarian their credentials, the kidnapping of Brian Keenan and John McCarthy only increased Waite's difficulties. Having picked up reports in the Middle East that there was more to Waite's mission than he was prepared to admit in public, Irish government officials persuaded Keenan's relatives to have nothing to do with Waite.

'We had the distinct feeling that Waite was not the full shilling,' explained an Irish diplomat who worked closely on getting Keenan released. 'We were getting all these reports that there was more to his relationship with the Americans than he was prepared to admit, and we felt we stood a better chance of getting Keenan released if we did not get Waite involved.' Waite did however meet with John McCarthy's father Patrick at Lambeth Palace. He offered Mr McCarthy his sincere commiserations about the abduction of his son and said he would like to help. Waite said he was concerned about the 'recent phenomenon' of the British hostages, which only served to make his task more difficult. But he stressed that his primary obligation was to work for the release of the Americans.

'We've going to get them out, you know,' Waite confided to Mr McCarthy, without specifying what he meant by 'we'. As had been the case with Alec Collett, Waite was too involved with the Americans to worry about British hostages.

If Waite was kept completely in the dark about Oliver North's secret arms deals with Iran, the same could not be said of the British government. Mrs Thatcher, Geoffrey Howe, Michael Heseltine, the then defence secretary, and William Whitelaw, Leader of the House, were all provided by MI5, Britain's internal security service, with a full transcript of a meeting which took place on Sunday December 8, 1985, at the palatial West End apartment of a leading Israeli arms dealer. Bud McFarlane had flown to London three days after formally handing in his notice as National Security Adviser for one last meeting with Ghorbanifar to see if there was any possibility of securing the release of the American hostages without resorting to further arms deals. The unusual collection of American officials and Middle Eastern arms dealers inevitably caught the attention of MI5, which arranged to have the apartment bugged for the meeting, which started at 3 pm and lasted several hours. As a consequence the British government was furnished with all the details of the arms shipments which the Americans had already sent to Iran, and the attitudes of the various participants to future arms sales. Having had their appetites whetted by this meeting, MI5 continued to monitor all of North's subsequent meetings at Ghorbanifar's suite at the Churchill Hotel, at which the details for all North's early arms shipments were worked out.

Throughout this period Terry Waite was in regular contact with the Foreign Office. Lord Runcie recalls that Lambeth Palace always had better relations with the Foreign Office than with Downing Street. When he was in London, Waite had regular meetings at the Foreign Office. Initially he would liaise with Foreign Office officials about the Archbishop's forthcoming trips abroad. During his missions to Iran and Libya, he had worked closely with British diplomats. And when he agreed to accept the Lebanese assignment, he stayed in regular contact with Sir David Miers, the former British ambassador to Lebanon who had been placed in charge of the Middle East desk. For the Lebanon mission, Waite saw his visits to the Foreign Office very much as a courtesy call. His primary responsibility was to his new-found American friends who had introduced him to a lifestyle infinitely more dynamic and exciting than anything he had ever experienced working with the staid old Foreign Office.

'He was very good at keeping his cards close to his chest,' recalled Sir David. 'He knew people had placed their trust in him and he knew how to respect that.' If Waite kept his cards close to his chest, so did the British government. From December 1985, Thatcher and Howe had all the details concerning North's arms deals. The British authorities were also well aware that Waite was working closely with Oliver North, even though Waite tried to conceal the fact at his meetings with Miers. Once MI5 was on North's trail, it could hardly fail to notice two such unlikely characters as North and Nir trotting across Lambeth Bridge for afternoon tea with Terry Waite. But at no point was Waite warned of the dangers of working with North, even though he was meeting with senior Foreign Office officials on average once every two weeks.

At first the information provided by MI5 was confined to a small group of senior ministers and advisers within the British government on the strict understanding that no action be taken on the information. One of the worst-kept secrets of the intelligence world is that intelligence services spend as much time spying on their allies as on their enemies, the only difference being that they need to be more circumspect about how they use information they have acquired about friendly nations. Thus, having learned what North and McFarlane were up to, Thatcher felt no need to raise the issue with her close friend and ally, President Reagan. To do so would have been highly embarrassing. At the time Britain learned about North's arms deals, it was of little consequence for the British. The only British hostage in Lebanon was Alec Collett. He was held by a Palestinian group, so that his chances of release would not be affected by the Americans shipping arms to Iran. How far the information was passed down the hierarchy of the Foreign Office is an open question. Sir David Miers, who as head of the Middle East desk should have been privy to the information, said he didn't know the full picture until late 1986.

'Stories often surfaced through our contacts in London that

something was going on,' said Sir David. 'But when we raised the matter with the Americans, we got no satisfaction. We were asking people who knew as little about the North operation as we did.'

The kidnapping of John McCarthy in April 1986, however, changed the picture entirely for the British government. After the public outcry which had greeted the murders of Padfield, Douglas and Collett, the British government was now required to enter the quicksands of the Lebanese hostage crisis to secure McCarthy's release. From the outset Mrs Thatcher was insistent that no deals would be done. But in order for her to maintain this position, she needed to be sure she could count on her closest ally, the United States, to stand by its public statements that it would pursue the same policy. Mrs Thatcher's position, however, would become untenable if Oliver North continued with his arms deals. In order to make sure the Americans supported the British position, Mrs Thatcher sent two of her most senior advisers to see Admiral John Poindexter, the US National Security Adviser. Sir Percy Cradock was a distinguised diplomat whose primary responsibility at Downing Street was to handle all intelligence reports, and decide which ones were worthy of the prime minister's attention, whether they concerned undercover operations against the IRA or Oliver North's arms deals. Sir Percy flew to Washington at the end of May 1986, one month after McCarthy's kidnapping. On June 1, accompanied by Sir Anthony Acland, the British ambassador in Washington, Sir Percy attended a meeting at Admiral John Poindexter's office at the White House.

Robert Oakley, a no-nonsense Texan who was then in charge of the State Department's counter-terrorism department and attended the preliminary meeting, said Cradock and Acland quickly came to the point.

'They came in to see us and said: "What the hell are you

people up to?" Oakley recalled.' Acland and Cradock made no mention of the meetings that had been bugged in London, but said they had received information from Tiny Rowland, the British entrepreneur, that the Americans were 'shipping arms all over the place' in an attempt to get their hostages released. The British delegation forcibly made the point that, only a month previously, the Thatcher government had stuck its neck out by supporting the American raid against Libya, and had had to face the consequences when three British citizens were murdered in retaliation. According to another American diplomat present at the meeting, Cradock and Acland made no secret of their disquiet at what the Americans were up to.

'They had accepted risks on our behalf,' the diplomat explained. 'And here we were doing a deal. They could tell what was going on, and they were very upset.'

Poindexter heard the envoys out in stony silence. The British delegation asked him to confirm, categorically, that the United States would never pay a ransom, even indirectly, for the release of the hostages. Poindexter tried to turn the question aside. 'We are looking at a variety of ways to get the hostages out,' he acknowledged, playing with his pipe.

'But an arms deal?' Cradock persisted.

'No,' Poindexter said calmly. 'There's no arms deal in the works.'

As Oakley later said of the meeting: 'Cradock and Acland came to see Poindexter to find out what was going on. They did not get a satisfactory answer.' The meeting nevertheless showed the much-vaunted 'special relationship' between Britain and the United States in an interesting light. The British spied on the Americans, but would not admit it. The Americans doublecrossed the British, and lied through their teeth about it. It was what is known by the French as *raison d'état*.

The British delegation were not the only ones who did not

receive a satisfactory explanation from the NSC. The US State Department, the institution responsible for running American foreign policy, knew nothing about the scope of North's activities which, if anything, were expanding rather than contracting, as he continued to pursue the twin goals of freeing the American hostages and providing funds for the Contra guerrillas.

Although McFarlane and his team had returned to Washington in a state of deep depression following the Teheran meeting, McFarlane's principled stand of shipping no more arms until the hostages were freed paid one small dividend in July with the release of Lawrence Jenco, the Roman Catholic priest who had been kidnapped in Beirut eighteen months previously. As was the kidnappers' custom, Jenco was given hardly any warning of his impending release. The kidnappers had told all the hostages in May that they would all soon be going home. Clearly word had filtered through from Iran about the anticipated success of the McFarlane visit. As suddenly as the guards had raised the prospect of freedom, they dropped it. Then two months later they raised the subject again, and asked David Jacobsen to make a video, in which he once again spelt out the kidnappers' conditions and called on Reagan to negotiate for the hostages' release. Having made the video, Jacobsen thought he might be the lucky hostage being released, but without any explanation they told Jenco he was going home. After saying a few prayers with his companions, Jenco was bound head to foot with masking tape so that he resembled a mummy, packed into the back of a car and driven to the Bekaa Valley where the kidnappers removed the tape, handed him the videotape, and gave him some Lebanese money to get a taxi. They then left the elderly priest to stumble around in the dark for several hours before he came across some Lebanese children who raised the alarm.

At the moment Jenco was released, Waite was in Jordan on official Church business. North had been in touch with Waite and told him that a release was likely, and that if it happened he wanted Waite to fly directly to Damascus. Waite said he would be happy to oblige, and as soon as news reached him that Jenco had been set free, he took the first flight to Damascus. Waite's transportation was organised by Robert Oakley. 'I got a call from Ollie saying that we had to find Waite and get him to Damascus because another hostage was coming out and North needed him to handle the publicity,' Oakley recalled. 'Now this is not an easy proposition at the best of times. We tracked Waite down to Amman, but he had no visa for Damascus. We had to pull a lot of strings to get him a visa, and arrange the transportation. But we managed it. We got him to the church on time.' At the time Oakley, who knew very little about the arms deals, thought there was nothing unusual about Waite going to Damascus. 'There were all kinds of people trying to get involved, and we didn't turn any of them away in case they could be of some use. But when you look back at it, none of them did any damn good.'

When Waite arrived at the American ambassador's residence in Damascus, he embraced Jenco warmly. Then, as he engaged him in conversation, he said something which confused Jenco.

'He told me he'd been waiting for my release in Amman. Then he said, "You do believe me, don't you?" I had no reason not to believe him. I knew absolutely nothing about what was going on, except that I was free. It struck me as a very odd thing to say.'

On Oliver North's instructions, briefings given by White House spokesman Larry Speakes about Jenco's release attempted to ensure that Waite received all the credit. 'Terry Waite was instrumental in Jenco's release,' said Speakes, 'and I don't think he has really gotten the proper credit yet.' For the next few days, every time Jenco appeared in public, Waite was at his side. And every time someone asked a question about Jenco's release, Waite gave the distinct impression that he, and he alone, had been responsible. Waite accompanied Jenco to the American military base at Wiesbaden in West Germany for his debriefing and reunion with his family. He then flew with Jenco to the Vatican to see the Pope. Jenco told Waite he had a message to the Pope from the kidnappers. Waite asked him to say there was also a message for the Archbishop of Canterbury, a request which further confused Jenco. Waite explained that this would enable him to make a new appeal to the kidnappers. At the press conference in Rome, Waite made a fresh appeal to the kidnappers to renew the dialogue which had been so abruptly terminated the previous Christmas so that a solution to the problem could be found 'based on the tenets common to Islam and Christianity'. Waite also told the press that his presence in the Middle East at the time of Jenco's release was 'not a coincidence'. To Waite's surprise, the kidnappers responded, but not in the way Waite had intended. A terse statement issued in Beirut denied the kidnappers had sent any message to the Archbishop of Canterbury through Jenco. The leaders of Islamic Jihad clearly had no desire to engage in further discussions with Terry Waite.

Jenco's release gave Waite a new lease of life. His mission had looked to be going nowhere; all his initiatives had failed, and the Libyan raid had made his task infinitely more difficult. Waite had indicated that he was getting tired of his globe-trotting role, and was putting out feelers for a new job. 'It's such an obsessively demanding job,' Waite said in a candid interview in June. 'There are too many strains and pressures. There's a limit to how long anyone can do it. It's terrible not to be able to be a normal human being.' He fancied working for a well-established charity such as the Prince of Wales Trust which would give him a high profile.

He was also looking for a job with better remuneration. He privately complained that his £16,000-a-year salary was insufficient given his international status. He considered the possibility of working for a private American company which specialised in international hostage negotiations. Waite also complained in private that he did not get sufficient credit from Runcie for his efforts, although this was probably due to the fact that Runcie knew so little about what Waite was up to. Waite felt he was a worthy contender for the Nobel peace prize, and was disappointed that he had not been adopted as a candidate.

With Jenco's release, however, Waite was back in the limelight. For the first time in a long while the British tabloids were able to garland Waite with praise. 'Hero Waite helps free priest', said one headline, while another read: 'Thank God for Mr Fixit Terry Waite'. When Waite was asked at a press conference how he had managed to get Jenco free, he merely looked at the ground and replied: 'Wouldn't you like to know.' At the start of August Waite read the lesson at a memorial service at St Martin-in-the-Fields on behalf of Padfield, Douglas and Collett, the murdered Britons, an ironic choice given how little interest Waite had shown in the fate of the British hostages. But Waite's public persona knew no bounds. In Britain and America he had become a celebrity. When he bought an MGB roadster which was specially converted to take his large frame, all the national newspapers sent photographers to record the event. He even hosted a six-part television talk show, in which he interviewed the great and the good, such as Princess Anne and the mountaineer Chris Bonington. The show was an unmitigated disaster. One newspaper referred to him as a 'bearded blancmange' while another critic thought the host of the show was too self-obsessed to pay sufficient regard to his guests. 'Self-effacement was not one of Waite's strong suits,' the critic wrote. 'He talked as much about himself as about his interviewee.'

In mid-August Waite accompanied Runcie to San Francisco for a Church conference. It was the first time Runcie had been in close proximity with Waite for many months, and he used the opportunity to express his reservations about Waite continuing to work on the Lebanon mission.

'I was still unhappy about Terry being involved in Lebanon, and I wanted him to concentrate his efforts at Lambeth Palace,' said Runcie. 'But Terry persuaded me that the hostage releases were all his own work, and I believed him.' While in San Francisco, Runcie was irritated when Waite used a press conference called by the Church to make a direct appeal to the kidnappers for the release of all American hostages.

'To be honest I was a bit miffed about the whole thing,' said Runcie. 'We had come to San Francisco to talk about serious Church matters, and here was Terry issuing statements about Lebanon. It was not appropriate.' Waite issued a further statement when the Church party arrived in New York. Waite was now an instantly recognisable celebrity in the US as well as Britain, and he hated to disappoint the camera crews who followed him everywhere. 'Let's get out of the problem in Lebanon with honour and with dignity and move forward,' he said on arrival in New York. Waite clearly had plans to return to Beirut for another meeting with the kidnappers. Islamic Jihad, however, issued a statement, together with a picture of David Jacobsen, which left no one in any doubt about what the kidnappers thought of Waite's performance. The statement did not mention Waite by name, but it was clear to whom it was referring.

'As for those who are issuing repeated publicity plans,' the statement read, 'we say: "You know our demands perfectly well and how they can be met. So why don't you take effective action to produce a solution? You must know that empty publicity goes with the wind. Or do you want to reap personal gain?"'

While Waite was getting excited about the possibility of another visit to Lebanon, North was continuing with the arms shipments to Iran. North, with Poindexter's backing, had persuaded President Reagan that the hostages might be harmed if the arms sales did not continue. The consignment of Hawk missile parts McFarlane had prevented being sent in May were delivered to Teheran in August. The Iranians were happy, Ghorbanifar made a handsome profit and North received a healthy contribution for the Contras' war chest.

While North and Waite in their different ways believed they were making a positive contribution to resolving the hostage crisis, events in Beirut suggested otherwise. On September 9, Frank Reed, an American who ran his own language school in Beirut, was kidnapped as he was being driven by his chauffeur to play golf near Beirut airport. Given the number of people who had already been kidnapped in Lebanon, it was inconceivable that there were still Americans living in Beirut, let alone Americans who played golf less than a mile from the southern suburbs. Reed, who was in his mid-fifties, had lived in Beirut for eight years and married a Lebanese woman, by whom he had a son. Reed had converted to Islam and felt he was safe because he was married to a Lebanese.

Nor was he the only American citizen still in West Beirut. Three days after Reed's abduction, Joseph Cicippio was kidnapped from outside his office at the AUB. A close friend of David Jacobsen, Cicippio had been in Lebanon for two years. He too had converted to Islam and married a Lebanese woman, Elham Ghandour, who was working at the American embassy in East Beirut. Cicippio thought he was safe so long as he did not leave the AUB campus. But in a well-executed operation the kidnappers broke into the campus and kidnapped Cicippio as he was walking to his office. A month later a third American, Edward Tracy, was kidnapped as he sat drinking coffee in his favourite West Beirut café. Tracy was a wanderer who had travelled the world in search of his fortune. The fortune had proved elusive, but he settled in Beirut where he made a modest income selling the *Encyclopedia Britannica*. When sales declined because of the war, Tracy took to selling Bibles. When this did not work, he sold copies of the Koran. In addition he wrote several books of poetry. By the time he was abducted, he was already showing signs of mental illness. Having seized Reed, Cicippio and Tracy, the kidnappers had more Americans in their possession than they did when North and Waite first started their mission to Lebanon. As far as the kidnappers were concerned, hostage-taking was a profitable business.

The continuing abduction of American citizens seemed to make little impression on either Waite or North. Waite went on giving press conferences offering to return to Beirut while North planned more arms deals with the Iranians. After all the problems North and McFarlane had experienced over the May trip to Teheran, North had decided to find a more reliable intermediary than Ghorbanifar, whom he thought was too much driven by his own profit motive to be reliable. Using a series of intermediaries, North was introduced to Ali Hashemi Bahremani, an up-and-coming Iranian official who was also the nephew of Hashemi Rafsanjani. Bahremani impressed the Americans with his intelligence and common sense, and was invited to Washington where he agreed to help free the hostages in return for further arms supplies. Unlike Ghorbanifar, Bahremani did not promise the earth, only what was feasible. From the outset he made it clear he could not secure the release of all the hostages, an indication of the real relationship between Teheran and Hizbollah. Bahremani also told North that a rival faction was responsible for the kidnapping of Reed, Cicippio and Tracy because they were annoyed North would no longer do business with them. An arms deal needed to be concluded quickly if the hostages were to be released.

On October 28, 1986, an Israeli plane flew to Teheran with a further shipment of 500 TOW missiles as part of a deal arranged between North and Bahremani. Two days later, at North's request, Terry Waite flew to Cyprus to be available for a further hostage release. He did not have long to wait. On November 2, David Jacobsen, the director of the American Hospital, was released in Beirut after eighteen months in captivity. Waite flew with North in an American military helicopter from Cyprus to Beirut to collect Jacobsen. As they did so the first copies of *Ash-Shiraa* were delivered to the Lebanese news-stands.

17

THE LAST SUPPER

When Terry Waite stood up to say grace at his Lebanese friend's well-appointed Kensington flat, his thoughts were more on the perilous journey ahead than on the sumptuous spread upon the table. The next morning Waite was to set off on by far the most dangerous journey of his jet-setting career. He had decided to return alone to West Beirut in an attempt to salvage his reputation and to secure the release of the hostages. In an attempt to raise everyone's spirits, Kamal Khoury, a successful London-based Lebanese businessman and former cabinet minister who had helped Waite plan his mission, threw a dinner party for a select group of friends. There was not a guest present that Sunday evening, January 11, 1987, who had not attempted to persuade Waite against returning to Lebanon. But Waite had set his heart on going back and now was not the time for backsliding. Now was the time to offer Waite support, and to pray that his visit would pass quickly and without incident.

Ever since *Ash-Shiraa* had revealed the Iran-Contra scandal, as it was quickly to become known, the previous November, Waite had been obsessed with the idea of returning to West

Beirut. Once the full story of North's arms shipments was revealed, Waite's position seemed to have been seriously compromised. The more serious newspapers, which had become distinctly cool towards Waite the more he cultivated his populist image, published articles raising questions not only about his judgement, which seemed to have been seriously at fault as far as North was concerned, but about his real motives for wanting to hog the limelight. Waite felt the only way to confound the critics was to go back to Beirut and prove that he did not need the assistance of Oliver North, or anyone else for that matter, to deliver the goods.

This was a very dangerous undertaking for Waite. On the several occasions he had returned to the Lebanese capital at North's behest to supervise a release, he had travelled to East Beirut, the Christian and, to a certain extent, pro-West sector of the city where foreigners were generally immune from the attentions of the Shia gangs. The last time he had been in West Beirut was in December 1985 when the kidnappers had given him twenty-four hours to leave the city on pain of death. For all Waite's bravura, returning to West Beirut was an exceedingly hazardous proposition and one not made any easier now that the hostage situation had become immensely more complicated. Of the original group of Americans he had sought to release, Terry Anderson and Thomas Sutherland were still in captivity. In addition, three more Americans were being held; Reed, Cicippio and Tracy – at least two of them, Cicippio and Tracy, by a different group to the one Waite had been dealing with. Add to this list John McCarthy, Brian Keenan, half-a-dozen Frenchmen and a brace of other luckless nationalities, and it was clear that Waite faced an almost impossible task.

Trying to get the hostages released, however, was not high on Waite's list of priorities. His primary purpose was to salvage his reputation. In effect he was conducting a glorified public relations exercise solely engineered for the rehabilitation of Terry Waite. If he managed to get some hostages released into the bargain, all well and good. But Waite knew in his heart of hearts that this was a remote possibility. He admitted as much when Khoury, who as a Lebanese citizen would never have dreamt of going to Lebanon at that time, tried to persuade him to reconsider his position.

'None of us wanted Terry to go back to Lebanon,' said Khoury, whose urbanity and sophistication is a testament to the more attractive side of the Lebanese national character. 'But once he decided to go back, we had to do everything we could to help him. Beirut was at its lowest ebb and he needed all the help he could get. Terry wanted to go back to prove his innocence. He had been used and he wanted to show he had nothing to do with North.'

When Khoury asked Waite what he hoped to achieve, Waite replied: 'I've just got to demonstrate I can go to places like Beirut of my own accord. All I want is to spend five minutes in Beirut to show the world that Terry Waite is his own man. Then I'll jump on the next plane home. I promise you I won't take any risks.'

Khoury had only become involved with Waite at the end of 1986 when he was contacted by Habiby, with whom he had previously worked in Lebanon, and asked if he could be of assistance. Khoury was a personal friend of Walid Jumblatt, and thought he would be able to get the Druze to protect Waite.

Waite's initial plan was to make a repeat trip to Beirut for Christmas 1986, a dubious proposition indeed given the response his hostage-for-Christmas ploy had evoked the previous year.

'I really would like to be there over Christmas because these Islamic groups know how they feel about their religious festivals and they recognise the importance of Christmas for us,'

Waite said at press conference in London in mid-December. 'It leads to a bit more flexibility.' It almost defies belief that Waite could seriously propose that the kidnappers had any interest in a Christian festival when they were coming to terms with the implications of the Iran-Contra revelations. Fortunately for Waite, security in Lebanon was so dire that a repeat Christmas visit was ruled out of the question. But the fact that Waite had even considered going to Lebanon on such a flimsy pretext demonstrated that he was prepared to clutch at straws to save his reputation.

Right up until the moment the Iran-Contra scandal broke, Waite had behaved as though every hostage release from Lebanon was entirely his own doing, and he did his utmost to obtain maximum publicity. As soon as he arrived at the American embassy in early November 1986, having flown into East Beirut with Oliver North in preparation for David Jacobsen's release, Waite telephoned the AP office in West Beirut and announced: 'I'm here. Something might happen.' Within minutes journalists were heading for the Middle East from all over the world. North made no secret of the fact to his American colleagues that Waite had been brought along simply to handle the publicity, a role Waite seemed happy to fulfil.

Waite flew with North and Jacobsen by helicopter from Beirut to Larnaca for Jacobsen's first press conference since being set free. When the helicopter landed, North ducked out of sight while Waite and Jacobsen faced the press. Waite looked relaxed and confident. I had not seen him since we had been trapped in the Commodore Hotel together the year previously, and I remained bemused about how he was still managing to secure the release of hostages when I knew for a fact that he had not set foot in West Beirut for twelve months. When I put this to him briefly at Larnaca, he just laughed and said, 'You know full well I cannot divulge the details of my mission.'

At the press conference Jacobsen, still clearly under the impression that Waite alone was responsible for his release, paid the Anglican churchman a fulsome tribute. 'This man did something that we really appreciated. He gave us hope that we would be free men again. We love this guy.' Waite ended the press conference by holding out the prospect that the five other Americans might soon be released, saying he would know within twenty-four hours whether he would be returning to Beirut. This statement raised more questions than it answered. If Waite was hoping to bring five Americans out, he must have made contact with an entirely separate group of kidnappers without going to West Beirut. And if he could do this, why was he not working for the release of Keenan and McCarthy, or even the French hostages for that matter? Whenever Waite spoke publicly about his mission, he never made any mention of McCarthy and Keenan, an omission which did not seem to square with the amount of enthusiasm he was devoting to the American hostages.

The arms-for-hostages scandal broke while Waite was flying from Larnaca to Wiesbaden where Jacobsen was to undergo his official debriefing and medical examination, and when the media began to ask him about his involvement in the arms deals, Waite's attitude towards the publicity he had so rigorously courted changed radically. Waite could hardly avoid the media, but when he arrived for the press conference at Wiesbaden, his demeanour had altered. Gone was the ebullient and confident Waite who had actively sought the media in Beirut. Here a cautious, defensive man who looked as though he had suffered a severe loss of self-confidence.

'Quite frankly speculation as far as I'm concerned is so dangerous because it's putting further at risk the lives of the hostages in Lebanon,' said Waite. It was a favourite fall-back position of his, as it had been for Oliver North, to raise the prospect of hostages' lives being in danger whenever awkward questions were asked. 'There are a lot of people trying to make political capital,' Waite continued. 'There are a lot of people trying to sabotage honest and straightforward efforts. There are a lot of people muscling in on this whole thing for a variety of reasons best known to themselves.'

By the time he got back to London, Waite had become decidedly ratty. 'Do these people who write such speculative comments realise that such comments could cost me my life?' he snapped at Heathrow. By way of highlighting his personal bravery, Waite revealed how Islamic Jihad had threatened to kill him the previous year. At the time, of course, Waite had made no mention of the kidnappers' threats; on the contrary, he said that he had made 'good progress' and that his mission was continuing.

For the first few weeks of the Iran-Contra scandal, Waite managed to distance himself from the political fall-out which swept through Washington as the true extent of North's activities was revealed. North's parting words to Waite in Wiesbaden were for him to keep his head down while North was still hopeful that more hostages would be released, and he wanted to be able to call on Waite again to handle the publicity. But events were quickly to overtake North. Despite the frantic effort by him and his secretary Fawn Hall to consign to the shredding machine all the most sensitive documents relating to the arms deals and the diversion of the profits to the Contras, William Bradford Reynolds, the Assistant Attorney General, managed to uncover a document on November 25 which clearly showed that at least $12 million in profits from the sales to Iran had been channelled by North to finance the Contras. Reynolds was acting on behalf of President Reagan, who had asked for a thorough investigation of the National Security Council's activities. This was not a document that could be swept under the carpet. By the end of November North had been sacked, Admiral Poindexter had resigned and Reagan had appointed a trusted Republican senator, John Tower, to conduct a full inquiry into the activities of the NSC.

Had North been able to resist the temptation to use the profits of the arms trade to finance the Contras, it is interesting to consider whether the revelations would have caused such a major political scandal, a scandal which was to ruin the last two years of Reagan's presidency. Although the American government had passed legislation banning arms sales to Iran, it would have been very difficult for US congressmen to pillory the administration for undertaking a course of action designed to effect the release of American citizens from Lebanon. Thanks to the efforts of the hostages' relatives, in particular Terry Anderson's sister Peggy Say, there was considerable public pressure on the government to get the hostages freed. The real problem with the arms sales was that, rather than resolving the hostage crisis, they prolonged it. For every American North and Waite brought home, another was taken captive.

As the political crisis deepened in Washington, Waite was summoned before the Archbishop of Canterbury to give a full account of his actions. Runcie had only allowed Waite to continue with the mission because Waite had insisted he was directly responsible for the release of the Americans.

'Terry misled me,' said Runcie. 'On several occasions during the summer of 1986 I suggested to him that he should give up the Lebanon mission, but I was misled about the degree to which he was in direct contact with the kidnappers. When Weir, Jenco and Jacobsen came out, I had been led to believe by Terry that he had been a significant factor. In those circumstances I could hardly tell him to stop working for the release of the American hostages. He always gave me the impression he was able to travel backwards and forwards to Beirut as he chose. He never told me that he had been ordered out of Beirut by the kidnappers.'

But Runcie was becoming increasingly irritated that Waite was neglecting his duties for the pursuit of international glory. 'This was a source of constant disagreement between us because Terry was becoming an international figure and there was a whole area of his work he was neglecting at Lambeth Palace from 1986,' said Runcie. 'He did not keep me in touch and I, to my great regret, did not do enough to find out what he was up to. I had many other more important matters to attend to, and I trusted Terry's judgement. If I had known more about what he was up to, I would have been a lot more firm with him.'

When news of the arms-for-hostages scandal reached Runcie, however, with all its political implications, the Archbishop was faced with no alternative other than to summon Waite to his office and demand a full explanation. 'It was all rather unpleasant, really,' said Runcie, 'and I was annoyed that it had reached this stage. But I had to have him in and thrash the whole matter out.'

During a heated discussion, Waite gave Runcie a categorical assurance that he had nothing to do with North's arms deals. Waite was insistent that his only contact with the Americans had been to use their transport facilities to get in and out of Beirut. Runcie replied that even this compromised Waite's status as a representative of the Church. If Waite was unable to go to Beirut without the assistance of the American government, said Runcie, he should never have gone.

As all the details of Waite's mission over the previous eighteen months became clear, Runcie reluctantly came to the conclusion that he would have to sack Waite. 'The basic fact of the matter was that he had been working independently of me, which was something he should never have been allowed to do. I never employed him as an envoy. I employed him to work for me for the Church and to keep me informed of developments taking place throughout the Anglican Communion. I think both Terry and I recognised that we would have to part company.'

Runcie attributes the failure of Waite's Lebanon mission to two main factors: his inability to make any progress with the Kuwaitis; and Waite's use of publicity for his own ends. 'I disapproved of him not winding up the Lebanon mission after the 1985 trip, but he remained determined to continue to work for the American hostages.' Runcie also believes Waite was a victim of American duplicity. 'His love of publicity and lack of sophistication about what was being worked on him by the Americans were the cause of all his difficulties.' Despite the problems in their working relationship Runcie still retains an affection for Waite, and acknowledges that he must accept some of the blame for allowing Waite to run out of control. 'If only I'd known more, I would have acted. But I was too busy with other matters to spend my time tracking Terry, and he did not feel inclined to let me know what he was up to. But I remain affectionately loyal to him. He was someone who genuinely cared for the underdog, and no one who had worked with him had any doubts about the depth of his compassion and commitment.'

The only reason Runcie and Waite did not part company immediately the Iran-Contra scandal broke was that Waite insisted he must make one more trip to Lebanon. 'He felt it was very important both for himself and the Church that he be allowed to return to Beirut as soon as possible,' Runcie explained. 'He felt that if he could go back, it would absolve the Church from any accusations that it could only take on foreign missions with the help of governments or other institutions. I was very much against it, and tried to persuade him not to go. In the circumstances I felt that he would need all the protection he could get, and that this was not the moment to withdraw the protection of the Church. But we both agreed that he would not be working for the Church once the Beirut trip had been completed.' In effect, before sacking Waite, Runcie was allowing him an opportunity to vindicate himself, an opportunity to which, strictly speaking, Waite was not entitled. But Runcie's dislike of taking hard and fast decisions had been the hallmark of his tenure as Archbishop, and his failure to refuse Waite permission to return to Beirut as a representative of the Church was something he would regret for years to come.

On the other side of the Atlantic, the Iran-Contra revelations had had a similarly devastating impact upon the headquarters of the Episcopal Church in Manhattan, which had funded Waite's mission for the past eighteen months. Father William Dearnaly, who had worked as Waite's press officer in the US, was on sick leave when the story broke. 'I first saw it in the *New York Times*, and when I saw the name Oliver North I turned green,' Dearnaly recalled. 'I knew we had been in contact with North as part of Waite's mission. It was the first time that I realised Waite's humanitarian mission was in fact something entirely different.' The immediate fear within the hierarchy of the Episcopal Church was that Church officials faced the possibility of being subpoenaed to appear before the congressional committees set up to investigate North's activities. Such an eventuality would be disastrous for a church which prided itself on being independent of the government. It would also jeopardise the credibility of the Church's foreign relief operations, many of which were only tolerated by the local authorities because the Church was able to demonstrate its independence of American government policy.

The Church needed a scapegoat, and Samir Habiby fitted the bill perfectly. Habiby had initially become involved with Waite at the request of the then Presiding Bishop, John Allen. Allen, however, had retired at the end of 1985, and Edmund Browning, his successor, did not see eye to eye with Habiby whom he found abrasive and self-willed. As with Waite at Lambeth Palace, Habiby's superiors had failed either to set out the parameters within which Waite's mission should be conducted, or to exercise proper control over Habiby's activities. Thus when Iran-Contra broke, the Church was thrown into confusion because no one knew what Habiby or Waite had been up to. Bishop Browning is said to have uttered a most unecclesiastical 'Oh, shit' when informed of the Church's involvement with North. Habiby was asked for a full account of all the meetings he and Waite had had with North, and a full explanation of how Waite's mission had been linked to the American government. Browning also sent one of his close advisers, Father Charles Cesaretti, to London for consultations with Lambeth Palace. Cesaretti was a sophisticated bureaucrat who had observed Waite establishing close links with the American Church with growing unease. 'The problem with Waite and Habiby was that no one was monitoring them,' Cesaratti explained, 'and as their terms of reference were changing all the time, some sort of supervision over their activities should have been imposed. We simply did not have the resources to handle a problem of the magnitude of the Lebanon hostage crisis. I was beginning to feel that with the Waite mission we were beginning to act more like a government than a church. The Episcopal Church normally has nothing to do with a government institution like the National Security Council, and yet here we were on the phone to people like Oliver North every day.'

Cesaretti attended a crisis meeting at Lambeth Palace to work out how the Church should respond to the Iran-Contra scandal. Waite again assured Cesaretti that he had done nothing wrong, but Cesaretti remained unconvinced. When he heard Waite was planning to return to Lebanon, he did his best to persuade Waite not to go. 'We were not in a position where we could tell Waite he could not go back to Lebanon, but I felt we had a moral responsibility for his safety, and I told him we were against the idea,' said Cesaretti. 'As far as we were concerned the Church's involvement in the issue of the American hostages in Lebanon was at an end.' Cesaretti returned to New York and sought out Habiby. Cesaretti did not want to talk inside the office, fearing it might be bugged. So he took Habiby for a walk in Manhattan to brief him on the conclusions he had drawn from the crisis meeting at Lambeth. 'Samir, we are in deep trouble,' Cesaretti gloomily confided.

Apart from being required to justify his actions to Runcie and other senior churchmen, Waite managed to weather the political storm without suffering much damage to his public reputation. When asked by interviewers, he would refuse to be drawn on the subject of his relations with Oliver North. To reinforce his own role in the hostage releases, Waite got Weir, Jenco and Jacobsen to fly to London. Together with Runcie, they posed for the press. Waite read out a brief statement in which he said his mission was 'continuing', but, uniquely in Waite's dealings with the press, he refused to answer questions. Runcie also remembers that there was an element of tension to Waite's meetings with the hostages. 'Benjamin Weir, in particular, was very upset about the arms sales, and could not understand how Terry could have been involved in something like that. Terry tried to explain, but I don't think Weir really understood,' said Runcie.

Then in mid-December Robert Oakley, who as head of counter-terrorism at the State Department was assisting the inquiry into North's activities, made the first public confirmation that Waite had met with North 'on several occasions'. Oakley's admission hit Waite like a bombshell. Waite later confided to his friends that he felt he had been 'betrayed' by the Americans. 'I invested a lot of trust in the Americans, and then they go and destroy my reputation when it suits them,'

Waite complained. Oakley's admission was picked up and published in all the main British newspapers, and it was not long before journalists were in contact with Lambeth Palace asking Waite about the extent of his involvement with North. Why had Waite taken the credit for the release of Americans when it now transpired they had been freed in return for shipments of arms to Teheran? How much did Waite know about the arms shipments during the eighteen months he was in contact with North? Waite refused to discuss in detail his relationship with North, except to deny he knew anything about the arms shipments, and to reiterate his view that many factors contributed to the release of the hostages, not just the arms shipments.

The only person who can say precisely what Waite was told about the arms shipments is Oliver North, and he denies giving Waite any information. Waite himself has repeatedly denied knowing anything about North's arms transfers. North claims that McFarlane and Casey told him not to tell Waite about the shipments. North also maintains that he never gave Waite a bugging device. 'Waite was essential to the release of three American hostages,' North has written. 'If we had not used Terry Waite, we would have needed to use *a* Terry Waite.'[1] He does not, however, specify the precise nature of Waite's role.

Casey died of a brain tumour before giving a full account of his role in Iran-Contra. McFarlane, however, who attempted to kill himself with an overdose of sleeping tablets rather than face the congressional inquiry, contests North's claim that he was ordered not to tell Waite anything about the arms transfers. McFarlane, who after all was North's boss,

[1]North's comments on Waite are taken from the manuscript seen by the author of a chapter on Waite which was to be included in a future edition of North's autobiography *Under Fire*.

remains bitter at the way a genuine initiative to open a line of communication to Iran was hijacked by North, and he harbours a strong suspicion that Waite knew much more about the arms deals than he has ever admitted.

'I never had any dealings with Waite personally,' said McFarlane. 'I knew North was meeting with him often and he would tell me what was going on with Waite. The general idea was that Waite would be the ostensible broker of the hostages' release, while North arranged the deal with Iran. North also told me that he shared intelligence material with Waite. Waite would give North intelligence, and North would respond in kind. I am in no doubt that Waite knew a lot more about North's activities than he has ever been prepared to admit.' Certainly, the very fact that North and Waite were swapping intelligence data thoroughly undermined Waite's claim to be an 'independent humanitarian'.

Robert Oakley, who as head of the State Department's counter-terrorism unit regularly joined North for meetings on the hostage crisis in 1985–86 when Waite was devoting his energies full-time to Lebanon, also believes Waite was not entirely unaware of North's activities. 'Waite was a front man and was very helpful in easing the anxieties of the families,' said Oakley, who was appointed US ambassador to Pakistan after Iran-Contra, where he supervised the CIA's operation to supply the Afghanistan resistance movement. 'Waite was also very useful in diverting attention from what was really going on between North and the Iranians. We hoped but never believed that he could exert some humanitarian influence and get people out. Waite knew bloody well that the US government was doing things to get the hostages out. Waite knew he had nothing to do with it. And he didn't mind taking the credit for it.'

Oakley, who retired from the American diplomatic service after his posting to Pakistan, feels no regrets about revealing

Waite's contacts with North. Oakley was one among many career diplomats at the State Department who were outraged that a lowly lieutenant-colonel at the NSC had conducted an alternative, and legally dubious, foreign policy. 'When North was exposed, I felt the best thing was for as much detail as possible to come out. Terry Waite was sincere in wanting to be helpful. He may even have thought he was helpful in trying to release the hostages. And to be fair to him, if he had spoken up publicly and said he had nothing to do with the release of the hostages, it would have undermined North's deal. But if Waite did not like what was happening, no one forced him to go along with it. But Waite had built himself up into an international figure, and he loved the publicity, for goodness' sake. That's why he did it, and he really worked very hard at it. That is probably why he was so humiliated by the Iran-Contra revelations. He never fully understood that, as far as the American government was concerned, he was nothing more than a front man.'

This, then, was the political reality behind Waite's grand adventure to work for the Americans in Lebanon, an adventure over which he had fought tooth and nail to overcome Runcie's resistance, and which he saw as the pinnacle of his career. For all the photo-calls at the White House with Vice-President Bush, for all the urgent phone calls from Oliver North at the Old Executive Building seeking his advice and co-operation, for all the jet-setting and press conferences at which Waite had been universally acclaimed a hero, the plain fact was that, as far as the Americans were concerned, Waite was nothing more than a willing stooge who happened to fit into a far more important American initiative. Waite had made it quite clear that he did not mind being used in order to pursue his humanitarian goals, and the Americans, in their characteristically forthright manner, had no compunction about using him. When the whole edifice came crumbling down around

Oliver North's shredding machine, Waite had no cause to demand an apology, and the Americans felt no obligation to offer one.

Contemplating this dismal scenario at his musty, cold office at Lambeth Palace in the depths of a London winter, it is easy to imagine Waite's desperation to pull off a remarkable act which would confound his critics and prove, once and for all, that the career he had built for himself as a mediator was not entirely without validity. There was certainly an air of desperation about Waite as he contemplated returning to Beirut after his links with North had been exposed, a desperation which, in part, was manifested in the announcement that he intended to go back to the city for Christmas. He grasped any opportunity to prove his credentials had not been undermined by the Iran-Contra affair. In a pre-Christmas interview with the BBC Waite claimed: 'My contacts in Lebanon in the last two weeks have indicated it [Iran-Contra] has not been a major setback for me personally.' It is difficult to accept that, by that stage, Waite had any 'contacts in Lebanon' worthy of the name. He had not been in direct contact with the kidnappers for more than a year. Everyone he had contacted in Lebanon to explore the possibility of a return trip warned him not to come. And Waite's claim that Iran-Contra had 'not been a major setback for me personally' was to be seen in an entirely different light once he went back to Lebanon.

Between mid-December 1986, when Waite's links with North were exposed, and January 12, 1987, when he set off for Beirut, Waite's office was besieged with people trying to persuade him not to go. Sir David Miers met him several times to urge against the trip. Apart from the anarchic security situation in Beirut, a bitter battle had erupted between the Amal militiamen and the Palestinians at the refugee camps on the outskirts of the city. Waite's main difficulty was to find someone to meet him at the airport and get him into Beirut.

He then intended to have a series of meetings with Lebanese leaders, which he hoped would provide a sufficient number of photo-opportunities for the media to see that he was still capable of independent action. He would then return home.

Kamal Khoury thought Jumblatt was the best option for an escort because the Druze were generally regarded as the most disciplined Lebanese militia, and because they controlled the area of West Beirut Waite intended to visit. When first contacted by Khoury, Jumblatt was incredulous that Waite should want to return. 'He told me that it would be madness for Terry to return to Lebanon,' said Khoury, 'but when I passed on the message to Terry, he told me to tell Walid that he was going to return whether the Druze protected him or not. Walid is a man of honour, and if Terry was going, the Druze would look after him. But they agreed to do this with a heavy heart.'

Once he knew the Druze would meet him at the airport, Waite presented his Beirut visit to Miers as a *fait accompli*. 'He phoned me one day and said he had found someone to look after him,' said Miers. 'There was nothing much else I could do about it.' Miers said his approach to Waite was similar to the way one would treat a daughter who had decided to marry someone of whom one did not approve. 'You might not approve of the choice, but once the wedding has taken place you just have to get on with it. Once Waite made his decision to go back, our job was to try to look after him and make sure he was all right.'

Miers even got John Gray, the British ambassador to Lebanon who had returned to London for Christmas, to see Waite at Lambeth in a last-ditch effort to stop him going. Before flying to London, Gray had checked with Jumblatt to see what he felt about Waite's coming and was told bluntly that Jumblatt thought the whole idea preposterous. Gray passed this message to Waite, but Waite was unmoved. 'There was little I could tell him that he didn't already know,' said Gray. 'He was determined to carry out what he called his "mission". He was determined to go back.' At one point while Gray was talking to Waite, Runcie poked his head around the door of Waite's office. 'Are you really sure about this, Terry?'

Waite replied sharply that he was.

In an attempt to give Waite's mission extra substance, Habiby, who was trying to save his job in Manhattan, suggested that Khoury, who had good contacts in Kuwait, should travel to the emirate and see if the Kuwaitis were prepared to reconsider Waite's visa application. The very suggestion that the Kuwaitis would consider a *volte face* was naive. The Iran-Contra revelations had made the Kuwaitis more, not less, resolute in their determination to hold onto the 17. But Khoury agreed to go to Kuwait while Waite was in Lebanon, a decision which raised Waite's hopes that he might, after all, be able to achieve something from his trip.

Kamal Khoury and Samir Habiby drove Waite to Heathrow on the morning of January 12 to catch a direct MEA flight to Beirut. It was thirteen months since Waite had last flown from London to Beirut, and this time the atmosphere was very different compared with the heyday of Waite's Lebanon mission when the first-class cabin was crammed with cameras and the champagne flowed. None of the big television companies thought Waite's return to Beirut was worth risking the lives of a crew. Nor would there be any last-minute delay for consultation with Oliver North. For this trip, Waite was on his own. A sombre mood descended on the small group as Waite bade farewell.

'Please, Terry, promise me you'll take care,' pleaded Khoury.

'Don't worry, Kamal, I'm going to be all right. I'll be back in a few days,' Waite replied.

For the first few days of Waite's Lebanon mission, it seemed on the surface as though the fears about his return had been exaggerated. Ten Druze bodyguards met him at the airport and drove him to the Riviera Hotel on the West Beirut seafront; the Commodore had been ruled out because it was in an area now controlled by Hizbollah. Waite was given a two-room suite overlooking the Mediterranean. The security operation mounted by the Druze was so tight that the few journalists in Beirut, most of them Lebanese, had difficulty getting to see Waite. Waite had meetings with prominent Lebanese leaders such as Jumblatt, many of whom he had not previously met. Waite, in his Druze cocoon, continued to issue statements saying he was making progress.

Outside the safety of the Riviera, however, there were signals coming from the kidnap groups which suggested otherwise. The day Waite arrived in Lebanon, Dakr Damanhouri, who worked at the Saudi Arabian cultural centre, was kidnapped. The following day Roger Auque, a French cameraman, one of the few foreign journalists left in West Beirut, was kidnapped as he returned home from taking pictures of Waite taking his morning constitutional along the seafront. Waite was the only person in Beirut who thought it a good idea to take an early morning stroll through the war-ravaged city; surrounded by Druze bodyguards, it seemed a good photo-opportunity. The other journalists saw Auque's abduction as a clear warning to Waite. They told Waite as much, and he issued a warning to foreign journalists to stay away.

While Waite was doing the rounds of Lebanese leaders, Islamic Jihad, the group he hoped to meet, issued a statement which made no mention of Waite or his presence in Beirut. The statement, directed towards the Kuwaiti government which was hosting the Conference of Islamic Nations, carried a photograph of Terry Anderson, and promised that action would be taken against any country which attended the conference. When the next day a group calling itself the Revolutionary Justice Organisation issued pictures of Jo Cicippio and Edward Tracy, Waite said this was 'a very good sign'. That afternoon he met Cicippio's wife, Elham, who wanted to know what Waite was doing for the hostages, such as her husband, who were not held by Islamic Jihad. Mrs Cicippio, who had wanted a quiet, private meeting, was surprised when Waite insisted that she join him in the hotel lobby so that the photographers could take pictures of them together.

'I told him that while he was in Beirut he should work for the release of all the hostages,' said Mrs Cicippio. 'I was not very impressed with him. He wanted us to have our picture taken. I was very surprised by all the media. I didn't expect it. Waite said it would be a good idea to let the photographers shoot us. It would show the world he was working for the hostages. I agreed, but I was not very happy.'

The arrest at Frankfurt airport of Mohammed Ali Hamadi, the Hizbollah militiaman who had masterminded the 1985 TWA hijack, the day after Waite's arrival in Lebanon also had implications which Waite did not immediately grasp. If Islamic Jihad had kidnapped a group of Westerners to get their comrades released from Kuwait, there was a strong likelihood that the kidnap groups would pursue a similar policy to get Hamadi released. A few days later Rudolf Cordes, a fifty-three-year-old West German businessman, was kidnapped as he arrived at Beirut airport. When Waite heard the news he said he was 'saddened' and repeated his call for foreigners to stay away from Beirut. But he refused to accept the logical consequences of what was happening in Lebanon. The fact that a Frenchman and a German had been kidnapped within a week of Waite's arrival should have told him that there was absolutely no possibility of negotiating the release of hostages. But Waite was too obsessed with his own public rehabilitation to pay attention to the gathering stormclouds. When reporters phoned him up from London and America, all Waite wanted to know was how 'my story' was being reported. The truth was rather disappointing. The media has a highly developed sense of a story that will not stand up, and most of Waite's statements and activities in Beirut merited only the briefest mentions in the British and American press compared with the acres of space devoted to fresh allegations concerning the Iran-Contra scandal. If Waite was putting his life on the line for the hostages, the rest of the world was not taking much notice.

Waite even received a direct call from an official at the British embassy who, believing Waite's phone was tapped, took the absurd precaution of introducing himself in Latin before warning Waite in English that the arrest of Hamadi in Frankfurt could seriously jeopardise his own safety. Waite rejected the advice, but after a week the strain was beginning to show. Habiby and Khoury were still in constant contact with Waite, and were anxious that he had strayed beyond the period of a few days originally agreed upon in London. 'I kept trying to get Terry to agree to leave, but he always had an excuse for staying one more day,' said Habiby. In private Waite succumbed to bouts of self-pity which he shared with some of the journalists who interviewed him. He complained of being alone all the time, of not having any support from Lambeth Palace or the Foreign Office, forgetting that the reason they kept their distance was because he insisted on acting alone.

Waite's spirits were at a low ebb when he sensed the breakthrough he had been looking for. One week after his arrival, Waite finally received an audience with Sheikh Mohammed Fadlallah at his apartment in the southern suburbs. Waite was in no doubt that Fadlallah, for all his denials, had close links to the group holding Anderson and Sutherland. Fadlallah could contact Mugniyeh just by picking up the telephone. When

Waite was shown into the Sheikh's apartment in Bir al-Abed, Shia Muslim militiamen were sitting in the same room as the Sheikh. Some were his bodyguards, others his personal assistants. It is more than likely one of the kidnappers was also present. Fadlallah was frosty and to the point. Why had Waite returned to Lebanon? Waite explained he had returned on a humanitarian mission to bring the hostage issue to an end. Fadlallah wanted to know why he should help when so many promises had been broken in the past. Waite replied that he still hoped to go to Kuwait, a statement upon which Fadlallah made no comment, but which may well have aroused the suspicions of others present who had previous experience of Waite's promises concerning Kuwait. Fadlallah brought the audience to a speedy conclusion. He told Waite that he was welcome to stay in Beirut as a man of the Church, and that if the kidnappers wanted to get in touch with him, they knew where to find him.

At his hotel room, Waite still had the shortwave radio he had brought the year previously to contact the kidnappers. He had tuned it in to the agreed frequency at the start of his trip, but there had been no word from the kidnappers. Soon after he returned from seeing Fadlallah, however, a man claiming to be a representative of the kidnap gangs called up and asked for a meeting with Waite. As before, Waite was told to go to the surgery of Dr Adnan Mroueh at the American Hospital, where the kidnappers would verify their credentials by producing pictures of the hostages. Waite was delighted. It was just the opportunity he had been seeking, though he had mentioned it to no one. A visit to the kidnappers would verify his credentials as an independent operator; no one would be able to accuse him of being merely a front man for Oliver North.

Waite telephoned Akram Shehayeb, a respected Druze politician who had been deputed by Jumblatt to take personal responsibility for Waite's safety. He wanted Shehayeb to provide a leather jacket and a pair of dark glasses. When Shehayeb heard what Waite planned to do, he did everything he could to persuade him not to go.

'Terry, if you go to see these people, they will kidnap you,' said Shehayeb. 'I know them better than you do. Times have changed in Beirut.'

'I have to make my own judgements, Akram, but thank you for your advice,' said Waite.

'But if you go to see them, Terry, we will not be able to protect you. Druze militiamen cannot go into those areas.'

'I don't want any protection,' replied Waite. 'If I am going to see these people, I must do it of my own accord.'

Shehayeb contacted Jumblatt to tell him what Waite was planning, and Jumblatt told him to prevent Waite from attending the meeting. Shehayeb had had many previous dealings with Mugniyeh in negotiations for the release of Druze prisoners, and he knew what a difficult man Mughiyeh could be. But when Waite insisted that there was no reason for the Druze to prevent him going to the meeting, Shehayeb relented.

'But Terry, why are you doing this?' reasoned Shehayeb. 'Do you really want to be a hostage yourself?'

'Please don't worry yourself about me, Akram,' Waite replied. 'If I pull this one off I'll be *Time* magazine's Man of the Year.'

The Druze drove Waite to Dr Mroueh's surgery. At that point they parted company with Waite, who said he would contact them once the meeting finished. Waite went to the surgery, and within minutes the door opened and Imad Mugniyeh walked in. Mugniyeh was taking just as big a risk as Waite in making so public a visit, even if Waite had tried to keep the meeting secret – but at least Mugniyeh had his bodyguards with him. The three men sat chatting for a few minutes, until the phone on Dr Mroueh's desk rang, calling him away to conduct an emergency operation. Mroueh left, saying he would be back in ten minutes and telling Waite not to leave the room until he returned. When Mroueh came back an hour and a half later, the room was empty. Terry Waite had joined the wretched ranks of the hostages.

18

TO BE A HOSTAGE

If Oliver North and Terry Waite felt they had suffered from the exposure of the Iran-Contra scandal, the hostages still in Lebanon suffered much more. For Terry Anderson and Thomas Sutherland in particular, the revelation that the American government had sold arms to Iran in return for the release of three American hostages shattered all hope of imminent release. For more than a year, these two had had to swallow their disappointment as first Benjamin Weir, then Lawrence Jenco and finally David Jacobsen were freed. Anderson, who had broken down in tears when Weir was released after it had been agreed among the hostages that Anderson should be the one to go, slowly adjusted to the fact that the kidnappers valued him too highly to let him go. The guards also led Sutherland to believe he would be one of the last to be released because they still suspected he was a spy. When Jenco and Jacobsen were released, Anderson and Sutherland could only comfort themselves that at least the freed men would be able to do something for them when they got home to the United States.

Throughout the period that North and Waite were working

for their release, the hostages did their best to maintain each other's morale. They were all middle-aged men who, with the exception of Father Jenco, were married with children, and mature enough to lend each other support rather than fret about their own predicaments. Even so, being together in a confined space day after day, under the constant threat of being beaten if a guard discovered one of them not wearing a blindfold, it was not surprising that personalities sometimes clashed. With any group, the first major psychological battle is for the election of a leader. When the Americans had first been brought together in the summer of 1985, Ben Weir felt he had best claim to be their unofficial representative. Apart from being the longest-held, Weir was the eldest of the five and, as head of a large seminary, was used to responsibility. Marty Jenco, as the priest liked to be called, had a far more unassuming nature, and was content for others to take control of worldly decision-making. Tom Sutherland's academic mind, trained to weigh opposing arguments carefully in order to reach a rational and fair decision, caused his fellow captives too much anguish for them to accept him as leader. Weir's position, then, was primarily challenged by Anderson and Jacobsen, two obstinate and self-willed men who invariably found themselves taking diametrically opposed views.

Although Anderson's educational achievements were modest, he possessed a bright intellect. A widely-travelled journalist, he had a tendency to assume he was an authority on any given subject. Aggressive by nature, Anderson was a formidable opponent in any argument, as had been witnessed by his holding forth at the bar of the Commodore Hotel. From the moment he met up with Jacobsen, there was hardly anything that Jacobsen could say or do that Anderson did not find intensely irritating. One of the underlying reasons for this personality clash was the fact that Anderson, who was more akin to the archetypal, mid-Western redneck than he ever cared to admit, was utterly intolerant of the superficial Californian lifestyle Jacobsen seemed to represent. On the first occasion the two were allowed to talk to each other, Jacobsen told him of the passion he had developed, when living in Saudi Arabia, of going for a jog in the desert.

'It's a really difficult sensation to describe,' he told Anderson. 'You have all this space around you and all you can see for miles and miles is sand. You have the sun on your back and the sweat is pouring off your body, and it's an experience unlike anything else.' Anderson quickly formed the opinion that Jacobsen was a bit soft in the head, and described him to the other hostages as a 'typically vacuous and shallow Californian'.

Anderson and Jacobsen were soon having lengthy, heated arguments almost daily. They would argue over how to manage a hospital. As a trained hospital administrator, Jacobsen had a fairly good idea of what he was talking about. But that did not prevent Anderson from giving his opinion. Nothing is more irritating for a hospital administrator than to hear a lay person express the commonly held belief that doctors, not bureaucrats, run hospitals. When Anderson said exactly that, Jacobsen hit the roof. They also argued about politics. Anderson was no fan of Ronald Reagan, having witnessed the terrible mess the American government had made of foreign policy in Lebanon. Whenever Anderson made a scathing remark about Reagan, Jacobsen, a committed Republican, would leap to his president's defence. When Weir and Jenco were there, they acted as a buffer between the two.

On the rare occasions that Sutherland also became involved in an argument, he tended to side with Jacobsen, his colleague from the American University, because he felt that Anderson was being over-belligerent. Sutherland even got into an argument with Anderson over the position of the wing-flaps of an aircraft on landing and take-off. Anderson thought the flaps were up, and Sutherland that they were down. Because the hostages had no access to reference books, there was no way they could check out who was right, and the argument continued on and off for months.

No matter how much the others tried to take the heat out of the arguments, Anderson would continue until he forced Jacobsen to give in. Jacobsen would be close to tears, and occasionally would thump the wall in anger, when he finally gave up.

'Well, fuck you anyway, Terry,' he would shout. 'Just go fuck yourself and leave me alone.' Anderson would remain quite passive, a smile of triumph breaking out across his face.

Jacobsen was undoubtedly a very trying person to share a confined space with. Apart from being a committed Republican, he was a born-again Christian, and never ceased telling less devout hostages such as Anderson the value of Christianity. Jacobsen was also a fitness fanatic, and would organise a whole range of callisthenic exercises to keep his body in trim. Another familiar ploy of Jacobsen's was to attempt to improve his eyesight by taking his plastic spoon, hold it at eye level and at arm's length, and focus on it intensely while drawing the spoon towards him. The exercise would be repeated several times, and the sight of this somewhat imbecilic gesture drove the other hostages to distraction. Jacobsen was probably at his most difficult when he decided to try to escape following the failure of Waite's mission in late 1985. The others were set against any kind of escape attempt because they believed they had no chance of overpowering the guards. Any such attempt would most likely result in some or all of them being shot. But Jacobsen insisted on his right to plan an escape; he intended to overpower one of the guards, then make a break for freedom. Anderson, who had trained as a marine, offered to teach Jacobsen how to throttle a man with a swift, forearm blow from behind, and over a period of days Anderson took great pleasure in hitting Jacobsen very hard as part of the mock training. Jacobsen also embarked on his own physical fitness programme, assigning himself six hundred push-ups and six hundred sit-ups. Fortunately for all concerned, Jacobsen never put his plan into action.

From the summer of 1985 until the summer of 1986 the American hostages were held together in two apartments. The first apartment, where Sutherland was introduced to Weir, Jenco, Anderson and Jacobsen, was situated close to Beirut airport. In October, following Weir's release, they were moved to the southern suburbs. In fact, after every release the remaining captives were moved to a new hideout as a precaution against a possible rescue operation. The moves were often the most traumatic part of the hostages' experience. For a short journey they would be blindfolded and moved in the back of a van. For a longer journey, however, each would be tightly bound with masking tape and placed in a false compartment under a lorry. Often they were bound so tightly it was a wonder they were not asphyxiated.

But for the rest of the time, their main priority was to find ways of occupying the interminable hours in their cells. None of them enjoyed the periods where they were held alone; at least if they were with someone else they could maintain some sort of human dialogue. Once they were all together, the guards provided them with a Bible and some scraps of paper. Depending on the mood of the guards, the hostages were even allowed to make their own card games, but when the guards noticed that the hostages were having too much fun, they confiscated them. Despite the general effort not to cause offence, the most trivial matters could provoke a dispute. Marty Jenco, for example, suffered from a weak bladder, and quickly filled the plastic bottle provided for use during the day. When he could not get the attention of the guards to empty his bottle, Jenco would try to use another hostage's bottle, which would be met with stiff resistance. There was also the considerable problem of flatulence from which nearly all the hostages suffered. Sutherland believed this resulted from a combination of anxiety and the constant diet of beans. Although the thought of five grown men, two of them men of the cloth, sitting in a small cell succumbing to repeated, violent attacks of flatulence might seem amusing, for those concerned it was a constant source of irritation, not least because of the all-pervading intensity of the intestinal gas some of the worst offenders, such as Sutherland, produced. It was hardly surprising that sex was not a matter that dominated the hostages' thoughts. The constant fear of what might happen to them, together with the anxiety they felt for their families and friends, meant that their libidos essentially went into hibernation. Occasionally the subject would arise when, for example, they speculated that two of the guards might be homosexual lovers, but in general sex was a taboo subject.

The hostages enjoyed a mixed relationship with the guards. For the first couple of years they were looked after by the same group, never more than four at a time. The leaders, such as Mugniyeh, made infrequent appearances, usually when something was about to happen, such as the seizure or release of a hostage. But when nothing much was happening on the hostage front, Mugniyeh could spend several months without seeing the captives.

Most of the guards were in their early twenties. Some were ordinary working-class Lebanese who had worked as barbers or car mechanics before joining the militia; others were well-educated and had graduated from the AUB. The fact that they belonged to a group committed to the destruction of American interests in the Middle East did not prevent them from following all the latest trends in American pop culture. They wore jeans, tee-shirts and Reebok track shoes. They amused themselves during the long, tedious hours guarding the hostages by watching American soaps such as *Dallas*. They nicknamed the hostages after their favourite American movie-stars – David Jacobsen was Clint Eastwood, and Terry Anderson was Charles Bronson. They carried out their duties for the grand sum of about $25 a month.

Some of the guards were quite well-disposed towards the hostages, and would talk to them at length about their families and personal problems. They could even display touching signs of humanity. One hot summer's day in 1985, for example, David Jacobsen playfully asked the guard to get the hostages an ice cream. To their amazement, he returned fifteen minutes later – with an ice cream. On another occasion when the heat in the hostages' cell became unbearable, one guard got a large sheet of cardboard and waved it over them like a fan. The guards also responded to the hostages' request to be allowed to read and brought them a varied collection of books, which included the Bible, Emily Brontë's *Wuthering Heights*, Homer's *Odyssey*, and Mervyn Peake's *Gormenghast* trilogy. On other occasions they could turn ugly, such as when Anderson, early in his captivity, tried to bribe one of them to free him. The guard immediately reported Anderson to Mugniyeh, who saw to it that Anderson was severely beaten for his impudence. Jenco lost twenty per cent of his hearing after receiving open-handed slaps across his ears when the guards accused him of trying to peep through his blindfold to see them.

No matter how intimate the dialogue became between hostages and guards (Jacobsen even advised one of the guards, who was newly-married, about birth control), the hostages maintained a 'them and us' approach, which became most pronounced when the guards attempted to victimise one of the captives. One of the few tangible successes of Waite's mission to Beirut in 1985 was that he was able to get a bag of mail from families and friends delivered to the hostages. But when, two months later, the guards finally delivered the mail, they refused to give any to Tom Sutherland, probably because of their suspicions that he was a spy. When the others realised what was going on, they refused to accept their mail unless Sutherland was included. The guards, surprised at the strength of feeling, relented and gave Sutherland mail from his wife and three daughters, for which he was eternally grateful.

In the summer of 1986, when Jenco was released, the kidnappers turned their ire on David Jacobsen. This followed a videotape Jacobsen had made prior to Jenco's release in which he read out a prepared statement and gave some details about the death of William Buckley. He then expressed his condolences to Buckley's family, not knowing that the CIA man was a bachelor. When the tape was shown on American television, some of the more imaginative American journalists speculated that the reference to Buckley's family was a coded message from Jacobsen to the CIA. Such was the organisation of the Lebanese kidnap groups, that they soon had in Lebanon a videotape of the news reports broadcast in the US, which they played back to the hostages. The kidnappers were not pleased with what they saw. A few days later the three Americans were roused from sleep and told they were going home. It was yet another lie. The guards just wanted the hostages to give as little trouble as possible while they were being moved. The hostages were taken to another building and put in a cell six feet by six feet, with a ceiling under six feet high. Gone were all privileges; the only furnishings were two mattresses; the only light came from the hallway. When the electricity generator was not switched on, the Americans could hear the sea, and heavy traffic. They inferred that they were still near the airport. They were not the only hostages there, a fact they deduced by counting the pairs of feet passing their cell on the way to the bathroom.

Although they did not know it at the time, the Americans were in the same building as John McCarthy and Brian Keenan. McCarthy, in the cell next to the three Americans, had been brought to this building soon after his abduction in April. For the first few months he was held by himself in a tiny cell, in the building where Brian Levick and Geoffrey Nash had been held a year previously. McCarthy was never given an explanation as to why he had been kidnapped. Keenan was further down the corridor close to the South Korean diplomat who had been abducted at the start of the year. After three months, the guards decided that McCarthy, at twenty-nine the youngest hostage in the building, deserved some company, so they brought Brian Keenan to join him in his cell. Keenan, in ragged clothes, his beard wild and unkempt, was sat down next to McCarthy. After the door closed, both men sat in silence with their blindfolds on, fearful that the guard might still be watching them. After a few minutes, however, they both nervously peeped under their blindfolds. As McCarthy set eyes on Keenan for the first time, he exclaimed: 'Fuck me, it's Ben Gunn!'

The two had not previously met. McCarthy said he had originally come to Lebanon to make a film about Keenan's abduction. 'It is the worst thing I have ever done,' he said. It took time for them to get to know each other properly. Each having being held alone for three months, it was difficult at first to communicate. Each was apprehensive of giving too much away to the other, for fear of his reaction. But over the months they came to understand one another, even though they had markedly different characters. Keenan, even in captivity, found it difficult to keep his temper, and would often shout at the guards if he felt he was being mistreated, an attitude which often provoked the guards to a violent response. McCarthy, on the other hand, displayed the tact he had learned at his English public school and was often able to calm down an ugly situation created by Keenan's bad temper.

A few days after his arrival at 'the prison', Jacobsen was woken early one morning by a guard and asked to follow him. Ever since he had been shown the videotape, Jacobsen had been dreading this moment, and fully expected the guards to kill him. He was blindfolded and taken to a room which contained about six people, including Ali, the mysterious Iranian who appeared whenever a release was in the offing. Some of the guards who were well-disposed towards the hostages were in the room, but on this occasion there was no hint of friendship. Jacobsen was invited to sit down, but before he could do so white flashes ripped through his skull as a pair of open hands cuffed him across the head. A shower of blows fell upon his head, and while someone screamed at him in Arabic, a guard grabbed his feet and forced them between the strap and barrel of an automatic rifle. The assailant then twisted the weapon until his feet were painfully bound. Jacobsen's legs were lifted until only his head and shoulders touched the floor. At that point everyone in the room laid into him. Two guards used lengths of rubber hose to beat the soles of his feet, while the others used him as a punch-bag. Jacobsen shouted at the guards he knew well to save him, but they replied, 'You have embarrassed us by sending a coded message in the video.' The beating lasted for about ten minutes. When it stopped, the guards insisted on inflicting one final torture; they forced Jacobsen to stand up and made him jog for five minutes on his bloody, battered feet. Jacobsen was then taken back to his cell to recover. As he lay convulsed with pain, one of the guards who had taken part in the attack arrived with a glass of cold water and a bunch of grapes.

'Here, Mr David. Take these. We are sorry, Mr David.'

This was the only beating Jacobsen received during the eighteen months he was held, but it reinforced the conviction of all the hostages that the guards could just as easily beat them as humour them. After the beating Jacobsen was held separately, probably because the guards did not want the others to see what they had done. Despite the mistake Jacobsen had made on the video, the guards asked him to make another recording in October 1986, in which he made an impassioned plea for the American government to do something to free the hostages. He drew a parallel between the plight of the hostages in Lebanon and the action the American government had taken to free an American journalist, Nicholas Daniloff, who had been seized by the KGB in Moscow. When Anderson and Sutherland got to hear of what Jacobsen had said, they were furious, for they had agreed amongst themselves that they would do nothing more than the bare minimum demanded by the kidnappers. They did not want to give the impression that they were co-operating with the kidnappers. Jacobsen, they believed, was going out of his way to co-operate.

'The kidnappers thought they would let Jacobsen out because he would shit on Reagan once he was free,' said Sutherland. But when Jacobsen was freed a few weeks later, he retracted all the criticisms he had made of Reagan in the videotape, saying he had been forced to make them by the kidnappers.

'I thought, God damn that man,' said Sutherland. 'No one forced him to say anything. He did it of his own volition to get himself released. He was thinking only about himself. He didn't care if Terry and myself were left to rot.'

The guards were also disappointed by Jacobsen's performance after his release. One of them complained to Sutherland, 'Mr David cheated us. He said he was going to say many things against Reagan, but he said nothing. He did not do what we told him to do.' The guards made no mention to the hostages about the Iran-Contra revelations which had emerged as Jacobsen was flying to freedom. All the hostages knew at the time was that the guards' attitude towards them changed considerably. Up until Jacobsen's release, the guards had been increasingly more friendly, telling them that they would all be home for Christmas. The guards even seemed genuinely pleased that the hostages would be going home to their families. From early November, however, their attitude changed radically. One night a guard went into the cell where McCarthy and Keenan were sleeping and started hitting the two hostages all over the body with his rifle butt. He left them, bruised and covered with blood, promising to return for a repeat performance, but without any explanation for the attack.

It is highly probable that the first the kidnap gangs knew of the arms-for-hostages deals was when, like the rest of the world, they read about them in *Ash-Shiraa*. Throughout the arms deals, the Iranians always insisted that they did not have total control over the kidnap groups, but that they could exercise a certain degree of influence over them. The Iranians were certainly desperate for American weapons and spare parts, but it is doubtful whether the kidnappers would have been prepared to release their hostages solely to help the Iranian war effort. Their priority was to get their comrades released from jail in Kuwait, and it is unlikely that they would have had much interest in any deal with the Americans that did not include that condition.

Certainly, as soon as details of the arms shipments were made public, any prospects Anderson and Sutherland may have entertained of an early release were completely torpedoed; perhaps fortunately, they did not know at the time how close they had come to freedom. Had details of the shipments not been revealed in *Ash-Shiraa* two days after Jacobsen's release, it is probable that their release would have been secured by further arms deals. Instead, the guards became increasingly more threatening towards them from the middle of November. As a result of the activities of North and Waite, the hostages faced the worst period of their captivity. Apart from withdrawing all privileges, such as their books and home-made games, the guards would constantly scream at them: 'You are spies. You are all spies, and we will make you pay.'

It was about this time that Sutherland suffered a beating similar to Jacobsen's. Sutherland had been in his cell for thirteen hours and was desperate to urinate. He pulled up his blindfold to look around. At that moment a guard let out a war whoop; he had been watching Sutherland for this for several hours. Sutherland did not give a damn about looking at the guard, so urgent was his desire to go to the bathroom. A group of guards seized him and beat the soles of his feet with a rubber hose until he could no longer stand the pain and began to scream. 'You cannot imagine the agony of being beaten like that,' said Sutherland. 'It sets your whole body on fire.' When Sutherland asked why they were doing this to him, the guards repeated the old charge that he was a spy.

'It really bugged me that they kept going on about me being a spy,' said Sutherland. 'I kept telling them that a university teacher would not have anything to do with the CIA, but they would not believe me. They went on like this for four years.'

After the beating Sutherland and Anderson were put in separate cells which had no light and were so small they could hardly move. This was by far the most difficult period of Sutherland's years in captivity. He became so depressed that on three occasions he tried to kill himself.

'They wouldn't even give me a candle to eat by,' said Sutherland. 'I thought to myself, I'll be damned if I'm going to put up with this, I'd sooner die.

'So I put a plastic bag over my head and tried to suffocate myself, but I found out on each try that it got very painful

(Above) Margaret Thatcher flew to Washington to lend Ronald Reagan her unequivocal support after the Iran-Contra scandal broke. *(UPI/Bettmann Newsphotos)*

(Above) Terry Waite arranged for the three American hostages freed as part of the arms-for-hostages deals to visit Lambeth Palace for a 'debriefing'. (Left to right: Father Lawrence Jenco, Dr Robert Runcie, Waite, Dr David Jacobsen and Rev. Benjamin Weir.) He later dressed up as a London bus conductor to take part in the 'Crisis at Christmas' charity *(left)*. *(Group photo: Press Association/Topham; photo of Waite: Press Association)*

Walid Jumblatt, the head of the Druze, reluctantly agreed to protect Waite on his last visit to Lebanon. He is pictured here *(above)* meeting with Druze religious leaders and with Waite outside his Mukhtara fiefdom *(below)*. *(Lena Kara)*

Less than 24 hours before his abduction, Waite met with Sheikh Fadlallah, the spiritual leader of the Hizbollah *(above)*. This meeting sealed his fate as a hostage. Later that evening Waite left for a secret meeting with the kidnappers *(below)*. *(Lena Kara)*

(Right) The hostages were moved regularly from one building to another. At one point some of the Western hostages were held in this building in Beirut's southern suburbs. *(Lena Kara)*

(Above) UN troubleshooter Giandomenico Picco was given the job of securing the release of the Western hostages. Unlike Terry Waite, he kept his activities a closely guarded secret. He is pictured here with Joseph Cicippio, one of the last American hostages to be released. *(Reuters/Bettmann)* *(Below)* Jill Morrell formed the campaign 'The Friends of John McCarthy' after becoming disillusioned with the impotence of the British government to secure her boyfriend's release.

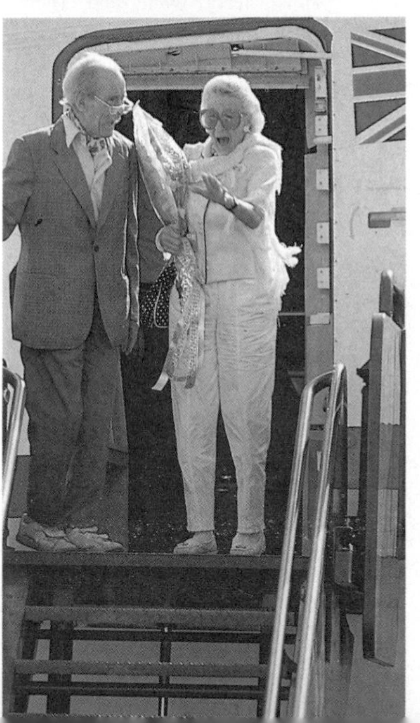

(Above) John McCarthy celebrates his new-found freedom with his father Pat *(left)* and brother Terence *(right)* at the residence of the British ambassador to Syria, August 1991. *(Reuters/Bettmann)*

(Left) A Spitfire did a victory roll over RAF Lyneham as Jackie Mann, the oldest of the British hostages, flew home with his wife Sunnie. *(Frank Spooner Pictures)*

Not all the hostages returned home alive. The remains of William Buckley *(inset)*, the former CIA station chief in Beirut, were dumped outside the southern suburbs at the end of December 1991. He was buried with full military honours in Washington *(above)*. *(Reuters/Bettmann Newsphotos)* *(Below)* Terry Waite and Thomas Sutherland were released together in November 1991, but the bonhomie did not last for long.

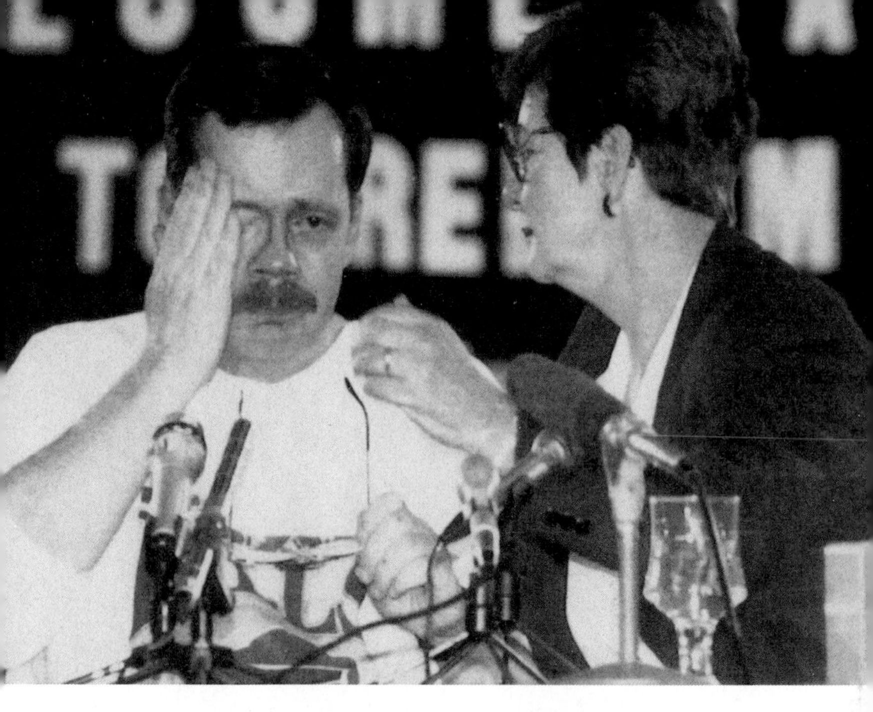

(Above) Terry Anderson, the longest-serving hostage after seven years in captivity, is overcome with emotion after being reunited with his sister Peggy Say. *(Below)* George Bush and Javier Perez de Cuellar, the UN secretary-general, welcome the American hostages back to Washington. Standing left to right: Joseph Cicippio, Terry Anderson, Thomas Sutherland, Alann Steen and Jesse Turner. *(UPI/Bettmann)*

(Above) Shortly before the mysterious murders in November 1992 of Ian Spiro's wife Gail and their three children, he confided to friends: 'My past has come back to haunt me.' Three days later, his body was found in the Californian desert. *(Below)* The author with Lebanese tribesmen in the Bekaa Valley, spring 1992. *(Lena Kara)*

and as it got more painful, the vision of my wife and three daughters appeared before me ever more clearly. And I decided each time, Gee, I can't go through with this, and I would pull it off.'

The Iran-Contra revelations effectively put the hostages in Lebanon into cold storage. For the next two years they saw nothing of Mugniyeh or the mysterious Iranian, Ali. The only news they were given of the outside world was when a guard appeared in their cell to tell them that Terry Waite had gone missing.

'He was laughing, and that was unusual in itself at that time,' said Sutherland. 'He said "Waite has disappeared. Perhaps he has gone to Washington." Then he gave another chuckle and left.' Neither hostage understood the guard's comment because they knew nothing about the Iran-Contra affair.

In early January 1987, five hostages were moved out of 'the prison' and taken to the port of Tyre; they were McCarthy, Keenan, Anderson, Sutherland and Frank Reed, who had been in a cell close to the other Americans since November. The hostages were moved out of Beirut because fierce street battles had broken out between the Amal and Druze militias, and the kidnappers felt the hostages' lives might be at risk. For the journey, the hostages were bound with tape and placed in a false compartment in the floor of a lorry. The space was so confined that the hostages called it 'the coffin'. For five weeks they were held in a miserable dungeon which was the worst of all the sixteen different locations experienced in seven years in captivity by Anderson and Sutherland, the longest-serving hostages. Throughout this period the guards victimised Reed, who for some unexplained reason had upset them. They made him lie in such a position that he had no alternative but to look up at a hole through which he could see the guards outside. They would then drag him out of the cell and beat him.

Anderson and Sutherland had by now become close friends.

At first they had been wary of each other; Sutherland, in particular, was offended by Anderson's opinionated belligerence. But with time, Sutherland learnt to appreciate the more sensitive and caring side of Anderson's nature. A typical example of Anderson's generosity occurred when the hostages were being taken to southern Lebanon in the spring of 1987. It was cold and dark, and Anderson and Sutherland had been left sitting in the back of a van. Anderson noticed Sutherland was feeling the cold very badly and, despite shivering himself, gave Sutherland his own coat. On another occasion Anderson gave Sutherland his mattress after Sutherland had worn out his own. As a result Anderson had to sleep on a hard tile floor. When Sutherland tried to protest, Anderson refused to give in.

'In the marines I slept in worse places than this,' he said. 'Your need is greater than mine, Tom.' Sutherland was overwhelmed by Anderson's genuine acts of friendship, and the strong bond of mutual respect and affection that grew between them helped them to survive the long years of captivity. 'I'm so glad I had Terry with me as a companion. If it had been David Jacobsen, the next five years would have been a very different proposition,' said Sutherland.

In early April the hostages were moved again, this time to an apartment in the centre of Tyre. Anderson, Sutherland and Reed were held in one room, Keenan and McCarthy in a small utility room. The five were held at this apartment, which was close to a mosque, for six months, but the two groups, the Americans and the British, never met. Each group, however, could hear the other talking to the guards. Living conditions improved considerably. They were given access to a television – McCarthy and Keenan during the day, the Americans the rest of the time. Despite this, morale remained low. Their hopes had been raised that they would be home for Christmas, and they found it difficult to come to terms with the fact that they were just marking time. The guards would try to raise their spirits by telling them progress was still being made.

'The negotiations are very good, believe me,' one would say. After so many disappointments, the hostages were not going to be taken in.

'That's just fine,' Anderson would reply, his sarcasm lost on the guards. 'We'll all go home tomorrow, if that's all the same with you.'

'Yes, tomorrow, you'll go home tomorrow,' the guard would promise with a smile. The next day the guard would behave as though the conversation had never taken place.

By now McCarthy and Keenan were getting on like a house on fire. McCarthy's natural civility and good humour made a deep impression on the guards, who generally treated him with respect. A heavy smoker, he was even able to persuade them to give him extra rations of cigarettes. The fact that McCarthy was able to establish such a good rapport with the guards took some of the pressure off Keenan, whose quick temper was constantly in danger of provoking the guards to violence. But even McCarthy's charm was of no avail in August 1987, after the hostages had been in the apartment for four months, when Keenan finally overstepped the mark and grabbed one of the guards.

In Tyre, the hostages were joined by a new set of guards. One of them, a short man, was nicknamed Ghost by the hostages because he had a habit of sneaking up on them to see if he could catch them out. One day Ghost told Keenan to stand up in the utility room cell. As he got up, the guard accused him of trying to open the small window. Keenan became so irate that, despite his chains, he lunged at the guard, grabbed hold of him and started to shake him. McCarthy, who was sitting on the floor, called out to him to let go, that it would only make matters worse. But the damage had been done. The diminutive guard left the room. A few minutes later he returned with another guard who was built like an ox. While the larger guard held Keenan, Ghost set about him with a broom handle, landing a series of savage blows to his body. To the Americans in the room next door, it sounded as if someone was hammering on the wall. The beating continued for several minutes, but throughout the ordeal Keenan did not make a sound. He did not want to give the guards the satisfaction. McCarthy, who was chained to the wall, could only watch. The guards left Keenan, bleeding and bruised, crumpled in the corner. Having worked himself almost into a frenzy, Ghost then went next door to the Americans.

'Anybody here want to fight me?' he screamed, brandishing the bloody broomstick. 'British meat is good meat, but American meat is no good. You want to fight me? You're all dogs.' Having heard the punishment inflicted on Keenan, the Americans had the good sense not to say a word. For weeks afterwards, Keenan groaned in agony every time he moved, but the experience did not make him any more respectful of the guards.

Although the American and British hostages were held only a few yards apart, they did not meet each other until the following year, by which time they had all been moved to the Bekaa Valley. Keenan, McCarthy, Anderson, Sutherland and Reed were all moved out of Tyre towards the end of November 1987 when the guards decided it was safe to take them back to Beirut. Keenan and McCarthy were taken to an apartment close to Sheikh Fadlallah's headquarters, while Sutherland and Anderson were put in with a group of French hostages. A pattern gradually emerged where a group of hostages would be held in one place for a few months, then, without warning, the kidnappers would announce they were being moved, and the group would be broken up. In general, the kidnappers allowed hostages linked by nationality or age to stay together; if a hostage had company, it made looking after him easier. Thus Keenan and McCarthy were kept together, as were Anderson and Sutherland, with the exception of one five-month period between November 1987 and April 1988 when they were separated and put with different groups of French hostages. It was while Sutherland and Anderson were with the French in late 1987 that they first learned of the Iran-Contra scandal.

'When I heard about the Iran-Contra affair for the first time, it just blew my mind apart,' Sutherland recalled. 'Everything began to fit into place and make sense.'

From late 1986, the hostage issue was further complicated by the fact that more than one group were kidnapping foreigners in Beirut. The Revolutionary Justice Organisation claimed responsibility for the kidnapping of Joseph Cicippio, Edward Tracy and seven Frenchmen. Although the RJO undoubtedly had close links with Islamic Jihad, it also had its own identity and agenda. It was rumoured that the RJO was being run by dissident Iranians opposed to Rafsanjani's attempts to improve relations with the West. One indication that the group pursued its own agenda was that throughout the five years they were held captive, Cicippio and Tracy saw none of the other American hostages.

Joseph Cicippio had a particularly hard time in capitivity. He had had enough warnings of the risks he faced by staying on in Beirut, especially after his close friend David Jacobsen was kidnapped. But he was happy with his new wife, Elham, and was determined not to desert his post at the university. 'I felt at the time that I was at the Alamo,' recalled Cicippio. 'Here was a piece of America surrounded by hostile forces, and I felt just like Davy Crockett, and I was not going to leave.' It was a decision he would long regret. Immediately after his abduction, Cicippio was subjected to a terrifying interrogation. His interrogators pursued the familiar line of accusing him of working for the CIA and demanding to know why he had remained in Beirut so long. When dissatisfied with his answers, they made him watch as they placed a single bullet in a revolver, spun the chamber, placed the gun to his head and pulled the trigger. This game of Russian roulette went on for several hours. At another point when they were unhappy with Cicippio's answers, the kidnappers put a knife to his testicles and threatened to castrate him. Tracy was put through a similar ordeal, which served only to confuse a man who was already mentally disturbed at the time of his abduction.

For five years Cicippio was chained to Tracy day and night, and had to tolerate the rantings of a man who had no idea what was happening to him. As if this were not bad enough, Cicippio and Tracy were held for the first two years on the balcony of a high-rise building in Beirut. During the winter months Cicippio became so cold he was afraid to go to sleep, for fear that he would not wake up: 'I didn't realise how cold a man could get.' He suffered permanent frostbite damage to his hands and feet. The two men had just two blankets and some plastic sheeting to protect them from the elements. Cicippio also had to cope with the constant threat of violence from the kidnappers. When they heard Tracy ranting, they would come out and tell him to shut up. Tracy, of course, would have no idea what they were saying to him, and would continue his mumbling regardless. This would infuriate the guards, who would seize a length of telephone cable and whip Tracy mercilessly. But the beatings only made Tracy more confused, which in turn caused the guards to become more frustrated. On one occasion the guards became so exasperated by Tracy's behaviour that they placed both men up against the wall and threatened to shoot them. It took the kidnappers, most of whom were young, working-class Lebanese, many months to realise that Tracy was genuinely sick.

Yet another group of Americans were held by a group which went by the name of the Islamic Jihad for the Liberation of Palestine (IJLP). Four days after Terry Waite went missing, the IJLP pulled off the most audacious kidnap of the whole crisis. On the morning of January 24, 1987, a group of men dressed in the uniform of the Lebanese security police arrived at Beirut University College (BUC) and asked to see all the teachers holding American passports. BUC lived very much in the shadow of its more famous neighbour, the AUB, and essentially provided higher education for the sons and daughters of wealthy Lebanese who did not have the academic qualifications to attend the American University. Despite the chaotic situation in Beirut, four American teachers – Jesse Turner, Robert Polhill, Mitheleshwar Singh and Alann Steen – had stayed on at the BUC. But as the activities of the kidnap gangs intensified in January 1987, college officials thought it prudent to ask the Lebanese police to provide extra protection. Thus the college authorities saw nothing untoward in the arrival of a group of security police at the main college entrance.

The security police asked the four Americans to assemble in one of the conference rooms to advise them and co-ordinate the security arrangements. The head officer said they wanted to conduct a drill to show the teachers how they should behave in the event of someone trying to kidnap them. The first rule, said the policeman, was not to resist, as to do so was to run the risk of being shot. To reinforce his point he produced four sets of handcuffs, and asked the teachers to put them on. They readily obliged, and when the policeman then produced an automatic rifle, pointed it at them and ordered them to climb into the back of a waiting police van, they still did not realise what was happening. It was only as the van sped off through the college gates that they realised they were the victims of an elaborate sting. It later transpired that the Lebanese who carried out the kidnapping were genuine policemen who had been employed by Hussein Musawi, the Hizbollah leader in the Bekaa Valley. Musawi, apparently jealous at the mounting influence the other kidnap groups had acquired in Iran, felt the time had come to get some hostages of his own. Needless to say, the security police were never seen again at their barracks.

The American and British hostages held by Islamic Jihad were formally introduced to each other in May 1988 when they were all put in the same room in a filthy cell in the Bekaa Valley they called the 'pigpen'. Keenan and McCarthy endured one of their worst journeys in the 'coffin' on the way to the Bekaa. Normally on such a journey, Keenan and McCarthy, despite being bound like mummies, would kick or touch each other to reassure themselves that they were surviving the terrible ordeal. But on this particular seven-hour trip, McCarthy lay motionless and did not make a sound, leading Keenan to fear the worst. When they finally got to the Bekaa and the guards pulled McCarthy out and removed his bindings, McCarthy was traumatised. He stumbled around in the fresh air muttering, 'Where are we? Are they going to shoot us?'

The cell was called the pigpen because it lay directly underneath the guards' toilet. Sometimes water would overflow and fall onto the hostages chained below. Not surprisingly, all the hostages suffered bouts of extreme diarrhoea. The guards showed no sympathy. Rather than allow the hostages frequent access to the toilet, they provided a plastic garbage bag in which to defecate.

Despite such indignities, Keenan and McCarthy helped to raise the spirits of the older Americans. After being together for nearly two years, Keenan and McCarthy had developed a zany sense of humour where they would shout abuse at each other, Keenan in his thick, Belfast accent, and McCarthy in the clipped tones of the English public schoolboy. At first this banter confused the Americans; when they argued, it was for real. In time, however, the Americans warmed to their new companions. Keenan endeared himself to them with his endless string of shaggy-dog stories which could each last for up to an hour and helped to kill the time. McCarthy earned their respect because for them, even during the darkest moments of their captivity, he maintained all the traits of a perfect English gentleman.

By the time Keenan and McCarthy joined the Americans, Keenan's behaviour had become markedly more eccentric. When he was not telling stories, Keenan would talk for hours about politics. No one would have guessed he was an Ulster Protestant. The tenor of his remarks was that he had been forced to flee Belfast because of his Republican sympathies. Whenever the subject of Ireland came up, Keenan made it quite clear that he firmly supported the armed struggle. To reinforce his commitment to the Republican cause in Ireland, Keenan decided to go 'on the blanket' in sympathy with all the Irish political prisoners jailed in Britain. Going on the blanket was a form of protest devised by IRA prisoners in Northern Ireland during the late 1970s as part of their campaign to have the status of political prisoners. Republican prisoners refused to wear prison uniform, and instead covered themselves with a blanket. In time, the protest escalated into the dirty protest, culminating in the notorious hunger strikes. Given the appalling sanitary conditions in the Lebanon cells, Keenan could hardly go on a dirty protest. But he did refuse to wear the few items of underwear provided, and covered himself only with a blanket. When Keenan decided upon his protest, McCarthy saw no point in objecting to something which Keenan felt strongly about and which enabled him to come to terms with his captivity. When the Americans first met Keenan, they could not understand the point of conducting a protest in a Lebanese dungeon on behalf of people thousands of miles away, especially as the outside world had no way of knowing what Keenan was up to. But ultimately the Americans took the view that if it made Keenan happy, it was best to let him get on with it.

Keenan's going on the blanket only made his life in captivity harsher. At the best of times the Shia Muslim guards were unpredictable, and they did not take kindly to Keenan's open defiance of their wishes. Working-class Lebanese Shias know next to nothing about the intricacies of Irish politics. Arabs are also by nature extremely modest, and the guards found Keenan's refusal to wear any clothes not only a challenge to their authority, but an insult to their religious beliefs. As a result, there was an underlying tension to Keenan's relationship with the guards which often exploded in violence. One such occasion was on Christmas Eve 1988 when all the hostages, faced with yet another Christmas in captivity, were in low spirits. As the guards were chaining them up for the night, one, whether by accident or design, gave a sharp pull on Keenan's chain.

'Hey, you, watch that,' shouted Keenan. The guard, a particularly paranoid individual, immediately spun round and challenged Keenan to repeat what he had said.

'I said don't you pull that chain again or you'll regret it,' Keenan shouted. The guard gave Keenan's chain an even harder tug. At that, even though he was blindfolded and chained up, Keenan leapt to his feet and sprang at the guard, who jumped back like a frightened rabbit. The guard left the room, but returned a few minutes later with two of his colleagues, who were armed with belts and broom handles. They proceeded to lay into the defenceless Keenan, delivering sickening blows to his legs, arms and shoulders. As the guards hit him, they seemed to become more and more excited, working themselves into a frenzy. In that mood, they might well have beaten Keenan to death, had not another, more senior guard, walked in to see what was going on. He called a halt to the assault and, after shouting a few curses at Keenan, they left the cell, covered in sweat. Keenan lay motionless on the floor, his body covered in bruises from head to toe. It was a high price to pay for a small political gesture.

19

THE LOST YEARS

It was several days before the realisation began to dawn that Terry Waite would not be returning from his secret meeting with the kidnappers. The Druze bodyguards had watched Waite's meeting with Mugniyeh from a nearby building. They had watched as Dr Mroueh left his office, and then as Mugniyeh escorted Waite out of the room. They were immediately suspicious, and a few hours later called Mroueh to see when Waite would be back. Mroueh was hesitant, and said Waite had ignored his instructions not to leave the room without him. He did not know when Waite would be back. The Druze knew Waite wanted to see the kidnappers, but had not expected him to leave the room. At first they assumed Waite had gone to see the hostages. Although they started to become concerned when he did not return that evening, the Druze refused to admit publicly that Waite was missing. They put out a statement that he was having 'marathon talks' with the kidnappers. 'We're waiting for a call from him to go and pick him up,' said an official.

The security situation in Beirut continued to deteriorate. The day after Waite went missing a forty-seven-year-old West

German businessman, Alfred Schmidt, was kidnapped when three men broke into his hotel room, put a hood over his head and drove him away. But still the Druze continued to insist nothing untoward had happened to the Anglican churchman. 'Mr Waite is still having a meeting with the hostage-holders,' the next Druze statement reported. Waite was being allowed to 'see and converse' with the American hostages, said the Druze. They even phoned Lambeth Palace to assure the Archbishop that Waite was 'safe and well'. It was only on the third day after Waite went missing that the first hint of doubt appeared in the Druze statements. 'Terry Waite is still negotiating with the kidnappers, as far as we can tell,' the statement read.

While in public the Druze tried to present a brave face, in private they were engaged in a frantic search. Responsibility for trying to rescue Waite was given to Akram Shehayeb, the Druze politician who had been deputed by Jumblatt to guard Waite. Shehayeb had had previous dealings with the Mugniyeh clan over hostages. In 1983 he managed to persuade Mugniyeh to release a cameraman with an American network who had been kidnapped by Shia gunmen. Shehayeb had made contact with Mugniyeh, and a few days later he was surprised to find Mugniyeh and the cameraman walking into his office. 'This is the man you're looking for,' said Mugniyeh, and left without another word.

Three days after Waite went missing Shehayeb had a meeting with Mugniyeh at Beirut's Summerland Hotel, which lasted for seven hours. Mugniyeh did not say that he definitely had Waite, although Shehayeb had personally watched Mugniyeh leading Waite out of Mroueh's surgery. Mugniyeh told Shehayeb that if he wanted to get Waite back, he would have to get his seventeen 'brothers' released from Kuwait. Shehayeb protested that the Druze had no influence over Kuwait, and that the fate of the 17 was not a Druze concern. Mugniyeh shrugged his shoulders, and said that if the Druze could not help with the prisoners then Waite would not be freed. At this point Shehayeb began to lose his temper, and threatened Mugniyeh that if he did not release Waite immediately, he would send Druze militiamen into the southern suburbs to rescue him forcibly. By taking Waite, said Shehayeb, Mugniyeh had insulted the honour of the Druze who had pledged themselves to guarantee Waite's safety. Mugniyeh said he would need time to consult with other Hizbollah leaders, and left.

The following day Shehayeb received a call asking him to attend a meeting with Sheikh Fadlallah. When Shehayeb arrived, Fadlallah informed him that nothing could be done about Terry Waite.

'Akram, this matter is far bigger than both of us,' Fadlallah confided in almost parental tones. 'There is no point sending your fighters against us. It will only cause unnecessary bloodshed. The Englishman has been taken, and there is nothing you or I can do about it.' Fadlallah did not say who had Waite, but Shehayeb assumed that, if Fadlallah was involved, the Iranians must have had a hand in the abduction. Shehayeb reported back to Jumblatt who, in a typically dramatic gesture, offered himself as a hostage if the kidnappers would release Waite.

Meanwhile John Gray, the British ambassador, was becoming increasingly concerned about Waite's whereabouts. Because the embassy had been moved to the Christian enclave in East Beirut, it was difficult for officials to find out what was going on in the Muslim quarter. The last Gray had heard of Waite was when he got one of his staff to phone Waite to tell him to leave the city. Gray knew the Druze were looking after Waite, and every time he phoned their headquarters he was told Waite was working with 'other people' and was quite safe. Eventually Gray was left with no option but to drive over to West Beirut, a highly risky undertaking, to find out what was going on. Accompanied by four SAS-trained bodyguards, Gray drove to Shehayeb's office in West Beirut in a bullet-proof Jaguar.

'I just had to go over to his office to have it out with him,' said Gray. 'Eventually he conceded he didn't have a clue where Waite had gone.' It was another two weeks before a senior official with the Amal militia, who had close contacts with Hizbollah, confirmed that Waite had been kidnapped. 'My information is that Terry Waite will not be returning as he is kidnapped,' the official told the Reuters news agency. 'He has been added to the list of hostages. He became one the day he left his bodyguard.'

When Waite left Mroueh's surgery with Mugniyeh, he knew there was a good chance he might not come back. But when Mugniyeh offered him the chance to see Anderson and Sutherland, Waite thought it was too good an opportunity to miss. It might be a trap, but if he pulled it off he would be a hero once more. And Sutherland and Anderson might even be released. Mugniyeh searched him for weapons and asked him to wear a blindfold. Waite was driven to a flat somewhere in the southern suburbs. When they arrived Waite was asked to strip for another search. Waite was not put out, as he had been through this routine once before when he met Mugniyeh in 1985. The kidnappers took Waite's clothes and gave him new ones, then left him alone. As the hours passed, Waite fell asleep on the couch. Eventually the kidnappers returned and took him to another building where he was again required to wait. Finally they drove him to a garage and told him to get out of the car. Waite still thought there was a slim chance he might be going to meet the hostages, but his hopes were quickly destroyed. The kidnappers opened a trapdoor and ordered Waite, who was still wearing a blindfold, to enter. He clambered onto a wardrobe and into the basement. He was then led to a cell and chained to a wall. Waite's mission to free the hostages in Lebanon had finally come to an end.

To help him survive the ordeal ahead, Waite made three resolutions: he would not allow himself to have any regrets, to be sentimental or to indulge in self-pity. He suspected he would be put through a rigorous interrogation concerning the exact nature of his dealings with Oliver North. Mugniyeh and the rest of Islamic Jihad were convinced that Waite was an American spy, and they also believed he had deceived them over his promise to free the prisoners from Kuwait. As the kidnappers had told the American hostages the year previously, Waite was a 'bad man', and now they had him captive, they would deal with him accordingly. For the first few months of his captivity, Waite was subjected to a series of beatings such as had been given to Jacobsen and Sutherland. His legs were bound to the barrel of a gun, and his legs raised into the air, no mean feat given Waite's weight and size. The kidnappers then pounded the soles of his feet with rubber hose. On other occasions the guards would appear in the middle of the night, unchain his hands and tell him to face the wall. They would then fire questions at him, beating him if they were not satisfied with his answers.

When he was not being interrogated, Waite was chained hand and foot so that he could not lie straight. The kidnappers' treatment of Waite was considerably harsher than their treatment of the other hostages, a reflection of the anger they felt towards him for letting them down, and because of his links with Oliver North. At one point they told Waite he had only a few hours left to live; he could write one letter before his execution. Waite wanted to write to several people. He condensed his thoughts into a single missive to the effect that he had no regrets for what he had done, and that he had only been trying to do what he believed was right. He was then asked if he had any last requests. He asked for a cup of tea, because his throat was parched from the emotional exertion of writing his last letter. When he had drunk his tea, they told him to stand up and face the wall. As he did so he felt a gun being pressed against his head. The kidnappers asked if he had anything left to say, and Waite replied, 'Nothing'. He then said his prayers, fully expecting to be shot at any moment. But they put the gun down, saying they would carry out the execution later. After that terrifying experience, the kidnappers ceased their interrogation of Terry Waite.

For the first four years of his captivity, Waite was held in solitary. For much of the time he was given nothing, no pen, paper, pencil, radio or books. He was left chained and blindfolded in a tiny cell. In such circumstances it is easy for a man either to lose his wits or to lose the will to live, but Waite was sustained by his faith and his determination to survive. Even in the darkest moments, Waite would think to himself, You can do your worst but you cannot destroy me. Never. He wrote a novel in his mind. He became so involved with the plot which, true to Waite's character, was about himself, that he carried on writing it for three days. On another occasion he imagined himself sailing around the world, and made a list of all the provisions he would need to take. He would do mental arithmetic which would require memorising long lists of numbers. When he got to the solution he would go back to the roots of the equation, a process which could occupy him for days. When he was eventually given a Bible, it did not give him quite the solace he had hoped. Far from being comforted, Waite was angered as he read through the Old Testament, with all its tales of treachery and vice.

Waite found himself in some peculiar situations. During the early part of his captivity, the kidnappers would dress him as a woman when they wanted to move him from one prison to another – some undertaking, given that Waite stands six foot seven inches in his socks. Somehow the kidnappers found a long black cloak and a veil to cover him. At other times when the kidnappers wanted to move him, they would bind him with masking tape and stuff him in a chest. Finding that Waite was too big for one chest, they put him in a fridge. The fridge had only recently been turned off, and was still frosted. Fortunately, Waite was able to force open the door, otherwise he might have suffocated. When, a few years later, the Beirut apartment in which Waite was being held was in the middle of a ferocious artillery battle, the kidnappers put him in a bath for safety, chaining his feet to the taps. For several days shells landed all around, one of them in the next building. As Waite listened to the screams of the injured, he realised he was not the only person suffering in Lebanon.

The prospect of any of the hostages being released rapidly receded as the American government broke off its discussions with the Iranian government. Even after North's deals had been exposed, the US attempted to continue a dialogue with the Iranian contacts who had managed to arrange David Jacobsen's release. But with more experienced State Department officials representing the Americans instead of Oliver North, the negotiations quickly ground to a halt. A team of officials met with the Iranians at Frankfurt's Park Hotel on December 13, 1986. The Iranians, believing they were still working on the basis established with North, said they would try to secure the release of more American hostages in return for the delivery of 1,500 TOW missiles; the Iranians also wanted the US to put pressure on Kuwait to release the 17. The State Department officials were horrified by the Iranian demands. As far as they were concerned, the US government policy specifically forbade pressuring other governments to free prisoners in exchange for hostages. When they reported back to Shultz, he gave immediate orders to return to Washington and have nothing further to do with the Iranians. There were to be no more American arms sold to Iran in return for hostages. For the next year the Americans were so consumed by the excitement of the Congressional hearings into Iran-Contra that efforts to seek the release of the captives virtually ceased. And when the hearings concluded and criminal proceedings were instigated against the principal architects of the Iran-Contra deals, the bitter lessons learned meant that Washington had very limited room for manoeuvre in any future attempts to free the hostages.

If Margaret Thatcher privately allowed herself a smug sense of satisfaction at the furore created across the Atlantic by Iran-Contra, out of respect for Reagan she kept her thoughts to herself. Thatcher happened to be in Washington on a far more important mission in mid-November 1986, at the very moment the scandal was beginning to break. Alarmed by the commitments Reagan had unwittingly made at the Reykjavik summit with Mikhail Gorbachev to remove all American nuclear weapons from Europe, Thatcher had come to Washington to make Reagan aware of his responsibilities to NATO and the importance of Britain maintaining its independent nuclear capability. Thus, when asked by reporters in Washington what she thought of Reagan's involvement in Iran-Contra, Thatcher conveniently forgot that, only six months previously, she had personally sent Sir Percy Cradock and Sir Anthony Acland to complain to the Americans about the secret arms-for-hostages deals. Instead she went on record with a statement hardly a single American politician of either party would at that moment have been prepared to sign. 'I believe implicity in the President's total integrity on that subject,' she proclaimed. Such unequivocal support from the Iron Maiden gave the beleaguered President a much-appreciated fillip.

The only dealings Mrs Thatcher had with the hostage issue on that trip was to invite Elaine Collett to afternoon tea at the British ambassador's residence in Washington. Though Alec Collett's children, David and Suzie, had concluded that their father was dead after watching the grisly video which purported to show him being hanged, Mrs Collett continued to cling to the hope that her husband was alive. Until his body was produced, she would not give up hope. This had the potential to embarrass the Thatcher government; the murder of three British hostages after the American raid on Libya was, after all, one of the more embarrassing episodes of Thatcher's premiership. To placate Mrs Collett, British officials arranged to fly her from New York to Washington. No publicity was given to the visit; it was not the kind of publicity Bernard Ingham, Thatcher's press secretary, wanted to encourage. The visit would, however, give Mrs Thatcher a convenient fall-back position in the event of difficult questions being raised about what the British government was doing for the hostages. Ingham could reply that the Prime Minister was deeply committed to the hostage issue; she had even broken off from an important Washington visit to see Mrs Collett. Mrs Collett was shown into the British embassy by the back door.

'She was a very pleasant woman,' Mrs Collett recalled. 'She was very cordial towards me and she said she was genuinely concerned about my situation. She accepted my argument that Alec might still be alive, although she was noncommittal about what the British government could do about it. All she would say to me was, "We don't negotiate with terrorists." When I left I was surprised there was no publicity given to the meeting.'

Mrs Thatcher's hardline policy on terrorism was to dominate the way in which the British authorities set about trying to secure the release of Waite and McCarthy. Mrs Thatcher had a natural antipathy towards any group or institution associated in any way with acts of terrorism. Official British contact with the PLO and the African National Congress, not to mention the Irish Republican Army, was not on any agenda after Thatcher came to power. Her repugnance of terrorism was strengthened by the murder of Airey Neave, one of her closest political allies, by the IRA, and her own lucky escape when the IRA blew up Brighton's Grand Hotel in October 1984 during the Conservative Party conference. When in later years people asked her advisers why she was utterly obdurate, far more so than the leaders of most other governments, in her refusal to contemplate talking to foreign 'terrorist' organisations, her experience at Brighton was cited as the explanation.[1]

Mrs Thatcher's absolute insistence that no British official become involved in any negotiations for the release of the British hostages left little room for manoeuvre, and probably partly explains why the kidnappers, during the five years they held McCarthy and Waite, never once issued demands for them. Even after the Iran-Contra débâcle, the American, French and West German governments continued to receive regular demands from the kidnappers. Although the governments concerned might not be able to act on any of the demands, it nevertheless gave them an opportunity to assess who was holding the hostages, and to explore the possibility of opening a dialogue. Once a dialogue was established, the chances of securing the hostages' release were greatly improved. But the kidnappers regarded Thatcher's public attitude as so intransigent that it did not even seem worth their while to make demands.

The kidnappers' attitude was no doubt influenced by the uncompromising manner in which Thatcher responded to the conviction, in October 1986, of Nizar Hindawi at the Old Bailey on charges of trying to blow up an El Al jumbo jet at

---

[1]Young, *op. cit.*

Heathrow Airport. Hindawi, a Palestinian from Jordan, had persuaded his Irish girlfriend to board an El Al flight from London to Tel Aviv with a parcel containing a bomb. The bomb was set to explode when the aircraft was airborne. The attack was planned two days after the American raid against Libya in April 1986, but was foiled by the vigilance of El Al security guards as the Irish woman boarded the plane. Hindawi was arrested, and in their subsequent inquiries, British officials found that the operation had been planned with the active assistance of the Syrian ambassador in London. Even though it became clear some form of action would need to be taken against the Syrians, the Foreign Office was opposed to cutting all diplomatic relations with Damascus. To do so would be to deprive Britain of access to one of the most strategically important countries in the Middle East and make it immeasurably more difficult to work for the release of British hostages in Lebanon. But for all the arguments advanced by the Foreign Office, Mrs Thatcher was adamant that the British government must cut all diplomatic relations with Syria.

Nor were Britain's relations with Iran at this time much better. Since she had sent in the SAS to end the siege of the Iranian embassy in London in 1980, Iran had every reason to be thankful to Mrs Thatcher for her determined stand against terrorism. But throughout the 1980s relations between the two countries had declined to the extent that by the time McCarthy and Waite were kidnapped, Britain's diplomatic representation in Teheran had been reduced to a small interests section housed in the Swedish embassy. To show their disapproval of Mrs Thatcher's policies in the Middle East, Iranian students had sacked the British embassy several times. The road outside the embassy had been renamed Bobby Sands Road, after the IRA hunger-striker, and a mural of Mrs Thatcher was painted on the wall outside the embassy which depicted her with the

Jewish Star of David around her neck and smiling as she perched on a bloody claw painted with the American stars and stripes. Four months after Waite's abduction, moreover, relations between Britain and Iran reached an all-time low after the Iranian vice-consul in Manchester, Ali Qassemi, was arrested for shoplifting. The following day Edward Chaplin, the British chargé d'affaires in Teheran, was seized as he drove to work by a group of Revolutionary Guards and beaten up. As a consequence Britain severed all diplomatic relations with Iran.

Not that, given what was going on in Teheran at the time, British officials stood much chance of persuading the Iranians to help with the British hostages. The leak of the details of the arms deals between the US and Iran to *Ash-Shiraa* had constituted a dangerous challenge to the power of Hashemi Rafsanjani. The purpose of the leak was to embarrass Rafsanjani in the eyes of Ayatollah Khomeini in the hope that Rafsanjani would be disgraced and forced from office. In the aftermath of the revelations, however, it soon became apparent to the group which had leaked the story, the supporters of Ali Montazeri, Khomeini's designated successor, that Khomeini himself had approved the arms deals. For all his public pronouncements against the US, Khomeini was experienced enough to know that politics is often a choice between two evils and, as far as Khomeini was concerned, buying weapons from the US was preferable to defeat by Saddam Hussein. Rafsanjani moved quickly to consolidate his position. It is said that he personally ordered the kidnapping of Terry Waite to protect his nephew, Ali Hashemi Bahremani, who had been negotiating the last arms deal with Oliver North. Rafsanjani also asserted his authority over the Montazeri camp by ordering the execution of Mehdi Hashemi, the radical Revolutionary Guard whose arrest had sparked the power struggle and the leaking of the story to

Ash-Shiraa. Hashemi was duly executed by firing squad at Evin prison in October 1987. At about the same time Hassan Sabra, the editor of *Ash-Shiraa*, miraculously survived an assassination attempt when a team of Iranian hitmen fired three shots at his head at close range. The gunmen pulled up alongside Sabra's car on a motorcycle as he was driving his daughter home from school. One bullet went through his cheek, another the back of his head, while the third hit his daughter in the leg. Both father and daughter survived.

The chances of the Iranians using their influence to get the hostages freed were further diminished by the build-up in tension in the Gulf in the summer of 1987 following Washington's decision to use the US navy to provide Kuwaiti oil tankers with an escort through the Straits of Hormuz. Throughout the Iran-Iraq war the Iranians accused Kuwait of siding with Iraq, and threatened to attack Kuwaiti ships passing through the Gulf. These threats only served to reinforce the Kuwaitis' resolve not to give in to the Iranians, which meant, in particular, not releasing the Dawa 17. The fact that the Americans were actively protecting Kuwaiti interests in the Gulf only made the Iranians less inclined to use their 'good offices' on behalf of Western hostages.

Given this unpromising diplomatic backdrop, it was hardly surprising that the hostages were put into cold storage. From 1987, the only references the kidnappers made to the hostages was when they issued threats against the involvement of the US in the Gulf. At various times statements issued in the name of groups claiming to hold the hostages made threats to the effect that hostages would be killed if the Americans continued to protect Arab shipping from attack by the Iranians.

In the absence of any hard information on the fate of the hostages, the Middle East became an enormous rumour-mill in which the slightest piece of gossip about a likely release was snapped up and became copper-bottomed fact. Even the faintest suggestion that Terry Waite had been seen taking a walk along the Green Line – and there were many – was sufficient to bring hordes of journalists flocking to Cyprus's Larnaca airport. Beirut was now considered off-limits to all but the most foolhardy journalists, and Larnaca was regarded as the best location for anticipating a hostage release on the basis that they would be flown to Cyprus upon their release. A room was hired close to the control tower to enable camera crews to get the best possible picture. Depending on how co-operative the Syrians were feeling, they would provide a selected number of journalists with visas for Damascus. When the Syrians realised how much foreign currency they could earn from the media – they charged $800 each time a television crew brought its equipment into Syria – it became much easier to obtain a Syrian visa. As the hostage who attracted the most media interest and excitement was Terry Waite, the media circus which travelled regularly between Damascus and Larnaca came to be known as 'the Waite-watchers'.

One of the few journalists to return to Beirut at this time was Charles Glass, a distinguished correspondent with the American ABC television station. Glass, who was half-Lebanese, knew Lebanon well, and had taken leave from the company to write a travel book on the Levant. From personal experience Glass knew how dangerous Lebanon had become, so he took the precaution of arranging to visit Beirut with Ali Osseiran, the son of the Lebanese defence minister. With his dark hair and complexion, Glass hoped he would pass as an ordinary Lebanese. He also thought that, by travelling in a car driven by the defence minister's personal chauffeur, he was safe from the kidnap gangs. But on June 17, 1987, the kidnappers managed to capture Glass, Osseiran and the chauffeur in Beirut in broad daylight within a few hundred yards of a Syrian checkpost. Osseiran and the driver were released one week later, but for two months it looked as though Glass had joined the ranks of the long-term hostages. He even appeared in a videotape in which he looked haggard and admitted he was working for the CIA.

Just when everybody had given up hope of seeing him again, Glass turned up at the Summerland Hotel claiming he had escaped from the kidnappers. Glass later wrote a detailed account of how he freed himself from his chains by tying the links together with thread, until he had made enough room to slip his arms and legs through the manacles. Whether Glass genuinely escaped or was allowed to escape, however, became a lively topic for debate, especially after one of America's most respected anchormen, who also happened to work for a rival news company, introduced the item on Glass with the words: 'Charles Glass, the young American journalist who *claims* he escaped from captivity in Beirut . . .' Certainly the Syrians, with whom the Lebanese defence minister was on friendly terms, were so annoyed by Glass's abduction that they launched a massive search to set him free. And if the Syrians were able to assist in Glass's liberation, it raised the question as to how much pressure they could bring to bear, if the mood took them, to free the other Western hostages.

With the British government stymied in its efforts to free McCarthy and Waite, one of the few channels which remained open was Lambeth Palace. There was no longer any Terry Waite at Lambeth to negotiate on behalf of the Church, so the task fell to John Lyttle, a wily behind-the-scenes political operator who had been hired by Runcie to keep him posted on any domestic political developments which might affect the Church. Previously there had been no one on the staff of Lambeth Palace with any experience of politics and government. Lyttle had never met Waite, and started work in January 1987 while Waite was still working on his Beirut mission. Lyttle, a contemporary of Roy Hattersley from Sheffield, had spent most of his working life with the

Labour Party, before following Shirley Williams to the SDP. A bachelor and compulsive smoker, Lyttle decided to accept the Lambeth job after he had suffered a heart attack. 'I thought it was time I took things a bit easy,' Lyttle confided to his friends.

Within days of his appointment, Lyttle's sole responsibility was to try and locate the missing churchman, hardly the easygoing job he had anticipated. It was several days before Lambeth woke up to the fact that Waite had been kidnapped. It then fell to Lyttle to go through Waite's documents for any clues as to why Waite might have been abducted. As a highly-trained and experienced political officer, Lyttle knew the importance of keeping a detailed record of meetings, and was dumbfounded at how little documentation Waite had kept of his mission. There were a few discarded air tickets and a few diary notes, but nothing of any substance. And the more Lyttle inquired into Waite's activities, the less he liked what he found. As with many others who had worked with Waite on the Lebanon mission, Lyttle came to the conclusion that Waite had been beguiled by flattery.

'If someone asked me into the White House and told me there was a special job that only I could do, my nose would quiver so much it would fall off,' Lyttle confided to his friends. He was also privately enraged that Waite had preferred to spend time abroad on his missions than with his family. 'That man would prefer to sit in a tent with Gaddafi in the desert than around the Christmas tree with his own family,' he exploded.

Once he had pieced together the sorry facts of Waite's last mission, Lyttle confronted Runcie to find out why he had allowed Waite to return to Beirut in the first place.

'I could hardly stand in his way,' Runcie protested.

'Oh yes you bloody well could,' Lyttle replied in characteristically blunt Yorkshire fashion. 'You're his bloody boss, after all.'

In February Runcie wrote to both Rafsanjani and Fadlallah appealing for their help in securing Waite's release, but received no reply. Lyttle began work on a variety of schemes, including one by which the Church would raise money for medical equipment for Lebanon's Shia community. The equipment would not be a ransom, but a gift from the Church to the Lebanese people. Such a gesture might encourage the kidnappers to view the Church and Waite more favourably. But on no account was any ransom to be paid to Hizbollah.

A whole range of characters came forward to offer their services to Lambeth, and much of Lyttle's time was taken up with trying to work out who could and who could not be taken seriously. In March 1987 Lambeth was approached by John Entwistle and Charles Armstrong. If Lambeth would foot the bills, they told Lyttle, they could fly some of their Shia friends from Lebanon to meet the Archbishop. These Shias had close contacts with Hizbollah and could organise Waite's release. Lyttle was suspicious and contacted both the Foreign Office and Scotland Yard. The Foreign Office confirmed that Entwistle had a criminal record for petty crime, although he had not been involved in serious crimes such as kidnapping or terrorism. A commander at Scotland Yard encouraged Lyttle to play along with the two men with the words, 'Kidnapping is a very dirty business and you don't make much progress if you only talk to archangels and archbishops.' Lambeth paid them £10,000 in air fares and £2,000 in cash. The two men were never seen at Lambeth again.

Lyttle received a more serious approach in the autumn of 1987; a message that Mustafa Tlass, the Syrian defence minister, would like to see Lyttle in Damascus. Lyttle was taking a holiday in Cyprus at about that time, and sent word that if Tlass was serious, he could arrange a visa for Lyttle to collect in Cyprus. When Lyttle arrived for his holiday, a Syrian visa was awaiting him. He flew to Damascus the following

Monday. When Lyttle met Tlass, the Syrian asked him if he would be prepared to go to Lebanon, under Syrian protection, to meet some of the Hizbollah leaders. Lyttle readily agreed, and the next day he was taken for an uncomfortable ride in a Range Rover, wedged between two well-armed soldiers of the Syrian special forces. Although the soldiers were clearly nervous about meeting Hizbollah, they drove like maniacs over the mountain road to Beirut. When they got there, however, Fadlallah, the man they had come to see, was out. So the party piled back into the Range Rover and drove back across the mountain to Baalbek, where they had arranged a meeting with Sheikh Subhi Tufayli, the secretary-general of Hizbollah and the kidnappers' paymaster. Lyttle had a cordial meeting with Tufayli, but when the Lebanese cleric realised Lyttle had nothing to offer in return for the release of the hostages, Tufayli brought the meeting to an abrupt end, saying he had no knowledge where the captives were located.

Had Lyttle consulted Samir Habiby before going to Lebanon, he might have made more of the opportunity. Habiby, with his Palestinian roots, knew how deals were done in the Middle East; arriving for such an important meeting emptyhanded was not on. But Lyttle had cut Habiby out of the picture, as had the rest of the Church establishment, both in Britain and America. After Waite's kidnap, Bishop Browning unceremoniously relieved Habiby of his job at the Presiding Bishop's Fund without explanation. He also authorised a secret investigation into how the fund had been managed under Habiby, the implication being that funds had somehow been misappropriated while Habiby and Waite were working on the Lebanon mission. It later transpired that the fund had contributed $18,000 dollars to Waite's travelling expenses. This had been approved by the presiding bishop when the Episcopal Church first asked for Waite's assistance. Habiby was nevertheless ostracised from the Episcopal Church headquarters, hardly reasonable treatment for someone who had devoted so much energy to Waite's cause. It was the Church, after all, which asked Habiby to assist Waite, and he had done so with enthusiasm. He had opposed Waite's returning to Beirut, and had nothing to do with Waite's suicidal decision to meet the kidnappers. And yet Habiby was made to pay for Waite's folly. Moreover, the Episcopal Church told Runcie to have nothing further to do with Habiby. 'I was warned off him,' said Runcie. 'I never got to the bottom of it, but in the circumstances it seemed the right thing to do.' Despite being cold-shouldered by the Church establishment, Habiby continued to work tirelessly for the release of his friend, undertaking several trips to the Middle East at his own expense.

While the British and Americans were, for their own reasons, incapable of making progress, the French and Germans showed that it was not necessary for Westerners held in Lebanon to be left to rot indefinitely. In November 1987, two Frenchmen, Roger Auque and Jean-Louis Normandin, who had been held for ten months and twenty months respectively, were flown to Paris for a heroes' welcome. Normandin had been held for a few months with Jo Cicippio and Edward Tracy, while Auque had been held by Islamic Jihad. Throughout the course of the crisis, as many French were kidnapped as Americans. At least fifteen French were kidnapped between 1985 and 1987 by the main kidnap groups. But unlike the Americans, the French government was able to get its hostages out without causing a national scandal.

The French government had many advantages over the British and Americans when it came to confronting the hostage issue. France still maintained the close cultural and political ties with Lebanon which had been established during the colonial period. French was, with Arabic, Lebanon's official language; the French government still maintained an active diplomatic role in Lebanon, mainly to assist those parties, such as the Christians and the Sunni Muslims, which supported the French-designed constitution, where, as in Paris, all real political power was vested in the office of the president. It was precisely this French-inspired status quo which the radical Shia Muslims were trying to destroy, and kidnapping Frenchmen, of whom there were many still in Lebanon, was seen as one way of putting pressure on both Paris and the Lebanese government to accept the need for reform. Nor was it only French policy in Lebanon to which the Shia Muslims took exception. Under the rule of the Shah, French President Valéry Giscard d'Estaing had committed French industry to a massive development programme in Iran. The French then did a *volte-face*, and encouraged the Ayatollah's revolution by encouraging him to reside in exile in Paris. Once the revolution had been accomplished, however, the Ayatollah repaid his hosts by cancelling billions of dollars' worth of French contracts, notably in nuclear power. As a consequence, the French moved to open support for Iraq. The French built the experimental nuclear research centre on the outskirts of Baghdad which was later destroyed by the Israelis. And when war broke out between Iraq and Iran, the French became Iraq's main arms suppliers. As with the Royal Navy during the Falklands War, many Iranian oil tankers and oil installations in the Gulf were destroyed by French-made Exocet missiles fired from French-built super-Etendard and Mirage fighters. The Shia Muslims of Lebanon and Iran consequently had many reasons for wanting to take Frenchmen hostage.

It was precisely because France, unlike Britain and the US, had historic ties in Lebanon that the French government was able to take an active role in getting its hostages freed. Although the members of the European Community had signed an agreement in London in December 1986 'to make no concessions under duress to terrorists and their sponsors', Jacques Chirac, the right-wing French prime minister, was prepared to make a far more liberal interpretation of this edict than Mrs Thatcher. Chirac argued that there was a distinction between treating directly with hostage-takers, which was plainly unacceptable, and dealing with other states – in this case, Syria and Iran – which might be able to influence the kidnap gangs. In 1987, the British government flatly rejected this argument; the close identification of Iran with hostage-taking made such a distinction meaningless in British eyes.

Chirac, more to the point, was under considerably more pressure to get the French hostages released than either Thatcher or Reagan. In the summer of 1986, Shia extremists had subjected Paris to a ferocious bombing campaign which had virtually reduced the city to a state of terror. And every evening before the news, the main French television stations carried harrowing pictures of the French hostages, giving the precise number of days they had been held. With presidential elections due in May 1988, it was imperative that Chirac came to terms with the Shia extremist groups in order to prevent any further terrorist attacks on mainland France and to secure the release of the French hostages.

The job of getting the French hostages freed was entrusted to Jean-Charles Marchiana, a veteran of French undercover operations in the Middle East who, because of his close contacts with the Lebanese Shia, was able to deal directly with Hizbollah. During his negotiations, which started in earnest in the summer of 1987, Marchiana learned that the French hostages had been held, at various times, with the Americans. He also learned what the kidnappers wanted in return for the American hostages. The demands were not very different to those made in the kidnappers' statements. When he returned to Paris to report to Chirac, Marchiana had meetings with American diplomats at which he indicated it would be possible to get some hostages released in return for certain concessions. The Americans, still embroiled in the Iran-Contra hearings, declined Marchiana's offer of assistance.

The British authorities were also aware of Marchiana's activities, but kept their distance because they still had no proof that the British hostages were even alive, and because they were naturally suspicious of French motives. Britain had cause to be suspicious of its European allies doing deals behind its back after the West Germans managed to get Alfred Schmidt released in September 1987. At first Bonn insisted that no deals had been struck, but then the kidnappers rather embarrassed the Germans by issuing a statement to the effect that certain 'guarantees' had been provided in return for Schmidt's release. The most likely explanation was that Schmidt's company, the electronics giant Siemens, paid a substantial ransom while the West German authorities quietly turned a blind eye.

Having offered to help their allies, the French saw no reason not to press ahead with Marchiana's initiative. The precise details have never been made public, but in return for the release of Augue and Normandin, the French set free Wahid Gordji, an official at the Iranian embassy in Paris who was being held for his role in the bomb attacks in Paris in 1986. At the same time the French aircraft carrier *Clemenceau*, which had supported the US effort to keep the Straits of Hormuz open during the Iran–Iraq war, was withdrawn, and the Iraqi government quietly informed that it could no longer count on the delivery of twenty Mirage F-1 fighter bombers. When details of the deal were leaked, Mrs Thatcher immediately accused the French of being 'soft' on terrorism. Sir Ewen Fergusson, the British ambassador, paid a visit to the Quai d'Orsay where he delivered a strongly worded protest on behalf of Mrs Thatcher.

When, on May 3, 1988, the last three French hostages – journalist Jean-Paul Kauffmann, and diplomats Marcel

Carton and Marcel Fontaine – were released on the eve of the French presidential election, Chirac was universally condemned outside France for his brazen opportunism; in France he was hailed as a national hero. Charles Pasqua, the interior minister who had supervised the operation, went on television to insist that no cash had been paid. 'Not a franc, not a dollar, not a deutschmark. If you like, not even an Iranian rial.' But it soon transpired Chirac had promised both Iran and the Lebanese kidnap groups a wide-ranging package to be implemented as soon as he was elected president. These included restoring full diplomatic relations with Iran, releasing Shia Muslims jailed in France on terrorist offences, and the favourable settlement of a one-billion-dollar financial dispute between Iran and France. Unfortunately for Chirac, the late surge in his opinion poll popularity prompted by the release of the hostages fell short of securing him victory in the elections. Not all of his promises were fulfilled by François Mitterrand, who secured a second term in the final round of the election on May 10. But France did agree to restore diplomatic relations with Teheran.

The British government made no attempt to hide its contempt for the manner in which the French had secured the hostages' release. Sir Ewen Fergusson was again required to inform the Quai d'Orsay that the French had incurred the displeasure of his prime minister. Officials in Whitehall complained bitterly of being betrayed by the French, and argued that they now faced an immeasurably more difficult task in trying to get the British hostages freed. 'All this kind of thing does is to raise the expectations of the kidnappers that they will get something for all the hostages they hold,' complained one senior Foreign Office official. 'It just means it will be a lot harder to convince them we are not in the business of doing a deal.'

While British and American officials decried the perfidy of the

French, the fact remained that, had the British and American governments been more co-operative with the French, they might well have been able to make progress on behalf of their own hostages. Carton, Fontaine and Kauffmann were all held by Islamic Jihad, the same group which held McCarthy, Waite, Keenan, Sutherland, Anderson and Reed. The three Frenchmen had, at various times, been held in the same cell as Anderson, Sutherland and Reed, who in turn had been held with McCarthy and Keenan. At the precise moment the three Frenchmen were being released, Anderson, Sutherland, Reed, McCarthy and Keenan were being held together at the 'pigpen' on the outskirts of Baalbek. While the British government was still insisting that it had no idea whether McCarthy and Waite were even alive, the French had managed to secure the release of three men who had been held in the same apartment as the British. Moreover, the 'deal' by the French bore a striking resemblance to the manner in which the British government would ultimately secure the release of its hostages. The principal concession made by the French was to restore diplomatic relations with Iran. In 1990, Britain would do likewise, paving the way for the release of McCarthy and Waite.

The release of the Frenchmen turned out to be the watershed for the British government in the issue of the British hostages. Suddenly the government found itself under pressure to act, particularly in the case of John McCarthy who, unlike Terry Waite, was an innocent victim of the kidnap gangs. In the two years since McCarthy had been kidnapped, the government had refused to discuss his case in public, mainly to avoid reviving painful memories of Thatcher's role in the Libyan raid and of the three murdered Britons. But the sight of all the French hostages returning home meant the government could no longer avoid the issue, especially as Jill Morrell, McCarthy's redoubtable girlfriend, was no longer prepared to toe the Foreign Office line.

Morrell had got to know McCarthy through her work as a scriptwriter at WTN. The couple had been going out for several months before McCarthy was sent on the Lebanon assignment. On the day of his kidnap, Morrell had bought food for a 'welcome home' supper and was preparing to leave for Heathrow to meet him when she received a call saying McCarthy had been kidnapped. 'It seemed like an awful mistake. It didn't seem possible,' said Morrell. 'The truth only sank in later.' Morrell and McCarthy's best friend from university, Chris Pearson, resolved to do their best to get McCarthy freed. Morrell, describing herself as McCarthy's fiancée, made several emotional public appeals to the kidnappers. Hearing her described as McCarthy's fiancée came as a surprise to Pat and Sheila McCarthy who had no idea the relationship had advanced so far. In fact Morrell had merely assumed the title because she thought it might lend weight to her appeals.

For the first two years Morrell and Pearson accepted the Foreign Office's request to keep quiet. They were assured that the FO was pursuing private discussions, secretly investigating every avenue. Publicity, they were told, might endanger the delicacy of the government's investigations. Then they were told that official British policy was to do absolutely nothing for the hostages, to give the kidnappers the notion that the hostages were of no significance, in the hope that they would decide the hostages were of no value and release them. By the spring of 1988, however, Morrell and Pearson had finally lost patience with the FO, and decided to launch their own campaign; The Friends of John McCarthy was set up in January 1988 to put pressure on the government to get the hostages released. If the Germans, French and Americans could get their hostages out, why not the British?

By the time Carton, Fontaine and Kauffmann were released the campaign was well-established, and Morrell, an attractive, quietly spoken blonde, was able to present a convincing case to the media. Her message was blunt and powerful. 'The policy of the government is literally to leave the British hostages there to rot,' she announced the day after the Frenchmen were freed. 'They may not do deals, but they still have a responsibility to talk to anyone that can help.' Morrell's broadside had the desired effect. David Mellor, the Foreign Office minister, hurriedly agreed to see her, the first time a British minister had officially acknowledged her existence. Mellor even went on breakfast television to defend the government's record. 'We would like to have Terry Waite and John McCarthy back,' he announced. 'We will pursue all legitimate means to do that.' All of a sudden, thanks to the commitment of McCarthy's friends, the fate of the British hostages had become a national priority.

20

LET'S BE FRIENDS

In the spring of 1989, John McCarthy and Brian Keenan received the distinct impression that they were on the point of being released. After all the indignities they had suffered in the 'pigpen' with the Americans, they had been moved back to Beirut to an apartment which, by comparison with some of the places they had been kept in, verged on the acceptable. The food improved, the beatings stopped, although Keenan was still feeling the effects of the savage beating he had received at Christmas, and they were even given a television for an hour each evening. By listening to the guards' radio they were able to pick up titbits of news, which they would discuss for hours. They were even provided with copies of *Time* and *Newsweek* magazines. The guards seemed more amiably disposed towards them, and every indication suggested they would soon be set free.

Although they did not realise it at the time, the improvement in living conditions was the result of a radical transformation in the relationship between Iran and Britain which had started in the summer of 1988 and resulted in the two countries, at a meeting in Vienna in November 1988, agreeing to the restoration of full diplomatic relations. Of all factors that led to this remarkable turnaround, by far the most important was the emergence of Hashemi Rafsanjani as a person of considerable power and influence in Iran. The first hint that Iran was losing interest in the hostage crisis had come in early 1988 when Rafsanjani admitted publicly that 'mistakes' had been made in relations between the Middle East and the West. Not too much credence was given to Rafsanjani's comments initially, mainly because no one was sure how much weight his comments carried in Teheran. Rafsanjani had had a narrow escape with the Iran-Contra affair which, if nothing else, had revealed the hazards of the West becoming involved in the perennial infighting of Iranian politics. Then in the summer of 1988 Iran and Iraq signed a ceasefire agreement which effectively ended the war which had raged between them for eight years.

The ceasefire agreement freed Rafsanjani to undertake a thorough review of Iran's foreign policy initiatives. His main priority was to repair the damage done to Iran's infrastructure during the war – in particular, the oil industry. To do this he needed Western technology, but the West was unlikely to co-operate so long as Iran was perceived as responsible for holding Western hostages in Lebanon. Freeing the hostages, therefore, became a priority for Rafsanjani. His main problem was to overcome the resistance of people like Ali Akbar Mohtashemi, the Iranian interior minister who had helped to set up Hizbollah when he was Iran's ambassador to Damascus, and who maintained close links with Mugniyeh and the other leaders of the kidnap groups. Mohtashemi was very much in league with the radical Islamic groups around Montazeri, Khomeini's designated successor, and it was by no means a foregone conclusion that Rafsanjani could override their wishes and set the hostages free. There was also the question of placating the actual kidnap groups who, after all, had their own reasons for holding on to the hostages.

In her forthright manner, Mrs Thatcher came close to wrecking the change in Iran's attitude towards Britain before it had had a chance to take root. When on July 3, 1988, the USS *Vincennes*, an American naval destroyer, accidentally shot down an Iranian airliner as it took off from the Iranian port of Bandar Abbas, killing the 290 passengers and crew, Thatcher enraged the Iranians by claiming the warship's action had been entirely legitimate in the circumstances. There had been no need for Mrs Thatcher to say anything; it was an issue between the Iranians and the Americans, and there was absolutely no reason for Britain to comment.

Thatcher's remarks nearly wrecked a highly delicate initiative John Lyttle had been working on for several months, with the active encouragement of the Foreign Office, to establish a dialogue with Rafsanjani. The initial approach had been made by the Iranians when, in March, Lyttle received a call out of the blue from a man who said he had been sent from Teheran to talk to him. The caller said it was imperative that he was not identified – he did not want to end up in front of a firing squad at Evin prison. So Lyttle arranged to meet him at a coffee shop at Victoria Station in London. As Lyttle himself admitted, his early contacts with the Iranians seemed to have been taken straight from the pages of a Jeffrey Archer novel. After the initial meeting at Victoria, the two men continued to meet in the lobbies of various London hotels, with the Iranian wearing a variety of disguises to conceal his identity from the vigilant attentions of MI5.

During the course of their conversations, the Iranian told Lyttle that Iran was willing to help free Waite, McCarthy and Keenan, but that Rafsanjani would first require some official British gesture of support for the Islamic revolution. As such a gesture was unlikely to be forthcoming from Mrs Thatcher, Lyttle suggested taking a parliamentary delegation to Teheran. The Iranians accepted the idea, and Lyttle led a delegation of five MPs to Teheran in the spring of 1988. Lyttle was surprised, when he was handed the tickets for the trip by the staff at Lambeth, to find he had been booked to fly first class. When he queried the cost, however, he was told: 'Well, that's the way Terry Waite always used to travel.'

Lyttle's contact was in fact working for the newly-established National Security Service which had been established in Teheran by Rafsanjani. The NSS was part of the Iranian foreign ministry, and Lyttle was introduced in Teheran to two officials personally seconded by Rafsanjani to arrange the release of the hostages. In return, Rafsanjani wanted a wide-ranging package of financial assistance, mainly in the form of export credit guarantees and the freeing of Iranian assets seized during the revolution. Rafsanjani's survival depended on the speed with which he could get the economy functioning again. And as the West had no desire to see the more radical elements, such as Montazeri, replace Rafsanjani, a deal was to everyone's advantage.

The talks between the British delegation and Rafsanjani progressed well. The Iranians indicated that they were keen to restore diplomatic relations so that normal trading ties could be resumed. The British said they were happy to consider Iran's request, so long as Iran gave a firm undertaking to help free the British hostages. It was at this delicate juncture that the Americans accidentally shot down the Iranian airbus and Thatcher made her injudicious comments – before even Reagan had been given a chance to say anything. The Iranians were angrier with Thatcher for speaking out of turn than they were with the Americans for killing 290 innocent Iranians. David Waite, Terry Waite's brother who acted as official spokesman for the Waite family, wrote to Thatcher saying how upset the family was by her comments and expressing the hope that she would find some way to put things right. Waite never received a reply, but a month later, when Lyttle was preparing to return to Teheran, Geoffrey Howe, the foreign secretary, arranged for Thatcher to sign a letter expressing her wish for Britain to have better relations with Iran. Following the parliamentary visit, the next step to improved relations was the decision by the Foreign Office to send a diplomat, David Reddaway, on a three-week fact-finding mission. His visit to Teheran was portrayed as an attempt by both sides to bury their differences and establish some semblance of normality in their relations.

As a result of Reddaway's visit and Lyttle's hard work, Geoffrey Howe finally met with Ali Akbar Velayati, the Iranian foreign minister, at the United Nations in September. At a businesslike meeting, they agreed to appoint teams of officials to work out the details for restoring diplomatic relations in the new year. Sir David Miers was appointed to head the British delegation. For all the criticism that had been levelled at Chirac for restoring relations with Iran to get the French hostages released, the British government was pursuing a similar line; the only difference being that all the French hostages were free and all the British hostages were still captive.

'I didn't really think that offering to open relations with Iran was the same as "doing a deal"', explained Sir David. 'It is something the British government would do anyway, so why not do it and see what happens? It is always better to keep a line open to a country like Iran than to close it off.'

It is a measure of the pressure the government felt itself to be under that Geoffrey Howe visited the campaign bus the Friends of John McCarthy had brought to the Conservative Party conference at Blackpool in October. Mrs Thatcher refused point-blank to meet Morrell and Pearson; Howe, on the other hand, agonised with his senior advisers over whether he should show his face. Eventually he decided that, as it was ultimately his responsibility to get the hostages released, he should. Government sensitivity on the issue was clearly mounting.

During the autumn, British and Iranian officials had a series of meetings in Geneva and Vienna to discuss the restoration of diplomatic relations. Sir David and his team raised the question of the British hostages every time they met. 'It was one of several issues we raised, and we left them in no doubt that we expected their co-operation in getting our hostages released,' said Sir David. The Iranians indicated they were prepared to help, and also provided the British delegation with the first concrete information that Waite, McCarthy and Keenan were still alive. 'The Iranians told us that if any of these three had died in captivity, they would know about it,' said a British official. 'They had not heard anything, so they assumed they were all alive. It was certainly the most encouraging news we had received about the British hostages in two years, and it was a start.' But while the Iranians said they might be able to get McCarthy and Keenan released, Waite would be a different matter. Waite, the Iranians explained, was considered to be an American hostage because of his links with Oliver North. He would only be freed when the Americans were. But to encourage the British and help persuade the Americans to pursue a similar policy, on October 3 the kidnappers released Mitheleshwar Singh, the Indian-American who was one of the four teachers kidnapped from Beirut University College in January 1987.

The Iranians' main concern during the normalisation negotiations was to get the British to make a public apology for cutting diplomatic ties with Teheran. Such gestures were considered crucial to Iranian leaders such as Rafsanjani, who had to justify all his moves in Teheran's highly emotional political climate. A public apology from Britain would greatly assist

Rafsanjani when he came to explain his decision to resume relations. The text of the 'apology' became a major stumbling block; Britain made it clear it felt it had nothing to apologise for, while the Iranians insisted they must have some public concession from the British to justify the move. Eventually a formula was agreed, and on November 11 the British and Iranian governments signed an agreement for the restoration of diplomatic relations. As a direct result of this, McCarthy and Keenan were taken to a new apartment in Beirut a couple of months later in anticipation of their release.

By early 1989 everything was going according to plan; the Iranian delegation had arrived in London and three British diplomats had arrived in Teheran to reopen the British embassy. The restoration of relations went ahead despite the destruction of Pan Am flight 103 as it flew over the Scottish village of Lockerbie in late December 1988, killing 276 people, including 259 passengers and crew. In the immediate aftermath of the crash, it was impossible to tell who or what was responsible, although the better-informed conspiracy theorists were quick to suggest that the attack had been carried out by Iran as a reprisal for the destruction of the Iranian airbus by the USS *Vincennes* the previous summer. It later transpired that the bombing was the work of Colonel Gaddafi in retaliation for the 1986 raid on Tripoli. But in the absence of hard facts, the British government decided to press ahead with restoring relations with Iran. The immediate priority was to get the hostages freed. If information was forthcoming at a later date of Iranian involvement in the Lockerbie attack, Britain could then take the appropriate action.

In February 1989, however, another disaster struck in the form of the publication of Salman Rushdie's *The Satanic Verses*, in which the Anglo-Indian novelist managed to profane most of the holiest tenets of Islam. Radical Islamic fundamentalists drew the offending material to the attention of Ayatollah Khomeini who, as anticipated, issued a *fatwa*, or edict, authorising Muslims to kill Rushdie. Try as it might, this was not something the British government could ignore. While few government officials had any great respect for either Rushdie or his tortuous prose, they were obliged, as a matter of principle, to resist any deliberate attempt by a foreign country to murder a British citizen. Britain had no alternative but to break diplomatic relations. Within just a few weeks, the team of British diplomats who had arrived in Teheran with such high hopes of opening a new chapter in Britain's relations with Iran were on their way home.

The Rushdie affair created the biggest crisis in Britain's relations with the Middle East for several years. Warnings were issued by the Foreign Office for Britons living, working or travelling in the Middle East to take extra care. The British embassy in Beirut was once again forced to close its visa and consulate section in West Beirut. More to the point, Rushdie's literary whim ended the prospects of Brian Keenan and John McCarthy being freed. Lambeth Palace put the word around that the Rushdie affair had affected Waite's chances of release. But had any of the British hostages been freed, Waite would not have been among them. Waite was still being held in solitary confinement and, as far as the kidnappers were concerned, he would be one of the last to leave. The Rushdie affair, however, meant that Keenan and McCarthy were placed back in cold storage.

As if the British government did not have trouble enough with publication of *The Satanic Verses*, the addition of yet another Briton to the ranks of the hostages made its task immeasurably more difficult. It remains unclear whether Jackie Mann was kidnapped as a direct result of *The Satanic Verses*, as his abductors never made any demands; but the climate of hostility towards Britain and the British the book created in Beirut no doubt played some part in the calculations of the kidnappers to seize a seventy-four-year-old retired RAF Spitfire pilot. Certainly the quality of life for the last English couple in West Beirut was a far cry from the halcyon days of the 1960s when they lived the textbook expatriate lifestyle: sunshine, picnics and large gin and tonics at embassy parties. The couple had met at a wartime dance at the Dorchester Hotel in London. He was the dashing Battle of Britain hero who had been shot down six times. On one occasion he had been so afraid of being captured by the Germans that he flew his blazing Spitfire back across the Channel. After one particularly lucky escape, Mann had undergone the agony of having his face and legs surgically reconstructed. Sunnie was the upper-class ambulance driver doing her bit in the blitz. While the band played the Vera Lynn hit, 'Yours till the Stars Lose Their Glory', they fell, if not desperately in love, into deep admiration for each other.

After the war Jackie became a commercial airline pilot and, to escape the drabness of ration-book Britain, jumped at the chance to join Lebanon's national carrier, Middle East Airlines. For the next thirty years the Manns came to terms with the fact that theirs was not exactly a marriage made in heaven. He liked going to parties; she was devoted to the riding school she ran for wealthy Lebanese. They rarely saw eye-to-eye, and there were frequent fights and arguments; for a while they even maintained separate apartments. Then the civil war erupted. Jackie and Sunnie Mann remained in West Beirut after the rest of the British community had departed basically because they had nowhere else to go. By 1989 the couple had been reduced to a state of genteel poverty. After retiring as a pilot, Mann had opened the Pickwick bar, but that source of income dried up when the pub was blown up by Islamic terrorists who objected to the sale of liquor. Sunnie's riding school had also fallen on hard times because, being close to the Green Line, it attracted fewer and fewer customers.

In the spring of 1989, the civil war entered a dramatic new phase with the emergence of General Michel Aoun as the self-proclaimed saviour of Lebanon. As a first step towards re-establishing government authority, Aoun attempted to close down the illegal ports used by the militias to import and export arms. Aoun's action not surprisingly met with stiff resistance from the militias which by now had become a law unto themselves, with the result that Beirut was plunged into another round of fighting. Due to the ferocity of the bombardment General Aoun was directing towards the western sector of the city – the worst bombardment Beirut had suffered in fourteen years of civil war – the electricity supply was, at best, intermittent. It became almost impossible to buy fresh fruit and vegetables, even fresh bread. Sunnie spent her days, shelling permitting, checking on the horses or taking her pet poodle for a walk. Jackie would potter about the house, waiting for Sunnie to bring him *L'Orient du Jour*, the only foreign newspaper on sale in Beirut. Although Jackie couldn't read French, he'd worked out a way to do the word puzzle, which occupied him for about half an hour a day. Apart from that he would sit around drinking bottles of local beer until the time came to cook dinner.

On the day of his abduction Jackie set off for the bank in his battered old Simca to draw money from the couple's dwindling savings account. From there he intended to drop by one of the bars still operating for a few drinks with some old Lebanese friends. Before he left the apartment, Sunnie nagged him to take care.

'Be careful,' she warned. 'I don't want you getting kidnapped. Just watch what you're doing and where you go.'

'Who'd want to kidnap me?' Jackie snapped. 'I'll be back

around three, as usual.' So saying, he set off.[1] It would be the last time the couple saw each other for over two years.

The abduction followed the familiar pattern. As Mann drove away from the bank on Hamra Street, a large white American car drove in front of him and forced him to a halt. Four or five men jumped out of the car, some carrying handguns, and waved them at Mann. Mann opened the car door to find out what was going on, and was immediately seized by two of the men. They dragged him across the road, forced him into the boot of their car and drove off.

Even by hostage standards, Mann's captivity was particularly exacting. On the day he was seized, he was driven from Beirut to Sidon. Mann had been kidnapped by a maverick group of Palestinians who called themselves the Union of Palestine Refugees. He was taken to one of the Palestinian refugee camps on the outskirts of Sidon. The group holding him appeared to be particularly paranoid. Although they had entered the hostage game of their own choice, they seemed to be in awe of all the other hostage groups. They were afraid of Hizbollah, the main Shia militia; they were afraid of the PLO, the main Palestinian militia; and of course they were scared of the Israelis. They took every precaution to ensure that Mann was not discovered, so that no allowances were made for his age.

In all he was held at five different locations, most of them in southern Lebanon and the Chouf mountains. For the first three and a half months he was kept in isolation in a room the size of a cupboard. Throughout his captivity he never once saw daylight, he saw no other hostages, and had no access to television, radio or books. Occasionally he was allowed to walk around the guards' room, and even to venture down a

[1] Jackie and Sunnie Mann, *Yours Till the End*, Heinemann, 1992.

corridor to stretch his legs. A guard would accompany him with a loaded gun to make sure the frail septuagenarian did not try to escape. But for most of the time Mann was forced to lie on an old mattress chained to a wall. He was fed on a meagre diet of bread and Arabic cheese, which he detested.

Beatings were administered regularly. Whenever Mann did something which displeased the guards, they would punch and kick him. Once, when Mann grabbed the legs of a guard as he was about to kick him, the guard nearly poured a kettle of boiling water over Mann's face, but was persuaded against it by another guard.

Mann also became convinced that the leader of the Palestinian group was intent on raping him, and made several unsuccessful assaults. In one incident, Mann became suspicious that the guards were trying to drug him. He pretended to be asleep, giving the impression that the drugs had worked. Four or five guards came into the room. The chain around his leg was unlocked, and he was eased away from the wall. Mann opened his eyes very slightly, so that he could just see. Standing at the bottom of his mattress was one of the guards, his jacket removed. He was unbuttoning his trousers and unbuckling his belt, and Mann was convinced the guard intended to rape him while he was asleep. Mann leapt up, and a struggle ensued in which Mann lost two teeth. Eventually the guards left the room and did not bother Mann again. Given the circumstances in which Mann was held, it is entirely feasible that the alleged rape attempt was merely a figment of Mann's imagination; on other occasions he believed he heard American and British intelligence officers in the next room discussing their plans to rescue him. True or not, it all contributed to the considerable distress Mann suffered in captivity.

The abduction of Jackie Mann effectively brought the British government back to square one. After nearly a year of intensive diplomatic efforts, Britain was no closer to getting any of its hostages freed. A report commissioned by the Foreign Office in the spring of 1989 to assess exactly how much new information the government had about the fate of the hostages made depressing reading. Britain was no wiser than it had been the previous year; it did not even know for sure whether Keenan, McCarthy, Waite and now Mann were alive. Kauffmann, one of the last three Frenchmen to be released, had hinted that he thought British hostages were being held by Islamic Jihad, but he had not seen them. The Iranians, in their elliptical way, had hinted they were alive, but had produced no firm evidence.

The lack of any concrete information gave rise to a string of speculative stories, most without the slightest foundation of truth, on the fate of the hostages. Ever since Waite's abduction in January 1987, there had been wild stories about his fate: that he had been shot while fleeing; that he had died of a heart attack; that he had been taken to Teheran for interrogation and that he would be freed for a ransom of $5 million. Because there was no way of checking out these stories, most serious journalists were circumspect about how they used them. But by 1989 journalists who were more concerned with making a name for themselves than with the feelings of the hostages' families produced a plethora of stories which were pure fiction. Brent Sadler, for example, came up with a story, which was run on the ten o'clock news, that Waite had been shipped by sea to Teheran in a crate; ITN provided a graphic to illustrate Waite's clandestine passage. Another example of irresponsible sensationalism regarding Waite was a story submitted to the *Observer* by Shyam Bhatia, its Middle East correspondent. For several months the rumour had been circulating that Terry Waite had been killed, either by accident or design, and had been buried at a village in the Bekaa Valley called Nabi Sheet, the home of the Musawi clan. Because it was impossible to verify such a story, most journalists left it alone, mainly so as not to cause unnecessary distress to the Waite family. Bhatia, however, whose Anglo-Indian features enabled him to move freely around Lebanon without being identified as a foreigner, travelled to Nabi Sheet and triumphantly informed his office that he had found the grave of Terry Waite. The initial reaction among the more experienced journalists at the *Observer* was that the story contained too much supposition and not enough fact. But Bhatia demanded to talk to the editor, Donald Trelford, whom he attempted to persuade to print the story. Assured the story would run, Bhatia returned to the bar of the Cavalier Hotel where he had been drinking with his colleagues and bought champagne to celebrate his big scoop.

As the British authorities pondered what to do next, the pressure on them to produce results increased with the news in the spring of 1989 that Sheila McCarthy, John's mother, had terminal cancer and had only a few months to live. The family had maintained a dignified silence since the abduction of their son. Pat McCarthy, who had retired after a successful career in business, had implicit trust in the ability of the government to act on his son's behalf. He had kept his distance when the Friends of John McCarthy was formed because its stance seemed to differ from that propounded by the government. But when it was discovered that Mrs McCarthy was seriously ill, the family decided to make a direct appeal to the kidnappers to release their son so that he could see his mother before she died. Mrs McCarthy recorded a message to be shown on Lebanese television on the third anniversary of her son's abduction in April 1989 in which she made a blunt appeal to the kidnappers: 'Please let him go.' The family received no response, and two months later, when it was clear Mrs McCarthy had only a few days to live, Pat McCarthy made a second video. Again the appeal was met with stony silence. On July 8,

Sheila McCarthy died not knowing whether her beloved son was alive.

Just when the British and American governments were beginning to despair of ever making progress on the hostages, the possibility was raised of a new era of good relations between the West and Iran when Ayatollah Khomeini finally succumbed to the ill health which had dogged his final years. It had been widely anticipated that, following the old man's death, Iran would be thrown into a bitter power struggle between the Rafsanjani and Montazeri factions. In fact, the emergence of Rafsanjani as Khomeini's political heir had been set in train by Khomeini himself. Rafsanjani was appointed as commander of the armed forces and given other positions of genuine political influence by Khomeini, so that when the Ayatollah died Rafsanjani was able to take the reins of government without too much opposition. Montazeri was allowed an important spiritual role in guiding the Iranian Revolution, but Rafsanjani made it increasingly clear that all key political decisions would be taken by him. Once the traditional period of mourning was over, Rafsanjani set to work once more to effect a reconciliation with the West, with the freeing of the hostages from Lebanon a priority.

In a sense Rafsanjani's rise to power was a vindication of the policy that had been initiated by Bud McFarlane in 1985. McFarlane had been convinced that there were 'moderate' elements in the Iranian leadership who would take a more pragmatic view of Iran's relationship with the US. McFarlane's original concept had become obscured after Oliver North used it as a justification for his arms sales to Iran. But the emergence of Rafsanjani, the man McFarlane had identified as someone the US could do business with, showed that it was not McFarlane's policy that had been wrong, but the manner in which it had been hijacked by Oliver North.

Before Rafsanjani could renew his efforts to improve

relations with the West, he had to overcome yet another crisis in relations between the West and the Middle East when the Israelis stirred up a hornets' nest of Shia outrage in southern Lebanon by abducting Sheikh Abdul Karim Obeid from his home at Jibchit in late July. The Israelis seized Sheikh Obeid as part of their efforts to locate seven Israeli servicemen missing in Lebanon. Obeid, a prominent Lebanese Shia cleric known to have close links with Hizbollah, was suspected of being involved in the abduction of two Israeli soldiers on patrol in southern Lebanon in 1986. He was also said to be behind the kidnapping of Lieutenant-Colonel William Higgins, an American marine attached to the UN force in southern Lebanon, in January 1987. The Israelis hoped that by taking Obeid they would be able both to discover Hizbollah's strategy in Lebanon and to put pressure on the kidnap groups to free the Israeli prisoners. But the Israelis, as so often in their relations with Lebanon's Shia Muslims, gravely miscalculated the impact of their action.

Within days the Israelis had provoked a major international crisis which threatened the lives of all the hostages. The first move in the crisis was the threat by a group calling itself the Organisation of the Oppressed of the Earth to 'execute' Lieutenant-Colonel Higgins if Obeid was not released immediately by the Israelis. A deadline of 12.00 GMT on July 31 was set by the kidnappers. Twenty minutes after it expired, Yitzhak Rabin, the Israeli defence minister, announced on Israeli radio that Israel was willing to free all Shia prisoners in exchange for the release of the Israeli servicemen and all Western hostages. Even if Rabin's offer had been serious, it came too late. An hour later the kidnappers issued a statement saying that Higgins had been executed. A video released at the same time showed Higgins dangling from a makeshift scaffold with a rope around his neck. This time the body was clearly identified.

At the same time another group, the Revolutionary Justice

Organisation, threatened to murder Jo Cicippio if Obeid were not released immediately. The Americans responded by ordering US navy warships to sail for the Lebanese coast. The kidnapping of Obeid highlighted the strains in the relationship between Israel and the US, for the first time in many years. Israel's right-wing dominated government was totally unrepentant about its abduction of Obeid, and resisted strong American pressure to release him. The Israelis insisted that Obeid would only be freed in exchange for the return of the missing Israeli servicemen. 'Do you think the Israeli forces grabbed the Sheikh only to free the Western hostages and leave the Israelis behind?' asked a senior Israeli official. For the next few days the West was kept on tenterhooks as the deadline for Cicippio's 'execution' approached. His wife Elham made a dramatic appeal on Lebanese television for the kidnappers to save her husband's life; the kidnappers responded by saying they would extend the deadline by another forty-eight hours.

The drama continued until the Revolutionary Justice Organisation, having extended the deadline by a further forty-five minutes, handed a note to a news agency in Beirut saying the execution had been 'frozen' indefinitely. It was, perhaps, no coincidence that at the very moment the kidnappers aborted the planned murder of Cicippio, Hashemi Rafsanjani was being sworn in as the new president of Iran, having won an outright victory in the presidential election. Rafsanjani was among the first to condemn the hanging of William Higgins, and while the failure of the Americans to put pressure on Israel to secure Obeid's release made Rafsanjani's task more difficult, the process by which the remaining American and British hostages finally came to be released was set in train on August 3, 1989 when Rafsanjani became the official leader of Iran.

The day after his election Rafsanjani told a Friday prayer

meeting in Teheran: 'I address the White House: there is a solution for Lebanon, a solution for freeing the hostages. Take a sensible attitude and we will help to solve the problems there so the people of the region may live in peace and friendship.' The same day Sheikh Fadlallah seemed to echo Rafsanjani's sentiments when he addressed a prayer service in south Lebanon. 'Let's be loftier. Let's be more humanitarian,' he told his Islamic fundamentalist audience. Finally the *Teheran Times*, Iran's English-language newspaper which was to become Rafsanjani's official mouthpiece, carried an article to the effect that the Iranian government would definitely intercede to free hostages if the American government made a guarantee that Iranian assets frozen at the time of the Iranian Revolution would be released. A small chink of light had appeared at the end of the diplomatic tunnel through which the hostages would one day walk to freedom.

21

HOMEWARD BOUND

In early 1990 the Foreign Office received an unexpected phone call from Mustafa Saad, the Lebanese Sunni Muslim leader from Sidon who had helped British officials in their abortive negotiations to free Alec Collett. Saad had been handed a letter, apparently written by John McCarthy. The letter was hand-written and addressed to McCarthy's parents. Saad inquired whether the Foreign Office was interested in seeing the letter. Yes, the Foreign Office was very interested in seeing it; so interested that the British government would be only too pleased to pay for Saad to fly to London directly and present the letter in person.

Saad duly delivered the letter to Whitehall, and on close examination it was found to be genuine. It bore no date, and Saad had no idea where it had come from. It had been passed by hand through a chain of intermediaries in Lebanon which made it almost impossible to ascertain its origins.

FROM: JOHN McCARTHY

TO: THE BRITISH GOVERNMENT

My name is John McCarthy. I am O.K. but I am living in very difficult and bad conditions. You must understand the following. My release with the others is impossible if the prisoners in Kuwait and in some European countries are not released. You must keep this letter secret otherwise my life will be in danger.

JOHN McCARTHY

It was clear that McCarthy was unaware of his mother's death; that he had not seen the videos she and his father had made the previous summer. But Pat McCarthy was able to overcome the pathos of reading his son's warm greetings to his dead mother. After four years of not knowing whether John was even alive, Pat McCarthy finally had irrefutable proof that he was.

The Foreign Office in its inimitable way cautioned against excessive enthusiasm; there was no way of telling when the letter had been written. As delicately as possible, the officials hinted that the possibility remained that McCarthy might have died since writing it. They need not have bothered. Pat McCarthy was not the type to let his emotions run away with him. But he preferred to look on the positive side. Someone had gone to the trouble of delivering a letter written by his son, and that in itself was cause for encouragement.

McCarthy's letter, which was concealed from the public at the time, was just one of many signs in the spring of 1990 that an end to the hostage crisis was in sight. Since the crisis over Sheikh Obeid's abduction the previous year had subsided, those involved in trying to secure the hostages' release had several grounds for cautious optimism. After assuming the office of president, Rafsanjani moved quickly to isolate his opponents. In particular Ali Akbar Mohtashemi, the leader of the hard core of Iranian radicals who supported the hostage-taking policy, was sacked as interior minister, although he was allowed to keep his seat in the Majlis. Without a ministry at his disposal, Mohtashemi was in no position to undermine Rafsanjani's policy. The execution of Mehdi Hashemi for running a rogue foreign policy had demonstrated what happened to those who did not accept official policy in Iran. Influential Iranian leaders, such as Ahmad Khomeini, the late Ayatollah's son, continued to rail against Iran having any contact with Washington, but they were very much in the minority as Rafsanjani asserted his more pragmatic policy of rapprochement with the West.

The momentum continued through the spring of 1990 as, first, the *Teheran Times* carried an editorial calling for the unconditional release of all hostages in Lebanon. 'Regardless of the West's propaganda ploys, Muslim forces, out of Islamic and humanitarian considerations, should work to get the hostages free with no preconditions. Maybe 1990 will be the year for the release of all the hostages.' Rafsanjani was clearly beginning to feel sufficient confidence in his position to express his opinions openly. A few weeks later he publicly stated his desire to resolve the hostage issue. 'My feeling is that the issue of the hostages is moving towards a solution. I and my friends would like the issue to be settled, since the US and others are exploiting the matter as a means of branding the Lebanese as terrorists.'

It was all very well Rafsanjani talking about getting the hostages released, but there still remained the question of how the Iranians were going to persuade the kidnap groups to set their captives free. There were now three main kidnap groups active in Lebanon: Islamic Jihad, the original group led by Mugniyeh, which held Anderson, Sutherland, Reed, McCarthy, Keenan and Waite; Islamic Jihad for the

Liberation of Palestine, which was holding the three BUC teachers Alann Steen, Jesse Turner and Robert Polhill; and the Revolutionary Justice Organisation, which was holding Americans Jo Cicippio and Edward Tracy. Although these groups had their separate identities, in that they issued their own statements and had their own sets of guards for the hostages, all of them came under the aegis of Hizbollah and ultimately took their orders from the Hizbollah leadership.

Hizbollah depended almost entirely on financial support from Iran, which put Rafsanjani in a powerful bargaining position. Until Rafsanjani came to power, Hizbollah had been able to take advantage of the endless factional in-fighting in Teheran to do much as it pleased in Lebanon. Once Rafsanjani had consolidated his power base, however, the Iranians were able to exert a far greater degree of control over the kidnap groups, so that by 1990 the Iranians effectively controlled the fate of the remaining hostages. Rafsanjani's ability to influence the hostage issue was greatly assisted by the fact that Imad Mugniyeh had been forced to seek sanctuary in Teheran. Western intelligence services had directed so much effort towards killing or capturing this notoriously successful master terrorist that it was virtually impossible for him to set foot in his home country. He therefore took up residence at a modest hotel on the outskirts of Teheran at the Iranian government's expense. If Rafsanjani wanted to talk to the leader of the Lebanese kidnap groups, he did not have far to travel.

The only outstanding demand of the kidnappers worthy, in Teheran's eyes, of consideration, was the issue of the Dawa prisoners in Kuwait. Two of the original 17 had now been released after serving their sentences, but among those in jail were Mugniyeh's brother-in-law, Mustapha Badreddin, and Hussein Youssef Musawi, the cousin of Hussein Musawi, one of Hizbollah's leading officials in the Bekaa Valley. In early

April 1990 the Iranian government began a fresh diplomatic initiative to get the prisoners released. Rather than using threats, as they had done in the past, this time the Iranian approach was altogether more supplicatory. The prisoners were being held because of 'mistakes' that had been made in the past, the Iranians argued. Now that the international climate had changed, it was time to bury the past and look to the future. The Kuwaitis could help build a new future in the relations between the two countries by releasing the prisoners. At the same time as the Iranians were talking privately to the Kuwaitis, Hizbollah was taking delivery of supplies of tanks, artillery, armoured personnel carriers and multi-barrelled rocket launchers. The equipment arrived following a visit to Beirut by Mahmoud Hashemi, Rafsanjani's brother, in early April. The new weapons were duly paraded before the faithful at Friday prayers in Beirut. The arms would be used by Hizbollah to continue its guerrilla campaign against Israel. In return Hizbollah would 'assist' Iran in helping to free the Western hostages.

The breakthrough came at the end of April when a lone car pulled up about forty yards from Beirut's Summerland Hotel. A black Mercedes driven by Syrian intelligence officers pulled alongside it in a cloud of dust, and seconds later pulled away at high speed with an extra passenger in the back seat. Robert Polhill, one of the three teachers held by the Islamic Jihad for the Liberation of Palestine, had been set free. The transfer of the thin and unsteady figure of Polhill from one car to the next took no more than three seconds, the shortest walk to freedom of any Beirut hostage. The operation was so well executed that it had clearly been planned in advance by the Syrians and the kidnappers, raising the question of how much the Syrians really knew about the kidnap groups. Polhill was immediately driven to Damascus where he gave a press conference at the Syrian foreign ministry at which he gave fulsome praise to the

Syrian government for assisting in his release. Polhill said little about his release, mainly because he was suffering from what later turned out to be throat cancer.

The *Teheran Times* now called for the release of a second American hostage, and an Iranian diplomat reacted to the article by predicting that a second American hostage would be released within a few days. Exactly one week after Polhill's release, Frank Reed, the director of the Lebanese International School, was handed over to the Syrians in Beirut and driven to Damascus to be officially handed over to the American embassy. Since his abduction in September 1986, nothing had been heard of Reed until a group calling itself the Organisation of Islamic Dawn issued a statement that it was going to release him in twenty-four hours' time. In fact Reed had been held throughout his captivity by Islamic Jihad.

The release of Polhill and Reed represented a dramatic breakthrough in the hostage crisis for several reasons. It was the first time in more than three years that the main Lebanese kidnap groups had freed American hostages. The fact that Polhill and Reed were held by different groups but were released as part of the same package revealed the level of co-operation between the kidnappers. Teheran's involvement indicated without doubt that Iran ultimately controlled the fate of the hostages. And unlike the deals that had been worked out between Oliver North and the Iranians, the kidnappers were fully aware of all the factors involved in future hostage releases. In the build-up to the release of Polhill and Reed, there had been a constant procession of senior Iranian officials travelling to Lebanon and Damascus, while leading Lebanese Shias, such as Sheikh Fadlallah, made the return trip to Teheran.

Both Teheran and Washington categorically refuted the suggestion that any deal had been done; nevertheless, the releases took place within the context of the most constructive dialogue that had taken place between the two countries since the Iranian Revolution. Following the release of Polhill and Reed, George Bush, the American President, referred to the 'process' by which the hostages had been released, and indicated that Washington had not been entirely passive. The most important American contribution was to resume the discussions in the Netherlands to settle the mutual financial claims that had been outstanding since the Iranian Revolution. The Iran–US claims tribunal set up under President Carter was the only official link between Iran and the US. In ten years the tribunal had made little progress. As Iran had most to gain from the tribunal, Rafsanjani had indicated that American hostages could be released if Iran's frozen assets were released. Thus on the day Frank Reed arrived at the US airforce base at Wiesbaden for a debriefing and medical check-up, Abraham Sofaer, the State Department's top legal adviser, met with Ali Heyrani Noobari, Iran's agent to the claims tribunal, at a secret location at The Hague.

The role the Syrians played revealed that Damascus also was not entirely without influence in the question of the hostages. For the past three years – since Terry Waite's abduction – the Syrians had been gradually extending their influence throughout the Muslim areas of Lebanon, and by the spring of 1990 they had a military presence in all the main areas used by the kidnap gangs to hold the hostages – the Bekaa Valley, the southern suburbs of Beirut and south Lebanon. Syrian intelligence knew exactly who was running the groups and where to find them, so that the Syrians, if they so chose, could have made life extremely difficult for the kidnap groups. But the Syrians treasured their diplomatic alliance with Iran more highly than they did the freedom of the hostages, though they were not averse to giving the impression that they had used their 'good offices' to assist in the releases. With the Soviet Union no longer either willing or able to sustain its support for Syria's radical Arab position, President Assad was obliged to acknowledge the political realities of the post-Cold War Middle East. After years of undermining every attempt by Washington to extend its influence in the region, Assad now had to face the fact that, for the foreseeable future, he would need to be on talking terms with the US. The Syrians' insistence that all hostages should be paraded before a carefully stage-managed press conference in Damascus, where the bemused captive would, on cue, pay tribute to the assistance provided by President Assad, was a priceless exercise in public relations for a man regarded throughout most of the civilised world as the architect of modern international terrorism.

From the British point of view, however, the most dramatic aspect of the release of the two Americans was the confirmation by Frank Reed that Keenan and McCarthy were alive. Apart from McCarthy's letter at the start of the year, this was the first independent confirmation their families had received that the two were still alive more than four years after their abduction. Reed, who had been held with Anderson and Sutherland for most of his captivity, had seen both on the Saturday before his release, although he had no word on Terry Waite or Jackie Mann. Reed telephoned Pat McCarthy and Brian Keenan's two sisters, who had mounted a campaign in Ireland for their brother's release. Reed told McCarthy's father that John had grown a beard, that he had been chained and blindfolded on occasions, but was in good physical health.

Keenan and McCarthy were being allowed six cigarettes each day, and Keenan gave McCarthy most of his ration because he was not a heavy smoker. They had got into the habit of reading a book a day. With their blindfolds pushed up, and still chained to the wall, they read whatever the guards brought them. Some of the books were readable, such as John Steinbeck's *Cannery Row*, while others were just plain pulp. At one point they had been brought an American encyclopaedia, but only the section K-Z. For an hour each evening they were allowed to watch television after the news; a favourite programme of all the hostages was the Benny Hill Show. For a spell in the summer of 1988, the hostages had been allowed a radio, but this had been taken away after the USS *Vincennes* shot down the Iranian airbus. One other luxury they were allowed was the freedom to exercise for an hour each afternoon, free of their chains. McCarthy and Keenan had become fitness fanatics, encouraging each other to do ever greater numbers of push-ups and sit-ups, and running around the room until they were exhausted. According to Reed, both Keenan and McCarthy were in excellent physical condition, with bulging biceps and 'muscles everywhere'. They also kept each other going with a constant stream of good-natured banter. For example, they had resolved that when their ordeal was over, rather than write a book, they would compose an operetta, with the working title *Gilbert and Sullivan meet the Ayatollah*. The production would end with the two of them dancing down a staircase in black tie and tails, shaking their top hats and singing: 'Goodbye, Hizbollah'.

For the last few months of his captivity, Reed was held in an apartment with Keenan and McCarthy close to Sheikh Fadlallah's home. Reed had been taken away from Anderson and Sutherland because he had fallen out with them. Reed's whole attitude had changed after he attempted to escape. The guards put him in a cell and beat him for four days continuously. When they had finished with him, they put him in a cell with Anderson and Sutherland. Whether because he was embarrassed that his escape attempt had failed, or bitter about the way the guards had treated him, Reed developed a deep dislike of Anderson and Sutherland, whom he seemed to believe were somehow responsible for this treatment. By the time they got to know Reed, Anderson and Sutherland had become as inseparable as Keenan and McCarthy. During their five years together, Sutherland had taught Anderson French. Anderson had also been given a primitive exercise bicycle, which he made good use of. After his severe beating, Reed did not trust anyone, and it is probable that at some point during his captivity he became mentally unstable. Try as Anderson and Sutherland might to make Reed accept them, he just lay on his mattress and refused to have anything to do with either them or the guards. When, after his release, Reed met Peggy Say, Anderson's sister, Reed caused her immense distress by saying bluntly what he thought of Anderson and Sutherland. Reed particularly disliked Sutherland, and refused to speak with him during the last four months they were held together.

'How can you not speak to somebody held with you under those circumstances?' Peggy Say asked Reed.

'Because I hated him,' Reed replied.[1] After the initial euphoria of Reed's release, his mental instability increased markedly until he was admitted to a psychiatric hospital for treatment.

The news that Keenan and McCarthy were alive put added pressure on the Irish and British governments to get them freed. From the outset the Irish government had assumed responsibility for securing Keenan's release, a fact much appreciated by Keenan, the arch-Republican, who constantly told his fellow hostages he did not want to be released by the 'fucking Brits'. Although tied by the same European Community constraint as the British government with regard to the Middle East, the Irish government, which maintained its

---

[1]Say, *op. cit.*

own considerable diplomatic presence in the region, was able to pursue its own policy in the matter. The Irish, for example, were able to host a meeting between EC and Iranian officials in Dublin in the summer of 1990 aimed at improving trade ties between Brussels and Teheran. Irish diplomats could also point out that the policies of the Irish government towards the Middle East were significantly different to those of the British. The Irish maintained a permanent military presence in south Lebanon as part of the contingent established to protect Shia villages. Indeed, scores of young Irish soldiers had been killed in the process. Unlike the American and French troops which had sided with the Lebanese Christians against the Shia Muslims, the Irish were on the side of the Shias. The determination of the Irish government to free Keenan was made all the greater because of the constant pressure applied to Dublin by Keenan's sisters, Elaine Spence and Brenda Gillham.

As had happened two years previously with the French hostages, the release of two more Americans provoked a flurry of accusations that the British government was failing in its duty. Even after the Iran-Contra controversy, the Americans had managed to get two more hostages out without compromising their principles; what had the British achieved? The criticism might have been justified two years earlier, when the British government had attempted to pretend there were no British hostages in Lebanon, but by spring 1990 securing the hostages' release had become a major priority at the Foreign Office. A Gallup poll carried out in May 1990 for the *Daily Telegraph* showed that 75 per cent of the British public was in favour of Britain talking with Syria and Iran to resolve the hostage issue.

The departure of Geoffrey Howe from the Foreign Office, and the arrival of Douglas Hurd in the autumn of 1989 (John Major spent a month as foreign secretary before being moved on to the Exchequer), marked a change of emphasis in Britain's approach to the issue. Until he fell out with Thatcher over Europe and her famous Bruges speech, Howe had very much followed his leader's line on foreign policy issues, especially with regard to the Middle East, which was not one of his major areas of interest. When, for example, Thatcher asked Howe to cancel a meeting with a joint Jordanian–Palestinian delegation in October 1985 because of the PLO's continued involvement in terrorism, Howe was happy to comply. Thus when Thatcher insisted on cutting diplomatic relations with Syria and Iran, and categorically refused to embark on any course of action in pursuit of the hostages, no matter how innocent, that might result in the British government having a dialogue with the kidnappers, Howe complied without demur. When Douglas Hurd, a former diplomat, arrived at the Foreign Office, however, he initiated a more humanitarian approach, irrespective of what Mrs Thatcher might think. Hurd, who was more to the centre of the Conservative Party, understood the need to free the British hostages on humanitarian grounds alone. He also appreciated that, in an area of such immense complexities as the Middle East, it was unrealistic to pursue any issue in simple terms of black and white. There were many ways of approaching the hostage problem without negotiating with the kidnap groups, and improving relations with Iran was as good a way as any to start.

Since Rafsanjani's personal intervention to defuse the crisis following the abduction of Sheikh Obeid, Iran had put out several feelers to the British government about the possibility of restoring diplomatic relations if Britain showed a willingness to 'respect Islamic values and principles'. Basically the Iranians, who remained convinced that the West was intent on destroying their Islamic revolution, sought reassurance. At first the Foreign Office, still smarting from the ignominious conclusion of its previous attempt to re-open relations, was distinctly frosty. Then, in November 1989, following a meeting with Waite's brother David and Pat McCarthy, Hurd indicated a change of emphasis in Britain's policy towards Iran. When relations had been broken off in March, Howe had insisted that Iran must revoke the *fatwa* against Salman Rushdie before Britain would even consider restoring relations. Hurd restated the main principles as set out by Howe, namely that it would be wrong to make substantial concessions to Hizbollah. But while he affirmed Howe's view that Iran held the key to the hostages' future, he avoided blaming the Iranian government, speaking instead of 'some Iranians'. The *fatwa* against Rushdie nevertheless remained a major obstacle. Though Khomeini had died, the decree had been upheld by Ayatollah Ali Khamenei, who had succeeded Khomeini as Iran's spiritual guide. And the *fatwa* remained in force in spite of a scrupulous defence Rushdie made of his book in early 1990. The other main concern of British officials was the case of Roger Cooper, a British freelance journalist who had been incarcerated in Evin prison in 1986 on trumped-up spying charges.

The release of Polhill and Reed and the news that McCarthy was alive added new impetus to the British government's attempts to improve relations with Iran. Britain still had no diplomatic links with Iran, Syria or Libya, which suggested that the British hostages would remain low on the kidnappers' list of priorities for releases. But with pressure mounting for action, Hurd indicated the British government was prepared to take a more positive approach to its relations with Iran. 'I do not rule out direct talks – but one needs to be clear that they are likely to be successful,' he said after meeting James Baker, the American Secretary of State, in Brussels after the release of the two Americans. 'The risk of direct talks is that you entrench attitudes and stiffen them and delay progress.' The release of the Americans even prompted Mrs Thatcher to thank Syria and Iran for their assistance when the subject was raised during prime minister's question time. The pressure on the government, however, intensified even further when Runcie, who had fully supported Lyttle's efforts to improve contacts with Iran, weighed in with his own call for the government to adopt a new approach. 'I believe the time has come for the governments of the UK and Iran to talk directly to each other to see how progress can be made,' he said.

For the next few months there were encouraging signs that progress, of sorts, was being made. One of Britain's biggest defence contractors, Lucas Industries, was revealed to be negotiating a contract worth £270 million as part of a deal to improve trade relations between Iran and Britain. In early July 1990, Ali Akbar Velayati, the Iranian foreign minister, made the first official visit to Kuwait by an Iranian since the conclusion of the Iran–Iraq war. The Iranians made it clear that one of the subjects at the top of Velayati's agenda was the question of the fifteen remaining prisoners who had now served seven years in jail; long enough for the Iranians to argue that the Kuwaitis could release them without losing face. While Velayati was visiting Kuwait, rumours began to circulate that Brian Keenan, who had been held for four years, was on the point of release.

Just at that point, however, the Middle East was plunged into another international crisis, this time of its own making, when President Saddam Hussein of Iraq ordered his army to invade Kuwait on August 2, 1990. The great irony of Hussein's decision was that, throughout the eight-year war between Iran and Iraq, Kuwait had been terrorised by the Iranians for supporting Iraq. Hussein, however, who had ruined his country's economy in his attempts to become the undisputed leader of the Arab world, was jealous of the wealth the other oil-rich Arab states had accumulated during the war, and was determined to redress the balance. In launching his attack on

Kuwait, however, Hussein unwittingly helped resolve the one major impediment to the release of the hostages in Lebanon. For as the elite units of Iraq's Republican Guards made their way towards the centre of Kuwait, the guards at the central prison followed the rest of the Kuwaiti nation in fleeing for their lives. As they abandoned the prison, they were hotly pursued by the 2,000-odd inmates who did not relish the prospect of having Hussein as their jailer. And among the first to escape were the fifteen remaining Dawa prisoners; the men who had been the focus of one of the most devastating campaigns of terrorism ever conducted in the Middle East were free at last.

Saddam Hussein's troops made a bee-line for the prison to try to capture the Dawa prisoners. Had they succeeded, it is interesting to consider what Hussein would have done with them. Most of the fifteen were dissident Shia Iraqis, and as such could expect no mercy from one of the world's most tyrannical leaders. Hussein, on the other hand, was well aware of their importance with regard to the fate of the Lebanon hostages. In the early months of the Gulf crisis Hussein held hundreds of American and British expatriate workers hostage in Iraq to dissuade the allies from taking military action over Kuwait, and it is quite possible that he would have used the Dawa prisoners for the same ends. In the event, all the prisoners escaped, making their way across the Iraqi border to Iran where most settled down to a life in exile. One exception was Mustafa Badreddin, one of the ring-leaders and Mugniyeh's brother-in-law, who was sighted in south Lebanon in October. With the ban on Mugniyeh's conjugal rights now presumably lifted, the most important obstacle to the release of the remaining Western hostages had been removed.

When Tom Sutherland heard on his short-wave radio that the Dawa prisoners had escaped, he immediately awoke Anderson who was still asleep in the corner.

'Hey, Terry,' cried Sutherland. 'You'll never guess what's happened.' Both men became excited as they considered the implications of the news. If there were no longer any prisoners in Kuwait, there was no need for the guards to hold them. Sutherland asked a guard to come over to their cell.

'Where are my new shoes? I'm going home,' he called. When Sutherland explained what he was talking about, the guard laughed and shook his head.

'Oh no, Mr Tom,' the guard replied. 'But the US had nothing to do with this.'

22

ENDGAME

Despite the dramatic breakthrough achieved by Hussein's invasion of Kuwait, it was generally accepted that the issue of the Western hostages would be put on ice until the Gulf crisis had been resolved. With thousands of troops streaming to the Gulf to save the Arabian oil fields from Saddam Hussein, Iran had every reason to be deeply concerned about the likely implications of the military build-up. Iran, after all, had bad memories of the last Western military deployment in the Gulf, three years previously. There was considerable surprise, therefore, when Brian Keenan was set free at the end of August after four and a half years in captivity.

It was perhaps not surprising that Keenan gave one of the most publicly emotional displays of all the hostages released from Lebanon. At his welcome-home press conference in Dublin, Keenan, often close to tears, spoke of the deep, enduring and unbreakable 'bond' between himself and McCarthy, whom he called John Boy. McCarthy had been Keenan's 'soul-mate' in captivity, and when the kidnappers had first told Keenan that they were going to free him, Keenan had refused to go, and had pleaded to be allowed to stay with McCarthy. But the kidnappers gave him no option. For Keenan, leaving McCarthy had been like having his right arm ripped off. Later Keenan was to provide probably the most illuminating insight into what it felt like to be a hostage. The desperation of a hostage, said Keenan, was that of a man 'hanging by his fingernails over the edge of chaos, and feeling his fingernails straightening.' In the months after his release, Keenan was to experience the same difficulty coming to terms with his freedom as he had coming to terms with captivity. After the euphoria surrounding his return, Keenan turned his back on his two sisters, Elaine and Brenda, who had campaigned so hard for his release, and withdrew to the wilds of the west of Ireland to resume his old drinking habits.

The one positive piece of news Keenan brought with him was the confirmation that Terry Waite was alive, and in the cell next to the one where Keenan had spent the last few months of his captivity with McCarthy. After Frank Reed was released, Keenan and McCarthy had realised there was another hostage in the cell next to theirs. Keenan knocked on the wall and received a response. By painstakingly tapping, using one tap for A, two taps for B and so on, Keenan was able to identify himself and McCarthy to Waite. On several occasions Keenan had also heard Waite crying out 'Oh no, oh no,' in the early hours of the morning. Keenan's main concern, however, was to lend momentum to the campaign to get John McCarthy released. Both Keenan and the Foreign Office were anxious about the psychological effect Keenan's release might have had on McCarthy, his close companion.

In fact McCarthy spent hardly any time on his own. Just two hours after Keenan's release, McCarthy was reunited with Anderson and Sutherland who, as McCarthy later said, became 'two right arms' to replace the one he had lost when Keenan was freed. McCarthy told the Americans that

Keenan had made contact with Waite, who was still being held alone, and they all agreed to try and persuade the guards to let Waite join them. After a few days, the guards acceded to their request and Terry Waite was brought into their cell. It was the first time Waite had seen any other hostages in nearly four years in captivity. Over the previous few months his treatment had gradually improved; he had been allowed books and had even been offered the opportunity of watching television for certain periods of the day, an offer he politely declined. But Waite's guards denied him the one luxury he wanted, a shortwave radio, so that he could listen to the news. During the months he was held next to Keenan and McCarthy, who had learnt much of what was going on in the world from Anderson and Sutherland, Waite brought himself up-to-date with current affairs by knocking on the wall to Keenan. When he was introduced to Anderson, Sutherland and McCarthy, Waite finally had access to a radio.

In the eighteen or so months since McCarthy had last seen Anderson and Sutherland, his mother had died. The guards had told him nothing about her television appeals or her death. The two Americans knew she had died, and discussed among themselves whether to tell him. Finally they resolved that they should, and so one evening when the four hostages were sitting in their cell, Anderson gently broke the news to McCarthy. When McCarthy had come to terms with his own loss, a few days later he quietly told Tom Sutherland when Anderson was in the bathroom that Anderson's father and brother had died while he was in captivity. Anderson too had been kept in the dark about the deaths of his relatives; the guards did not like to give the hostages bad news because they were afraid of the adverse effect it might have on their morale. Sutherland, who was closest to Anderson, agreed that he should be told, and so the bad news was duly broken. It was at moments such as these that the deep bonds of affection and respect were forged between the captives.

While the Americans were pleased at first to have Waite join them, after a few weeks they began to regret their decision. After nearly six years in captivity together, Anderson and Sutherland had become very set in their ways. McCarthy, who was much younger, and by nature more accommodating, was able to fit into the Americans' routine without causing too much disruption. But Waite, whose ordeal had been much the worst, managed to disturb the Americans' equilibrium by the size both of his physique and of his personality. Waite had been taken seriously ill with asthma at various times during his captivity – his damp, dusty cell provoked a violent allergic reaction. His asthma made it difficult for the other hostages to sleep, so every night Anderson would calm Waite, keeping up a hypnotic patter of 'take it easy, breathe easy, exhale' until Waite fell asleep. It was yet another example of the more understanding side of Anderson's nature that had developed in captivity. Sutherland, however, found virtually everything Waite did intensely irritating. For example, he was offended at the loud noise Waite made when he blew his nose. 'Christ, it sounds like a herd of elephants in the jungle,' Sutherland used to complain. But Waite would not be intimidated, and retorted that Sutherland, who still suffered from severe flatulence, was hardly one to complain.

More irritating for the Americans was the fact that Waite always wanted to be the centre of attention, which was hardly surprising given that he had just spent four years in isolation. Anderson and Sutherland were disinclined to believe Waite's horror story of being shipped bound and gagged in 'the coffin', when in fact he had been in Beirut throughout his captivity. 'He would never talk to us straight,' complained Sutherland. 'When we asked about his role in the Iran-Contra affair, he replied, "Ah, you don't want to know about that sort of thing."' Anderson and Sutherland still harboured resentment about the failure of Waite's mission to get them released in December 1985. The Americans' hopes of release had been dashed when Waite ended his mission, and they had suffered the worst period of their entire captivity at Christmas 1986 when North's arms deals had been exposed. Now that they could talk to him in person, Anderson and Sutherland, who had both lived in the Middle East for several years before their abduction, felt Waite did not know enough about the region to negotiate on their behalf. 'I can't think of a more inappropriate person to send on the kind of mission Waite was doing in Lebanon,' Sutherland complained to Anderson.

After a few months there was hardly anything that Waite said or did that did not annoy the Americans. Once, when Waite was regaling them with stories of the high points of his career, he boasted about how he always insisted on travelling first class. 'It's really the only way to travel,' Waite pronounced. 'For someone of my size, I just need the leg room. And, of course, when people know who you are, the service is so much better.' It was not perhaps the most tactful remark to make to two men who had been chained up and blindfolded in dank Lebanese cells for six years. Waite also upset the Americans by arguing with them over what they should listen to on the radio. Anderson and Sutherland were sports fans and liked to listen to the BBC World Service sports coverage on a Saturday afternoon. Whenever the sport came on, however, Waite would complain. 'Oh no, not sport again. What a waste of time. I must have a word with the BBC when I get out.'

The friction between Waite and the Americans did not make life easy for McCarthy, who was much younger than the others. McCarthy handled the situation like a master diplomat, distancing himself from the unseemly bickering of the older men and behaving like a proper English gentleman which, in the circumstances, was quite some achievement. McCarthy lost his composure only on those occasions when he heard Jill Morrell mentioned on the radio. During the long years of captivity, McCarthy had come to appreciate the deep love he felt for Morrell, and had learned about the campaign she was running on his behalf in London. But from 1989, when Morrell and the campaigners had received no evidence that McCarthy was still alive, she had quietly asked the media not to describe her as McCarthy's girlfriend in future. Her reasons were sound. If McCarthy were one day released, there was no telling how he would respond to her. After the long years of separation, they might both feel differently about each other. Morrell wanted to settle down and have a family, and it was only sensible that she continue to live her own life. But in his cell in Beirut, McCarthy was quick to pick up on the fact that she was no longer being described as his girlfriend, but simply as a friend.

'What the hell is this all about?' McCarthy would explode, becoming genuinely upset at the suggestion that Morrell was no longer waiting for him. At such moments the wisdom and experience of the older men enabled them to comfort McCarthy and help him through the hard time he was giving himself. Sutherland in particular, a father of three grown-up daughters and a university professor, would quietly talk McCarthy through his frustration.

'Don't worry about it, John,' Sutherland would say. 'She's just playing it safe. She doesn't know what kind of a guy she's going to meet when you get out. But she's sure going to get one hell of a surprise!'

The decision of the United Nations to use the threat of military force to liberate Kuwait if Hussein refused to withdraw his troops brought about a dramatic political and diplomatic realignment in the Middle East which also worked for the benefit of the hostages. One of the least expected aspects of the military build-up in the Gulf was the decision of the Syrians to join the American-led military coalition. For the better part of twenty years, the Syrians had devoted considerable energy to undermining American influence in the region. But as far as the Syrian leadership was concerned, Saddam Hussein constituted a far greater menace than George Bush and, to assure Syria a place in Bush's 'new world order', Assad agreed to send troops. The Syrian decision to take up arms against Iraq coincided with the decision by General Michel Aoun, the self-proclaimed Lebanese president, to step down, presaging the end of the Lebanese civil war and heralding the start of a new era in Lebanese politics in which the Syrians would effectively make Lebanon their own. The Syrians began by deploying troops throughout Lebanon and disarming the militias in an attempt to curtail the indiscriminate violence which was still claiming lives up until the end of 1990. In September, for example, Amin Sleit, a Druze who had been Waite's personal bodyguard, was shot dead when he opened the door of his apartment to two men he apparently knew. The rumour immediately began to circulate in Beirut that he had been murdered because he knew too much about Waite's kidnapping, but, like all rumours in Beirut, it was impossible to verify.

With Syrian soldiers taking up position alongside the 25,000 British Desert Rats sent to the Gulf to join the allied force, and with Syrian soldiers controlling the areas where the British hostages were held, it became a matter of acute necessity for the British government to restore diplomatic relations with Syria. It was, perhaps, no coincidence that, the day after Mrs Margaret Thatcher resigned as prime minister in November 1990, Douglas Hurd formally announced the restoration of full diplomatic links with Syria. The Foreign Office had reached a similar agreement with Iran earlier in the month; if British troops were going into battle less than a hundred miles from the Iranian border, it made sense for Britain to keep a watchful eye on Teheran. The Gulf crisis thus enabled the diplomatic stage to be set for a speedy conclusion of the hostage issue once the crisis was over.

Although the liberation of Kuwait was achieved by the end of February 1991, it was another couple of months before the Iranians felt comfortable enough to renew contacts with the American and British governments to resolve the hostage issue once and for all. To get the ball rolling, in April the Iranians released Roger Cooper, who had spent five years in Evin prison on false spying charges. Cooper's release had been one of the main British conditions for the restoration of relations. A few days later, Ali Akbar Velayati, the Iranian foreign minister, publicly called on the West to break the deadlock in the hostage crisis by persuading Israel to release all the Arab prisoners it was holding in south Lebanon. The British government responded by telling the Iranians to do more to get the hostages freed. Hurd said he looked to Teheran 'to use its undoubted and potentially decisive influence' to end the captivity of Waite, McCarthy and Mann. A month later, a clear indication that the Foreign Office was becoming actively engaged in the process of releasing the hostages came when it was announced that Douglas Hogg, the Foreign Office minister, was going to Beirut to meet Lebanese leaders. It was the first time a British minister had visited Beirut since 1985 – before any of the current hostages were abducted. After a four-day visit in which he held meetings with senior Lebanese officials, Mr Hogg professed his confidence that the 'tragic chapter' of the British hostages was heading towards a conclusion.

Mr Hogg's prophetic words were justified little more than a month later when in early August John McCarthy was handed over to the Syrians in Lebanon and driven to Damascus to be officially presented to the British authorities. McCarthy, who looked fit and healthy, had been chosen because the kidnappers felt they could trust him to deliver a lengthy statement to Javier Perez de Cuellar, the UN secretary-general, and because they knew he would make a good impression on the world's media. McCarthy did not disappoint them. He was charm itself when he appeared before the television cameras both at the press conference at Damascus and later at the more informal gathering at RAF Lyneham.

In preparation for the return of the British hostages, the Foreign Office had arranged, with the assistance of the Ministry of Defence, a psychological debriefing programme to enable the returnees to make the difficult adjustment from captivity to freedom. The British were unique in providing this facility. American hostages spent a couple of days at Wiesbaden where they were given a series of medical tests, and then, assuming they were not suffering from any serious ailment, they were released to the outside world. Many of the American hostages found it difficult to adjust to the shock of suddenly being the focus of intense media attention after spending such a long period in isolation. 'We were just thrown to the wolves,' complained David Jacobsen after his release. 'One minute we were sitting in a cell in Beirut, and the next we were the stars of the evening television news. We were not given a proper opportunity to come to terms with the disorientation of being released.' Brian Keenan, who spent his first few days of freedom closeted away in Dublin Castle, also complained of the suffering he experienced from being the centre of so much media attention upon his release. On the advice of RAF psychiatrists, the

Foreign Office arranged for all the British hostages to be taken to RAF Lyneham where they would be put through a gentle debriefing and would be allowed to stay for as long as they wanted, protected from the unwanted intrusion of the media.

At Lyneham, McCarthy enjoyed a private reunion with his father, brother and close friends. With the entire officers' mess at his disposal, he was able to have a quiet drink and reconcile himself to the death of his mother. Away from the cameras, he was finally reunited with Jill Morrell who, from the first moment she set eyes on him, realised that she felt herself to be much more than a mere girlfriend. When she appeared after a brief reunion with McCarthy, Morrell, by nature a shy woman, said she had been 'overwhelmed' by the experience. McCarthy confided to friends that the best aspect of being apart from someone you love deeply was the pleasure of falling in love with them all over again. That was how he felt about Jill Morrell. McCarthy stayed at Lyneham for a week, and even after he left he followed the advice of the psychiatrists and made a strenuous effort to keep out of the public eye, so that he could gradually rebuild his life.

McCarthy's only public appearance at Lyneham was when Perez de Cuellar flew to the British airbase to collect the letter which McCarthy had brought with him from the kidnappers. The letter had in fact been written by Sheikh Fadlallah, a fact Fadlallah unwittingly confirmed in a conversation with a young Lebanese Shia journalist after the letter had been published in New York.

'That was a great letter,' said the journalist, who was sympathetic to Hizbollah's cause. 'It said everything that needed to be said.'

'Why, thank you,' replied Fadlallah. 'It's very kind of you to say so.'

The fact that the letter was addressed to Perez de Cuellar

took no one at the UN by surprise. Ever since the end of the Gulf War one of Perez de Cuellar's most trusted aides, Giandomenico Picco, had been shuttling between Teheran, Beirut, Tel Aviv, Damascus and New York to get the hostage negotiations back on track. The Iranians had made the first soundings through their diplomatic mission in New York at the start of April, but it had been the British government's idea for the UN to oversee negotiations for the hostage endgame. Washington, with its deep aversion to any projects initiated at United Nations Plaza, was at first reluctant to allow the UN such an important role, fearing that the UN might somehow compromise Washington's interests in the Middle East. But the British argument prevailed, and Picco was detailed to pursue the Iran approach. Picco, who was regarded by some colleagues as a Venetian diplomat in the Byzantine tradition, was well qualified to undertake such a delicate enterprise. Unusually tall for an Italian and bearing the dark good looks more commonly found in Hollywood than the UN, Picco had won the confidence of senior Iranian leaders in 1988 by the skill and delicacy with which he had helped to negotiate the ceasefire agreement in the Iran–Iraq war. As a result of these contacts Picco was able not only to see the key figures in Iran, but also to travel to Lebanon for face-to-face meetings with the kidnappers.

Picco was the first Western intermediary to see the kidnappers in Lebanon since Terry Waite, and his approach was the antithesis of Waite's publicity-orientated mission of 1985. When I met Picco at his office on the thirty-fifth floor of United Nations Plaza, he explained that when he accepted the hostage portfolio, he made a conscious effort to avoid the mistakes Waite had made. 'I arrived in Beirut from the opposite direction Waite and North had taken,' said Picco. 'I was able to succeed because North and Waite were not able to use the tools I used. I arrived in Beirut from the

East, with the full support of the Iranians, while North and Waite arrived from the West, with all the difficulties that that posed. I had developed contacts with Iran over many years which were invaluable to my mission. They were not the sort of contacts you make every day. This was a tremendous asset that Waite and North did not have at their disposal. The Iranians were on my side. When I went into Beirut, I had the full backing of the Iranians. It would have been foolish for anyone to attempt to go to Lebanon without the support of Iran.'

Unlike Waite, who had a single meeting with the kidnappers, Picco had a succession of meetings, which began in the summer of 1991 and continued until the last hostages had been released. And whereas Waite had conducted his mission in the full blaze of publicity, Picco kept his so secret that no one even knew he had been to Beirut until long after he had left. The media only picked up on Picco's role after McCarthy's release, by which time he had been working in the Middle East for several months. Picco insists that it was more of a personal adventure than a diplomatic mission. 'I was only able to succeed because of the close relationship I had established with the Iranians over many years, and because I worked closely with Perez de Cuellar,' said Picco. Such was the sensitivity of his mission, moreover, that he felt obliged to keep it secret from most of his colleagues at the UN for fear that information might fall into the wrong hands. 'You could say that the mission was a success in spite of the UN bureaucracy,' said Picco. 'If the details of my mission had become known at the UN, I would have been killed.' Indeed, such was Picco's disenchantment with the UN that he resigned from the organisation immediately the last remaining Western hostages, two Germans, were released in June 1992.

Picco's mission to Lebanon required a great deal of

personal courage. He had many more meetings with the kidnap groups than there were hostage releases – and there were many of those in the autumn of 1991. Each time Picco went to see the kidnappers he was effectively kidnapped himself. 'I never knew if I would come back. I was in their hands for long periods with no contact with the outside world.' Picco claims he was never threatened, although militia officials in Beirut believe the kidnappers came close to seizing him when they felt they had been double-crossed by the Israelis.

The decision to set McCarthy free was taken only after most of the crucial negotiations with the kidnap groups had taken place. Picco refused to disclose details of the negotiations, but even after the escape of the Dawa prisoners, the kidnappers believed that they should get something in return for the hostages. At the local level, the kidnappers changed their demands. Their main concern now was to have Israel release all Shia prisoners under their control; the leaders also wanted guarantees for their safety once all the hostages had been set free. The Iranians, on the other hand, had their own agenda which primarily focused on the release of frozen Iranian assets and a guarantee that the US would co-operate fully at the Hague tribunal. The American and British governments reiterated their opposition to doing any deal with the kidnappers directly, but hinted to Picco that progress could be made to improving relations with Iran on a broad scale if the hostages were released.

By far the most difficult aspect of Picco's mission was to bring the Israelis into the equation. Ever since the abduction of Sheikh Obeid in 1989, the suspicion had remained that the Israelis had take him more to play themselves into the hostage game than because of Obeid's knowledge of Hizbollah's military operations. Israel still had seven servicemen missing in Lebanon and Syria, and the government was under considerable domestic pressure to locate them. By kidnapping Obeid and holding several hundred Shia Muslims from southern Lebanon prisoner, the Israelis had many cards to play in any hostage deal. Uri Lubrani, who as Israel's acting ambassador to Teheran in the late 1970s had predicted the fall of the Shah, had been given the task of finding the missing Israeli servicemen because of his unsurpassed knowledge of Shia culture. Lubrani, a small, rotund man in his early sixties with piercing brown eyes and a kindly countenance, had been dealing with the Shias of southern Lebanon since the 1982 Israeli invasion. He had more experience of hostage negotiations in the Middle East than anyone, and viewed his task as an intellectual challenge.

'Playing the hostage game is like playing a game of chess,' is how Lubrani explained his approach when I met him at his office deep within the bowels of the Israeli defence ministry in Tel Aviv. On the wall outside his office was a photograph of Masada, where the ancient Jews chose to commit mass suicide rather than capitulate to their Roman besiegers. Lubrani takes a similarly uncompromising approach to the hostage game. 'You make a move, and then you must work out what the other person's move will be. If we are honest, no one has any idea how to deal with hostage-taking. Every case is different and depends on the circumstances – how much you know about the kidnappers, where they are, what they want, etc. Then you have other factors such as how much pressure the families can bring to bear on the government. In a small country like Israel, the pressure can be very considerable.' In Lubrani's view, the Iranians released the hostages because they decided that holding them was a liability. 'Iran wanted better relations with the West, and it could not have those good relations while the hostages were still being held.' Nor did Lubrani have much respect for

Imad Mugniyeh, the mastermind behind the kidnappings: 'Mugniyeh is not a decision-maker, he is a trouble-maker.'

At first Picco was happy to involve the Israelis, but as his mission progressed he discovered, as is too often the case with the Jewish state, that the Israelis were working to their own agenda. At the time of McCarthy's release, however, Picco thought he was the undisputed master of negotiations, and even believed he could pull off a hostage deal to end all hostage deals – a one-off exchange of hostages and prisoners in the Middle East which would resolve the long-running saga at a stroke. He therefore regarded McCarthy's release as the first step in a 'schedule' which would result in all the hostages being freed. Picco has refused to provide specific details of the deals negotiated for each of the hostages, except to say that after McCarthy's release the schedule began to fall apart, mainly because of Israel's insistence that it reserved the right to act in what it considered to be the best interests of its missing servicemen, irrespective of what Picco was up to. For the first few weeks, however, Picco's schedule proceeded according to plan. There was a minor scare on the day of McCarthy's release when a group of gunmen kidnapped a French aid worker, Jérôme Leyraud. But the Syrians, anxious to ensure the hostage issue was closed, acted quickly, and Leyraud was released within forty-eight hours.

A few days later Edward Tracy, the eccentric bookseller held by the Revolutionary Justice Organisation for five years with Jo Cicippio, was freed. Tracy's release was the most poignant of them all. When he was handed over to the Americans it was immediately apparent that he had little idea where he was or what had happened to him. When he was flown to Wiesbaden there was no warm reunion with family and friends. He had led such a peripatetic existence prior to his capture that he had no family to speak of, and the large numbers of nurses and medical staff who gathered to welcome him at the airbase only served to confuse him further. He celebrated his first day of freedom with a Big Mac and a Coke, but within days he was referred to a psychiatric institution in the US where he was detained indefinitely. For Jo Cicippio, the release of Edward Tracy was the best thing that happened in five years in captivity. 'I didn't care what happened to me after he went,' said Cicippio. 'Nothing could be worse than being chained to a mad man for five years.'

After Tracy's release, the Israelis fulfilled their part of the bargain by releasing fifty-one Arab prisoners held in southern Lebanon. The Israelis said they had made the gesture after being told that an Israeli soldier missing in Lebanon had been killed. A few days later Israel took possession of the body of the dead soldier, and in return allowed a deported Palestinian to return to his home. Throughout this process all the different kidnap groups were vying with each other by issuing statements, accompanied by photographs of hostages, which made either fresh demands or statements in support of the UN's efforts to resolve the hostage issue. Then at the end of September the Revolutionary Justice Organisation, which had apparently purchased Jackie Mann from the radical Palestinian group which initially abducted him, announced that the seventy-year-old retired pilot would be released.

Jackie Mann weighed just eight stone three pounds after his 865-day ordeal. When he made his first public appearance outside the ambassador's residence in Damascus, he was clearly very weak. 'I'm very, very happy,' he said in a faint voice, before being led away to a waiting car by his indomitable wife Sunnie, who, with her outrageous glasses and thick red lipstick, had become something of a media celebrity during her husband's captivity. Mann was flown back to Britain on an RAF VC 10 and, as the plane arrived at RAF Lyneham, a lone Spitfire did a low, lazy victory roll as Mann took his first steps on British soil. To everyone's surprise, despite his physical frailty Mann had mentally survived his ordeal remarkably well.

With Mann's release, however, Picco's delicate negotiating act came to a shuddering halt. Picco refuses to go into detail about what went wrong, but it is clear that it was at about this point that the Israelis, frustrated at how little information they were receiving about their missing servicemen, began to renege on some of the pledges they had given to Picco. 'Picco had his agenda and we were happy to work with him,' explained Lubrani, 'but we also had our own agenda, and we had a duty to the families of the missing Israelis to do what we thought was best for them.'

Picco will not discuss how the Israelis acted. 'All I can say is that the Israelis ended up nearly destroying the whole mission.' He had assumed that the original schedule for the releases would need, on occasion, to be modified, but he was now required to pull out all the stops to save the negotiations. 'There were some hostages who came out for free, and there were others were very expensive,' he said. 'The next hostage to come out, Jesse Turner, cost me a great deal.'

Whether Picco paid in mental anguish, or some more tangible price was paid, is not clear, but the release of Jesse Turner, one of the two remaining BUC professors, in late October was a significant breakthrough. From now on the Israelis would play no further role in the hostage releases, much to the anger of both the Israelis, who were still keen to find out about their missing servicemen, and Lebanon's Shias, whose only remaining demand was the release of Shia Muslims held by Israel in return for the last hostages. Once Picco felt he could no longer rely on the Israelis, his main task was to persuade the kidnap groups to release the hostages, knowing that they would get nothing from the Israelis in return. The decision to let the remaining hostages go was effectively taken by Rafsanjani, who agreed to give the Hizbollah leaders several million dollars' worth of arms for each hostage freed. In a sense it was the logical extension of the policy Oliver North had pursued: Iran now gave weapons to Hizbollah to secure the release of American hostages.

At some point in early November, Ali, the smiling Iranian who always seemed to turn up when a hostage release was imminent, appeared in the building in the Bekaa Valley where Waite, Anderson and Sutherland were being held. Waite was taken out of the room, and the guards explained in detail to Anderson and Sutherland the timetable for their release. Having heard about all the other releases, this time Anderson and Sutherland were prepared to believe what they were being told. Waite had been excluded as a deliberate snub. After holding him for five years, the kidnappers still had little respect for him. They explained to Terry Anderson that he would be the last to leave because they did not want to give Waite the opportunity of claiming any credit for getting the hostages out. The ultimate humiliation for Waite, as far as the kidnappers were concerned, would be for him to be released before one of the men he had come to Lebanon to rescue.

Waite had to learn from Anderson and Sutherland what was going on. One of the guards also had a quiet word with him. 'We told you not to come back to Lebanon, but you ignored us,' he said. 'We gave you our trust, and you betrayed us. That is why we have held you here.' It was the first and only time that the guards explained to any hostage why he had been kidnapped.

A few days later a guard announced that Sutherland and Waite were to be released. This time Sutherland, who had been told this so many times, believed he was really going to be set free. Waite and Sutherland were provided with new clothes, and allowed to take an extra long shower. A barber was brought in to tend Waite's beard. The two were then allowed to say their farewells to Terry Anderson. Before they left, Waite got into an argument with a guard.

'You stole my watch,' he declared. 'When you took me I had a nice watch, and you've taken it from me. I want you to replace it.' The guard merely shrugged and disappeared. A few minutes later he returned with three Citizen quartz watches, one for each hostage.

Waite and Sutherland were then led, blindfolded, out of the room and placed in the boot of a waiting Mercedes, Waite lying on top of Sutherland. They were driven out of Baalbek for about five minutes, then were transferred to another car, a BMW, driven by a Syrian intelligence officer. 'Welcome to freedom,' said the Syrian with a large smile, and sped off in the direction of Damascus. An hour later the small group arrived at the headquarters of Syrian intelligence, where they were only supposed to rest for a few minutes before being taken to the Syrian foreign ministry to be paraded before the world's press. But there was yet another hold-up when Waite asked for a mirror. Before appearing before the cameras, he wanted to see what he looked like. He was horrified at what he saw, and demanded that the Syrians find another barber to trim his beard, though it was late at night.

'This is disgraceful,' said Waite. 'I can't possibly face my public looking like this.' The constant delays drove Sutherland, who knew his wife would be waiting at the press conference, wild. 'Terry Waite is the most egotistical bastard I have ever had the misfortune to meet,' Sutherland would later tell his wife. Half an hour later, after Waite's beard had received its second trim of the day, the two were driven to the Syrian foreign ministry, where they were presented to the press. Waite readily seized the microphone.

The showman in Waite immediately came to the fore the

moment he was able to face the press. Both in Damascus, where Waite spoke of how he had experienced 'some of the suffering of the people of Lebanon', and at the speech he gave at his arrival at Lyneham, Waite impressed everyone in his first public appearance for nearly five years. It was classic Terry Waite. Put him in front of a camera, and he came alive. He spent his first twenty minutes at Lyneham giving a press conference before going off to the officers' mess for a reunion with his wife, Frances, and the couple's four children. Waite stayed at Lyneham for three weeks, longer than any of the other British hostages, mainly because he discovered he was still very weak from the long period he had spent in solitary confinement, and because he had more reason than any of the other hostages for wanting to avoid the attentions of the media. While there was a general acknowledgement that Waite had paid a terrible price for his folly in returning to Lebanon, there was also a strong desire to set the record straight on his involvement in the Iran-Contra affair. Closeted at Lyneham, Waite was saved the difficulty of having to answer awkward questions about the nature of his mission to Lebanon. When he did appear before the press, it was in a carefully stage-managed interview with the BBC, which had been arranged by his cousin, John Waite, who worked for BBC Radio. In the interview, which in characteristic Waite fashion was shown on the Sunday before Christmas, Waite gave an often emotional account of his period in captivity in which he categorically refuted any suggestion that he had been involved in North's arms deals.

Oliver North, who by pure coincidence happened to be visiting London the week after Waite's release to promote his book, gave probably the most detailed explanation of Waite's role in his arms deals that he is ever likely to provide.[1] Waite's role, said North, had been much the same as the one the United Nations had played in getting the hostages released: to provide a point of contact which was not the American government. Waite understood, said North, that he was the independent churchman required. But, North said, he never told Waite about the missile shipments to Iran, which he admitted were the real reason for the releases. Did that mean that Waite did not know?

'That's a different question,' said North. 'I never told him. I don't know what Terry knew.' And even if he had known, it would not have made any difference to the way Waite would have acted. 'I'm not asking anyone to endorse what I did or what I failed to do,' said North. 'But think about this. If I had told Waite all of it, it would have placed him at far greater risk. He was going to continue what he was doing anyway. In many respects he would have worked with anyone who could have helped get those men free, because that's what his purpose in life was.' North admitted he had cried when he heard about Waite's release while on a book promotion tour in Kansas – 'I'm human, notwithstanding what's been written' – and had left a number at RAF Lyneham where Waite could contact him. Waite did not take up the opportunity.

The need for Waite to maintain his privacy was increased in the days immediately after his release as his public reputation came under attack. The first knock to his image was provided by Shamseddin Khareghani, the Iranian chargé d'affaires in London, who told Sky Television that he still believed there was a link between Waite and the CIA, and that Waite's links with the CIA were the main reason why he was

[1]Interview in the *Daily Telegraph*, November 26, 1991.

kidnapped in Beirut. And then Tom Sutherland vented in public the personal antipathy he felt towards Waite. In a series of interviews Sutherland first indicated that Waite's mediation effort had been totally ineffectual, and then he told a conference in Washington that he had come close on several occasions to striking Waite because of his insensitivity to the other hostages. 'Waite was afraid he would get abrupt replies from Anderson and McCarthy so he picked on me to talk to,' said Sutherland. 'He is a super-egoist. I'm convinced he negotiated for hostages for the publicity value.' Waite was deeply hurt by Sutherland's comments, and contacted John McCarthy to see if he would have a quiet word with Sutherland to ask him to tone down his comments. McCarthy duly phoned Sutherland at his home in Denver and asked him to lay off Waite.

'Tom, we all feel the same way about Waite, but it's really not fair to go on at him in public like this,' said McCarthy who, four months after his release, had successfully adjusted to freedom. 'Give him a break. He needs it after what he's been through.'

Any fears that Anderson might once more miss out on being released at the last minute were removed ten days later when the final act in the saga rapidly drew to a close. On December 2, Jo Cicippio, the last hostage held by the Revolutionary Justice Organisation, was freed. The following day the Islamic Jihad for the Liberation of Palestine closed its hostage file by releasing Alann Steen, the last of the four BUC teachers. And on December 4, Terry Anderson, who had spent six and three-quarter years as a hostage, the longest period any of the Western hostages spent in captivity, was finally set free. Even on the day of his release, there was a last-minute hitch when the convoy bringing Anderson from the Bekaa Valley to Damascus got caught up in a snowdrift in the ante-Lebanon mountain range. Finally the small party reached Damascus where Anderson, looking pale and wearing a white shirt with a black jumper, appeared in public for the first time at the Syrian foreign ministry. Anderson's emotions got the better of him as he was reunited with Peggy Say, his sister, and his fiancée, Madeleine, and Sulome, the six-year-old daughter he had never seen. 'I'm going to call you "button",' Anderson told the little girl. 'All the time I was held I knew you had been born, but I did not know your name. So I called you "button" because it appealed to me, and that's what I'll call you from now on.' Anderson also helped to take some of the sting out of the comments Sutherland had made about Waite. Anderson publicly thanked Waite 'who risked his life for me'.

Before his release, Anderson confided that his guards, some of whom had been within him for the duration of his captivity, had come as close as they knew how to apologising to Anderson for holding him hostage.

'Hostage-taking is a waste of time,' one of the guards told Anderson the day before he was freed. 'We didn't get what we thought out of this. We are not going to take any more hostages.'

Perhaps the most poignant moment in the whole of Picco's hostage-release programme came at the end of December. Although Picco's main priority was to free the living, he was also mindful of those who had not survived the ordeal, and throughout his negotiations with the kidnappers sought to retrieve the bodies of those who had died in captivity. On December 27, a news agency in Beirut received a call that the body of William Buckley, the CIA station chief who had died of pneumonia in the summer of 1985, had been dumped at the side of the airport road. A team of American officials drove to the site, and on a stretch of wasteground opposite the 'champagne mosque' on the outskirts of Beirut's southern suburbs, they found a canvas sack filled with Buckley's remains. A similar call led American officials to recover the bones of Lieutenant-Colonel William Higgins, whom a group calling itself the Organisation of the Oppressed of the Earth had claimed to have executed in the summer of 1989. The remains were flown back to the United States where they were buried with full military honours in flag-draped coffins.

EPILOGUE

That sweet bondage which is freedom's self.
– Percy Bysshe Shelley, 1792–1822

A thick blanket of snow covered the Bekaa Valley, and for as far as the eye could see Lebanese tribesmen and their families lined the road. While the children played with their fathers' Kalashnikov rifles, the old men stood silently, holding pots of cold, bitter coffee, the traditional Islamic drink of mourning. It was as though the entire population of the Valley had forsaken the comfort of their homes to pay their respects to the latest casualty of the interminable war between Arab and Jew. A few days previously, in the middle of February 1992, a squadron of Israeli helicopter gunships had ambushed a convoy of cars on a remote stretch of road in southern Lebanon. Abbas Musawi, the recently elected general-secretary of Hizbollah, was killed instantly as his black Mercedes was destroyed by a barrage of Israeli missiles. His wife and five-year-old daughter were also killed in the attack, which lasted no more than a few seconds.

Like so many episodes in the Arab–Israeli conflict, the assassination of Musawi proved to be counter-productive. The

Israelis killed Musawi because they were angry at his decision, taken during Giandomenico Picco's hostage mission, not to include Israeli servicemen in the deal for the release of the last hostages. Lebanon's Shia Muslims reacted to the attack by staging the largest demonstration of support for Hizbollah ever seen in Lebanon. Nothing inspires the Islamic fundamentalist tendency so much as the 'martyrdom' of one of its leaders, and Musawi's death gave Hizbollah precisely the renewed sense of purpose it had been searching for since the release of the hostages. The day following the attack the streets of Beirut's southern suburbs were packed with thousands of outraged Shias vowing to avenge the latest addition to the canon of Hizbollah martyrs. On the day of Musawi's funeral, the long, black flag of Hizbollah hung from every rooftop along the road from Baalbek to the site of Musawi's burial at Nabi Sheet. Interspersed among the Hizbollah flags were banners bearing inscriptions from the Koran, such as: 'Should I cry for you or for the living?' Occasionally the distinctive orange, white and green of the Iranian national flag was to be seen. As the coffins of Musawi and his family were borne aloft by the mourners, they filled the air with their chants. 'We are marching to Jerusalem,' they shouted, working themselves into a frenzy.

To judge by the impressive demonstration of support for Hizbollah, Iran's investment in Lebanon's Shia Muslim community had paid off handsomely from the time ten years before when a few hundred Iranian guards had pitched camp on the outskirts of Baalbek. At the time of Musawi's assassination I happened to be in Lebanon researching for this book. Indeed I had arranged an interview with Musawi to discuss Hizbollah's role in the hostage crisis, but the Israelis struck two days before our appointment. So, with some trepidation, I travelled to the Bekaa for Musawi's funeral. Though Hizbollah officials insisted I would be quite safe, it was only natural to feel uneasy about returning to an area where, only months previously, a group of Westerners had been chained and blindfolded in basement cells. 'You have nothing to fear,' insisted the Hizbollah official who was to be my guide. 'Today is a great day in the history of our movement. You are welcome as the guest of Hizbollah.' Certainly the Lebanese Shia knew how to extract every last morsel of propaganda from Musawi's demise. Hizbollah's television channel, whose main antenna was situated on the minaret of a mosque in the southern suburbs, broadcast endless replays of the charred and mutilated remains of Musawi's child being removed from the car, while the announcer intoned: 'Congratulations. The martyr Sheikh Abbas Musawi rests in paradise. *Alluah Akbar*, God is great.'

If the size of the demonstrations revealed the extent to which Hizbollah's support had grown, the number of dignitaries who travelled to Nabi Sheet for the funeral emphasised just how important the militia had become. Apart from the Iranian ambassador to Damascus, representatives of both Ayatollah Ali Khameini, Iran's spiritual leader, and President Rafsanjani flew from Teheran for the service. As I watched the demonstrations, I fell into conversation with several young Hizbollah militiamen, people who it was easy to believe knew more about the captivity of the Western hostages than they were prepared to admit. They all made the same point. Hostage-taking, I was assured, was no longer on the Hizbollah agenda. 'This phase is at an end,' said one young official. 'Taking hostages proved to be of no value. Today Hizbollah has a different set of objectives.'

It was comforting to hear this, but it was hard to accept that the exercise had not been of some benefit to the development of the militia. When I had last visited Lebanon six years previously – at the time of John McCarthy's kidnapping – Hizbollah had been very much the poor relation compared with the main Muslim militias, the Druze and Amal. In the intervening period Hizbollah had emerged as one of the most important political forces in Lebanon. The key to Hizbollah's success was its ability to provide tangible assistance to the Lebanese Shia, the country's least privileged group. In the southern suburbs and the Bekaa Valley, Hizbollah created an impressive social services structure; there was hardly a school, hospital or road that was not the work of Hizbollah. Increased influence had also led to increased sophistication on the part of the Hizbollahis. Gangs of bearded militiamen no longer roamed the streets of West Beirut randomly smashing up liquor stores and harassing immodestly dressed women. Hizbollah's leadership had accepted the fact that Lebanon was essentially secular in nature, and that for the Shia Muslims to make progress, they needed to work within the Lebanon status quo, not against it.

The kidnapping campaign had been invaluable in raising the militia's profile. If a small group of Islamic fundamentalists could inspire fear in the West, it was worthy of serious consideration in Lebanon. Any young Shia man who wanted to prove himself was more likely to join Hizbollah than any other Muslim militia. But the hostage issue for Hizbollah, and for the Iranians, was a sideshow; for Iran the priority was to export the Islamic revolution, and for the Lebanese the main goal was to construct an infrastructure which would give the Shia a better deal. Not all the tribesmen who lined the road to Nabi Sheet on the day of Musawi's funeral were regular attenders at the mosque; but they recognised that, by supporting the Iranians, they had a better chance of getting the roads, schools and hospitals denied them for generations by the Christian and Sunni authorities in Beirut. The closeness of the links between Iran and Hizbollah were confirmed, moreover, when the State Department acknowledged that Teheran had paid $1 million for each of the hostages released in the autumn of 1991.

In many respects the kidnappers took advantage of the radical Islamic tide to pursue their own ends; no one was going to criticise them in Lebanon for attacking Western interests. But while the kidnappers liked to wrap themselves in a cloak of revolutionary Islamic rhetoric, they were little better than criminals. Once the hostages were released, most of the kidnappers simply went back to their families and continued with their lives as though nothing had happened. The ringleaders, however, people like Mugniyeh, who had gained a reputation among the world's intelligence agencies, had to be more circumspect, and many of them sought sanctuary in Iran. An official with one of the main militias, who had made a new career as a lawyer and politician, described Imad Mugniyeh as 'about as worthless as a shoe'. The official, whose contacts with Hizbollah were such that he was able to provide the first confirmation in 1987 that Terry Waite had been kidnapped, was scathing about the way the West had handled the hostage crisis. 'We knew these people were nobodies,' he said. 'But the hostage card became a winning card all the time. The big mistake of the West was to make Hizbollah bigger and bigger by sending all the envoys and missionaries to Beirut. It made these people seem like big-shots. The only "real man" in the West was Margaret Thatcher. She stood up to them.'

Faced with a phenomenon as complicated as this, it is not surprising that so many governments got in a mess over the hostage issue. It was easy for militia officials to ascertain that the kidnappers were little better than common criminals; they knew who they were and where they came from. They had grown up with them, amidst the carnage and disruption of the Lebanese civil war. But for those Western governments whose embassies had been blown up, and who had no way of knowing what was going on in West Beirut, it was a different proposition. Sophisticated institutions such as the Foreign Office, the State Department or the Quai d'Orsay are well-equipped to negotiate disarmament treaties, trade agreements and strategic alliances, but when it comes to dealing with anonymous, fanatical gunmen in a no-man's-land, the system does not function at its best. Taking to the moral high ground, as the Thatcher government did, and refusing point-blank to negotiate with terrorists is all very well, but it does not make locating the hostages any easier. And in the end public pressure for the government to act on humanitarian grounds ultimately becomes irresistible.

The Americans were the first to crack, not so much because of the campaigns run by Peggy Say and relatives of the other hostages, but because of the extreme emotional sensitivity of Ronald Reagan. Jacques Chirac's efforts amounted to a cynical exercise in political opportunism designed to win him the French presidency. The British might claim they held firm, but from the moment the Friends of John McCarthy campaign got into its stride in spring 1988, there was an unmistakable change of emphasis in the way Britain approached the issue. Rather than banging the table at every opportunity, as had so often been the case when Mrs Thatcher had her way, a dialogue was established, in spite of the provocation of the Lockerbie bombing and the Salman Rushdie *fatwa*, which resulted in Britain restoring diplomatic relations with Teheran and the hostages returning home. Though British politicians and officials may have prided themselves that Britain alone got its hostages out without doing a deal, the question remains whether it was necessary for John McCarthy, the innocent victim of an international battle of wills, to spend five years in a Beirut dungeon. 'It was tough on the hostages, but the policy of not doing deals with terrorists proved right in the end,' was how one senior Foreign Office official justified the British position. But this does not take account of the fact that, in many respects, the British hostages were released in spite of the activities of their government. Had the Dawa prisoners not managed to escape, and if Iran had not decided it needed the West more than the West needed Iran, it is extremely doubtful whether all American and British hostages would have been freed by the autumn of 1991. The refusal of the German authorities to release the Hamadi brothers meant that two German aid workers, Heinrich Struebig and Thomas Kemptner, remained in captivity. They were finally released in June 1992, prompting Giandomenico Picco to tender his resignation in disgust at the way he had been treated by Boutros Boutros-Ghali, the new secretary-general.

By the time the last hostages were released, of course, the world was a very different place to the one from which they had been taken. The end of the Cold War, the collapse of the Iron Curtain and the Soviet Union meant that many of the political tensions between the West and the Middle East which had contributed to the hostages being taken in the first place had passed. The changes in the balance of world power, however, were of little consequence to the freed hostages, who were more concerned with rebuilding their lives. Jo Cicippio had to learn to live with the pain of permanent frostbite damage. Alann Steen had to come to terms with the seizures he suffered as a result of a severe beating. When Steen accidentally prolonged his exercise period, a guard hit him in the face, knocking his head against the wall. He suffered permanent brain damage, and would require medical treatment for the rest of his life.

Terry Anderson emerged from his ordeal a far more fragile character. Gone was the feisty belligerence. As his sister, Peggy Say, commented after spending some time with the kid brother she had worked so hard to release, Anderson was a far softer person for his experience. 'And I like this version a lot better,' she said. Anderson faced many difficult decisions. It was more than twenty years since he had lived in the US. Shortly before his abduction he had left his wife and child. He had no roots to talk of. He had to decide whether he wanted to continue being a journalist, where to live and a whole range of crucial questions which most men of forty-four had resolved years previously. For the first few months after his release Anderson went to recuperate with Madeleine and Sulome on the Caribbean island of Antigua and work out what he wanted to do.

Thomas Sutherland probably made the easiest adjustment to freedom. When I visited him at his home at Fort Collins, Colorado, it was hard to imagine he had ever been away. As he padded about in his carpet slippers fixing 'old-fashioneds' and shouting at the cat to get off the furniture, he appeared the typical family man, with pictures of his daughters in their graduation gowns fixed proudly on the wall. He admitted to being slightly overwhelmed by his reception, especially when he was made guest of honour for the day at Glasgow Rangers Football Club, where as a boy he had dreamed of playing for the first team. As he walked out onto the pitch before the start of a game in January 1992, he was greeted by the famous Hampden roar, a terrifying sound even when it is well-meant. During a visit to a British Aerospace factory in Scotland, Sutherland was even able to resolve a question which had troubled him for years – ever since he had had an argument with Anderson on the subject: the position of the wing-flaps on an aircraft on landing and take-off. The only aspect of his captivity that Sutherland was unable to come to terms with was his deep dislike of Terry Waite. 'That man is the most despicable bastard I have ever met, and I hope I never again have the misfortune to see him,' he said.

Thanks to the professional help they received at Lyneham, all the British hostages appeared to make a smooth transition back to normal life. John McCarthy turned down the opportunity to become a media star by shutting himself away, and quietly rebuilding his life with Jill Morrell, his family and close friends. McCarthy's worst fears about what the media really wanted from him were confirmed when he gave a small press conference a few weeks after his release. While McCarthy, with Morrell at his side, tried to explain the difficulties of life after captivity, the only subject of interest to the harridans from the *Daily Mirror* and the *News of the World*, who had been specially chosen for the assignment, was the state of McCarthy's sex life. 'Aren't you goin' ta marry 'er, John?' shouted one. 'Give her a kiss for the cameras,' pleaded another. After that performance, McCarthy decided to keep well out of the public eye.

One of the Manns' main worries after Jackie's release was their precarious financial situation. They had stayed on in Beirut because they had insufficient means to go anywhere else. But Sunnie displayed her considerable resourcefulness by signing a lucrative book contract and negotiating for a camera crew to film her husband's debriefing at Lyneham, thereby making enough money to ensure a comfortable retirement in Cyprus. The only setback occurred in February 1992 when Jackie was admitted to a military hospital at the British base at Akrotiri suffering from pneumonia. The fact that he was weak did not prevent him from snapping at his wife when she told him that Terry Waite had telephoned to ask if he could come to Cyprus to see Jackie.

'What the bloody hell does he want to come here for?' said Mann from his sick-bed. 'I've never met the man in my life. He's never done anything for me. All the other hostages were held together, but I was all alone. Tell him to stay away.'

Terry Waite was soon back to his old irrepressible self, once he had regained his physical strength. There was never any question of his returning to work at Lambeth Palace. He went through the motions of meeting George Carey, the new Archbishop of Canterbury, in early 1992, but it was very much a courtesy call. His job had been filled years previously, and besides, Waite had signed a publishing contract for his life story which would earn him £400,000. He no longer needed the modest Lambeth salary he had complained about regularly. Waite was also spared the embarrassment of meeting John Lyttle, the man who had done so much to gain Waite's release but who nevertheless had little respect for the churchman. Lyttle died in April 1991 from his heart condition, and did not live to see the fruits of all his hard work to rebuild Britain's relations with Iran.

Waite took possession of his old MGB sports car which had been reconditioned by motoring enthusiasts during his absence, and was made a visiting fellow at Trinity Hall, Cambridge, where he was given a room with bars across the window to write his memoirs. Waite quickly settled into the swing of life at Cambridge, and was often to be found doing a stiff-legged jive at student discos. His public appearances, however, were nothing more than photo-opportunities. He steadfastly declined to be interviewed about his role in North's arms deals. The nearest he came to making any comment about his Lebanon mission was when, in June 1992, he appeared on the BBC radio programme *Desert Island Discs*. Between his selections of Bach and Schubert, Waite admitted that he had liked the publicity which surrounded his missions and that, perhaps, he may have been stupid to return to Lebanon on that last occasion. But he made it clear he did not want to dwell in the past, and appeared to be more interested in entering the spirit of the famous programme. As a special luxury for his desert island he chose an electronic chess set. He also appeared on the American chat-show 20–20, broadcast on Good Friday, in which he revealed how he passed up the chance to escape because of his pacifist views. He had found a gun on top of the bathroom cistern one day, and for a brief moment contemplated using it. But he could not bring himself to shoot the man guarding him.

In November, however, Waite's past came back to haunt him in the most dramatic fashion when news emerged of a mass murder in California. The first I heard of the murders was when a relative of Ian Spiro, the British agent who had helped to set up Waite's meeting with the Lebanese kidnappers (see pages 229–30), telephoned me at the *Sunday Telegraph* to report that Spiro's second wife Gail and the couple's three children had been found murdered at their home in the exclusive suburb of Rancho Santa Fe, on the outskirts of San Diego, California. Spiro himself was missing, and the relative feared that he might be on the run from a Lebanese hit-squad. I had learned, during the course of researching this book, that Spiro had left Beirut at the end of 1988 and made a new life for himself in California. He was able to use his real name for the simple reason that throughout the period of his residence in Beirut he had used a variety of aliases and was never known as Ian Spiro. I had attempted, through an intermediary, to interview Spiro about his involvement with Waite, but he declined the approach, saying he did not believe the time was yet ripe to tell his story. Then, out of the blue, he telephoned me at my London home shortly after publication of the book.

'Hello, I'm Spiro. Do you know who I am?'

I replied that I did, and we had a short conversation in which he indicated his interest in reading the book. I offered to send him a copy, but he did not want to give an address or telephone number.

'Don't worry, I have ways of getting a copy. I'll be in London soon, and perhaps then we can get together.'

He hung up, and I thought little more of it. If he did turn up, I would happily see him. But I thought it to be an unlikely prospect given his rather shifty manner on the telephone.

It was just three weeks later that one of his daughters by his first marriage telephoned me to tell me of the brutal murders in California. Spiro's wife and three children had each been killed by a single bullet to the back of the head. I was immediately struck by the professionalism of the killings. It also reminded me of many similar assassinations which had been carried out during the course of the Lebanese civil war, where whole families had been killed by a rival group to emphasise their vengeful nature. The mystery about what had happened to Spiro himself was solved three days later when his body was found a three-hour drive from his home in the Californian desert. Spiro was found inside a locked four-wheel-drive jeep at a remote picnic spot. Cause of death was given as cyanide poisoning. Terry Waite's behaviour in the wake of the Spiro murders was entirely consistent with his determination to distance himself from the less palatable aspects of his involvement in Lebanon. At first he denied ever having met Spiro, but later was forced to admit he knew him. In fact Waite had known him to the extent that he had been on holiday with the Spiro family in the south of France.

The police authorities at first dismissed the case as a straightforward suicide/homicide. Spiro, it was said, was disillusioned about his failure to make a new life for himself in California. He had run up a mountain of debt, and was under pressure to repay outstanding loans. In the aftermath of the Iran-Contra scandal, the American intelligence network point-blank refused to have anything to do with him, and he found all his attempts to renew his business contacts in the Middle East stymied. His wife, concerned about his increasingly erratic behaviour, was also threatening to leave him. Certainly Spiro lacked no shortage of motives for killing his family, or so the police believed.

But when details of Spiro's rather lurid past as a spy and international arms dealer emerged, the police took a rather different view of the case, and before long the FBI had been called in to lend assistance. Among the more wild accusations that were made was that Spiro, after his links with the CIA were summarily terminated following the exposure of North's arms deals with Iran, had gone over to the other side and had become a double agent working for the Iranians. It was suggested that Spiro had played a key role in organising the Lockerbie air disaster. Spiro was aware that a team of CIA agents, who were returning from a hostage reconnaissance mission in Beirut, would be on the plane, and passed this information on to the bombers. It was also suggested that Spiro, desperate to earn money, was trying to take advantage of a bounty scheme operated by the American government whereby large sums of money would be paid for any information which resulted in the capture of the Lebanese kidnappers. The deaths of the Spiro family coincided with the publication of full-page advertisements in the Arabic press advertising the American offer. After weeks of investigation, however, the authorities were unable to reach a satisfactory conclusion. Certainly if Spiro and his family were murdered, it was carried out in a highly professional manner.

The political changes in the British government which had taken place during the hostages' captivity also had a bearing on the way they were treated after their release. It would have been inconceivable, had Margaret Thatcher still been in power, for the returning hostages to receive any public accolade. As far as she was concerned, they were nothing but an embarrassing reminder of the unfortunate consequences of her decision to allow the Americans to use their airbases in Britain to bomb Libya. But Margaret Thatcher was now Baroness Thatcher of Kesteven in the county of Lincolnshire, and her successor as prime minister, John Major, adopted a far more sympathetic approach towards the freed hostages. If the British government felt any slight pangs of guilt that it had taken so long to get its hostages released, it was never articulated. But Waite, McCarthy, Mann and Keenan who, for all his Republican sympathies, was happy to be considered British for the occasion, all received awards in the New Year honours list. Waite, McCarthy and Keenan were even invited to lunch at Buckingham Palace, while Waite, who had more need of privacy than the others, was offered the use of one of the Queen's hunting lodges at Balmoral.

Throughout all the fuss, not a word was said about the hostages who had died. Nor was any reference made to the fact that, out of six Britons abducted in Lebanon, only three returned. The Germans, French and Americans got ninety per cent of their hostages freed; the fact that the British government secured the release of only fifty per cent of its hostages was conveniently overlooked as British officials acclaimed their triumph in getting the captives home without doing any deals.

The fate of the Britons who had died in captivity was not forgotten, however, by their relatives. Although Elaine Collett had, in her head if not her heart, accepted the probability that Alec had died, she still felt it her duty to try and secure the return of his body so that he could be given a decent Christian burial. Though officials at the UN in New York and the Foreign Office in London continued to investigate the whereabouts of Collett's body, no information was forthcoming.

The friends and relatives of Leigh Douglas and Philip Padfield made their feelings known when McCarthy, Waite, Keenan and Mann were honoured by the government, but no posthumous award was made to the two British teachers killed as a result of Thatcher's decision to support the raid on Libya.

'It's as if they have tried to sweep Leigh's death under the carpet,' said Freda Douglas, whose house was full of mementoes of her son. A large oak Ottoman chest he purchased shortly before his death filled the hall, and a portrait of him, taken on the balcony of his apartment in Beirut, occupied pride of place in the living room. 'We wrote to Buckingham Palace and said that if they were going to give awards to the other British hostages, they should give one to Philip and Leigh as well. The Palace wrote us back a nice letter, but nothing ever happened.'

There were times during the crisis when details surfaced of the terrible conditions the hostages had to endure, when Freda and her husband thought it was better that their son had died rather than suffer such an ordeal. But as the elderly couple watched as the other hostages were freed and began to rebuild their lives, they felt the weight of their loss even harder. 'My Leigh would have been all right if he had been allowed to live,' said Mrs Douglas. 'He would have been able to build a new life for himself. He would have got over the experience. But he was never given the chance, and for that I feel very bitter, very bitter about the way Margaret Thatcher threw away the life of my son for a conflict that had nothing to do with him.'

To preserve the memory of Philip Padfield, the other innocent British victim of the bombing raid, his friends published a collection of poems which were found among his private papers. Padfield had told only his closest friends that he wrote poetry, and rarely showed them what he had written. Most of his poems were intensely personal, but a few, such as one of the last he wrote, 'Again Remembrance', revealed the inspiration he derived from Beirut, a city he loved.

So in the going down of this sun
I grieve
And in this evening remember
And with remembering resolve
Against all the odds – to love

To save this sunset for the ones to come
To sanctify this dying to the ones now gone.

APPENDIX I

KEY DATES

October 1965	–	Ayatollah Ruhollah Khomeini arrives in exile in Najaf, southern Iraq.
October 1978	–	Khomeini expelled from Najaf by Saddam Hussein. Renews exile in Paris.
January 1979	–	Abdication of Shah of Iran.
February 1979	–	Ayatollah Khomeini's triumphant return to Teheran from Paris.
October 1979	–	Iranian students seize control of American embassy in Teheran.
September 1980	–	Saddam Hussein invades Iran at start of Iran–Iraq war.
November 1980	–	Ronald Reagan elected President of the US.
December 1980	–	Terry Waite visits Teheran on behalf of British hostages.
January 1981	–	American embassy hostages released in Teheran.

		Terry Waite secures release of British hostages.
June 1982	–	Israeli invasion of Lebanon. Revolutionary Guards arrive at Baalbek.
July 1982	–	Four Iranians trying to enter Beirut kidnapped by Christian militiamen. David Dodge, American-born acting president of the American University of Beirut (AUB), kidnapped.
September 1982	–	Massacre of Palestinians by Christian militiamen at Sabra and Chatila refugee camps. Arrival of multinational peacekeeping force.
April 1983	–	American embassy destroyed by suicide truck-bomb.
October 1983	–	American and French military barracks in Beirut destroyed by suicide truck-bombs.
December 1983	–	Shia Muslim extremists bomb Kuwait.
January 1984	–	Hussein Farrash, consul at the Saudi Arabian embassy, kidnapped. Malcolm Kerr, acting president of the AUB, murdered.
February 1984	–	Frank Regier, American professor of electrical engineering at AUB, kidnapped. Christian Joubert, French engineer, kidnapped. British, American, Italian and French troops ordered to leave Beirut after Muslim militias seize control. Shia Muslim prisoners put on trial in Kuwait for bombings.

APPENDIX I

March 1984	–	Jeremy Levin, bureau chief of Cable News Network, kidnapped in Beirut. William Buckley, CIA station chief, kidnapped. 17 Shia Muslims convicted of Kuwait bombings.
April 1984	–	Regier and Joubert released.
May 1984	–	Benjamin Weir, American Presbyterian minister in Beirut, kidnapped.
August 1984	–	Jonathan Wright, British journalist, kidnapped.
September 1984	–	Jonathan Wright escapes.
October 1984	–	Suicide truck-bomb attack on American embassy in Beirut. IRA bomb attack at Conservative Party conference in Brighton.
December 1984	–	Waite visits Libya to negotiate for four Britons held without trial by Colonel Gaddafi. Peter Kilburn, librarian at AUB, kidnapped. Hijack of Kuwaiti jet to Teheran.
January 1985	–	Rev. Lawrence Jenco, Roman Catholic priest, kidnapped.
February 1985	–	Waite secures the release of four Britons from Libya. Jeremy Levin escapes.
March 1985	–	Terry Anderson, Associated Press bureau chief, kidnapped. Britons Brian Levick and Geoffrey Nash kidnapped and released. Alec Collett, British journalist, kidnapped. French diplomats Marcel Fontaine and Marcel Carton kidnapped.

May 1985	–	Waite arrives in New York for first meeting with Carol Weir. Terry Waite meets Oliver North. Videotape of Alec Collett released. Islamic Jihad releases photographs of four American hostages. Assassination attempt on Emir of Kuwait. Dennis Hill, British teacher in Beirut, murdered. French journalist Jean-Paul Kauffmann kidnapped. David Jacobsen, American director of American University Hospital, kidnapped.
June 1985	–	Thomas Sutherland, dean of agriculture at AUB, kidnapped. William Buckley dies in captivity. TWA hijack.
July 1985	–	Reagan approves plan for Israel to ship weapons to Teheran in return for release of American hostages. Waite has first London meeting with Oliver North.
August 1985	–	Israel sends first consignment of 96 TOW missiles to Teheran. Iran fails to release hostage.
September 1985	–	Second consignment of TOW missiles sent from Israel to Teheran. Benjamin Weir released.
October 1985	–	Two British women resident in Beirut, Amanda McGrath and Hazel Moss, kidnapped. Four Soviet diplomats kidnapped. One murdered, three rescued. North arranges interception of

		Palestinian terrorists accused of hijacking Italian cruise liner *Achille Lauro*. Israel bombs PLO headquarters in Tunis. Islamic Jihad announces William Buckley has been 'executed' in retaliation for Israeli raid.
November 1985	–	Waite flies to Lebanon for meeting with kidnappers. North arranges shipment of Hawk missiles to Iran. Brian Keenan takes up teaching post in Beirut.
December 1985	–	Waite refused Kuwait visa. North proposes third arms-for-hostages shipment to Iran. M15 bugs meetings held by Oliver North in London. Waite makes final visit to Lebanon. No hostages released.
January 1986	–	North and Waite meet in New York. Reagan approves further arms transfers to Iran. North meets Ghorbanifar in London and visits Waite at Lambeth Palace.
February 1986	–	North arranges third shipment of arms to Iran.
March 1986	–	British teachers Philip Padfield and Leigh Douglas kidnapped. French television journalist Jean-Louis Normandin kidnapped with crew. Crew later released.
April 1986	–	Thatcher allows Americans to use British airbases for attack on Libya. Padfield and Douglas murdered by

		Abu Nidal in retaliation for Libya raid together with Peter Kilburn, missing AUB librarian.
		Palestinian group produces video of Alex Collett being hanged.
		British journalist John McCarthy kidnapped as he tries to leave Lebanon.
		Nezar Hindawi, a Jordanian Palestinian, arrested in London after persuading his Irish girlfriend to carry bomb on board El Al jet at Heathrow.
May 1986	–	Robert McFarlane and Oliver North fly with cake to Teheran.
June 1986	–	Mrs Thatcher sends Sir Percy Cradock and Sir Anthony Acland to complain to Admiral John Poindexter, US National Security Director, about activities of Oliver North.
July 1986	–	Rev. Lawrence Jenco released.
		Waite joins Jenco for flight to freedom.
August 1986	–	North organises delivery of Hawk missile parts to Iran.
September 1986	–	Frank Reed, American director of Lebanese International School, kidnapped.
		Joseph Cicippio, American financial director at AUB, kidnapped.
		David Hirst, Middle East correspondent of the *Guardian*, escapes from attempted kidnap.
October 1986	–	Edward Tracy, American book salesman, kidnapped.
		Nezar Hindawi jailed for forty-five years at Old Bailey for attempted El

		Al bombing; Britain cuts diplomatic relations with Syria.
		Terry Waite returns to Beirut for hostage release.
		North ships 500 TOW missiles to Iran.
November 1986	–	American hostage David Jacobsen released.
		Ash-Shiraa reveals details of US official Robert McFarlane's secret visit to Teheran in May.
		Rafsanjani confirms McFarlane visited Teheran with a planeload of arms.
December 1986	–	Robert Oakley, head of counter-terrorism at State Department, confirms that Waite met North on 'several occasions'.
		Waite announces he will return to Beirut.
January 1987	–	Waite returns to Beirut.
		Saudi diplomat kidnapped.
		Roger Auque, French cameraman, kidnapped.
		Mohammed Ali Hammadi, Lebanese Hizbollah official, arrested in Germany for TWA hijack.
		Rudolf Cordes, West German businessman, kidnapped.
		Alfred Schmidt, West German businessman, kidnapped.
		Terry Waite kidnapped.
		Four American teachers at Beirut University College kidnapped.
May 1987	–	Iranian vice-consul arrested in Manchester.
		British diplomat Edward Chaplin beaten up in Teheran.

June 1987	–	Britain imposes diplomatic sanctions against Iran. American journalist Charles Glass kidnapped.
July 1987	–	Diplomatic relations between Iran and France severed.
August 1987	–	Charles Glass escapes.
September 1987	–	Alfred Schmidt, West German hostage, released.
November 1987	–	French hostages Jean-Louis Normandin and Roger Auque released.
January 1988	–	'Friends of John McCarthy' formed.
February 1988	–	Lt-Col. William Higgins, US marine working for UN, kidnapped in south Lebanon.
May 1988	–	French hostages Jean-Paul Kauffmann, Marcel Carton and Marcel Fontaine released.
July 1988	–	USS *Vincennes* shoots down Iranian airbus over the Gulf.
September 1988	–	German businessman Rudolf Cordes released. Sir Geoffrey Howe, British foreign secretary, meets his Iranian counterpart, Ali Akbar Velayati, in New York.
October 1988	–	American hostage Mitheleshwar Singh released.
November 1988	–	Britain and Iran agree to restore diplomatic relations.
December 1988	–	Britain formally opens embassy in Teheran. Pan Am flight 103 explodes in flight over Lockerbie, Scotland.
February 1989	–	Howe and Velayati meet in London. Ayatollah Khomeini issues *fatwa*

		against author Salman Rushdie for publication of *The Satanic Verses*.
March 1989	–	Diplomatic relations between Britain and Iran severed.
May 1989	–	Jackie Mann, retired British airline pilot, kidnapped.
June 1989	–	Ayatollah Khomeini dies in Teheran. Sheila McCarthy, mother of John, issues an appeal to see her son before she dies.
July 1989	–	Sheila McCarthy dies of cancer. Ali Akbar Rafsanjani elected President of Iran. Sheikh Abdul Karim Obeid kidnapped by Israel. Video released showing Lt-Col. Higgins being hanged.
February 1990	–	Salman Rushdie makes public apology for *Satanic Verses*. *Teheran Times* calls for unconditional release of all Western hostages in Lebanon.
March 1990	–	President Rafsanjani says the hostage issue will be solved.
April 1990	–	American hostages Robert Polhill and Frank Reed released.
May 1990	–	Rafsanjani claims credit for hostage releases.
July 1990	–	France releases Iranian terrorist Anis Naccache and four accomplices.
August 1990	–	Iraq invades Kuwait. Dawa prisoners escape from Kuwait. Brian Keenan released.
September 1990	–	European Community signals interest in restoring normal relations with Iran Terry Waite's Druze bodyguard

		murdered in Beirut. Britain and Iran restore diplomatic relations.
October 1990	–	General Michel Aoun steps down, signalling the end of Lebanese civil war.
November 1990	–	Thatcher resigns as prime minister. Britain restores diplomatic relations with Syria.
January 1991	–	Start of the Gulf War.
February 1991	–	Conclusion of the Gulf War.
April 1991	–	Roger Cooper freed from jail in Teheran.
June 1991	–	British Foreign Office minister Douglas Hogg makes official visit to Lebanon.
August 1991	–	John McCarthy released. Edward Tracy released.
September 1991	–	Jackie Mann released. Israel releases Arab prisoners and receives bodies of two missing Israeli soldiers.
October 1991	–	Jesse Turner released.
November 1991	–	Thomas Sutherland and Terry Waite released.
December 1991	–	Joseph Cicippio released. Alann Steen released. Terry Anderson released.
February 1992	–	Abbas Musawi, general secretary of Hizbollah, assassinated by Israel in southern Lebanon.
June 1992	–	German hostages Heinrich Struebig and Thomas Kemptner released. Giandomenico Picco, UN hostage negotiator, resigns.

APPENDIX II

DOCUMENT FACSIMILES

By the time Robert McFarlane led his ill-fated mission to Teheran in May 1986, Oliver North's arrangements for the release of the American hostages had reached the height of sophistication. In late May he submitted a memorandum [see (i) below] to Admiral John Poindexter, who had replaced McFarlane as National Security Adviser, setting out in detail how he expected the hostage release to proceed. This document, which was given as evidence at the Congressional hearings in Washington in the summer of 1987, gives the timings of the arms shipments to Iran, and the arrangements for American personnel to receive the released hostages. North also included in his 'Hostage Recovery Plan' details of how the international media should be handled once the hostages were freed. The 'Draft Press Guidance' [see (ii) below], which was circulated to American diplomats and White House staffers, showed the extent to which Terry Waite figured in North's planning. In order to prevent the press asking awkward questions about the circumstances surrounding a hostage release, North suggested that American officials steer all press inquiries to Waite. When, two months later, North's arms shipments resulted in the release of Lawrence Jenco, Waite was flown to Damascus by the State Department, where the Anglican churchman fulfilled his designated role to perfection. Even after the Iran-Contra scandal broke, North still sought to portray Waite as having played a central role in the hostage negotiations. In a briefing to Congressional leaders in mid-November 1986 [see (iii) below], North maintained that the reason some American hostages remained in captivity was because of Waite's inability to make progress on the Kuwait prisoners.

UNCLASSIFIED
~~TOP SECRET~~

N 9930

May 22, 1986

RECEIVED
FBI
NOV 29 1986
Copy is Receipt

~~TOP SECRET~~

ACTION

MEMORANDUM FOR JOHN M. POINDEXTER

FROM: OLIVER L. NORTH N

SUBJECT: Hostage Recovery Plan

Partially Declassified/Released on 17 Aug 1987 under provisions of E.O. 12356 by B. Reger, National Security Council

Attached for your information are papers which contain essential information and action requirements for the execution of the hostage recovery plan.

Tab I is the operation order and time table for the critical events of the plan. The following people will have copies of this timetable: Clair George, Dewey Clarridge, and Bob Earl. We have established a communications plan in which the travelling party will make routine contact in order to apprise the appropriate people of progress along the timetable.

Tab II is the U.S.-Iran Terms of Reference (TOR) that will be used by Bud during our discussions with the Iranians.

Tab III contains three different sets of press guidance for use:

-- upon release of the hostages in Beirut;
-- upon the non-hostile disclosure of the party's visit to Iran; and
-- the hostile discovery and abduction of the party while in Iran.

Tab VI is a memo from you to the Secretaries of State and Defense, the CJCS, and the Director, FBI to execute the established interagency plan (Tab A) to receive, debrief, and reunite our citizens. This memo will follow-up a secure conference call upon notification of the hostages release.

UNCLASSIFIED
~~TOP SECRET~~

~~TOP SECRET~~
Declassify: OADR

EXHIBIT
DRC-16

3580
T125

(i)

APPENDIX II

UNCLASSIFIED

N 9943

~~SECRET~~ (Until released by NSC) ~~SECRET~~

DRAFT PRESS GUIDANCE

RELEASE OF U.S. HOSTAGES IN BEIRUT

-- We are extremely pleased that the hostages have finally been released.

-- We do not yet know the precise circumstances and details leading to their release.

-- We note, however, that there have been a number of overtures over the past year, seeking to obtain release of the U.S. and other foreign hostages in Beirut.

-- 

-- In addition, there have been recent efforts by various humanitarian and other organizations to facilitate the release of the hostages.

-- We can only assume that the cumulative effect of all of these efforts over the past year have finally produced results.

-- I recommend you refer your questions to Mr. Waite and to the various organizations that have been making these overtures for release of the hostages.

-- They will be taken to a U.S. military hospital for a medical examination. Arrangements are being made to reunite them with their families as soon as possible.

UNCLASSIFIED

~~SECRET~~ (Until released by NSC) ~~SECRET~~

(ii)

EXHIBIT EM-21

NAT'L SCTY BRIEFING OF CONGRESSIONAL LEADERS – 12 Nov 86

2pm [Sit Rm]

RR

No laws broken
No ransom for hostages
No officials or agencies bypassed

RR, VP, GPS, CWW, EM, WJC, DTR, JMP — Byrd, Dole, Wright, Cheney, Thompson, Speakes, Ball, Keel

JMP

Objectives { Contact moderate elements. Stop Iranian spt of terrorism. Obtain hostages

EXHIBIT EM-21

Finding pursuant to § 662 For Asst Act of 1961 as amended

Channel 1 Dep to PM
Channel 2 Sr official

Terry Waite Efforts thwarted by demand for Kuwait prisoners

Actions: ① McF to Tehran May 86
REF: Talking Points
US believes USSR would intervene to prevent Iraqi defeat.
2 obstacles to US-Iran cooperation { Spt for terrorism; Hostages must be ret'd

② Trf'd to Iran (w/ help of Israel) { !!! 1000 TOWs; 240 types of Hawk missile parts

③ Info provided to Iran [illegible]

SELECT BIBLIOGRAPHY

Ajami, Fouad, *The Vanished Imam* (Cornell University Press, 1986).
Antonius, George, *The Arab Awakening* (Hamish Hamilton, London, 1938).
Bakhash, Shaul, *The Reign of the Ayatollahs* (Basic Books, New York, 1986).
Bradlee, Ben, Jr., *Guts and Glory* (Donald I. Fine, New York, 1988).
Brill, E.J., *Encyclopaedia of Islam* (Macmillan, New York, 1983).
Cobban, Helena, *The Making of Modern Lebanon* (Hutchinson, London, 1985).
Cooley, John K., *Payback* (Brasseys, New York, 1991).
Dobson, Christopher and Payne, Ronald, *War Without End* (Harrap, London, 1986).
Fisk, Robert, *Pity the Nation* (André Deutsch, London, 1990).
Friedman, Thomas L., *From Beirut to Jerusalem* (Farrar, Straus & Giroux, New York, 1989).

Fromkin, David, *A Peace to End All Peace* (Avon Books, New York, 1989).
Gilmour, David, *Lebanon: The Fractured Nation* (St Martin's Press, New York, 1983).
Glass, Charles, *Tribes With Flags* (Secker & Warburg, London, 1990).
Hennessy, Peter, *Whitehall* (Secker & Warburg, London, 1989).
Hewitt, Gavin, *Terry Waite: Why Was He Kidnapped?* (Bloomsbury, London, 1991).
Hiro, Dilip, *Iran Under the Ayatollahs* (Routledge & Kegan Paul, London, 1987).
Hourani, Albert, *A History of the Arab Peoples* (Faber & Faber, London, 1991).
Jacobsen, David, *Hostage: My Nightmare in Beirut* (Donald I. Fine, New York, 1991).
Kedourie, Elie, *Politics in the Middle East* (Oxford University Press, 1992).
Kinross, Lord, *The Ottoman Centuries* (Jonathan Cape, London, 1977).
Ledeen, Michael, *Perilous Statecraft* (Charles Scribner's Sons, New York, 1988).
Lewis, Bernard, *The Arabs in History* (Hutchinson, London, 1966).
——, *The Assassins* (Weidenfeld & Nicolson, London, 1967).
Mann, Jackie and Sunnie, *Yours Till the End* (Heinemann, London, 1992).
Mansfield, Peter, *The Arabs* (Allen Lane, 1976).
Mantle, Jonathan, *Archbishop* (Sinclair-Stevenson, London, 1991).
Mayer, Jane and McManus, Doyle, *Landslide* (Houghton Mifflin Company, Boston, 1988).
Mortimer, Edward, *Faith and Power: The Politics of Islam* (Faber & Faber, London, 1982).
North, Oliver L., *Under Fire* (HarperCollins, 1991).

——, *Taking the Stand* (Simon & Schuster Pocket Books, New York, 1987).
Randal, Jonathan, *The Tragedy of Lebanon* (Chatto & Windus, London, 1990).
Regan, Donald T., *For The Record* (Harcourt Brace Jovanovich, New York, 1988).
Rodinson, Maxime, *The Arabs* (Croom Helm, London, 1981).
Runciman, Sir Steven, *A History of the Crusades* (Cambridge University Press, 1951).
Salibi, Kamal, *The Modern History of Lebanon* (Weidenfeld & Nicolson, London, 1965).
Say, Peggy, *Forgotten* (Simon & Schuster, New York, 1991).
Schiff, Ze'ev and Ya'ari, Ehud, *Israel's Lebanon War* (Simon & Schuster, New York, 1983).
Seale, Patrick, *Asad of Syria: The Struggle for the Middle East* (I.B. Tauris and Co. Ltd, London, 1988).
——, *Abu Nidal: A Gun for Hire* (Random House, 1992).
Shawcross, William, *The Shah's Last Ride* (Chatto & Windus, London, 1989).
Sick, Gary, *All Fall Down* (I.B. Tauris, London, 1985).
——, *October Surprise* (Random House, New York, 1991).
Speakes, Larry, *Speaking Out* (Charles Scribner's Sons, New York, 1988).
Taheri, Amir, *The Cauldron: The Middle East Behind the Headlines* (Hutchinson, 1988).
——, *Nest of Spies* (Pantheon Books, New York, 1988).
Theroux, Peter, *The Strange Disappearance of Imam Moussa Sadr* (Weidenfeld & Nicolson, London, 1987).
Thomas, Gordon, *Journey Into Madness* (Bantam Press, 1988).
The Tower Commission Report (Bantam Books, 1987).
Vatikiotis, P.J., *The History of Egypt* (Weidenfeld & Nicolson, London, 1969).
Weir, Ben and Carol, *Hostage Bound, Hostage Free* (Lutterworth Press, 1987).
Woodward, Bob, *Veil: The Secret Wars of the CIA 1981–87*

(Simon & Schuster, New York, 1987).
Wright, Robin, *Sacred Rage: The Crusade of Modern Islam* (André Deutsch, London, 1986).
Young, Hugo, *One of Us* (Macmillan, London, 1991).

INDEX

INDEX

INDEX

INDEX

INDEX